Caesar: A Sketch

by James Anthony Froude

"Pardon, gentles all The flat unraised spirit that hath dared On this unworthy scaffold to bring forth So great an object."

--SHAKESPEARE, Henry V.

PREFACE.

I have called this work a "sketch" because the materials do not exist for a portrait which shall be at once authentic and complete. The original authorities which are now extant for the life of Caesar are his own writings, the speeches and letters of Cicero, the eighth book of the "Commentaries" on the wars in Gaul and the history of the Alexandrian war, by Aulus Hirtius, the accounts of the African war and of the war in Spain, composed by persons who were unquestionably present in those two campaigns. To these must be added the "Leges Juliae" which are preserved in the Corpus Juris Civilis. Sallust contributes a speech, and Catullus a poem. A few hints can be gathered from the Epitome of Livy and the fragments of Varro; and here the contemporary sources which can be entirely depended upon are brought to an end.

The secondary group of authorities from which the popular histories of the time have been chiefly taken are Appian, Plutarch, Suetonius, and Dion Cassius. Of these the first three were divided from the period which they describe by nearly a century and a half, Dion Cassius by more than two centuries. They had means of knowledge which no longer exist--the writings, for instance, of Asinius Pollio, who was one of Caesar's officers. But Asinius Pollio's accounts of Caesar's actions, as reported by Appian, cannot always be reconciled with the Commentaries; and all these four writers relate incidents as facts which are sometimes demonstrably false. Suetonius is apparently the most trustworthy. His narrative, like those of his contemporaries, was colored by tradition. His biographies of the earlier Caesars betray the same spirit of animosity against them which taints the credibility of Tacitus, and prevailed for so many years in aristocratic Roman society. But Suetonius shows nevertheless an effort at veracity, an antiquarian curiosity and diligence, and a serious anxiety to tell his story impartially. Suetonius, in the absence of evidence direct or presumptive to the contrary, I have felt myself able to follow. The other three writers I have trusted only when I have found them partially confirmed by evidence which is better to be relied upon.

The picture which I have drawn will thus be found deficient in many details which have passed into general acceptance, and I have been unable to claim for it a higher title than that of an outline drawing.

CONTENTS

CHAPTER I.

Free Constitutions and Imperial Tendencies.--Instructiveness of Roman History.--Character of Historical Epochs.--The Age of Caesar.--Spiritual State of Rome.--Contrasts between Ancient and Modern Civilization.

CHAPTER II.

The Roman Constitution.--Moral Character of the Romans.--Roman Religion.-- Morality and Intellect.--Expansion of Roman Power.--The Senate.--Roman Slavery.--Effects of Intercourse with Greece.--Patrician Degeneracy.--The Roman Noble.--Influence of Wealth.--Beginnings of Discontent.

CHAPTER III.

Tiberius Gracchus.--Decay of the Italian Yeomanry.--Agrarian Law.--Success and Murder of Gracchus.--Land Commission.--Caius Gracchus.--Transfer of Judicial Functions from the Senate to the Equites.--Sempronian Laws.--Free Grants of Corn.--Plans for Extension of the Franchise.--New Colonies.--Reaction.--Murder of Caius Gracchus

CHAPTER IV.

Victory of the Optimates.--The Moors.--History of Jugurtha.--The Senate corrupted.--Jugurthine War.--Defeat of the Romans.--Jugurtha comes to Rome.--Popular Agitation.--The War renewed.--Roman Defeats in Africa and Gaul.--Caecilius Metellus and Caius Marius.--Marriage of Marius.--The Caesars.--Marius Consul.--First Notice of Sylla.--Capture and Death of Jugurtha

CHAPTER V.

Birth of Cicero.--The Cimbri and Teutons.--German Immigration into Gaul.--Great Defeat of the Romans on the Rhone.--Wanderings of the Cimbri.--Attempted Invasion of Italy.--Battle of Aix.--Destruction of the Teutons.--Defeat of the Cimbri on the Po.--Reform in the Roman Army.-- Popular Disturbances in Rome.--Murder of Memmius.--Murder of Saturninus and

Glaucia

CHAPTER VI.

Birth and Childhood of Julius Caesar.--Italian Franchise.--Discontent of the Italians.--Action of the Land Laws.--The Social War.--Partial Concessions.--Sylla and Marius.--Mithridates of Pontus.--First Mission of Sylla into Asia.

CHAPTER VII.

War with Mithridates.--Massacre of Italians in Asia.--Invasion of Greece.--Impotence and Corruption of the Senate.--End of the Social War.--Sylla appointed to the Asiatic Command.--The Assembly transfer the Command to Marius.--Sylla marches on Rome.--Flight of Marius.--Change of the Constitution.--Sylla sails for the East.--Four Years' Absence.--Defeat of Mithridates.--Contemporary Incidents at Rome.--Counter Revolution.--Consulship of Cinna.--Return of Marius.--Capitulation of Rome.--Massacre of Patricians and Equites.--Triumph of Democracy.

CHAPTER VIII.

The Young Caesar.--Connection with Marius.--Intimacy with the Ciceros.--Marriage of Caesar with the Daughter of Cinna.--Sertorius.--Death of Cinna.--Consulships of Norbanus and Scipio.--Sylla's Return.--First Appearance of Pompey.--Civil War.--Victory of Sylla.--The Dictatorship and the Proscription.--Destruction of the Popular Party and Murder of the Popular Leaders.--General Character of Aristocratic Revolutions.--The Constitution remodelled.--Concentration of Power in the Senate.--Sylla's General Policy.--The Army.--Flight of Sertorius to Spain.--Pompey and Sylla.--Caesar refuses to divorce his Wife at Sylla's Order.--Danger of Caesar.--His Pardon.--Growing Consequence of Cicero.--Defence of Roscius.--Sylla's Abdication and Death

CHAPTER IX.

Sertorius in Spain.--Warning of Cicero to the Patricians.--Leading Aristocrats.--Caesar with the Army in the East.--Nicomedes of Bithynia.-- The Bithynian Scandal.--Conspiracy of Lepidus.--Caesar returns to Rome.-- Defeat of Lepidus.--Prosecution of Dolabella.--Caesar taken by Pirates.-- Senatorial

Corruption.--Universal Disorder.--Civil War in Spain.--Growth of Mediterranean Piracy.--Connivance of the Senate.--Provincial Administration.--Verres in Sicily.--Prosecuted by Cicero.--Second War with Mithridates.--First Success of Lucullus.--Failure of Lucullus, and the Cause of it.--Avarice of Roman Commanders.--The Gladiators.--The Servile War.--Results of the Change in the Constitution introduced by Sylla

CHAPTER X.

Caesar Military Tribune.--Becomes known as a Speaker.--Is made Quaestor.-- Speech at his Aunt's Funeral.--Consulship of Pompey and Crassus.--Caesar marries Pompey's Cousin.--Mission to Spain.--Restoration of the Powers of the Tribunes.--The Equites and the Senate.--The Pirates.--Food Supplies cut off from Rome.--The Gabinian Law.--Resistance of the Patricians.--Suppression of the Pirates by Pompey.--The Manilian Law.--Speech of Cicero.--Recall of Lucullus.--Pompey sent to command in Asia.--Defeat and Death of Mithridates.--Conquest of Asia by Pompey

CHAPTER XI.

History of Catiline.--A Candidate for the Consulship.--Catiline and Cicero.--Cicero chosen Consul.--Attaches Himself to the Senatorial Party.--Caesar elected Aedile.--Conducts an Inquiry into the Syllan Proscriptions.--Prosecution of Rabirius.--Caesar becomes Pontifex Maximus--and Praetor.--Cicero's Conduct as Consul.--Proposed Agrarian Law.--Resisted by Cicero.--Catiline again stands for the Consulship.-- Violent Language in the Senate.--Threatened Revolution.--Catiline again defeated.--The Conspiracy.--Warnings sent to Cicero.--Meeting at Catiline's House.--Speech of Cicero in the Senate.--Cataline joins an Army of Insurrection in Etruria.--His Fellow-conspirators.--Correspondence with the Allobroges.--Letters read in the Senate.--The Conspirators seized.-- Debate upon their Fate.--Speech of Caesar.--Caesar on a Future State.-- Speech of Cato--and of Cicero.--The Conspirators executed untried.--Death of Catiline.

CHAPTER XII.

Preparations for the Return of Pompey.--Scene in the Forum.--Cato and Metellus.--Caesar suspended from the Praetorship.--Caesar supports Pompey.-

-Scandals against Caesar's Private Life.--General Character of them.--Festival of the Bona Dea.--Publius Clodius enters Caesar's House dressed as a Woman.--Prosecution and Trial of Clodius.--His Acquittal, and the Reason of it.--Successes of Caesar as Propraetor in Spain.--Conquest of Lusitania.--Return of Pompey to Italy.--First Speech in the Senate.-- Precarious Position of Cicero.--Cato and the Equites.--Caesar elected Consul.--Revival of the Democratic Party.--Anticipated Agrarian Law.-- Uneasiness of Cicero.

CHAPTER XIII.

The Consulship of Caesar.--Character of his Intended Legislation.--The Land Act first proposed in the Senate.--Violent Opposition.--Caesar appeals to the Assembly.--Interference of the Second Consul Bibulus.--The Land Act submitted to the People.--Pompey and Crassus support it.--Bibulus interposes, but without Success.--The Act carried--and other Laws.--The Senate no longer being Consulted.--General Purpose of the Leges Juliae.-- Caesar appointed to Command in Gaul for Five Years.--His Object in accepting that Province.--Condition of Gaul, and the Dangers to be apprehended from it.--Alliance of Caesar, Pompey, and Crassus.--The Dynasts.--Indignation of the Aristocracy.--Threats to repeal Caesar's Laws.--Necessity of Controlling Cicero and Cato.--Clodius is made Tribune.--Prosecution of Cicero for Illegal Acts when Consul.--Cicero's Friends forsake him.--He flies, and is banished.

CHAPTER XIV.

Caesar's Military Narrative.--Divisions of Gaul.--Distribution of Population.--The Celts.--Degree of Civilization.--Tribal System.--The Druids.--The AEdui and the Sequani.--Roman and German Parties.--Intended Migration of the Helvetii.--Composition of Caesar's Army.--He goes to Gaul.--Checks the Helvetii.--Returns to Italy for Larger Forces.--The Helvetii on the Saine.--Defeated, and sent back to Switzerland.--Invasion of Gaul by Ariovistus.--Caesar invites him to a Conference.--He refuses.-- Alarm in the Roman Army.--Caesar marches against Ariovistus.--Interview between them.--Treachery of the Roman Senate.--Great Battle at Colmar.-- Defeat and Annihilation of the Germans.--End of the First Campaign.-- Confederacy among the Belgae.--Battle on the Aisne.--War with the Nervii.--Battle of Maubeuge.--Capture of Namur.--The Belgae conquered.-- Submission of Brittany.--End of the Second Campaign.

CHAPTER XV.

Cicero and Clodius.--Position and Character of Clodius.--Cato sent to Cyprus.--Attempted Recall of Cicero defeated by Clodius.--Fight in the Forum.--Pardon and Return of Cicero.--Moderate Speech to the People.--Violence in the Senate.--Abuse of Piso and Gabinius.--Coldness of the Senate toward Cicero.--Restoration of Cicero's House.--Interfered with by Clodius.--Factions of Clodius and Milo.--Ptolemy Auletes expelled by his Subjects.--Appeals to Rome for Help.--Alexandrian Envoys assassinated.-- Clodius elected aedile.--Fight in the Forum.--Parties in Rome.--Situation of Cicero.--Rally of the Aristocracy.--Attempt to repeal the Leges Juliae.--Conference at Lucca.--Caesar, Pompey, and Crassus.--Cicero deserts the Senate.--Explains his Motives.--Confirmation of the Ordinances of Lucca.--Pompey and Crassus Consuls.--Caesar's Command prolonged for Five Additional Years.--Rejoicings in Rome.--Spectacle in the Amphitheater.

CHAPTER XVI.

Revolt of the Veneti.--Fleet prepared in the Loire.--Sea-fight at Quiberon.--Reduction of Normandy and of Aquitaine.--Complete Conquest of Gaul.--Fresh Arrival of Germans over the Lower Rhine.--Caesar orders them to retire, and promises them Lands elsewhere.--They refuse to go--and are destroyed.--Bridge over the Rhine.--Caesar invades Germany.--Returns after a Short Inroad.--First Expedition into Britain.--Caesar lands at Deal, or Walmer.--Storm and Injury to the Fleet.--Approach of the Equinox.-- Further Prosecution of the Enterprise postponed till the following Year.-- Caesar goes to Italy for the Winter.--Large Naval Preparations.--Return of Spring.--Alarm on the Moselle.--Fleet collects at Boulogne.--Caesar sails for Britain a Second Time.--Lands at Deal.--Second and more Destructive Storm.--Ships repaired, and placed out of Danger.--Caesar marches through Kent.--Crosses the Thames, and reaches St. Albans.--Goes no further, and returns to Gaul.--Object of the Invasion of Britain.--Description of the Country and People.

CHAPTER XVII.

Distribution of the Legions after the Return from Britain.--Conspiracy among the Gallic Chiefs.--Rising of the Eburones.--Destruction of Sabinus, and a Division of the Roman Army.--Danger of Quintus Cicero.--Relieved by Caesar in Person.--General Disturbance.--Labienus attacked at Lavacherie.--Defeats and kills Induciomarus.--Second Conquest of the Belgae.--Caesar again crosses the Rhine.--Quintus Cicero in Danger a Second Time.--Courage of a Roman Officer.--Punishment of the Revolted Chiefs.--Execution of Acco.

CHAPTER XVIII.

Correspondence of Cicero with Caesar.--Intimacy with Pompey and Crassus.-- Attacks on Piso and Gabinius.----Cicero compelled to defend Gabinius--and Vatinius.--Dissatisfaction with his Position.--Corruption at the Consular Elections.--Public Scandal.--Caesar and Pompey.--Deaths of Aurelia and Julia.--Catastrophe in the East.--Overthrow and Death of Crassus.-- Intrigue to detach Pompey from Caesar.----Milo a Candidate for the Consulship.--Murder of Clodius.--Burning of the Senate-house.--Trial and Exile of Milo.--Fresh Engagements with Caesar.--Promise of the Consulship at the End of his Term in Gaul.

CHAPTER XIX.

Last Revolt of Gaul.--Massacre of Romans at Gien.--Vercingetorix.--Effect on the Celts of the Disturbances at Rome.--Caesar crosses the Cevennes.--Defeats the Arverni.--Joins his Army on the Seine.--Takes Gien, Nevers, and Bourges.--Fails at Gergovia.--Rapid March to Sens.--Labienus at Paris.--Battle of the Vingeanne.--Siege of Alesia.--Caesar's Double Lines.--Arrival of the Relieving Army of Gauls.--First Battle on the Plain.--Second Battle.--Great Defeat of the Gauls.--Surrender of Alesia.--Campaign against the Carnutes and the Bellovaci.--Rising on the Dordogne.--Capture of Uxellodunum.--Caesar at Arras.--Completion of the Conquest.

CHAPTER XX.

Bibulus in Syria.--Approaching Term of Caesar's Government.--Threats of Impeachment.--Caesar to be Consul or not to be Consul?--Caesar's Political Ambition.--Hatred felt toward him by the Aristocracy.--Two Legions taken from him on Pretense of Service against the Parthians.--Caesar to be recalled before the Expiration of his Government.--Senatorial Intrigues.-- Curio deserts the Senate.--Labienus deserts Caesar.--Cicero in Cilicia.-- Returns to Rome.--Pompey determined on War.--Cicero's Uncertainties.-- Resolution of the

Senate and Consuls.--Caesar recalled.--Alarm in Rome.-- Alternative Schemes.--Letters of Cicero.--Caesar's Crime in the Eyes of the Optimates.

CHAPTER XXI.

Caesar appeals to his Army.--The Tribunes join him at Rimini.--Panic and Flight of the Senate.--Incapacity of Pompey.--Fresh Negotiations.-- Advance of Caesar.--The Country Districts refuse to arm against him.-- Capture of Corfinium.--Release of the Prisoners.--Offers of Caesar.-- Continued Hesitation of Cicero.--Advises Pompey to make Peace.--Pompey, with the Senate and Consuls, flies to Greece.--Cicero's Reflections.-- Pompey to be another Sylla.--Caesar Mortal, and may die by more Means than one.

CHAPTER XXII.

Pompey's Army in Spain.--Caesar at Rome.--Departure for Spain.--Marseilles refuses to receive him.--Siege of Marseilles.--Defeat of Pompey's Lieutenants at Lerida.--The whole Army made Prisoners.--Surrender of Varro.--Marseilles taken.--Defeat of Curio by King Juba in Africa.-- Caesar named Dictator.--Confusion in Rome.--Caesar at Brindisi.--Crosses to Greece in Midwinter.--Again offers Peace.--Pompey's Fleet in the Adriatic.--Death of Bibulus.--Failure of Negotiations.--Caelius and Milo killed.--Arrival of Antony in Greece with the Second Division of Caesar's Army.--Siege of Durazzo.--Defeat and Retreat of Caesar.--The Senate and Pompey.--Pursuit of Caesar.--Battle of Pharsalia.--Flight of Pompey.--The Camp taken.--Complete Overthrow of the Senatorial Faction.--Cicero on the Situation once more.

CHAPTER XXIII.

Pompey flies to Egypt.--State of Parties in Egypt.--Murder of Pompey.--His Character.--Caesar follows him to Alexandria.--Rising in the City.-- Caesar besieged in the Palace.--Desperate Fighting.--Arrival of Mithridates of Pergamus.--Battle near Cairo, and Death of the Young Ptolemy.--Cleopatra.--The Detention of Caesar enables the Optimates to rally.--Ill Conduct of Caesar's Officers in Spain.--War with Pharnaces.-- Battle of Zela, and Settlement of Asia Minor.

CHAPTER XXIV.

The Aristocracy raise an Army in Africa.--Supported by Juba.--Pharsalia not to end the War.--Caesar again in Rome.--Restores Order.--Mutiny in Caesar's Army.--The Mutineers submit.--Caesar lands in Africa.-- Difficulties of the Campaign.--Battle of Thapsus.--No more Pardons.-- Afranius and Faustus Sylla put to Death.--Cato kills himself at Utica.-- Scipio killed.--Juba and Petreius die on each other's Swords.--A Scene in Caesar's Camp.

CHAPTER XXV.

Rejoicings in Rome.--Caesar Dictator for the Year.--Reforms the Constitution.--Reforms the Calendar--and the Criminal Law.-- Dissatisfaction of Cicero.--Last Efforts in Spain of Labienus and the Young Pompeys.--Caesar goes thither in Person, accompanied by Octavius.-- Caesar's Last Battle at Munda.--Death of Labienus.--Capture of Cordova.-- Close of the Civil War.--General Reflections.

CHAPTER XXVI.

Caesar once more in Rome.--General Amnesty.--The Surviving Optimates pretend to submit.--Increase in the Number of Senators.--Introduction of Foreigners.--New Colonies.--Carthage.--Corinth.--Sumptuary Regulations.--Digest of the Law.--Intended Parthian War.--Honors heaped on Caesar.--The Object of them.--Caesar's Indifference.--Some Consolations.--Hears of Conspiracies, but disregards them.--Speculations of Cicero in the Last Stage of the War.--Speech in the Senate.--A Contrast, and the Meaning of it.--The Kingship.--Antony offers Caesar the Crown, which Caesar refuses.--The Assassins.--Who they were.--Brutus and Cassius.--Two Officers of Caesar's among them.--Warnings.--Meeting of the Conspirators.--Caesar's Last Evening.--The Ides of March.--The Senate-house.--Caesar killed.

CHAPTER XXVII.

Consternation in Rome.--The Conspirators in the Capitol.--Unforeseen Difficulties.--Speech of Cicero.--Caesar's Funeral.--Speech of Antony.-- Fury of the People.--The Funeral Pile in the Forum.--The King is dead, but the Monarchy survives.--Fruitlessness of the Murder.--Octavius and Antony.--Union of Octavius, Antony, and Lepidus.--Proscription of the Assassins.--

Philippi, and the end of Brutus and Cassius.--Death of Cicero.--His Character.

CHAPTER XXVIII.

General Remarks on Caesar.--Mythological Tendencies.--Supposed Profligacy of Caesar.--Nature of the Evidence.--Servilia.--Cleopatra.--Personal Appearance of Caesar.--His Manners in Private Life.--Considerations upon him as a Politician, a Soldier, and a Man of Letters.--Practical Justice his Chief Aim as a Politician.--Universality of Military Genius.--Devotion of his Army to him, how deserved.--Art of reconciling Conquered Peoples.--General Scrupulousness and Leniency.--Oratorical and Literary Style.--Cicero's Description of it.--His Lost Works.--Cato's Judgment on the Civil War.--How Caesar should be estimated.--Legend of Charles V.-- Spiritual Condition of the Age in which Caesar lived.--His Work on Earth to establish Order and Good Government, to make possible the Introduction of Christianity.--A Parallel.

CAESAR: A SKETCH

CHAPTER I.

To the student of political history, and to the English student above all others, the conversion of the Roman Republic into a military empire commands a peculiar interest. Notwithstanding many differences, the English and the Romans essentially resemble one another. The early Romans possessed the faculty of self-government beyond any people of whom we have historical knowledge, with the one exception of ourselves. In virtue of their temporal freedom, they became the most powerful nation in the known world; and their liberties perished only when Rome became the mistress of conquered races, to whom she was unable or unwilling to extend her privileges. If England was similarly supreme, if all rival powers were eclipsed by her or laid under her feet, the Imperial tendencies, which are as strongly marked in us as our love of liberty, might lead us over the same course to the same end. If there be one lesson which history clearly teaches, it is this, that free nations cannot govern subject provinces. If they are unable or unwilling to admit their dependencies to share their own constitution, the constitution itself will fall in pieces from mere incompetence for its duties.

We talk often foolishly of the necessities of things, and we blame circumstances for the consequences of our own follies and vices; but there are faults which are not faults of will, but faults of mere inadequacy to some unforeseen position. Human nature is equal to much, but not to everything. It can rise to altitudes where it is alike unable to sustain itself or to retire from them to a safer elevation. Yet when the field is open it pushes forward, and moderation in the pursuit of greatness is never learnt and never will be learnt. Men of genius are governed by their instinct; they follow where instinct leads them; and the public life of a nation is but the life of successive generations of statesmen, whose horizon is bounded, and who act from day to day as immediate interests suggest. The popular leader of the hour sees some present difficulty or present opportunity of distinction. He deals with each question as it arises, leaving future consequences to those who are to come after him. The situation changes from period to period, and tendencies are generated with an accelerating force, which, when once established, can never be reversed. When the control of reason is once removed, the catastrophe is no longer distant, and then nations, like all organized creations, all forms of life, from the meanest flower to the highest human institution, pass through the inevitably recurring stages of growth and transformation and decay. A commonwealth, says Cicero, ought to be immortal, and for ever to renew its youth. Yet commonwealths have proved as unenduring as any other natural object:

Everything that grows Holds in perfection but a little moment, And this huge state presenteth nought but shows, Whereon the stars in silent influence comment.

Nevertheless, "as the heavens are high above the earth, so is wisdom above folly." Goethe compares life to a game at whist, where the cards are dealt out by destiny, and the rules of the game are fixed: subject to these conditions, the players are left to win or lose, according to their skill or want of skill. The life of a nation, like the life of a man, may be prolonged in honor into the fulness of its time, or it may perish prematurely, for want of guidance, by violence or internal disorders. And thus the history of national revolutions is to statesmanship what the pathology of disease is to the art of medicine. The physician cannot arrest the coming on of age. Where disease has laid hold upon the constitution he cannot expel it. But he may check the progress of the evil if he can recognize the symptoms in time. He can save life at the cost of an unsound limb. He can tell us how to preserve our health when we have it; he can warn us of the conditions under which particular disorders will have us at disadvantage. And so with nations: amidst the endless variety of circumstances there are constant phenomena which give notice of approaching danger; there are courses of action which have uniformly produced the same results; and the wise politicians are those who have learnt from experience the real tendencies of things, unmisled by superficial differences, who can shun the rocks where others have been wrecked, or from foresight of what is coming can be cool when the peril is upon them.

For these reasons, the fall of the Roman Republic is exceptionally instructive to us. A constitutional government the most enduring and the most powerful that ever existed was put on its trial, and found wanting. We see it in its growth; we see the causes which undermined its strength. We see attempts to check the growing mischief fail, and we see why they failed. And we see, finally, when nothing seemed so likely as complete dissolution, the whole system changed by a violent operation, and the dying patient's life protracted for further centuries of power and usefulness.

Again, irrespective of the direct teaching which we may gather from them, particular epochs in history have the charm for us which dramas have-- periods when the great actors on the stage of life stand before us with the distinctness with which they appear in the creations of a poet. There have not been many such periods; for to see the past, it is not enough for us to be able to look at it through the eyes of contemporaries; these contemporaries themselves must have been parties to the scenes which they describe. They must have had full opportunities of knowledge. They must have had eyes which could see things in their true proportions. They must have had, in addition, the rare literary powers which can convey to others through the medium of language an exact picture of their own minds; and such happy combinations occur but occasionally in thousands of years. Generation after generation passes by, and is crumbled into sand as rocks are crumbled by the sea. Each brought with it its heroes and its villains, its triumphs and its sorrows; but the history is formless legend, incredible and unintelligible; the figures of the actors are indistinct as the rude ballad or ruder inscription, which may be the only authentic record of them. We do not see the men and women, we see only the outlines of them which have been woven into tradition as they appeared to the loves or hatreds of passionate admirers or enemies. Of such times we know nothing, save the broad results as they are measured from century to century, with here and there some indestructible pebble, some law, some fragment of remarkable poetry which has resisted decomposition. These periods are the proper subject of the philosophic historian, and to him we leave them. But there are others, a few, at which intellectual activity was as great as it is now, with its written records surviving, in which the passions, the opinions, the ambitions of the age are all before us, where the actors in the great drama speak their own thoughts in their own words, where we hear their enemies denounce them and their friends praise them; where we are ourselves plunged amidst the hopes and fears of the hour, to feel the conflicting emotions and to sympathize in the struggles which again seem to live: and here philosophy is at fault. Philosophy, when we are face to face with real men, is as powerless as over the Iliad or King Lear. The overmastering human interest transcends explanation. We do not sit in judgment on the right or the wrong; we do not seek out causes to account for what takes place, feeling too conscious of the inadequacy of our analysis. We see human beings possessed by different impulses, and working out a pre-ordained result, as the subtle forces drive each along the path marked out for him; and history becomes the more impressive to us where it least immediately instructs.

With such vividness, with such transparent clearness, the age stands before us of Cato and Pompey, of Cicero and Julius Caesar; the more distinctly because it was an age in so many ways the counterpart of our own, the blossoming period of the old civilization, when the intellect was trained to the highest point which it could reach, and on the great subjects of human interest, on morals and politics, on poetry and art, even on religion itself and the speculative problems of life, men thought as we think, doubted where we doubt, argued as we argue, aspired and struggled after the same objects. It was an age of material progress and material civilization; an age of civil liberty and intellectual culture; an age of pamphlets and epigrams, of salons and of dinner-parties, of senatorial majorities and electoral corruption. The highest offices of state were open in theory to the meanest citizen; they were confined, in fact, to those who had the longest purses, or the most ready use of the tongue on popular platforms. Distinctions of birth had been exchanged for distinctions of wealth. The struggles between plebeians and patricians for equality of privilege were over, and a new division had been formed between the party of property and a party who desired a change in the structure of society. The free cultivators were disappearing from the soil. Italy was being absorbed into vast estates, held by a few favored families and cultivated by slaves, while the old agricultural population was driven off the land, and was crowded into towns. The rich were extravagant, for life had ceased to have practical interest, except for its material pleasures; the occupation of the higher classes was to obtain money without labor, and to spend it in idle enjoyment. Patriotism survived on the lips, but patriotism meant the ascendency of the party which would maintain the existing order of things, or would overthrow it for a more equal distribution of the good things which alone were valued. Religion, once the foundation of the laws and rule of personal conduct, had subsided into opinion. The educated, in their hearts, disbelieved it. Temples were still built with increasing splendor; the established forms were scrupulously observed. Public men spoke conventionally of Providence, that they might throw on their opponents the odium of impiety; but of genuine belief that life had any serious meaning, there was none remaining beyond the circle of the silent, patient, ignorant multitude. The whole spiritual atmosphere was saturated with cant--cant moral, cant political, cant religious; an affectation of high principle which had ceased to touch the conduct, and flowed on in an increasing volume of insincere and unreal speech. The truest thinkers were those who, like Lucretius, spoke frankly out their real convictions, declared that Providence was a dream, and that man and the world he lived in were material phenomena, generated by natural forces out of cosmic atoms, and into atoms to be again resolved.

Tendencies now in operation may a few generations hence land modern society in similar conclusions, unless other convictions revive meanwhile and get the mastery of them; of which possibility no more need be said than this, that unless there be such a revival in some shape or other, the forces, whatever they be, which control the forms in which human things adjust themselves, will make an end again, as they made an end before, of what are called free institutions. Popular forms of government are possible only when individual men can govern their own lives on moral principles, and when duty is of more importance than pleasure, and justice than material expediency. Rome at any rate had grown ripe for judgment. The shape which the judgment assumed was due perhaps, in a measure, to a condition which has no longer a parallel among us. The men and women by whom the hard work of the world was done were chiefly slaves, and those who constitute the driving force of revolutions in modern Europe lay then outside society, unable and perhaps uncaring to affect its fate. No change then possible would much influence the prospects of the unhappy bondsmen. The triumph of the party of the constitution would bring no liberty to them. That their masters should fall like themselves under the authority of a higher master could not much distress them. Their sympathies, if they had any, would go with those nearest their own rank, the emancipated slaves and the sons of those who were emancipated; and they, and the poor free citizens everywhere, were to a man on the side which was considered and was called the side of "the people," and was, in fact, the side of despotism.

CHAPTER II.

The Roman Constitution had grown out of the character of the Roman nation. It was popular in form beyond all constitutions of which there is any record in history. The citizens assembled in the Comitia were the sovereign authority in the State, and they exercised their power immediately and not by representatives. The executive magistrates were chosen annually. The assembly was the supreme Court of Appeal; and without its sanction no freeman could be lawfully put to death. In the assembly also was the supreme power of legislation. Any consul, any praetor, any tribune, might propose a law from the Rostra to the people. The people if it pleased them might accept such law, and senators and public officers might be sworn to obey it under pains of treason. As a check on precipitate resolutions, a single consul or a single tribune might interpose his veto. But the veto was binding only so long as the year of office continued. If the people were in earnest, submission to their wishes could be made a condition at the next election, and thus no constitutional means existed of resisting them when these wishes showed themselves.

In normal times the Senate was allowed the privilege of preconsidering intended acts of legislation, and refusing to recommend them if inexpedient, but the privilege was only converted into a right after violent convulsions, and was never able to maintain itself. That under such a system the functions of government could have been carried on at all was due entirely to the habits of self-restraint which the Romans had engraved into their nature. They were called a nation of kings, kings over their own appetites, passions, and inclinations. They were not imaginative, they were not intellectual; they had little national poetry, little art, little philosophy. They were moral and practical. In these two directions the force that was in them entirely ran. They were free politically, because freedom meant to them not freedom to do as they pleased, but freedom to do what was right; and every citizen, before he arrived at his civil privileges, had been schooled in the discipline of obedience. Each head of a household was absolute master of it, master over his children and servants, even to the extent of life and death. What the father was to the family, the gods were to the whole people, the awful lords and rulers at whose pleasure they lived and breathed. Unlike the Greeks, the reverential Romans invented no idle legends about the supernatural world. The gods to them were the guardians of the State, whose will in all things they were bound to seek and to obey. The forms in which they endeavored to learn what that will might be were childish or childlike. They looked to signs in the sky, to thunder-storms and comets and shooting stars. Birds, winged messengers, as they thought them, between earth and heaven, were celestial indicators of the gods' commands. But omens and auguries were but the outward symbols, and the Romans, like all serious peoples, went to their own hearts for their real guidance. They had a unique religious peculiarity, to which no race of men has produced anything like. They did not embody the elemental forces in personal forms; they did not fashion a theology out of the movements of the sun and stars or the changes of the seasons. Traces may be found among them of cosmic traditions and superstitions, which were common to all the world; but they added of their own this especial feature: that they built temples and offered sacrifices to the highest human excellences, to "Valor," to "Truth," to "Good Faith," to "Modesty," to "Charity," to "Concord." In these qualities lay all that raised man above the animals with which he had so much in common. In them, therefore, were to be found the link which connected him with the divine nature, and moral qualities were regarded as divine influences which gave his life its meaning and its worth. The "Virtues" were elevated into beings to whom disobedience could be punished as a crime, and the superstitious fears which run so often into mischievous idolatries were enlisted with conscience in the direct service of right action.

On the same principle the Romans chose the heroes and heroines of their national history. The Manlii and Valerii were patterns of courage, the Lucretias and Virginias of purity, the Decii and Curtii of patriotic devotion, the Reguli and Fabricii of stainless truthfulness. On the same principle, too, they had a public officer whose functions resembled those of the Church courts in mediaeval Europe, a Censor Morum, an inquisitor who might examine into the habits of private families, rebuke extravagance, check luxury, punish vice and self-indulgence, nay, who could remove from the Senate, the great council of elders, persons whose moral conduct was a reproach to a body on whose reputation no shadow could be allowed to rest.

Such the Romans were in the day when their dominion had not extended beyond the limits of Italy; and because they were such they were able to prosper under a constitution which to modern experience would promise only the most hopeless confusion.

Morality thus engrained in the national character and grooved into habits of action creates strength, as nothing else creates it. The difficulty of conduct does not lie in knowing what it is right to do, but in doing it when known. Intellectual culture does not touch the conscience. It provides no motives to overcome the weakness of the will, and with wider knowledge it brings also new temptations. The sense of duty is present in each detail of life; the obligatory "must" which binds the will to the course which right principle has marked out for it produces a fibre like the fibre of the oak. The educated Greeks knew little of it. They had courage and genius and enthusiasm, but they had no horror of immorality as such. The Stoics saw what was wanting, and tried to supply it; but though they could provide a theory of action, they could not make the theory into a reality, and it is noticeable that Stoicism as a rule of life became important only when adopted by the Romans. The Catholic Church effected something in its better days when it had its courts which treated sins as crimes. Calvinism, while it was believed, produced characters nobler and grander than any which Republican Rome produced. But the Catholic Church turned its penances into money payments. Calvinism made demands on faith beyond what truth would bear; and when doubt had once entered, the spell of Calvinism was broken. The veracity of the Romans, and perhaps the happy accident that they had no inherited religious traditions, saved them for centuries from similar trials. They had hold of real truth unalloyed with baser metal; and truth had made them free and kept them so. When all else has passed away, when theologies have yielded up their real meaning, and creeds and symbols have become transparent, and man is again in contact with the hard facts of nature, it will be found that the "Virtues" which the Romans made into gods contain in them the essence of true religion, that in them lies the special characteristic which distinguishes human beings from the rest of animated things. Every other creature exists for itself, and cares for its own preservation. Nothing larger or better is expected from it or possible to it. To man it is said, you do not live for yourself. If you live for yourself you shall come to nothing. Be brave, be just, be pure, be true in word and deed; care not for your enjoyment, care not for your life; care only for what is right. So, and not otherwise, it shall be well with you. So the Maker of you has ordered, whom you will disobey at your peril.

Thus and thus only are nations formed which are destined to endure; and as habits based on such convictions are slow in growing, so when grown to maturity they survive extraordinary trials. But nations are made up of many persons in circumstances of endless variety. In country districts, where the routine of life continues simple, the type of character remains unaffected; generation follows on generation exposed to the same influences and treading in the same steps. But the morality of habit, though the most important element in human conduct, is still but a part of it. Moral habits grow under given conditions. They correspond to a given degree of temptation. When men are removed into situations where the use and wont of their fathers no longer meets their necessities; where new opportunities are offered to them; where their opinions are broken in upon by new ideas; where pleasures tempt them on every side, and they have but to stretch out their hand to take them--moral habits yield under the strain, and they have no other resource to fall back upon. Intellectual cultivation brings with it rational interests. Knowledge, which looks before and after, acts as a restraining power, to help conscience when it flags. The sober and wholesome manners of life among the early Romans had given them vigorous minds in vigorous bodies. The animal nature had grown as strongly as the moral nature, and along with it the animal appetites; and when appetites burst their traditional restraints, and man in himself has no other notion of enjoyment beyond bodily pleasure, he may pass by an easy transition into a mere powerful brute. And thus it happened with the higher classes at Rome after the destruction of Carthage. Italy had fallen to them by natural and wholesome expansion; but from being sovereigns of Italy, they became a race of imperial conquerors. Suddenly, and in comparatively a few years after the one power was gone which could resist them, they became the actual or virtual rulers of the entire circuit of the Mediterranean. The south-east of Spain, the coast of France from the Pyrenees to Nice, the north of Italy, Illyria and Greece, Sardinia, Sicily, and the Greek Islands, the southern and western shores of Asia Minor, were Roman provinces, governed directly under Roman magistrates. On the African side Mauritania (Morocco) was still free. Numidia (the modern Algeria) retained its native dynasty, but was a Roman dependency. The Carthaginian dominions, Tunis and Tripoli, had been annexed to the Empire. The interior of Asia Minor up to the Euphrates, with Syria and Egypt, were under sovereigns called Allies, but, like the native princes in India, subject to a Roman protectorate. Over this enormous territory, rich with the accumulated treasures of centuries, and inhabited by thriving, industrious races, the energetic Roman men of business had spread and settled themselves, gathering into their hands the trade, the financial administration, the entire commercial control of the Mediterranean basin. They had been trained in thrift and economy, in abhorrence of debt, in strictest habits of close and careful management. Their frugal education, their early lessons in the value of money, good and excellent as those lessons were, led them, as a matter of course, to turn to account their extraordinary opportunities. Governors with their staffs, permanent officials, contractors for the revenue, negotiators, bill-brokers, bankers, merchants, were scattered everywhere in thousands. Money poured in upon them in rolling streams of gold. The largest share of the spoils fell to the Senate and the senatorial families. The Senate was the permanent Council of State, and was the real administrator of the Empire. The Senate had the control of the treasury, conducted the public policy, appointed from its own ranks the governors of the provinces. It was patrician in sentiment, but not necessarily patrician in composition. The members of it had virtually been elected for life by the people, and were almost entirely those who had been quaestors, aediles, praetors, or consuls; and these offices had been long open to the plebeians. It was an aristocracy, in theory a real one, but tending to become, as civilization went forward, an aristocracy of the rich. How the senatorial privileges affected the management of the provinces will be seen more particularly as we go on. It is enough at present to say that the nobles and great commoners of Rome rapidly found themselves in possession of revenues which their fathers could not have imagined in their dreams, and money in the stage of progress at which Rome had arrived was convertible into power.

The opportunities opened for men to advance their fortunes in other parts of the world drained Italy of many of its most enterprising citizens. The grandsons of the yeomen who had held at bay Pyrrhus and Hannibal sold their farms and went away. The small holdings merged rapidly into large estates bought up by the Roman capitalists. At the final settlement of Italy, some millions of acres had been reserved to the State as public property. The "public land," as the reserved portion was called, had been leased on easy terms to families with political influence, and by lapse of time, by connivance and right of occupation, these families were beginning to regard their tenures as their private property, and to treat them as lords of manors in England have treated the "commons." Thus everywhere the small farmers were disappearing, and the soil of Italy was fast passing into the hands of a few territorial magnates, who, unfortunately (for it tended to aggravate the mischief), were enabled by another cause to turn their vast possessions to advantage. The conquest of the world had turned the flower of the defeated nations into slaves. The prisoners taken either after a battle or when cities surrendered unconditionally were bought up steadily by contractors who followed in the rear of the Roman armies. They were not ignorant like the negroes, but trained, useful, and often educated men, Asiatics, Greeks, Thracians, Gauls, and Spaniards, able at once to turn their hands to some form of skilled labor, either as clerks, mechanics, or farm-servants. The great landowners might have paused in their purchases had the alternative lain before them of letting their lands lie idle or of having freemen to cultivate them. It was otherwise when a resource so convenient and so abundant was opened at their feet. The wealthy Romans bought slaves by thousands. Some they employed in their workshops in the capital. Some they spread over their plantations, covering the country, it might be, with olive gardens and vineyards, swelling further the plethoric figures of their owners' incomes. It was convenient for the few, but less convenient for the Commonwealth. The strength of Rome was in her free citizens. Where a family of slaves was settled down, a village of freemen had disappeared; the material for the legions diminished; the dregs of the free population which remained behind crowded into Rome, without occupation except in politics, and with no property save in their votes, of course to become the clients of the millionaires, and to sell themselves to the highest bidders. With all his wealth there were but two things which the Roman noble could buy, political power and luxury; and in these directions his whole resources were expended. The elections, once pure, became matters of annual bargain between himself and his supporters. The once hardy, abstemious mode of living degenerated into grossness and sensuality.

And his character was assailed simultaneously on another side with equally mischievous effect. The conquest of Greece brought to Rome a taste for knowledge and culture; but the culture seldom passed below the surface, and knowledge bore but the old fruit which it had borne in Eden. The elder Cato used to say that the Romans were like their slaves--the less Greek they knew the better they were. They had believed in the gods with pious simplicity. The Greeks introduced them to an Olympus of divinities whom the practical Roman found that he must either abhor or deny to exist. The "Virtues" which he had been taught to reverence had no place among the graces of the new theology. Reverence Jupiter he could not, and it was easy to persuade him that Jupiter was an illusion; that all religions were but the creations of fancy, his own among them. Gods there might be, airy beings in the deeps of space, engaged like men with their own enjoyments; but to suppose that these high spirits fretted themselves with the affairs of the puny beings that crawled upon the earth was a delusion of vanity. Thus, while morality was assailed on one side by extraordinary temptations, the religious sanction of it was undermined on the other. The, Romans ceased to believe, and in losing their faith they became as steel becomes when it is demagnetized; the spiritual quality was gone out of them, and the high society of Rome itself became a society of powerful animals with an enormous appetite for pleasure. Wealth poured in more and more, and luxury grew more unbounded. Palaces sprang up in the city, castles in the country, villas at pleasant places by the sea, and parks, and fish-ponds, and game-preserves, and gardens, and vast retinues of servants. When natural pleasures had been indulged in to satiety, pleasures which were against nature were imported from the East to stimulate the exhausted appetite. To make money--money by any means, lawful or unlawful--became the universal passion. Even the most cultivated patricians were coarse alike in their habits and their amusements. They cared for art as dilettanti, but no schools either of sculpture or painting were formed among themselves. They decorated their porticos and their saloons with the plunder of the East. The stage was never more than an artificial taste with them; their delight was the delight of barbarians, in spectacles, in athletic exercises, in horse-races and chariot-races, in the combats of wild animals in the circus, combats of men with beasts on choice occasions, and, as a rare excitement, in fights between men and men, when select slaves trained as gladiators were matched in pairs to kill each other. Moral habits are all-sufficient while they last; but with rude strong natures they are but chains which hold the passions prisoners. Let the chain break, and the released brute is but the more powerful for evil from the force which his constitution has inherited. Money! the cry was still money!--money was the one thought from the highest senator to the poorest wretch who sold his vote in the Comitia. For money judges gave unjust decrees and juries gave corrupt verdicts. Governors held their provinces for one, two, or three years; they went out bankrupt from extravagance, they returned with millions for fresh riot. To obtain a province was the first ambition of a Roman noble. The road to it lay through the praetorship and the consulship; these offices, therefore, became the prizes of the State; and being in the gift of the people, they were sought after by means which demoralized alike the givers and the receivers. The elections were managed by clubs and coteries; and, except on occasions of national danger or political excitement, those who spent most freely were most certain of success.

Under these conditions the chief powers in the Commonwealth necessarily centred in the rich. There was no longer an aristocracy of birth, still less of virtue. The patrician families had the start in the race. Great names and great possessions came to them by inheritance. But the door of promotion was open to all who had the golden key. The great commoners bought their way into the magistracies. From the magistracies they passed into the Senate; and the Roman senator, though in Rome itself and in free debate among his colleagues he was handled as an ordinary man, when he travelled had the honors of a sovereign. The three hundred senators of Rome were three hundred princes. They moved about in other countries with the rights of legates, at the expense of the province, with their trains of slaves and horses. The proud privilege of Roman citizenship was still jealously reserved to Rome itself and to a few favored towns and colonies; and a mere subject could maintain no rights against a member of the haughty oligarchy which controlled the civilized world. Such generally the Roman Republic had become, or was tending to become, in the years which followed the fall of Carthage, B.C. 146. Public spirit in the masses was dead or sleeping; the Commonwealth was a plutocracy. The free forms of the constitution were themselves the instruments of corruption. The rich were happy in the possession of all that they could desire. The multitude was kept quiet by the morsels of meat which were flung to it when it threatened to be troublesome. The seven thousand in Israel, the few who in all states and in all times remained pure in the midst of evil, looked on with disgust, fearing that any remedy which they might try might be worse than the disease. All orders in a society may be wise and virtuous, but all cannot be rich. Wealth which is used only for idle luxury is always envied, and envy soon curdles into hate. It is easy to persuade the masses that the good things of this world are unjustly divided, especially when it happens to be the exact truth. It is not easy to set limits to an agitation once set on foot, however justly it may have been provoked, when the cry for change is at once stimulated by interest and can disguise its real character under the passionate language of patriotism. But it was not to be expected that men of noble natures, young men especially whose enthusiasm had not been cooled by experience, would sit calmly by while their country was going thus headlong to perdition. Redemption, if redemption was to be hoped for, could come only from free citizens in the country districts whose manners and whoso minds were still uncontaminated, in whom the ancient habits of life still survived, who still believed in the gods, who were contented to follow the wholesome round of honest labor. The numbers of such citizens were fast dwindling away before the omnivorous appetite of the rich for territorial aggrandizement. To rescue the land from the monopolists, to renovate the old independent yeomanry, to prevent the free population of Italy, out of which the legions had been formed which had built up the Empire, from being pushed out of their places and supplanted by foreign slaves, this, if it could be done, would restore the purity of the constituency, snatch the elections from the control of corruption, and rear up fresh generations of peasant soldiers to preserve the liberties and the glories which their fathers had won.

CHAPTER III.

Tiberius Gracchus was born about the year 164 B.C. He was one of twelve children, nine of whom died in infancy, himself, his brother Caius, and his sister Cornelia being the only survivors. His family was plebeian, but of high antiquity, his ancestors for several generations having held the highest offices in the Republic. On the mother's side he was the grandson of Scipio Africanus. His father, after a distinguished career as a soldier in Spain and Sardinia, had attempted reforms at Rome. He had been censor, and in this capacity he had ejected disreputable senators from the Curia; he had degraded offending equites; he had rearranged and tried to purify the Comitia. But his connections were aristocratic. His wife was the daughter of the most illustrious of the Scipios. His own daughter was married to the second most famous of them, Scipio Africanus the Younger. He had been himself in antagonism with the tribunes, and had taken no part at any time in popular agitations.

The father died when Tiberius was still a boy, and the two brothers grew up under the care of their mother, a noble and gifted lady. They displayed early remarkable talents. Tiberius, when old enough, went into the army, and served under his brother-in-law in the last Carthaginian campaign. He was first on the walls of the city in the final storm. Ten years later he went to Spain as Quaestor, where he carried on his father's popularity, and by taking the people's side in some questions fell into disagreement with his brother-in-law. His political views had perhaps already inclined to change. He was still of an age when indignation at oppression calls out a practical desire to resist it. On his journey home from Spain he witnessed scenes which confirmed his conviction and determined him to throw all his energies into the popular cause. His road lay through Tuscany, where he saw the large-estate system in full operation--the fields cultivated by the slave gangs, the free citizens of the Republic thrust away into the towns, aliens and outcasts in their own country, without a foot of soil which they could call their own. In Tuscany, too, the vast domains of the landlords had not even been fairly purchased. They were parcels of the ager publicus, land belonging to the State, which, in spite of a law forbidding it, the great lords and commoners had appropriated and divided among themselves. Five hundred acres of State land was the most which by statute any one lessee might be allowed to occupy. But the law was obsolete or sleeping, and avarice and vanity were awake and active. Young Gracchus, in indignant pity, resolved to rescue the people's patrimony. He was chosen tribune in the year 133. His brave mother and a few patricians of the old type encouraged him, and the battle of the revolution began. The Senate, as has been said, though without direct legislative authority, had been allowed the right of reviewing any new schemes which were to be submitted to the assembly. The constitutional means of preventing tribunes from carrying unwise or unwelcome measures lay in a consul's veto, or in the help of the College of Augurs, who could declare the auspices unfavorable, and so close all public business. These resources were so awkward that it had been found convenient to secure beforehand the Senate's approbation, and the encroachment, being long submitted to, was passing by custom into a rule. But the Senate, eager as it was, had not yet succeeded in engrafting the practice into the constitution. On the land question the leaders of the aristocracy were the principal offenders. Disregarding usage, and conscious that the best men of all ranks were with him, Tiberius Gracchus appealed directly to the people to revive the agrarian law. His proposals were not extravagant. That they should have been deemed extravagant was a proof of how much some measure of the kind was needed. Where lands had been enclosed and money laid out on them he was willing that the occupants should have compensation. But they had no right to the lands themselves. Gracchus persisted that the ager publicus belonged to the people, and that the race of yeomen, for whose protection the law had been originally passed, must be re-established on their farms. No form of property gives to its owners so much consequence as land, and there is no point on which in every country an aristocracy is more sensitive. The large owners protested that they had purchased their interests on the faith that the law was obsolete. They had planted and built and watered with the sanction of the government, and to call their titles in question was to shake the foundations of society. The popular party pointed to the statute. The monopolists were entitled in justice to less than was offered them. They had no right to a compensation at all. Political passion awoke again after the sleep of a century. The oligarchy had doubtless connived at the accumulations. The suppression of the small holdings favored their supremacy, and placed the elections more completely in their control. Their military successes had given them so long a tenure of power that they had believed it to be theirs in perpetuity; and the new sedition, as they called it, threatened at once their privileges and their fortunes. The quarrel assumed the familiar form of a struggle between the rich and the poor, and at such times the mob of voters becomes less easy to corrupt. They go with their order, as the prospect of larger gain makes them indifferent to immediate bribes. It became clear that the majority of the citizens would support Tiberius Gracchus, but the constitutional forms of opposition might still be resorted to. Octavius Caecina, another of the tribunes, had himself large interests in the land question. He was the people's magistrate, one of the body appointed especially to defend their rights, but he went over to the Senate, and, using a power which undoubtedly belonged to him, he forbade the vote to be taken.

There was no precedent for the removal of either consul, praetor, or tribune, except under circumstances very different from any which could as yet be said to have arisen. The magistrates held office for a year only, and the power of veto had been allowed them expressly to secure time for deliberation and to prevent passionate legislation. But Gracchus was young and enthusiastic.

Precedent or no precedent, the citizens were omnipotent. He invited them to declare his colleague deposed. They had warmed to the fight, and complied. A more experienced statesman would have known that established constitutional bulwarks cannot be swept away by a momentary vote. He obtained his agrarian law. Three commissioners were appointed, himself, his younger brother, and his father-in-law, Appius Claudius, to carry it into effect; but the very names showed that he had alienated his few supporters in the higher circles, and that a single family was now contending against the united wealth and distinction of Rome. The issue was only too certain. Popular enthusiasm is but a fire of straw. In a year Tiberius Gracchus would be out of office. Other tribunes would be chosen more amenable to influence, and his work could then be undone. He evidently knew that those who would succeed him could not be relied on to carry on his policy. He had taken one revolutionary step already; he was driven on to another, and he offered himself illegally to the Comitia for re-election. It was to invite them to abolish the constitution and to make him virtual sovereign; and that a young man of thirty should have contemplated such a position for himself as possible is of itself a proof of his unfitness for it. The election-day came. The noble lords and gentlemen appeared in the Campus Martius with their retinues of armed servants and clients; hot-blooded aristocrats, full of disdain for demagogues, and meaning to read a lesson to sedition which it would not easily forget. Votes were given for Gracchus. Had the hustings been left to decide the matter, he would have been chosen; but as it began to appear how the polling would go, sticks were used and swords; a riot rose, the unarmed citizens were driven off, Tiberius Gracchus himself and three hundred of his friends were killed and their bodies were flung into the Tiber.

Thus the first sparks of the coming revolution were trampled out. But though quenched and to be again quenched with fiercer struggles, it was to smoulder and smoke and burst out time after time, till its work was done. Revolution could not restore the ancient character of the Roman nation, but it could check the progress of decay by burning away the more corrupted parts of it. It could destroy the aristocracy and the constitution which they had depraved, and under other forms present for a few more centuries the Roman dominion. Scipio Africanus, when he heard in Spain of the end of his brother-in-law, exclaimed, "May all who act as he did perish like him!" There were to be victims enough and to spare before the bloody drama was played out. Quiet lasted for ten years, and then, precisely when he had reached his brother's age, Caius Gracchus came forward to avenge him, and carry the movement through another stage. Young Caius had been left one of the commissioners of the land law; and it is particularly noticeable that though the author of it had been killed, the law had survived him being too clearly right and politic in itself to be openly set aside. For two years the commissioners had continued to work, and in that time forty thousand families were settled on various parts of the ager publicus, which the patricians had been compelled to resign. This was all which they could do. The displacement of one set of inhabitants and the introduction of another could not be accomplished without quarrels, complaints, and perhaps some injustice. Those who were ejected were always exasperated. Those who entered on possession were not always satisfied. The commissioners became unpopular. When the cries against them became loud enough, they were suspended, and the law was then quietly repealed. The Senate had regained its hold over the assembly, and had a further opportunity of showing its recovered ascendency when, two years after the murder of Tiberius Gracchus, one of his friends introduced a bill to make the tribunes legally re-eligible. Caius Gracchus actively supported the change, but it had no success; and, waiting till times had altered, and till he had arrived himself at an age when he could carry weight, the young brother retired from politics, and spent the next few years with the army in Africa and Sardinia. He served with distinction; he made a name for himself both as a soldier and an administrator. Had the Senate left him alone, he might have been satisfied with a regular career, and have risen by the ordinary steps to the consulship. But the Senate saw in him the possibilities of a second Tiberius; the higher his reputation, the more formidable he became to them. They vexed him with petty prosecutions, charged him with crimes which had no existence, and at length by suspicion and injustice drove him into open war with them. Caius Gracchus had a broader intellect than his brother, and a character considerably less noble. The land question he perceived was but one of many questions. The true source of the disorders of the Commonwealth was the Senate itself. The administration of the Empire was in the hands of men totally unfit to be trusted with it, and there he thought the reform must commence. He threw himself on the people. He was chosen tribune in 123, ten years exactly after Tiberius. He had studied the disposition of parties. He had seen his brother fall because the equites and the senators, the great commoners and the nobles, were combined against him. He revived the agrarian law as a matter of course, but he disarmed the opposition to it by throwing an apple of discord between the two superior orders. The high judicial functions in the Commonwealth had been hitherto a senatorial monopoly. All cases of importance, civil or criminal, came before courts of sixty or seventy jurymen, who, as the law stood, must be necessarily senators. The privilege had been extremely lucrative. The corruption of justice was already notorious, though it had not yet reached the level of infamy which it attained in another generation. It was no secret that in ordinary causes jurymen had sold their verdicts; and, far short of taking bribes in the direct sense of the word, there were many ways in which they could let themselves be approached and their favor purchased. A monopoly of privileges is always invidious. A monopoly in the sale of justice is alike hateful to those who abhor iniquity on principle and to those who would like to share the profits of it. But this was not the worst. The governors of the provinces, being chosen from those who had been consuls or praetors, were necessarily members of the Senate. Peculation and extortion in these high functions were offences in theory of the gravest kind; but the offender could only be tried before a limited number of his peers, and a governor who had plundered a subject state, sold justice, pillaged temples, and stolen all that he could lay hands on, was safe from punishment if he returned to Rome a millionaire and would admit others to a share in his spoils. The provincials might send deputations to complain, but these complaints came before men who had themselves governed provinces or else aspired to govern them. It had been proved in too many instances that the law which professed to protect them was a mere mockery.

Caius Gracchus secured the affections of the knights to himself, and some slightly increased chance of an improvement in the provincial administration, by carrying a law in the assembly disabling the senators from sitting on juries of any kind from that day forward, and transferring the judicial functions to the equites. How bitterly must such a measure have been resented by the Senate, which at once robbed them of their protective and profitable privileges, handed them over to be tried by their rivals for their pleasant irregularities, and stamped them at the same time with the brand of dishonesty! How certainly must such a measure have been deserved when neither consul nor tribune could be found to interpose his veto! Supported by the grateful knights, Caius Gracchus was for the moment all-powerful. It was not enough to restore the agrarian law. He passed another, aimed at his brother's murderers, which was to bear fruit in later years, that no Roman citizen might be put to death by any person, however high in authority, without legal trial, and without appeal, if he chose to make it, to the sovereign people. A blow was thus struck against another right claimed by the Senate, of declaring the Republic in danger, and the temporary suspension of the constitution. These measures might be excused, and perhaps commended; but the younger Gracchus connected his name with another change less commendable, which was destined also to survive and bear fruit. He brought forward and carried through, with enthusiastic clapping of every pair of hands in Rome that were hardened with labor, a proposal that there should be public granaries in the city, maintained and filled at the cost of the State, and that corn should be sold at a rate artificially cheap to the poor free citizens. Such a law was purely socialistic. The privilege was confined to Rome, because in Rome the elections were held, and the Roman constituency was the one depositary of power. The effect was to gather into the city a mob of needy, unemployed voters, living on the charity of the State, to crowd the circus and to clamor at the elections, available no doubt immediately to strengthen the hands of the popular tribune, but certain in the long-run to sell themselves to those who could bid highest for their voices. Excuses could be found, no doubt, for this miserable expedient in the state of parties, in the unscrupulous violence of the aristocracy, in the general impoverishment of the peasantry through the land monopoly, and in the intrusion upon Italy of a gigantic system of slave labor. But none the less it was the deadliest blow which had yet been dealt to the constitution. Party government turns on the majorities at the polling-places, and it was difficult afterward to recall a privilege which once conceded appeared to be a right. The utmost that could be ventured in later times with any prospect of success was to limit an intolerable evil; and if one side was ever strong enough to make the attempt, their rivals had a bribe ready in their hands to buy back the popular support. Caius Gracchus, however, had his way, and carried all before him. He escaped the rock on which his brother had been wrecked. He was elected tribune a second time. He might have had a third term if he had been contented to be a mere demagogue. But he, too, like Tiberius, had honorable aims. The powers which he had played into the hands of the mob to obtain he desired to use for high purposes of statesmanship, and his instrument broke in his hands. He was too wise to suppose that a Roman mob, fed by bounties from the treasury, could permanently govern the world. He had schemes for scattering Roman colonies, with the Roman franchise, at various points of the Empire. Carthage was to be one of them. He thought of abolishing the distinction between Romans and Italians, and enfranchising the entire peninsula. These measures were good in themselves--essential, indeed, if the Roman conquests were to form a compact and permanent dominion. But the object was not attainable on the road on which Gracchus had entered. The vagabond part of the constituency was well contented with what it had obtained--a life in the city, supported at the public expense, with politics and games for its amusements. It had not the least inclination to be drafted off into settlements in Spain or Africa, where there would be work instead of pleasant idleness. Carthage was still a name of terror. To restore Carthage was no better than treason. Still less had the Roman citizens an inclination to share their privileges with Samnites and Etruscans, and see the value of their votes watered down. Political storms are always cyclones. The gale from the east to-day is a gale from the west to-morrow. Who and what were the Gracchi, then?--the sweet voices began to ask--ambitious intriguers, aiming at dictatorship or perhaps the crown. The aristocracy were right after all; a few things had gone wrong, but these had been amended. The Scipios and Metelli had conquered the world: the Scipios and Metelli were alone fit to govern it. Thus when the election time came round, the party of reform was reduced to a minority of irreconcilable radicals who were easily disposed of. Again, as ten years before, the noble lords armed their followers. Riots broke out and extended day after day. Caius Gracchus was at last killed, as his brother had been, and under cover of the disturbance three thousand of his friends were killed along with him. The power being again securely in their hands, the Senate proceeded at their leisure, and the surviving patriots who were in any way notorious or dangerous were hunted down in legal manner and put to death or banished.

CHAPTER IV.

Caius Gracchus was killed at the close of the year 122. The storm was over. The Senate was once more master of the situation, and the optimates, "the best party in the State," as they were pleased to call themselves, smoothed their ruffled plumes and settled again into their places. There was no more talk of reform. Of the Gracchi there remained nothing but the forty thousand peasant-proprietors settled on the public lands; the jury law, which could not be at once repealed for fear of the equites; the corn grants, and the mob attracted by the bounty, which could be managed by improved manipulation; and the law protecting the lives of Roman citizens, which survived in the statute-book, although the Senate still claimed the right to set it aside when they held the State to be in danger. With these exceptions, the administration fell back into its old condition. The tribunes ceased to agitate. The consulships and the praetorships fell to the candidates whom the Senate supported. Whether the oligarchy had learnt any lessons of caution from the brief political earthquake which had shaken but not overthrown them remained to be seen. Six years after the murder of Caius Gracchus an opportunity was afforded to this distinguished body of showing on a conspicuous scale the material of which they were now composed.

Along the south shore of the Mediterranean, west of the Roman province, extended the two kingdoms of the Numidians and the Moors. To what race these people belonged is not precisely known. They were not negroes. The negro tribes have never extended north of the Sahara. Nor were they Carthaginians or allied to the Carthaginians. The Carthaginian colony found them in possession on its arrival. Sallust says that they were Persians left behind by Hercules after his invasion of Spain. Sallust's evidence proves no more than that their appearance was Asiatic, and that tradition assigned them an Asiatic origin. They may be called generically Arabs, who at a very ancient time had spread along the coast from Egypt to Morocco. The Numidians at this period were civilized according to the manners of the age. They had walled towns; they had considerable wealth; their lands were extensively watered and cultivated; their great men had country houses and villas, the surest sign of a settled state of society. Among the equipments of their army they had numerous elephants (it may be presumed of the African breed), which they and the Carthaginians had certainly succeeded in domesticating. Masinissa, the king of this people, had been the ally of Rome in the last Carthaginian war; he had been afterward received as "a friend of the Republic," and was one of the protected sovereigns. He was succeeded by his son Micipsa, who in turn had two legitimate children, Hiempsal and Adherbal, and an illegitimate nephew Jugurtha, considerably older than his own boys, a young man of striking talent and promise. Micipsa, who was advanced in years, was afraid that if he died this brilliant youth might be a dangerous rival to his sons. He therefore sent him to serve under Scipio in Spain, with the hope, so his friends asserted, that he might there perhaps be killed. The Roman army was then engaged in the siege of Numantia. The camp was the lounging-place of the young patricians who were tired of Rome and wished for excitement. Discipline had fallen loose; the officers' quarters were the scene of extravagance and amusement. Jugurtha recommended himself on the one side to Scipio by activity and good service, while on the other he made acquaintances among the high-bred gentlemen in the mess-rooms. He found them in themselves dissolute and unscrupulous. He discovered, through communications which he was able with their assistance to open with their fathers and relatives at Rome, that a man with money might do what he pleased. Micipsa's treasury was well supplied, and Jugurtha hinted among his comrades that if he could be secure of countenance in seizing the kingdom, he would be in a position to show his gratitude in a substantial manner. Some of these conversations reached the ears of Scipio, who sent for Jugurtha and gave him a friendly warning. He dismissed him, however, with honor at the end of the campaign. The young prince returned to Africa loaded with distinctions, and the king, being now afraid to pass him over, named him as joint-heir with his children to a third part of Numidia. The Numidians perhaps objected to being partitioned. Micipsa died soon after. Jugurtha at once murdered Hiempsal, claimed the sovereignty, and attacked his other cousin. Adherbal, closely besieged in the town of Cirta, which remained faithful to him, appealed to Rome; but Jugurtha had already prepared his ground, and knew that he had nothing to fear. The Senate sent out commissioners. The commissioners received the bribes which they expected. They gave Jugurtha general instructions to leave his cousin in peace; but they did not wait to see their orders obeyed, and went quietly home. The natural results immediately followed. Jugurtha pressed the siege more resolutely. The town surrendered; Adherbal was taken, and was put to death after being savagely tortured; and there being no longer any competitor alive in whose behalf the Senate could be called on to interfere, he thought himself safe from further interference. Unfortunately in the capture of Citra a number of Romans who resided there had been killed after the surrender, and after a promise that their lives should be spared. An outcry was raised in Rome, and became so loud that the Senate was forced to promise investigation; but it went to work languidly, with reluctance so evident as to rouse suspicion. Notwithstanding the fate of the Gracchi and their friends, Memmius, a tribune, was found bold enough to tell the people that there were men in the Senate who had taken bribes.

The Senate, conscious of its guilt, was now obliged to exert itself. War was declared against Jugurtha, and a consul was sent to Africa with an army. But the consul, too, had his fortune to make, and Micipsa's treasures were still unexpended. The consul took with him a staff of young patricians, whose families might be counted on to shield him in return for a share of the plunder. Jugurtha was as liberal as avarice could desire, and peace was granted to him on the easy conditions of a nominal fine, and the surrender of some elephants, which the consul privately restored.

Public opinion was singularly patient. The massacre six years before had killed out the liberal leaders, and there was no desire on any side as yet to renew the struggle with the Senate. But it was possible to presume too far on popular acquiescence. Memmius came forward again, and in a passionate speech in the Forum exposed and denounced the scandalous transaction. The political sky began to blacken again. The Senate could not face another storm with so bad a cause, and Jugurtha was sent for to Rome. He came, with contemptuous confidence, loaded with gold. He could not corrupt Memmius, but he bought easily the rest of the tribunes. The leaders in the Curia could not quarrel with a client of such delightful liberality. He had an answer to every complaint, and a fee to silence the complainer. He would have gone back in triumph, had he not presumed a little too far. He had another cousin in the city who he feared might one day give him trouble, so he employed one of his suite to poison him. The murder was accomplished successfully; and for this too he might no doubt have secured his pardon by paying for it; but the price demanded was too high, and perhaps Jugurtha, villain as he was, came at last to disdain the wretches whom he might consider fairly to be worse than himself. He had come over under a safe-conduct, and he was not detained. The Senate ordered him to leave Italy; and he departed with the scornful phrase on his lips which has passed into history: "Venal city, and soon to perish if only it can find a purchaser." [1]

A second army was sent across, to end the scandal. This time the Senate was in earnest, but the work was less easy than was expected. Army management had fallen into disorder. In earlier times each Roman citizen had provided his own equipments at his own expense. To be a soldier was part of the business of his life, and military training was an essential feature of his education. The old system had broken down; the peasantry, from whom the rank and file of the legions had been recruited, were no longer able to furnish their own arms. Caius Gracchus had intended that arms should be furnished by the government, that a special department should be constituted to take charge of the arsenals and to see to the distribution. But Gracchus was dead, and his project had died with him. When the legions were enrolled, the men were ill armed, undrilled, and unprovided--a mere mob, gathered hastily together and ignorant of the first elements of their duty. With the officers it was still worse. The subordinate commands fell to young patricians, carpet knights who went on campaigns with their families of slaves. The generals, when a movement was to be made, looked for instruction to their staff. It sometimes happened that a consul waited for his election to open for the first time a book of military history or a Greek manual of the art of war.[2]

[Sidenote: B.C 109.] An army so composed and so led was not likely to prosper. The Numidians were not very formidable enemies, but, after a month or two of manoeuvring, half the Romans were destroyed and the remainder were obliged to surrender. About the same time, and from similar causes, two Roman armies were cut to pieces on the Rhone. While the great men at Rome were building palaces, inventing new dishes, and hiring cooks at unheard-of salaries, the barbarians were at the gates of Italy. The passes of the Alps were open, and if a few tribes of Gauls had cared to pour through them, the Empire was at their mercy. Stung with these accumulating disgraces, and now really alarmed, the Senate sent Caecilius Metellus, the best man that they had and the consul for the year following to Africa. Metellus was an aristocrat, and he was advanced in years; but he was a man of honor and integrity. He understood the danger of further failure; and he looked about for the ablest soldier that he could find to go with him, irrespective of his political opinions.

Caius Marius was at this time forty-eight years old. Two thirds of his life were over, and a name which was to sound throughout the world and be remembered through all ages had as yet been scarcely heard of beyond the army and the political clubs in Rome. He was born at Arpinum, a Latin township, seventy miles from the capital, in the year 157. His father was a small farmer, and he was himself bred to the plough. He joined the army early, and soon attracted notice by his punctual discharge of his duties. In a time of growing looseness, Marius was strict himself in keeping discipline and in enforcing it as he rose in the service. He was in Spain when Jugurtha was there, and made himself especially useful to Scipio; he forced his way steadily upward, by his mere soldierlike qualities, to the rank of military tribune. Rome, too, had learned to know him, for he was chosen tribune of the people the year after the murder of Caius Gracchus. Being a self-made man, he belonged naturally to the popular party. While in office he gave offence in some way to the men in power, and was called before the Senate to answer for himself. But he had the right on his side, it is likely, for they found him stubborn and impertinent, and they could make nothing of their charges against him. He was not bidding at this time, however, for the support of the mob. He had the integrity and sense to oppose the largesses of corn; and he forfeited his popularity by trying to close the public granaries before the practice had passed into a system. He seemed as if made of a block of hard Roman oak, gnarled and knotted, but sound in all its fibres. His professional merit continued to recommend him. At the age of forty he became praetor, and was sent to Spain, where he left a mark again by the successful severity by which he cleared the province of banditti. He was a man neither given himself to talking nor much talked about in the world; but he was sought for wherever work was to be done, and he had made himself respected and valued in high circles, for after his return from the peninsula he had married into one of the most distinguished of the patrician families.

The Caesars were a branch of the Gens Julia, which claimed descent from Iulus the son of Aeneas, and thus from the gods. Roman etymologists could arrive at no conclusion as to the origin of the name. Some derived it from an exploit on an elephant-hunt in Africa--Caesar meaning elephant in Moorish; some to the entrance into the world of the first eminent Caesar by the aid of a surgeon's knife;[3]some from the color of the eyes prevailing in the family. Be the explanation what it might, eight generations of Caesars had held prominent positions in the Commonwealth. They had been consuls, censors, praetors, aediles, and military tribunes, and in politics, as might be expected from their position, they had been moderate aristocrats. Like other families they had been subdivided, and the links connecting them cannot always be traced. The pedigree of the Dictator goes no further than to his grandfather, Caius Julius. In the middle of the second century before Christ, this Caius Julius, being otherwise unknown to history, married a lady named Marcia, supposed to be descended from Ancus Marcius, the fourth king of Rome. By her he had three children, Caius Julius, Sextus Julius, and a daughter named Julia. Caius Julius married Aurelia, perhaps a member of the consular family of the Cottas, and was the father of the Great Caesar. Julia became the wife of Caius Marius, a _misalliance_ which implied the beginning of a political split in the Caesar family. The elder branches, like the Cromwells of Hinchinbrook, remained by their order. The younger attached itself for good or ill to the party of the people.

Marius by this marriage became a person of social consideration. His father had been a client of the Metelli; and Caecilius Metellus, who must have known Marius by reputation and probably in person, invited him to go as second in command in the African campaign. He was moderately successful. Towns were taken; battles were won: Metellus was incorruptible, and the Numidians sued for peace. But Jugurtha wanted terms, and the consul demanded unconditional surrender. Jugurtha withdrew into the desert; the war dragged on; and Marius, perhaps ambitious, perhaps impatient at the general's want of vigor, began to think that he could make quicker work of it. The popular party were stirring again in Rome, the Senate having so notoriously disgraced itself. There was just irritation that a petty African prince could defy the whole power of Rome for so many years; and though a democratic consul had been unheard of for a century, the name of Marius began to be spoken of as a possible candidate. Marius consented to stand. The law required that he must be present in person at the election, and he applied to his commander for leave of absence. Metellus laughed at his pretensions, and bade him wait another twenty years. Marius, however, persisted, and was allowed to go. The patricians strained their resources to defeat him, but he was chosen with enthusiasm. Metellus was recalled, and the conduct of the Numidian war was assigned to the new hero of the "populares."

A shudder of alarm ran, no doubt, through the senate-house when the determination of the people was known. A successful general could not be disposed of so easily as oratorical tribunes. Fortunately Marius was not a politician. He had no belief in democracy. He was a soldier, and had a soldier's way of thinking on government and the methods of it. His first step was a reformation in the army. Hitherto the Roman legions had been no more than the citizens in arms, called for the moment from their various occupations, to return to them when the occasion for their services was past. Marius had perceived that fewer men, better trained and disciplined, could he made more effective and be more easily handled. He had studied war as a science. He had perceived that the present weakness need be no more than an accident, and that there was a latent force in the Roman State which needed only organization to resume its ascendency. "He enlisted," it was said, "the worst of the citizens," men, that is to say, who had no occupation and who became soldiers by profession; and as persons without property could not have furnished themselves at their own cost, he must have carried out the scheme proposed by Gracchus, and equipped them at the expense of the State. His discipline was of the sternest. The experiment was new; and men of rank who had a taste for war in earnest, and did not wish that the popular party should have the whole benefit and credit of the improvements, were willing to go with him; among them a dissipated young patrician called Lucius Sylla, whose name also was destined to be memorable.

By these methods and out of these materials an army was formed such as no Roman general had hitherto led. It performed extraordinary marches, carried its water-supplies with it in skins, and followed the enemy across sandy deserts hitherto found impassable. In less than two years the war was over. The Moors to whom Jugurtha had fled surrendered him to Sylla, and he was brought in chains to Rome, where he finished his life in a dungeon.

So ended a curious episode in Roman history, where it holds a place beyond its intrinsic importance, from the light which it throws on the character of the Senate and on the practical working of the institutions which the Gracchi had perished in unsuccessfully attempting to reform.

[1] "Urbem venalem, et mature perituram, si emptorem invenenit."--Sallust, De Bello Jugurthino, c. 35. Livy's account of the business, however, differs from Sallust's, and the expression is perhaps not authentic.

[2] "At ego scio, Quirites, qui, postquam consules facti sunt, acta majorum, et Graecorum militaria praecepta legere coeperint. Homines praeposteri!"-- Speech of Marius, Sallust, Jugurtha, 85.

[3] "Caesus ab utero matris."

CHAPTER V.

The Jugurthine war ended in the year 106 B.C. At the same Arpinum which had produced Marius another actor in the approaching drama was in that year ushered into the world, Marcus Tullius Cicero. The Ciceros had made their names, and perhaps their fortunes, by their skill in raising cicer, or vetches. The present representative of the family was a country gentleman in good circumstances given to literature, residing habitually at his estate on the Liris and paying occasional visits to Rome. In that household was born Rome's most eloquent master of the art of using words, who was to carry that art as far, and to do as much with it, as any man who has ever appeared on the world's stage.

Rome, however, was for the present in the face of enemies who had to be encountered with more material weapons. Marius had formed an army barely in time to save Italy from being totally overwhelmed. A vast migratory wave of population had been set in motion behind the Rhine and the Danube. The German forests were uncultivated. The hunting and pasture grounds were too strait for the numbers crowded into them, and two enormous hordes were rolling westward and southward in search of some new abiding-place. The Teutons came from the Baltic down across the Rhine into Luxemburg. The Cimbri crossed the Danube near its sources into Illyria. Both Teutons and Cimbri were Germans, and both were making for Gaul by different routes. The Celts of Gaul had had their day. In past generations they had held the German invaders at bay, and had even followed them into their own territories. But they had split among themselves. They no longer offered a common front to the enemy. They were ceasing to be able to maintain their own independence, and the question of the future was whether Gaul was to be the prey of Germany or to be a province of Rome.

Events appeared already to have decided. The invasion of the Teutons and the Cimbri was like the pouring in of two great rivers. Each division consisted of hundreds of thousands. They travelled with their wives and children, their wagons, as with the ancient Scythians and with the modern South African Dutch, being at once their conveyance and their home. Gray-haired priestesses tramped along among them, barefooted, in white linen dresses, the knife at their girdle; northern Iphigenias, sacrificing prisoners as they were taken to the gods of Valhalla. On they swept, eating up the country, and the people flying before them. In 113 B.C. the skirts of the Cimbri had encountered a small Roman force near Trieste, and destroyed it. Four years later another attempt was made to stop them, but the Roman army was beaten and its camp taken. The Cimbrian host did not, however, turn at that time upon Italy. Their aim was the south of France. They made their way through the Alps into Switzerland, where the Helvetii joined them, and the united mass rolled over the Jura and down the bank of the Rhone. Roused at last into exertion, the Senate sent into Gaul the largest force which the Romans had ever brought into the field. They met the Cimbri at Orange, and were simply annihilated. Eighty thousand Romans and forty thousand camp-followers were said to have fallen. The numbers in such cases are generally exaggerated, but the extravagance of the report is a witness to the greatness of the overthrow. The Romans had received a worse blow than at Cannae. They were brave enough, but they were commanded by persons whose recommendations for command were birth or fortune; "preposterous men," as Marius termed them, who had waited for their appointment to open the military manuals.

Had the Cimbri chosen at this moment to recross the Alps into Italy, they had only to go and take possession, and Alaric would have been antedated by five centuries. In great danger it was the Senate's business to suspend the constitution. The constitution was set aside now, but it was set aside by the people themselves, not by the Senate. One man only could save the country, and that man was Marius. His consulship was over, and custom forbade his re-election. The Senate might have appointed him dictator, but would not. The people, custom or no custom, chose him consul a second time--a significant acknowledgment that the Empire, which had been won by the sword, must be held by the sword, and that the sword itself must be held by the hand that was best fitted to use it. Marius first triumphed for his African victory, and, as an intimation to the Senate that the power for the moment was his and not theirs, he entered the Curia in his triumphal dress. He then prepared for the barbarians who, to the alarmed imagination of the city, were already knocking at its gates. Time was the important element in the matter. Had the Cimbri come at once after their victory at Orange, Italy had been theirs. But they did not come. With the unguided movements of some wild force of nature they swerved away through Aquitaine to the Pyrenees. They swept across the mountains into Spain. Thence, turning north, they passed up the Atlantic coast and round to the Seine, the Gauls flying before them; thence on to the Rhine, where the vast body of the Teutons joined them and fresh detachments of the Helvetii. It was as if some vast tide-wave had surged over the country and rolled through it, searching out the easiest passages. At length, in two divisions, the invaders moved definitely toward Italy, the Cimbri following their old tracks by the eastern Alps toward Aquileia and the Adriatic, the Teutons passing down through Provence and making for the road along the Mediterranean. Two years had been consumed in these wanderings, and Marius was by this time ready for them. The Senate had dropped the reins, and no longer governed or misgoverned; the popular party, represented by the army, was supreme. Marius was continued in office, and was a fourth time consul. He had completed his military reforms, and the army was now a professional service, with regular pay. Trained corps of engineers were attached to each legion. The campaigns of the Romans were thenceforward to be conducted with spade and pickaxe as much as with sword and javelin, and the soldiers learnt the use of tools as well as arms. Moral discipline was not forgotten. The foulest of human vices was growing fashionable in high society in the capital. It was not allowed to make its way into the army. An officer in one of the legions, a near relative of Marius, made filthy overtures to one of his men. The man replied with a thrust of his sword, and Marius publicly thanked and decorated him.

The effect of the change was like enchantment. The delay of the Germans made it unnecessary to wait for them in Italy. Leaving Catulus, his colleague in the consulship, to check the Cimbri in Venetia, Marius went himself, taking Sylla with him, into the south of France. As the barbarian host came on, he occupied a fortified camp near Aix. He allowed the enormous procession to roll past him in their wagons toward the Alps. Then, following cautiously, he watched his opportunity to fall on them. The Teutons were brave, but they had no longer mere legionaries to fight with, but a powerful machine, and the entire mass of them, men, women, and children, in numbers which however uncertain were rather those of a nation than an army, were swept out of existence.

The Teutons were destroyed on the 20th of July, 102. In the year following the same fate overtook their comrades. The Cimbri had forced the passes through the mountains. They had beaten the unscientific patrician Catulus, and had driven him back on the Po. But Marius came to his rescue. The Cimbri were cut to pieces near Mantua, in the summer of 101, and Italy was saved.

The victories of Marius mark a new epoch in Roman history. The legions were no longer the levy of the citizens in arms, who were themselves the State for which they fought. The legionaries were citizens still. They had votes, and they used them; but they were professional soldiers with the modes of thought which belong to soldiers, and beside the power of the hustings was now the power of the sword. The constitution remained to appearance intact, and means were devised sufficient to encounter, it might be supposed, the new danger. Standing armies were prohibited in Italy. Victorious generals returning from campaigns abroad were required to disband their legions on entering the sacred soil. But the materials of these legions remained a distinct order from the rest of the population, capable of instant combination, and in combination irresistible save by opposing combinations of the same kind. The Senate might continue to debate, the Comitia might elect the annual magistrates. The established institutions preserved the form and something of the reality of power in a people governed so much by habit as the Romans. There is a long twilight between the time when a god is first suspected to be an idol and his final overthrow. But the aristocracy had made the first inroad on the constitution by interfering at the elections with their armed followers and killing their antagonists. The example once set could not fail to be repeated, and the rule of an organized force was becoming the only possible protection against the rule of mobs, patrician or plebeian.

The danger from the Germans was no sooner gone than political anarchy broke loose again. Marius, the man of the people, was the saviour of his country. He was made consul a fifth time and a sixth. The party which had given him his command shared, of course, in his pre-eminence. The elections could be no longer interfered with or the voters intimidated. The public offices were filled with the most violent agitators, who believed that the time had come to revenge the Gracchi and carry out the democratic revolution, to establish the ideal Republic and the direct rule of the citizen assembly. This, too, was a chimera. If the Roman Senate could not govern, far less could the Roman mob govern. Marius stood aside and let the voices rage. He could not be expected to support a system which had brought the country so near to ruin. He had no belief in the visions of the demagogues, but the time was not ripe to make an end of it all. Had he tried, the army would not have gone with him, so he sat still till faction had done its work. The popular heroes of the hour were the tribune Saturninus and the praetor Glaucia. They carried corn laws and land laws--whatever laws they pleased to propose. The administration remaining with the Senate, they carried a vote that every senator should take an oath to execute their laws under penalty of fine and expulsion. Marius did not like it, and even opposed it, but let it pass at last. The senators, cowed and humiliated, consented to take the oath, all but one, Marius's old friend and commander in Africa, Caecilius Metellus. No stain had ever rested on the name of Metellus. He had accepted no bribes. He had half beaten Jugurtha, for Marius to finish; and Marius himself stood in a semi-feudal relation to him. It was unlucky for the democrats that they had found so honorable an opponent. Metellus persisted in refusal. Saturninus sent a guard to the senate-house, dragged him out, and expelled him from the city. Aristocrats and their partisans were hustled and killed in the street. The patricians had spilt the first blood in the massacre in 121: now it was the turn of the mob.

Marius was an indifferent politician. He perceived as well as any one that violence must not go on, but he hesitated to put it down. He knew that the aristocracy feared and hated him. Between them and the people's consul no alliance was possible. He did not care to alienate his friends, and there may have been other difficulties which we do not know in his way. The army itself was perhaps divided. On the popular side there were two parties: a moderate one, represented by Memmius, who, as tribune, had impeached the senators for the Jugurthine infamies; the other, the advanced radicals, led by Glaucia and Saturninus. Memmius and Glaucia were both candidates for the consulship; and as Memmius was likely to succeed, he was murdered.

Revolutions proceed like the acts of a drama, and each act is divided into scenes which follow one another with singular uniformity. Ruling powers make themselves hated by tyranny and incapacity. An opposition is formed against them, composed of all sorts, lovers of order and lovers of disorder, reasonable men and fanatics, business-like men and men of theory. The opposition succeeds; the government is overthrown; the victors divide into a moderate party and an advanced party. The advanced party go to the front, till they discredit themselves with crime or folly. The wheel has then gone round, and the reaction sets in. The murder of Memmius alienated fatally the respectable citizens. Saturninus and Glaucia were declared public enemies. They seized the Capitol, and blockaded it. Patrician Rome turned out and besieged them, and Marius had to interfere. The demagogues and their friends surrendered, and were confined in the Curia Hostilia till they could be tried. The noble lords could not allow such detested enemies the chance of an acquittal. To them a radical was a foe of mankind, to be hunted down like a wolf, when a chance was offered to destroy him. By the law of Caius Gracchus no citizen could be put to death without a trial. The persons of Saturninus and Glaucia were doubly sacred, for one was tribune and the other praetor. But the patricians were satisfied that they deserved to be executed, and in such a frame of mind it seemed but virtue to execute them. They tore off the roof of the senate house, and pelted the miserable wretches to death with stones and tiles.

CHAPTER VI.

Not far from the scene of the murder of Glaucia and Saturninus there was lying at this time in his cradle, or carried about in his nurse's arms, a child who, in his manhood, was to hold an inquiry into this business, and to bring one of the perpetrators to answer for himself. On the 12th of the preceding July, B.C. 100,[1] was born into the world Caius Julius Caesar, the only son of Caius Julius and Aurelia, and nephew of the then Consul Marius. His father had been praetor, but had held no higher office. Aurelia was a strict stately lady of the old school, uninfected by the lately imported fashions. She, or her husband, or both of them, were rich; but the habits of the household were simple and severe, and the connection with Marius indicates the political opinions which prevailed in the family.

No anecdotes are preserved, of Caesar's childhood. He was taught Greek by Antonius Gnipho, an educated Gaul from the north of Italy. He wrote a poem when a boy in honor of Hercules. He composed a tragedy on the story of Oedipus. His passionate attachment to Aurelia in after-years shows that between mother and child the relations had been affectionate and happy. But there is nothing to indicate that there was any early precocity of talent; and leaving Caesar to his grammar and his exercises, we will proceed with the occurrences which he must have heard talked of in his father's house, or seen with his eyes when he began to open them. The society there was probably composed of his uncle's friends; soldiers and statesmen who had no sympathy with mobs, but detested the selfish and dangerous system on which the Senate had carried on the government, and dreaded its consequences. Above the tumults of the factions in the Capitol a cry rising into shrillness began to be heard from Italy. Caius Gracchus had wished to extend the Roman franchise to the Italian States, and the suggestion had cost him his popularity and his life. The Italian provinces had furnished their share of the armies which had beaten Jugurtha, and had destroyed the German invaders. They now demanded that they should have the position which Gracchus designed for them: that they should be allowed to legislate for themselves, and no longer lie at the mercy of others, who neither understood their necessities nor cared for their interests. They had no friends in the city, save a few far-sighted statesmen. Senate and mob had at least one point of agreement, that the spoils of the Empire should be fought for among themselves; and at the first mention of the invasion of their monopoly a law was passed making the very agitation of the subject punishable by death.

Political convulsions work in a groove, the direction of which varies little in any age or country. Institutions once sufficient and salutary become unadapted to a change of circumstances. The traditionary holders of power see their interests threatened. They are jealous of innovations. They look on agitators for reform as felonious persons desiring to appropriate what does not belong to them. The complaining parties are conscious of suffering and rush blindly on the superficial causes of their immediate distress. The existing authority is their enemy; and their one remedy is a change in the system of government. They imagine that they see what the change should be, that they comprehend what they are doing, and know where they intend to arrive. They do not perceive that the visible disorders are no more than symptoms which no measures, repressive or revolutionary, can do more than palliate. The wave advances and the wave recedes. Neither party in the struggle can lift itself far enough above the passions of the moment to study the drift of the general current. Each is violent, each is one-sided, and each makes the most and the worst of the sins of its opponents. The one idea of the aggressors is to grasp all that they can reach. The one idea of the conservatives is to part with nothing, pretending that the stability of the State depends on adherence to the principles which have placed them in the position which they hold; and as various interests are threatened, and as various necessities arise, those who are one day enemies are frightened the next into unnatural coalitions, and the next after into more embittered dissensions.

To an indifferent spectator, armed especially with the political experiences of twenty additional centuries, it seems difficult to understand how Italy could govern the world. That the world and Italy besides should continue subject to the population of a single city, of its limited Latin environs, and of a handful of townships exceptionally favored, might even then be seen to be plainly impossible. The Italians were Romans in every point, except in the possession of the franchise. They spoke the same language; they were subjects of the same dominion. They were as well educated, they were as wealthy, they were as capable as the inhabitants of the dominant State. They paid taxes, they fought in the armies; they were strong; they were less corrupt, politically and morally, as having fewer temptations and fewer opportunities of evil; and in their simple country life they approached incomparably nearer to the old Roman type than the patrician fops in the circus or the Forum, or the city mob which was fed in idleness on free grants of corn. When Samnium and Tuscany were conquered, a third of the lands had been confiscated to the Roman State, under the name of Ager Publicus. Samnite and Etruscan gentlemen had recovered part of it under lease, much as the descendants of the Irish chiefs held their ancestral domains as tenants of the Cromwellians. The land law of the Gracchi was well intended, but it bore hard on many of the leading provincials, who had seen their estates parcelled out, and their own property, as they deemed it, taken from them under the land commission. If they were to be governed by Roman laws, they naturally demanded to be consulted when the laws were made. They might have been content under a despotism to which Roman and Italian were subject alike. To be governed under the forms of a free constitution by men no better than themselves was naturally intolerable.

[Sidenote: B.C. 95.] [Sidenote: B.C. 91.] The movement from without united the Romans for the instant in defence of their privileges. The aristocracy resisted change from instinct; the mob, loudly as they clamored for their own rights, cared nothing for the rights of others, and the answer to the petition of the Italians, five years after the defeat of the Cimbri, was a fierce refusal to permit the discussion of it. Livius Drusus, one of those unfortunately gifted men who can see that in a quarrel there is sometimes justice on both sides, made a vain attempt to secure the provincials a hearing, but he was murdered in his own house. To be murdered was the usual end of exceptionally distinguished Romans, in a State where the lives of citizens were theoretically sacred. His death was the signal for an insurrection, which began in the mountains of the Abruzzi and spread over the whole peninsula.

The contrast of character between the two classes of population became at once uncomfortably evident. The provincials had been the right arm of the Empire. Rome, a city of rich men with families of slaves, and of a crowd of impoverished freemen without employment to keep them in health and strength, could no longer bring into the field a force which could hold its ground against the gentry and peasants of Samnium. The Senate enlisted Greeks, Numidians, any one whose services they could purchase. They had to encounter soldiers who had been trained and disciplined by Marius, and they were taught by defeat upon defeat that they had a worse enemy before them than the Germans. Marius himself had almost withdrawn from public life. He had no heart for the quarrel, and did not care greatly to exert himself. At the bottom, perhaps, he thought that the Italians were in the right. The Senate discovered that they were helpless, and must come to terms if they would escape destruction. They abandoned the original point of difference, and they offered to open the franchise to every Italian state south of the Po which had not taken arms or which returned immediately to its allegiance. The war had broken out for a definite cause. When the cause was removed no reason remained for its continuance. The Italians were closely connected with Rome. Italians were spread over the Roman world in active business. They had no wish to overthrow the Empire if they were allowed to share in its management. The greater part of them accepted the Senate's terms; and only those remained in the field who had gone to war in the hope of recovering the lost independence which their ancestors had so long heroically defended.

The panting Senate was thus able to breathe again. The war continued, but under better auspices. Sound material could now be collected again for the army. Marius being in the background, the chosen knight of the aristocracy, Lucius Sylla, whose fame in the Cimbrian war had been only second to that of his commander's, came at once to the front.

Sylla, or Sulla, as we are now taught to call him, was born in the year 138 B.C. He was a patrician of the purest blood, had inherited a moderate fortune, and had spent it like other young men of rank, lounging in theatres and amusing himself with dinner-parties. He was a poet, an artist, and a wit, but each and everything with the languor of an amateur. His favorite associates were actresses, and he had neither obtained nor aspired to any higher reputation than that of a cultivated man of fashion. His distinguished birth was not apparent in his person. He had red hair, hard blue eyes, and a complexion white and purple, with the colors so ill-mixed that his face was compared to a mulberry sprinkled with flour. Ambition he appeared to have none; and when he exerted himself to be appointed quaestor to Marius on the African expedition, Marius was disinclined to take him as having no recommendation beyond qualifications which the consul of the plebeians disdained and disliked.

Marius, however, soon discovered his mistake. Beneath his constitutional indolence Sylla was by nature a soldier, a statesman, a diplomatist. He had been too contemptuous of the common objects of politicians to concern himself with the intrigues of the Forum, but he had only to exert himself to rise with easy ascendency to the command of every situation in which he might be placed. He had entered with military instinct into Marius's reform of the army, and became the most active and useful of his officers. He endeared himself to the legionaries by a tolerance of vices which did not interfere with discipline; and to Sylla's combined adroitness and courage Marius owed the final capture of Jugurtha.

Whether Marius became jealous of Sylla on this occasion must be decided by those who, while they have no better information than others as to the actions of men, possess, or claim to possess, the most intimate acquaintance with their motives. They again served together, however, against the Northern invaders, and Sylla a second time lent efficient help to give Marius a victory. Like Marius, he had no turn for platform oratory and little interest in election contests and intrigues. For eight years he kept aloof from politics, and his name and that of his rival were alike for all that time almost unheard of. He emerged into special notice only when he was praetor in the year 93 B.C., and when he characteristically distinguished his term of office by exhibiting a hundred lions in the arena matched against Numidian archers. There was no such road to popularity with the Roman multitude. It is possible that the little Caesar, then a child of seven, may have been among the spectators, making his small reflections on it all.

[Sidenote: B.C. 120.] In 92 Sylla went as propraetor to Asia, where the incapacity of the Senate's administration was creating another enemy likely to be troublesome. Mithridates, "child of the sun," pretending to a descent from Darius Hystaspes, was king of Pontus, one of the semi-independent monarchies which had been allowed to stand in Asia Minor. The coast-line of Pontus extended from Sinope to Trebizond, and reached inland to the line of mountains where the rivers divide which flow into the Black Sea and the Mediterranean. The father of Mithridates was murdered when he was a child, and for some years he led a wandering life, meeting adventures which were as wild and perhaps as imaginary as those of Ulysses. In later life he became the idol of Eastern imagination, and legend made free with his history; but he was certainly an extraordinary man. He spoke the unnumbered dialects of the Asiatic tribes among whom he had travelled. He spoke Greek with ease and freedom. Placed, as he was, on the margin where the civilizations of the East and the West were brought in contact, he was at once a barbarian potentate and an ambitious European politician. He was well informed of the state of Rome, and saw reason, perhaps, as well he might, to doubt the durability of its power. At any rate, he was no sooner fixed on his own throne than he began to annex the territories of the adjoining princes. He advanced his sea frontier through Armenia to Batoum, and thence along the coast of Circassia. He occupied the Greek settlements on the Sea of Azof. He took Kertch and the Crimea, and with the help of pirates from the Mediterranean he formed a fleet which gave him complete command of the Black Sea. In Asia Minor no power but the Roman could venture to quarrel with him. The Romans ought in prudence to have interfered before Mithridates had grown to so large a bulk, but money judiciously distributed among the leading politicians had secured the Senate's connivance; and they opened their eyes at last only when Mithridates thought it unnecessary to subsidize them further, and directed his proceedings against Cappadocia, which was immediately under Roman protection. He invaded the country, killed the prince whom Rome had recognized, and placed on the throne a child of his own, with the evident intention of taking Cappadocia for himself.

This was to go too far. Like Jugurtha, he had purchased many friends in the Senate, who, grateful for past favors and hoping for more, prevented the adoption of violent measures against him; but they sent a message to him that he must not have Cappadocia, and Mithridates, waiting for a better opportunity, thought proper to comply. Of this message the bearer was Lucius Sylla. He had time to study on the spot the problem of how to deal with Asia Minor. He accomplished his mission with his usual adroitness and apparent success, and he returned to Rome with new honors to finish the Social war.

It was no easy work. The Samnites were tough and determined. For two years they continued to struggle, and the contest was not yet over when news came from the East appalling as the threatened Cimbrian invasion, which brought both parties to consent to suspend their differences by mutual concessions.

[1] I follow the ordinary date, which has been fixed by the positive statement that Caesar was fifty-six when he was killed, the date of his death being March, B.C. 44. Mommsen, however, argues plausibly for adding another two years to the beginning of Caesar's life, and brings him into the world at the time of the battle at Aix.

CHAPTER VII.

Barbarian kings, who found Roman senators ready to take bribes from them, believed, not unnaturally, that the days of Roman dominion were numbered. When the news of the Social war reached Mithridates, he thought it needless to temporize longer, and he stretched out his hand to seize the prize of the dominion of the East. The Armenians, who were at his disposition, broke into Cappadocia and again overthrew the government, which was in dependence upon Rome. Mithridates himself invaded Bithynia, and replied to the remonstrances of the Roman authorities by a declaration of open war. He called under arms the whole force of which he could dispose; frightened rumor spoke of it as amounting to three hundred thousand men. His corsair fleets poured down through the Dardanelles into the archipelago; and so detested had the Roman governors made themselves by their extortion and injustice that not only all the islands, but the provinces on the continent, Ionia, Lydia, and Caria, rose in revolt. The rebellion was preconcerted and simultaneous. The Roman residents, merchants, bankers, farmers of the taxes, they and all their families, were set upon and murdered; a hundred and fifty thousand men, women, and children were said to have been destroyed in a single day. If we divide by ten, as it is generally safe to do with historical round numbers, still beyond doubt the signal had been given in an appalling massacre to abolish out of Asia the Roman name and power. Swift as a thunderbolt Mithridates himself crossed the Bosphorus, and the next news that reached Rome was that northern Greece had risen also and was throwing itself into the arms of its deliverers.

The defeat at Cannae had been received with dignified calm. Patricians and plebeians forgot their quarrels and thought only how to meet their common foe. The massacre in Asia and the invasion of Mithridates let loose a tempest of political frenzy. Never was indignation more deserved. The Senate had made no preparation. Such resources as they could command had been wasted in the wars with the Italians. They had no fleet, they had no armies available; nor, while the civil war was raging, could they raise an army. The garrisons in Greece were scattered or shut in within their lines and unable to move. The treasury was empty. Individuals were enormously rich and the State was bankrupt. Thousands of families had lost brothers, cousins, or friends in the massacre, and the manifest cause of the disaster was the inefficiency and worthlessness of the ruling classes. In Africa, in Gaul, in Italy, and now in Asia it had been the same story. The interests of the Commonwealth had been sacrificed to fill the purses of the few. Dominion, wealth, honors, all that had been won by the hardy virtues of earlier generations, seemed about to be engulfed forever.

In their panic the Senate turned to Sylla, whom they had made consul. An imperfect peace was patched up with the Italians. Sylla was bidden to save the Republic and to prepare in haste for Greece. But Sylla was a bitter aristocrat, the very incarnation of the oligarchy, who were responsible for every disaster which had happened. The Senate had taken bribes from Jugurtha. The Senate had chosen the commanders whose blunders had thrown open the Alps to the Germans; and it was only because the people had snatched the power out of their hands and had trusted it to one of themselves that Italy had not been in flames. Again the oligarchy had recovered the administration, and again by following the old courses they had brought on this new catastrophe. They might have checked Mithridates while there was time. They had preferred to accept his money and look on. The people naturally thought that no successes could be looked for under such guidance, and that even were Sylla to be victorious, nothing was to be expected but the continuance of the same accursed system. Marius was the man. Marius after his sixth consulship had travelled in the East, and understood it as well as Sylla. Not Sylla but Marius must now go against Mithridates. Too late the democratic leaders repented of their folly in encouraging the Senate to refuse the franchise to the Italians. The Italians, they began to perceive, would be their surest political allies. Caius Gracchus had been right after all. The Roman democracy must make haste to offer the Italians more than all which the Senate was ready to concede to them. Together they could make an end of misrule and place Marius once more at their head.

Much of this was perhaps the scheming passion of revolution; much of it was legitimate indignation, penitent for its errors and anxious to atone for them. Marius had his personal grievances. The aristocrats were stealing from him even his military reputation, and claiming for Sylla the capture of Jugurtha. He was willing, perhaps anxious, to take the Eastern command. Sulpicius Rufus, once a champion of the Senate and the most brilliant orator in Rome, went over to the people in the excitement. Rufus was chosen tribune, and at once proposed to enfranchise the remainder of Italy. He denounced the oligarchy. He insisted that the Senate must be purged of its corrupt members and better men be introduced, that the people must depose Sylla, and that Marius must take his place. The Empire was tottering, and the mob and its leaders were choosing an ill moment for a revolution. The tribune carried the assembly along with him. There were fights again in the Forum, the young nobles with their gangs once more breaking up the Comitia and driving the people from the voting-places. The voting, notwithstanding, was got through as Sulpicius Rufus recommended, and Sylla, so far as the assembly could do it, was superseded. But Sylla was not so easily got rid of. It was no time for nice considerations. He had formed an army in Campania out of the legions which had served against the Italians. He had made his soldiers devoted to him. They were ready to go anywhere and do anything which Sylla bade them. After so many murders and so many commotions, the constitution had lost its sacred character; a popular assembly was, of all conceivable bodies, the least fit to govern an empire; and in Sylla's eyes the Senate, whatever its deficiencies, was the only possible sovereign of Rome. The people were a rabble, and their voices the clamor of fools, who must be taught to know their masters. His reply to Sulpicius and to the vote for his recall was to march on the city. He led his troops within the circle which no legionary in arms was allowed to enter, and he lighted his watch-fires in the Forum itself. The people resisted; Sulpicius was killed; Marius, the saviour of his country, had to fly for his life, pursued by assassins, with a price set upon his head. Twelve of the prominent popular leaders were immediately executed without trial, and in hot haste swift decisive measures were taken which permanently, as Sylla hoped, or if not permanently at least for the moment, would lame the limbs of the democracy. The Senate, being below its numbers, was hastily filled up from the patrician families. The arrangements of the Comitia were readjusted to restore to wealth a decisive preponderance in the election of the magistrates. The tribunes of the people were stripped of half their power. Their veto was left to them, but the right of initiation was taken away, and no law or measure of any kind was thenceforth to be submitted to the popular assembly till it had been considered in the Curia and had received the Senate's sanction.

Thus the snake was scotched, and it might be hoped would die of its wounds. Sulpicius and his brother demagogues were dead. Marius was exiled. Time pressed, and Sylla could not wait to see his reforms in operation. Signs became visible before he went that the crisis would not pass off so easily. Fresh consuls had to be elected. The changes in the method of voting were intended to secure the return of the Senate's candidates, and one of the consuls chosen, Cnaeus Octavius, was a man on whom Sylla could rely. His colleague, Lucius Cinna, though elected under the pressure of the legions, was of more doubtful temper. But Cinna was a patrician, though given to popular sentiments. Sylla was impatient to be gone; more important work was waiting for him than composing factions in Rome. He contented himself with obliging the new consuls to take an oath to maintain the constitution in the shape in which he left it, and he sailed from Brindisi in the winter of B.C. 88.

The campaign of Sylla in the East does not fall to be described in this place. He was a second Coriolanus, a proud, imperious aristocrat, contemptuous, above all men living, of popular rights; but he was the first soldier of his age; he was himself, though he did not know it, an impersonation of the change which was passing over the Roman character. He took with him at most 30,000 men. He had no fleet. Had the corsair squadrons of Mithridates been on the alert, they might have destroyed him on his passage. Events at Rome left him almost immediately without support from Italy. He was impeached; he was summoned back. His troops were forbidden to obey him, and a democratic commander was sent out to supersede him. The army stood by their favorite commander. Sylla disregarded his orders from home. He found men and money as he could. He supported himself out of the countries which he occupied, without resources save in his own skill and in the fidelity and excellence of his legions. He defeated Mithridates, he drove him back out of Greece and pursued him into Asia. The interests of his party demanded his presence at Rome; the interests of the State required that he should not leave his work in the East unfinished, and he stood to it through four hard years till he brought Mithridates to sue for peace upon his knees. He had not the means to complete the conquest or completely to avenge the massacre with which the Prince of Pontus had commenced the war. He left Mithridates still in possession of his hereditary kingdom, but he left him bound, so far as treaties could bind so ambitious a spirit, to remain thenceforward within his own frontiers. He recovered Greece and the islands, and the Roman provinces in Asia Minor. He extorted an indemnity of five millions, and executed many of the wretches who had been active in the murders. He raised a fleet in Egypt, with which he drove the pirates out of the archipelago back into their own waters. He restored the shattered prestige of Roman authority, and he won for himself a reputation which his later cruelties might stain but could not efface.

The merit of Sylla shows in more striking colors when we look to what was passing, during these four years of his absence, in the heart of the Empire. He was no sooner out of Italy than the democratic party rose, with Cinna at their head, to demand the restoration of the old constitution. Cinna had been sworn to maintain Sylla's reforms, but no oath could be held binding which was extorted at the sword's point. A fresh Sulpicius was found in Carbo, a popular tribune. A more valuable supporter was found in Quintus Sertorius, a soldier of fortune, but a man of real gifts, and even of genius. Disregarding the new obligation to obtain the previous consent of the Senate, Cinna called the assembly together to repeal the acts which Sylla had forced on them. Sylla, it is to be remembered, had as yet won no victories, nor was expected to win victories. He was the favorite of the Senate, and the Senate had become a byword for incapacity and failure. Again, as so many times before, the supremacy of the aristocrats had been accompanied with dishonor abroad and the lawless murder of political adversaries at home. No true lover of his country could be expected, in Cinna's opinion, to sit quiet under a tyranny which had robbed the people of their hereditary liberties.

The patricians took up the challenge. Octavius, the other consul, came with an armed force into the Forum, and ordered the assembly to disperse. The crowd was unusually great. The country voters had come in large numbers to stand up for their rights. They did not obey, They were not called on to obey. But because they refused to disperse they were set upon with deliberate fury, and were hewn down in heaps where they stood. No accurate register was, of course, taken of the numbers killed; but the intention of the patricians was to make a bloody example, and such a scene of slaughter had never been witnessed in Rome since the first stone of the city was laid. It was an act of savage, ruthless ferocity, certain to be followed with a retribution as sharp and as indiscriminating. Men are not permitted to deal with their fellow-creatures in these methods. Cinna and the tribunes fled, but fled only to be received with open arms by the Italians. The wounds of the Social war were scarcely cicatrized, and the peace had left the allies imperfectly satisfied. Their dispersed armies gathered again about Cinna and Sertorius. Old Marius, who had been hunted through marsh and forest, and had been hiding with difficulty in Africa, came back at the news that Italy had risen again; and six thousand of his veterans flocked to him at the sound of his name. The Senate issued proclamations. The limitations on the Italian franchise left by Sylla were abandoned. Every privilege which had been asked for was conceded. It was too late. Concessions made in fear might be withdrawn on the return of safety. Marius and Cinna joined their forces. The few troops in the pay of the Senate deserted to them. They appeared together at the gate's of the city, and Rome capitulated.

There was a bloody score to be wiped out. There would have been neither cruelty nor injustice in the most severe inquiry into the massacre in the Forum, and the most exemplary punishment of Octavius and his companions. But the blood of the people was up, and they had suffered too deeply to wait for the tardy processes of law. They had not been the aggressors. They had assembled lawfully, to assert their constitutional rights; they had been cut in pieces as if they had been insurgent slaves, and the assassins were not individuals, but a political party in the State.

Marius bears the chief blame for the scenes which followed. Undoubtedly he was in no pleasant humor. A price had been set on his head, his house had been destroyed, his property had been confiscated, he himself had been chased like a wild beast, and he had not deserved such treatment. He had saved Italy when but for him it would have been wasted by the swords of the Germans. His power had afterward been absolute, but he had not abused it for party purposes. The Senate had no reason to complain of him. He had touched none of their privileges, incapable and dishonest as he knew them to be. His crime in their eyes had been his eminence. They had now shown themselves as cruel as they were worthless; and if public justice was disposed to make an end of them, he saw no cause for interference.

Thus the familiar story repeated itself; wrong was punished by wrong, and another item was entered on the bloody account which was being scored up year after year. The noble lords and their friends had killed the people in the Forum. They were killed in turn by the soldiers of Marius. Fifty senators perished; not those who were specially guilty, but those who were most politically marked as patrician leaders. With them fell a thousand equites, commoners of fortune, who had thrown in their lot with the aristocracy. From retaliatory political revenge the transition was easy to pillage and wholesale murder, and for many days the wretched city was made a prey to robbers and cutthroats.

So ended the year 87, the darkest and bloodiest which the guilty city had yet experienced. Marius and Cinna were chosen consuls for the year ensuing, and a witch's prophecy was fulfilled that Marius should have a seventh consulate. But the glory had departed from him. His sun was already setting, redly, among crimson clouds. He lived but a fortnight after his inauguration, and he died in his bed on the 13th of January, at the age of seventy-one.

"The mother of the Gracchi," said Mirabeau, "cast the dust of her murdered sons into the air, and out of it sprang Caius Marius." The Gracchi were perhaps not forgotten in the retribution; but the crime which had been revenged by Marius was the massacre in the Forum by Octavius and his friends. The aristocracy found no mercy, because they had shown no mercy. They had been guilty of the most wantonly wicked cruelty which the Roman annals had yet recorded. They were not defending their country against a national danger. They were engaged in what has been called in later years "saving society;" that is to say, in saving their own privileges, their opportunities for plunder, their palaces, their estates, and their game-preserves. They had treated the people as if they were so many cattle grown troublesome to their masters, and the cattle were human beings with rights as real as their own.

The democratic party were now masters of the situation, and so continued for almost four years. Cinna succeeded to the consulship term after term, nominating himself and his colleagues. The franchise was given to the Italians without reserve or qualification. Northern Italy was still excluded, being not called Italy, but Cisalpine Gaul. South of the Po distinctions of citizenship ceased to exist. The constitution became a rehearsal of the Empire, a democracy controlled and guided by a popular dictator. The aristocrats who had escaped massacre fled to Sylla in Asia, and for a brief interval Rome drew its breath in peace.

CHAPTER VIII.

Revolutionary periods are painted in history in colors so dark that the reader wonders how, amidst such scenes, peaceful human beings could continue to exist. He forgets that the historian describes only the abnormal incidents which broke the current of ordinary life, and that between the spasms of violence there were long quiet intervals when the ordinary occupations of men went on as usual. Cinna's continuous consulship was uncomfortable to the upper classes, but the daily business of a great city pursued its beaten way. Tradesmen and merchants made money, and lawyers pleaded, and priests prayed in the temples, and "celebrated" on festival and holy day. And now for the first time we catch a personal view of young Julius Caesar. He was growing up, in his father's house, a tall, slight, handsome youth, with dark piercing eyes,[1] a sallow complexion, large nose, lips full, features refined and intellectual, neck sinewy and thick beyond what might have been expected from the generally slender figure. He was particular about his appearance, used the bath frequently, and attended carefully to his hair. His dress was arranged with studied negligence, and he had a loose mode of fastening his girdle so peculiar as to catch the eye.

It may be supposed that he had witnessed Sylla's coming to Rome, the camp-fires in the Forum, the Octavian massacre, the return of his uncle and Cinna, and the bloody triumph of the party to which his father belonged. He was just at the age when such scenes make an indelible impression; and the connection of his family with Marius suggests easily the persons whom he must have most often seen, and the conversation to which he must have listened at his father's table. His most intimate companions were the younger Marius, the adopted son of his uncle; and, singularly enough, the two Ciceros, Marcus and his brother Quintus, who had been sent by their father to be educated at Rome. The connection of Marius with Arpinum was perhaps the origin of the intimacy. The great man may have heard of his fellow-townsman's children being in the city, and have taken notice of them. Certain, at any rate, it is that these boys grew up together on terms of close familiarity.[2]

Marius had observed his nephew, and had marked him for promotion. During the brief fortnight of his seventh consulship he gave him an appointment which reminds us of the boy-bishops of the middle ages. He made him flamen dialis, or priest of Jupiter, and a member of the Sacred College, with a handsome income, when he was no more than fourteen. Two years later, during the rule of Cinna, his father arranged a marriage for him with a lady of fortune named Cossutia. But the young Caesar had more ambitious views for himself. His father died suddenly at Pisa, in B.C. 84; he used his freedom to break off his engagement, and instead of Cossutia he married Cornelia, the daughter of no less a person than the all-powerful Cinna himself. If the date commonly received for Caesar's birth is correct, he was still only in his seventeenth year. Such connections were rarely formed at an age so premature; and the doubt is increased by the birth of his daughter, Julia, in the year following. Be this as it may, a marriage into Cinna's family connected Caesar more closely than ever with the popular party. Thus early and thus definitively he committed himself to the politics of his uncle and his father-in-law; and the comparative quiet which Rome and Italy enjoyed under Cinna's administration may have left a permanent impression upon him.

The quiet was not destined to be of long endurance. The time was come when Sylla was to demand a reckoning for all which had been done in his absence. No Roman general had deserved better of his country than Sylla. He had driven Mithridates out of Greece, and had restored Roman authority in Asia under conditions peculiarly difficult. He had clung resolutely to his work, while his friends at home were being trampled upon by the populace whom he despised. He perhaps knew that in subduing the enemies of the State by his own individual energy he was taking the surest road to regain his ascendency. His task was finished. Mithridates was once more a petty Asiatic prince existing upon sufferance, and Sylla announced his approaching return to Italy. By his victories he had restored confidence to the aristocracy, and had won the respect of millions of his countrymen. But the party in power knew well that if he gained a footing in Italy their day was over, and the danger to be expected from him was aggravated by his transcendent services. The Italians feared naturally that they would lose the liberties which they had won. The popular faction at Rome was combined and strong, and was led by men of weight and practical ability. No reconciliation was possible between Cinna and Sylla. They were the respective chiefs of heaven and hell, and which of the two represented the higher power and which the lower could be determined only when the sword had decided between them. In Cinna lay the presumed lawful authority. He represented the people as organized in the Comitia, and his colleague in the consulship when the crisis came was the popular tribune Carbo. Italy was ready with armies; and as leaders there were young Marius, already with a promise of greatness in him, and Sertorius, gifted, brilliant, unstained by crime, adored by his troops as passionately as Sylla himself, and destined to win a place for himself elsewhere in the Pantheon of Rome's most distinguished men.

Sylla had measured the difficulty of the task which lay before him. But he had an army behind him accustomed to victory, and recruited by thousands of exiles who had fled from the rule of the democracy. He had now a fleet to cover his passage; and he was watching the movements of his enemies before deciding upon his own, when accident came suddenly to his help. Cinna had gone down to Brindisi, intending himself to carry his army into Greece, and to spare Italy the miseries of another civil war, by fighting it out elsewhere. The expedition was unpopular with the soldiers, and Cinna was killed in a mutiny. The democracy was thus left without a head, and the moderate party in the city who desired peace and compromise used the opportunity to elect two neutral consuls, Scipio and Norbanus. Sylla, perhaps supposing the change of feeling to be more complete than it really was, at once opened communications with them. But his terms were such as he might have dictated if the popular party were already under his feet. He intended to re-enter Rome with the glory of his conquests about him, for revenge and a counter-revolution. The consuls replied with refusing to treat with a rebel in arms, and with a command to disband his troops.

Sylla had lingered at Athens, collecting paintings and statues and manuscripts, the rarest treasures on which he could lay his hands, to decorate his Roman palace. On receiving the consuls' answer, he sailed for Brindisi in the spring of 83, with forty thousand legionaries and a large fleet. The south of Italy made no resistance, and he secured a standing-ground where his friends could rally to him. They came in rapidly, some for the cause which he represented, some for private hopes or animosities, some as aspiring military adventurers, seeking the patronage of the greatest soldier of the age. Among these last came Cnaeus Pompey, afterward Pompey the Great, son of Pompey, surnamed Strabo, or the squint-eyed, either from some personal deformity or because he had trimmed between the two factions and was distrusted and hated by them both.

Cnaeus Pompey had been born in the same year with Cicero, and was now twenty-three. He was a high--spirited ornamental youth, with soft melting eyes, as good as he was beautiful, and so delightful to women that it was said they all longed to bite him. The Pompeys had been hardly treated by Cinna. The father had been charged with embezzlement. The family house in Rome had been confiscated; the old Strabo had been killed; the son had retired to his family estate in Picenum,[3] where he was living when Sylla landed. To the young Roman chivalry Sylla was a hero of romance. Pompey raised a legion out of his friends and tenants, scattered the few companies that tried to stop him, and rushed to the side of the deliverer. Others came, like Sergius Catiline or Oppianicus of Larino,[4] men steeped in crime, stained with murder, incest, adultery, forgery, and meaning to secure the fruits of their villanies by well-timed service. They were all welcome, and Sylla was not particular. His progress was less rapid than it promised to be at the outset. He easily defeated Norbanus; and Scipio's troops, having an aristocratic leaven in them, deserted to him. But the Italians, especially the Samnites, fought most desperately. The war lasted for more than a year, Sylla slowly advancing. The Roman mob became furious. They believed their cause betrayed, and were savage from fear and disappointment. Suspected patricians were murdered: among them fell the Pontifex Maximus, the venerable Scaevola. At length the contest ended in a desperate fight under the walls of Rome itself on the 1st of November, B.C. 82. The battle began at four in the afternoon, and lasted through the night to the dawn of the following day. The popular army was at last cut to pieces; a few thousand prisoners were taken, but they were murdered afterward in cold blood. Young Marius killed himself, Sertorius fled to Spain, and Sylla and the aristocracy were masters of Rome and Italy. Such provincial towns as continued to resist were stormed and given up to pillage, every male inhabitant being put to the sword. At Norba, in Latium, the desperate citizens fired their own houses and perished by each other's hands.

Sylla was under no illusions. He understood the problem which he had in hand. He knew that the aristocracy were detested by nine tenths of the people; he knew that they deserved to be detested; but they were at least gentlemen by birth and breeding. The democrats, on the other hand, were insolent upstarts, who, instead of being grateful for being allowed to live and work and pay taxes and serve in the army, had dared to claim a share in the government, had turned against their masters, and had set their feet upon their necks. The miserable multitude were least to blame. They were ignorant, and without leaders could be controlled easily. The guilt and the danger lay with the men of wealth and intellect, the country gentlemen, the minority of knights and patricians like Cinna, who had taken the popular side and had deserted their own order. Their motives mattered not; some might have acted from foolish enthusiasm, some from personal ambition; but such traitors, from the Gracchi onward, had caused all the mischief which had happened to the State. They were determined, they were persevering. No concessions had satisfied them, and one demand had been a prelude to another. There was no hope for an end of agitation till every one of these men had been rooted out, their estates taken from them, and their families destroyed.

To this remarkable work Sylla addressed himself, unconscious that he was attempting an impossibility, that opinion could not be controlled by the sword, and that for every enemy to the oligarchy that he killed he would create twenty by his cruelty. Like Marius after the Octavian massacre, he did not attempt to distinguish between degrees of culpability. Guilt was not the question with him. His object was less to punish the past than to prevent a recurrence of it, and moderate opposition was as objectionable as fanaticism and frenzy. He had no intention of keeping power in his own hands. Personal supremacy might end with himself, and he intended to create institutions which would endure, in the form of a close senatorial monopoly. But for his purpose it would be necessary to remove out of the way every single person either in Rome or in the provinces who was in a position to offer active resistance, and therefore for the moment he required complete freedom of action. The Senate at his direction appointed him dictator, and in this capacity he became absolute master of the life and property of every man and woman in Italy. He might be impeached afterward and his policy reversed, but while his office lasted he could do what he pleased.

He at once outlawed every magistrate, every public servant of any kind, civil or municipal, who had held office under the rule of Cinna. Lists were drawn for him of the persons of wealth and consequence all over Italy who belonged to the liberal party. He selected agents whom he could trust, or supposed he could trust, to enter the names for each district. He selected, for instance, Oppianicus of Larino, who inscribed individuals whom he had already murdered, and their relations whose prosecution he feared. It mattered little to Sylla who were included, if none escaped who were really dangerous to him; and an order was issued for the slaughter of the entire number, the confiscation of their property, and the division of it between the informers and Sylla's friends and soldiers. Private interest was thus called in to assist political animosity, and to stimulate the zeal for assassination a reward of ?00 was offered for the head of any person whose name was in the schedule.

It was one of those deliberate acts, carried out with method and order, which are possible only in countries in an advanced stage of civilization, and which show how thin is the film spread over human ferocity by what is called progress and culture. We read in every page of history of invasions of hostile armies, of towns and villages destroyed and countries wasted and populations perishing of misery; the simplest war brings a train of horrors behind it; but we bear them with comparative equanimity. Personal hatreds are not called out on such occasions. The actors in them are neither necessarily nor generally fiends. The grass grows again on the trampled fields. Peace returns, and we forget and forgive. The coldly ordered massacres of selected victims in political and spiritual struggles rise in a different order of feelings, and are remembered through all ages with indignation and shame. The victims perish as the champions of principles which survive through the changes of time. They are marked for the sacrifice on account of their advocacy of a cause which to half mankind is the cause of humanity. They are the martyrs of history, and the record of atrocity rises again in immortal witness against the opinions out of which it rose.

Patricians and plebeians, aristocrats and democrats, have alike stained their hands with blood in the working out of the problem of politics. But impartial history declares also that the crimes of the popular party have in all ages been the lighter in degree, while in themselves they have more to excuse them; and if the violent acts of revolutionists have been held up more conspicuously for condemnation, it has been only because the fate of noblemen and gentlemen has been more impressive to the imagination than the fate of the peasant or the artisan. But the endurance of the inequalities of life by the poor is the marvel of human society. When the people complain, said Mirabeau, the people are always right. The popular cause has been the cause of the laborer struggling for a right to live and breathe and think as a man. Aristocracies fight for wealth and power, wealth which they waste upon luxury, and power which they abuse for their own interests. Yet the cruelties of Marius were as far exceeded by the cruelties of Sylla as the insurrection of the beggars of Holland was exceeded by the bloody tribunal of the Duke of Alva, or as "the horrors of the French Revolution" were exceeded by the massacre of the Huguenots two hundred years before, for which the Revolution was the expiatory atonement.

Four thousand seven hundred persons fell in the proscription of Sylla, all men of education and fortune. The real crime of many of them was the possession of an estate or a wife which a relative or a neighbor coveted. The crime alleged against all was the opinion that the people of Rome and Italy had rights which deserved consideration as well as the senators and nobles. The liberal party were extinguished in their own blood. Their estates were partitioned into a hundred and twenty thousand allotments, which were distributed among Sylla's friends, or soldiers, or freedmen. The land reform of the Gracchi was mockingly adopted to create a permanent aristocratic garrison. There were no trials, there were no pardons. Common report or private information was at once indictment and evidence, and accusation was in itself condemnation.

The ground being thus cleared, the Dictator took up again his measures of political reform. He did not attempt a second time to take the franchise from the Italians. Romans and Italians he was ready to leave on the same level, but it was to be a level of impotence. Rome was to be ruled by the Senate, and as a first step, and to protect the Senate's dignity, he enfranchised ten thousand slaves who had belonged to the proscribed gentlemen, and formed them into a senatorial guard. Before departing for the East he had doubled the Senate's numbers out of the patrician order. Under Cinna the new members had not claimed their privilege, and had probably been absent from Italy. They were now installed in their places, and the power of the censors to revise the list and remove those who had proved unworthy was taken away. The senators were thus peers for life, peers in a single chamber which Sylla meant to make omnipotent. Vacancies were to be supplied as before from the retiring consuls, praetors, aediles, and quaestors. The form of a popular constitution would remain, since the road into the council of State lay through the popular elections. But to guard against popular favorites finding access to the consulship, a provision was made that no person who had been a tribune of the people could be chosen afterward to any other office.

The Senate's power depended on the withdrawal from the assembly of citizens of the right of original legislation. So long as the citizens could act immediately at the invitation of either consul or tribune, they could repeal at their pleasure any arrangement which Sylla might prescribe. As a matter of course, therefore, he re-enacted the condition which restricted the initiation of laws to the Senate. The tribunes still retained their veto, but a penalty was attached to the abuse of the veto, the Senate being the judge in its own cause, and possessing a right to depose a tribune.

In the Senate so reconstituted was thus centred a complete restrictive control over the legislation and the administration. And this was not all. The senators had been so corrupt in the use of their judicial functions that Gracchus had disabled them from sitting in the law courts, and had provided that the judges should be chosen in future from the equites. The knights had been exceptionally pure in their office. Cicero challenged his opponents on the trial of Verres[5] to find a single instance in which an equestrian court could be found to have given a corrupt verdict during the forty years for which their privilege survived. But their purity did not save them, nor, alas! those who were to suffer by a reversion to the old order. The equestrian courts were abolished: the senatorial courts were reinstated. It might be hoped that the senators had profited by their lesson, and for the future would be careful of their reputation.

Changes were made also in the modes of election to office. The College of Priests had been originally a close corporation, which filled up its own numbers. Democracy had thrown it open to competition, and given the choice to the people. Sylla reverted to the old rule. Consuls like Marius and Cinna, who had the confidence of the people, had been re-elected year after year, and had been virtual kings. Sylla provided that ten years must elapse between a first consulship and a second. Nor was any one to be a consul who was not forty-three years old and had not passed already through the lower senatorial offices of praetor or quaestor.

The assembly of the people had been shorn of its legislative powers. There was no longer, therefore, any excuse for its meeting, save on special occasions. To leave the tribunes power to call the citizens to the Forum was to leave them the means of creating inconvenient agitation. It was ordered, therefore, that the assembly should only come together at the Senate's invitation. The free grants of corn, which filled the city with idle vagrants, were abolished. Sylla never courted popularity, and never shrank from fear of clamor.

The Senate was thus made omnipotent and irresponsible. It had the appointment of all the governors of the provinces. It was surrounded by its own body-guard. It had the administration completely in hand. The members could be tried only by their peers, and were themselves judges of every other order. No legal force was left anywhere to interfere with what it might please them to command. A senator was not necessarily a patrician, nor a patrician a senator. The Senate was,[6] or was to be as time wore on, a body composed of men of any order who had secured the suffrages of the people. But as the value of the prize became so vast, the way to the possession of it was open practically to those only who had wealth or interest. The elections came to be worked by organized committees, and except in extraordinary circumstances no candidate could expect success who had not the Senate's support, or who had not bought the services of the managers, at a cost within the reach only of the reckless spendthrift or the speculating millionaire.

What human foresight could do to prevent democracy from regaining the ascendency, Sylla had thus accomplished. He had destroyed the opposition; he had reorganized the constitution on the most strictly conservative lines. He had built the fortress, as he said; it was now the Senate's part to provide a garrison; and here it was, as Caesar said afterward, that Sylla had made his great mistake. His arrangements were ingenious, and many of them excellent; but the narrower the body to whose care the government was entrusted, the more important became the question of the composition of this body. The theory of election implied that they would be the best that the Republic possessed; but Sylla must have been himself conscious that fact and theory might be very far from corresponding.

The key of the situation was the army. As before, no troops were to be maintained in Italy; but beyond the frontiers the provinces were held by military force, and the only power which could rule the Empire was the power which the army would obey. It was not for the Senate's sake that Sylla's troops had followed him from Greece. It was from their personal devotion to himself. What charm was there in this new constructed aristocratic oligarchy, that distant legions should defer to it--more than Sylla's legions had deferred to orders from Cinna and Carbo? Symptoms of the danger from this quarter were already growing even under the Dictator's own eyes, and at the height of his authority. Sertorius had escaped the proscription. After wandering in Africa he made his way into Spain, where, by his genius as a statesman and a soldier, he rose into a position to defy the Senate and assert his independence. He organized the peninsula after the Roman model; he raised armies, and defeated commander after commander who was sent to reduce him. He revived in the Spaniards a national enthusiasm for freedom. The Roman legionaries had their own opinions, and those whose friends Sylla had murdered preferred Sertorius and liberty to Rome and an aristocratic Senate. Unconquerable by honorable means, Sertorius was poisoned at last. But his singular history suggests a doubt whether, if the Syllan constitution had survived, other Sertoriuses might not have sprung up in every province, and the Empire of Rome have gone to pieces like the Macedonian. The one condition of the continuance of the Roman dominion was the existence of a central authority which the army as a profession could respect, and the traditionary reverence which attached to the Roman Senate would scarcely have secured their disinterested attachment to five hundred elderly rich men who had bought their way into pre-eminence.

Sylla did not live to see the significance of the Sertorian revolt. He experienced, however, himself, in a milder form, an explosion of military sauciness. Young Pompey had been sent, after the occupation of Rome, to settle Sicily and Africa. He did his work well and rapidly, and when it was over he received orders from the Senate to dismiss his troops. An order from Sylla Pompey would have obeyed; but what was the Senate, that an ambitious brilliant youth with arms in his hands should send away an army devoted to him and step back into common life? Sylla himself had to smooth the ruffled plumes of his aspiring follower. He liked Pompey, he was under obligations to him, and Pompey had not acted after all in a manner so very unlike his own. He summoned him home, but he gave him a triumph for his African conquests, and allowed him to call himself by the title of "Magnus," or "The Great." Pompey was a promising soldier, without political ambition, and was worth an effort to secure. To prevent the risk of a second act of insubordination, Sylla made personal arrangements to attach Pompey directly to himself. He had a step-daughter, named Aemilia. She was already married, and was pregnant. Pompey too was married to Antistia, a lady of good family; but domestic ties were not allowed to stand in the way of higher objects. Nor did it matter that Antistia's father had been murdered by the Roman populace for taking Sylla's side, or that her mother had gone mad and destroyed herself, on her husband's horrible death. Late Republican Rome was not troubled with sentiment. Sylla invited Pompey to divorce Antistia and marry Aemilia. Pompey complied. Antistia was sent away. Aemilia was divorced from her husband, and was brought into Pompey's house, where she immediately died.

In another young man of high rank, whom Sylla attempted to attach to himself by similar means, he found less complaisance. Caesar was now eighteen, his daughter Julia having been lately born. He had seen his party ruined, his father-in-law and young Marius killed, and his nearest friends dispersed or murdered. He had himself for a time escaped proscription; but the Dictator had his eye on him, and Sylla had seen something in "the youth with the loose girdle" which struck him as remarkable. Closely connected though Caesar was both with Cinna and Marius, Sylla did not wish to kill him if he could help it. There was a cool calculation in his cruelties. The existing generation of democrats was incurable, but he knew that the stability of the new constitution must depend on his being able to conciliate the intellect and energy of the next. Making a favor perhaps of his clemency, he proposed to Caesar to break with his liberal associates, divorce Cinna's daughter, and take such a wife as he would himself provide. If Pompey had complied, who had made a position of his own, much more might it be expected that Caesar would comply. Yet Caesar answered with a distinct and unhesitating refusal. The terrible Sylla, in the fulness of his strength, after desolating half the homes in Italy, after revolutionizing all Roman society, from the peasant's cottage in the Apennines to the senate-house itself, was defied by a mere boy! Throughout his career Caesar displayed always a singular indifference to life. He had no sentimental passion about him, no Byronic mock-heroics. He had not much belief either in God or the gods. On all such questions he observed from first to last a profound silence. But one conviction he had. He intended, if he was to live at all, to live master of himself in matters which belonged to himself. Sylla might kill him if he so pleased. It was better to die than to put away a wife who was the mother of his child, and to marry some other woman at a dictator's bidding. Life on such terms was not worth keeping.

So proud a bearing may have commanded Sylla's admiration, but it taught him, also, that a young man capable of assuming an attitude so bold might be dangerous to the rickety institutions which he had constructed so carefully. He tried coercion. He deprived Caesar of his priesthood. He took his wife's dowry from him, and confiscated the estate which he had inherited from his father. When this produced no effect, the rebellious youth was made over to the assassins, and a price was set upon his head. He fled into concealment. He was discovered once, and escaped only by bribing Sylla's satellites. His fate would soon have overtaken him, but he had powerful relations, whom Sylla did not care to offend. Aurelius Cotta, who was perhaps his mother's brother, Mamercus Aemilius, a distinguished patrician, and singularly also the College of the Vestal Virgins, interceded for his pardon. The Dictator consented at last, but with prophetic reluctance. "Take him," he said at length, "since you will have it so--but I would have you know that the youth for whom you are so earnest will one day overthrow the aristocracy, for whom you and I have fought so hardly; in this young Caesar there are many Mariuses." [7] Caesar, not trusting too much to Sylla's forbearance, at once left Italy, and joined the army in Asia. The little party of young men who had grown up together now separated, to meet in the future on altered terms. Caesar held to his inherited convictions, remaining constant through good and evil to the cause of his uncle Marius. His companion Cicero, now ripening into manhood, chose the other side. With his talents for his inheritance, and confident in the consciousness of power, but with weak health and a neck as thin as a woman's, Cicero felt that he had a future before him, but that his successes must be won by other weapons than arms. He chose the bar for his profession; he resolved to make his way into popularity as a pleader before the Senate courts and in the Forum. He looked to the Senate itself as the ultimate object of his ambition. There alone he could hope to be distinguished, if distinguished he was to be.

Cicero, however, was no more inclined than Caesar to be subservient to Sylla, as he took an early opportunity of showing. It was to the cause of the constitution, and not to the person of the Dictator, that Cicero had attached himself, and he, too, ventured to give free expression to his thoughts when free speech was still dangerous.

Sylla's career was drawing to its close, and the end was not the least remarkable feature of it. On him had fallen the odium of the proscription and the stain of the massacres. The sooner the senators could be detached from the soldier who had saved them from destruction, the better chance they would have of conciliating quiet people on whose support they must eventually rely. Sylla himself felt the position; and having completed what he had undertaken, with a half-pitying, half-contemptuous self-abandonment he executed what from the first he had intended--he resigned the dictatorship, and became a private citizen again, amusing the leisure of his age, as he had abused the leisure of his youth, with theatres and actresses and dinner-parties. He too, like so many of the great Romans, was indifferent to life; of power for the sake of power he was entirely careless; and if his retirement had been more dangerous to him than it really was, he probably would not have postponed it. He was a person of singular character, and not without many qualities which were really admirable. He was free from any touch of charlatanry. He was true, simple, and unaffected, and even without ambition in the mean and personal sense. His fault, which he would have denied to be a fault, was that he had a patrician disdain of mobs and suffrages and the cant of popular liberty. The type repeats itself era after era. Sylla was but Graham of Claverhouse in a Roman dress and with an ampler stage. His courage in laying down his authority has been often commented on, but the risk which he incurred was insignificant. There was in Rome neither soldier nor statesman who could for a moment be placed in competition with Sylla, and he was so passionately loved by the army, he was so sure of the support of his comrades, whom he had quartered on the proscribed lands, and who, for their own interest's sake, would resist attempts at counter-revolution, that he knew that if an emergency arose he had but to lift his finger to reinstate himself in command. Of assassination he was in no greater danger than when dictator, while the temptation to assassinate him was less. His influence was practically undiminished, and as long as he lived he remained, and could not but remain, the first person in the Republic.

Some license of speech he was, of course, prepared for, but it required no small courage to make a public attack either on himself or his dependants, and it was therefore most creditable to Cicero that his first speech of importance was directed against the Dictator's immediate friends, and was an exposure of the iniquities of the proscription. Cicero no doubt knew that there would be no surer road to favor with the Roman multitude than by denouncing Sylla's followers, and that, young and unknown as he was, his insignificance might protect him, however far he ventured. But he had taken the Senate's side. From first to last he had approved of the reactionary constitution, and had only condemned the ruthless methods by which it had been established. He never sought the popularity of a demagogue, or appealed to popular passions, or attempted to create a prejudice against the aristocracy, into whose ranks he intended to make his way. He expressed the opinions of the respectable middle classes, who had no sympathy with revolutionists, but who dreaded soldiers and military rule and confiscations of property.

The occasion on which Cicero came forward was characteristic of the time. Sextus Roscius was a country gentleman of good position, residing near Ameria, in Umbria. He had been assassinated when on a visit to Rome by two of his relations, who wished to get possession of his estate. The proscription was over, and the list had been closed; but Roscius's name was surreptitiously entered upon it, with the help of Sylla's favorite freedman, Chrysogonus. The assassins obtained an acknowledgment of their claims, and they and Chrysogonus divided the spoils. Sextus Roscius was entirely innocent. He had taken no part in politics at all. He had left a son who was his natural heir, and the township of Ameria sent up a petition to Sylla remonstrating against so iniquitous a robbery. The conspirators, finding themselves in danger of losing the reward of their crime, shifted their ground. They denied that they had themselves killed Sextus Roscius. They said that the son had done it, and they charged him with parricide. Witnesses were easily provided. No influential pleader, it was justly supposed, would venture into antagonism with Sylla's favorite and appear for the defence. Cicero heard of the case, however, and used the opportunity to bring himself into notice. He advocated young Roscius's cause with skill and courage. He told the whole story in court without disguise. He did not blame Sylla. He compared Sylla to Jupiter Optimus Maximus, who was sovereign of the universe, and on the whole a good sovereign, but with so much business on his hands that he had not time to look into details. But Cicero denounced Chrysogonus as an accomplice in an act of atrocious villainy. The court took the same view, and the rising orator had the honor of clearing the reputation of the injured youth, and of recovering his property for him.

Sylla showed no resentment, and probably felt none. He lived for a year after his retirement, and died 78 B.C., being occupied at the moment in writing his memoirs, which have been unfortunately lost. He was buried gorgeously in the Campus Martius, among the old kings of Rome. The aristocrats breathed freely when delivered from his overpowering presence, and the constitution which he had set upon its feet was now to be tried.

[1] "Nigris vegetisque oculis."--Suetonius.

[2] "Ac primum illud tempus familiaritatis et consuetudinis, quae mihi cum illo, quae fratri meo, quae Caio Varroni, consobrino nostro, ab omnium nostrum adolescenti?fuit, praetermitto."--Cicero, De Provinciis Consularibus, 17. Cicero was certainly speaking of a time which preceded Sylla's dictatorship, for Caesar left Rome immediately after it, and when he came back he attached himself to the political party to which Cicero was most opposed.

[3] On the Adriatic, between Anconia and Pescara.

[4] See, for the story of Oppianicus, the remarkable speech of Cicero, Pro Cluentio.

[5] Appian, on the other hand, says that the courts of the equites had been more corrupt than the senatorial courts.--_De Bello Civili, i_. 22. Cicero was perhaps prejudiced in favor of his own order, but a contemporary statement thus publicly made is far more likely to be trustworthy.

[6] Sylla had himself nominated a large number of senators.

[7] So says Suetonius, reporting the traditions of the following century; but the authority is doubtful, and the story, like so many others, is perhaps apocryphal.

CHAPTER IX.

The able men of the democracy had fallen in the proscription. Sertorius, the only eminent surviving soldier belonging to them, was away, making himself independent in Spain. The rest were all killed. But the Senate, too, had lost in Sylla the single statesman that they possessed. They were a body of mediocrities, left with absolute power in their hands, secure as they supposed from further interference, and able to return to those pleasant occupations which for a time had been so rudely interrupted. Sertorius was an awkward problem with which Pompey might perhaps be entrusted to deal. No one knew as yet what stuff might be in Pompey. He was for the present sunning himself in his military splendors; too young to come forward as a politician, and destitute, so far as appeared, of political ambition. If Pompey promised to be docile, he might be turned to use at a proper time; but the aristocracy had seen too much of successful military commanders, and were in no hurry to give opportunities of distinction to a youth who had so saucily defied them. Sertorius was far off, and could be dealt with at leisure.

In his defence of Roscius, Cicero had given an admonition to the noble lords that unless they mended their ways they could not look for any long continuance.[1] They regarded Cicero perhaps, if they heard what he said of them, as an inexperienced young man, who would understand better by and by of what materials the world was made. There had been excitement and anxiety enough. Conservatism was in power again. Fine gentlemen could once more lounge in their clubs, amuse themselves with their fish-ponds and horses and mistresses, devise new and ever new means of getting money and spending it, and leave the Roman Empire for the present to govern itself.

The leading public men belonging to the party in power had all served in some capacity or other with Sylla or under him. Of those whose names deserve particular mention there were at most five.

Licinius Lucullus had been a special favorite of Sylla. The Dictator left him his executor, with the charge of his manuscripts. Lucullus was a commoner, but of consular family, and a thorough-bred aristocrat. He had endeared himself to Sylla by a languid talent which could rouse itself when necessary into brilliant activity, by the easy culture of a polished man of rank, and by a genius for luxury which his admirers followed at a distance, imitating their master but hopeless of overtaking him.

Caecilius Metellus, son of the Metellus whom Marius had superseded in Africa, had been consul with Sylla in 80 B.C. He was now serving in Spain against Sertorius, and was being gradually driven out of the peninsula.

Lutatius Catulus was a proud but honest patrician, with the conceit of his order, but without their vices. His father, who had been Marius's colleague, and had been defeated by the Cimbri, had killed himself during the Marian revolution. The son had escaped, and was one of the consuls at the time of Sylla's death.

More noticeable than either of these was Marcus Crassus, a figure singularly representative, of plebeian family, but a family long adopted into the closest circle of the aristocracy, the leader and impersonation of the great moneyed classes in Rome. Wealth had for several generations been the characteristic of the Crassi. They had the instinct and the temperament which in civilized ages take to money-making as a natural occupation. In politics they aimed at being on the successful side; but living as they did in an era of revolutions, they were surprised occasionally in unpleasant situations. Crassus the rich, father of Marcus, had committed himself against Marius, and had been allowed the privilege of being his own executioner. Marcus himself, who was a little older than Cicero, took refuge in Sylla's camp. He made himself useful to the Dictator by his genius for finance, and in return he was enabled to amass an enormous fortune for himself out of the proscriptions. His eye for business reached over the whole Roman Empire. He was banker, speculator, contractor, merchant. He lent money to the spendthrift young lords, but with sound securities and at usurious interest. He had an army of slaves, but these slaves were not ignorant field-hands; they were skilled workmen in all arts and trades, whose labors he turned to profit in building streets and palaces. Thus all that he touched turned to gold. He was the wealthiest single individual in the whole Empire, the acknowledged head of the business world of Rome.

The last person who need be noted was Marcus Aemilius Lepidus, the father of the future colleague of Augustus and Antony. Lepidus, too, had been an officer of Sylla's. He had been rewarded for his services by the government of Sicily, and when Sylla died was the second consul with Catulus. It was said against him that, like so many other governors, he had enriched himself by tyrannizing over his Sicilian subjects. His extortions had been notorious; he was threatened with prosecution as soon as his consulship should expire; and the adventure to which he was about to commit himself was undertaken, so the aristocrats afterward maintained, in despair of an acquittal. Lepidus's side of the story was never told, but another side it certainly had. Though one of Sylla's generals, he had married the daughter of the tribune Saturninus. He had been elected consul by a very large majority against the wishes of the

Senate, and was suspected of holding popular opinions. It may be that the prosecution was an after-thought of revenge, and that Lepidus was to have been tried before a senatorial jury already determined to find him guilty.

Among these men lay the fortunes of Rome when the departure of their chief left the aristocrats masters of their own destiny.

During this time Caesar had been serving his apprenticeship as a soldier. The motley forces which Mithridates had commanded had not all submitted on the king's surrender to Sylla. Squadrons of pirates hung yet about the smaller islands in the Aegean. Lesbos was occupied by adventurers who were fighting for their own hand, and the praetor Minucius Thermus had been sent to clear the seas and extirpate these nests of brigands. To Thermus Caesar had attached himself. The praetor, finding that his fleet was not strong enough for the work, found it necessary to apply to Nicomedes, the allied sovereign of the adjoining kingdom of Bithynia, to supply him with a few additional vessels; and Caesar, soon after his arrival, was despatched on this commission to the Bithynian court.

Long afterward, when Roman cultivated society had come to hate Caesar, and any scandal was welcome to them which would make him odious, it was reported that on this occasion he entered into certain relations with Nicomedes of a kind indisputably common at the time in the highest patrician circles. The value of such a charge in political controversy was considerable, for whether true or false it was certain to be believed; and similar accusations were flung indiscriminately, so Cicero says, at the reputation of every eminent person whom it was desirable to stain, if his personal appearance gave the story any air of probability.[2]

The disposition to believe evil of men who have risen a few degrees above their contemporaries is a feature of human nature as common as it is base; and when to envy there are added fear and hatred, malicious anecdotes spring like mushrooms in a forcing-pit. But gossip is not evidence, nor does it become evidence because it is in Latin and has been repeated through many generations. The strength of a chain is no greater than the strength of its first link, and the adhesive character of calumny proves only that the inclination of average men to believe the worst of great men is the same in all ages. This particular accusation against Caesar gains, perhaps, a certain credibility from the admission that it was the only occasion on which anything of the kind could be alleged against him. On the other hand, it was unheard of for near a quarter of a century. It was produced in Rome in the midst of a furious political contest. No witnesses were forthcoming; no one who had been at Bithynia at the time; no one who ever pretended to have original knowledge of the truth of the story. Caesar himself passed it by with disdain, or alluded to it, if forced upon his notice, with contemptuous disgust.

The Bithynian mission was otherwise successful. He brought the ships to Thermus. He distinguished himself personally in the storming of Mitylene, and won the oak-wreath, the Victoria Cross of the Roman army. Still pursuing the same career, Caesar next accompanied Servilius Isauricus in a campaign against the horde of pirates, afterwards so famous, that was forming itself among the creeks and river-mouths of Cilicia. The advantages which Servilius obtained over them were considerable enough to deserve a triumph, but were barren of result. The news that Sylla was dead reached the army while still in the field; and the danger of appearing in Rome being over, Caesar at once left Cilicia and went back to his family. Other causes are said to have contributed to hasten his return. A plot had been formed, with the consul Lepidus at its head, to undo Sylla's laws and restore the constitution of the Gracchi. Caesar had been urged by letter to take part in the movement, and he may have hurried home either to examine the prospects of success or perhaps to prevent an attempt which, under the circumstances, he might think criminal and useless. Lepidus was not a wise man, though he may have been an honest one. The aristocracy had not yet proved that they were incapable of reform. It might be that they would digest their lesson after all, and that for a generation to come no more revolutions would be necessary.

[Sidenote: B.C. 77. Caesar aet. 23.] Caesar at all events declined to connect himself with this new adventure. He came to Rome, looked at what was going on, and refused to have anything to do with it. The experiment was tried without him. Young Cinna, his brother-in-law, joined Lepidus. Together they raised a force in Etruria, and marched on Rome. They made their way into the city, but were met in the Campus Martius by Pompey and other consul, Catulus, at the head of some of Sylla's old troops; and an abortive enterprise, which, if it had succeeded, would probably have been mischievous, was ended almost as soon as it began. The two leaders escaped. Cinna joined Sertorius in Spain. Lepidus made his way to Sardinia, where in the next year he died, leaving a son to play the game of democracy under more brilliant auspices.

[Sidenote: Caesar aet. 24.] Caesar meanwhile felt his way, as Cicero was doing in the law-courts, attacking the practical abuses which the Roman administration was generating everywhere. Cornelius Dolabella had been placed by Sylla in command of Macedonia. His father had been a friend of Saturninus, and had fallen at his side. The son had gone over to the aristocracy, and for this reason was perhaps an object of aversion to the younger liberals. The Macedonians pursued him, when his government had expired, with a list of grievances of the usual kind. Young Caesar took up their cause, and prosecuted him. Dolabella was a favorite of the Senate; he had been allowed a triumph for his services, and the aristocracy adopted his cause as their own. The unpractised orator was opposed at the trial by his kinsman Aurelius Cotta and the most celebrated pleaders in Rome. To have crossed swords with such opponents was a dangerous honor for him; success against them was not to be expected, and Caesar was not yet master of his art. Dolabella was acquitted. Party feeling had perhaps entered into the accusation. Caesar found it prudent to retire again from the scene. There were but two roads to eminence in Rome--oratory and service in the army. He had no prospect of public employment from the present administration, and the platform alone was open to him. Plain words with a plain meaning in them no longer carried weight with a people who expected an orator to delight as well as instruct them. The use of the tongue had become a special branch of a statesman's education, and Caesar, feeling his deficiency, used his leisure to put himself in training and to go to school at Rhodes with the then celebrated Apollonius Molo. He had recovered his property and his priesthood, and was evidently in no want of money. He travelled with the retinue of a man of rank, and on his way to Rhodes he fell in with an adventure which may be something more than legend. When he was crossing the Aegean his vessel is said to have been taken by pirates. They carried him to Pharmacusa,[3] an island off the Carian coast, which was then in their possession, and there he was detained for six weeks with three of his attendants, while the rest of his servants were sent to the nearest Roman station to raise his ransom. The pirates treated him with politeness. He joined in their sports, played games with them, looked into their habits, and amused himself with them as well as he could, frankly telling them at the same time that they would all be hanged.

The ransom, a very large one, about ?0,000, was brought and paid. Caesar was set upon the mainland near Miletus, where, without a moment's delay, he collected some armed vessels, returned to the island, seized the whole crew while they were dividing their plunder, and took them away to Pergamus, the seat of government in the Asiatic province, where they were convicted and crucified. Clemency was not a Roman characteristic. It was therefore noted with some surprise that Caesar interceded to mitigate the severity of the punishment. The poor wretches were strangled before they were stretched on their crosses, and were spared the prolongation of their torture. The pirate business being disposed of, he resumed his journey to Rhodes, and there he continued for two years practising gesture and expression under the tuition of the great master.

[Sidenote: B.C. 78-72] During this time the government of Rome was making progress in again demonstrating its unfitness for the duties which were laid upon it, and sowing the seeds which in a few years were to ripen into a harvest so remarkable. Two alternatives only lay before the Roman dominion--either disruption or the abolition of the constitution. If the aristocracy could not govern, still less could the mob govern. The Latin race was scattered over the basin of the Mediterranean, no longer bound by any special ties to Rome or Italy, each man of it individually vigorous and energetic, and bent before all things on making his own fortune. If no tolerable administration was provided from home, their obvious course could only be to identify themselves with local interests and nationalities and make themselves severally independent, as Sertorius was doing in Spain. Sertorius was at last disposed of, but by methods promising ill for the future. He beat Metellus till Metellus could do no more against him. The all-victorious Pompey was sent at last to win victories and gain nothing by them. Six campaigns led to no result and the difficulty was only removed at last by treachery and assassination.

A more extraordinary and more disgraceful phenomenon was the growth of piracy, with the skirts of which Caesar had come in contact at Pharmacusa. The Romans had become masters of the world, only that the sea from one end of their dominions to the other should be patrolled by organized rovers. For many years, as Roman commerce extended, the Mediterranean had become a profitable field of enterprise for those gentry. From every country which they had overrun or occupied the conquests of the Romans had let loose swarms of restless patriots who, if they could not save the liberties of their own countries, could prey upon the oppressor. Illyrians from the Adriatic, Greeks from the islands and the Asiatic ports, Syrians, Egyptians, Africans, Spaniards, Gauls, and disaffected Italians, trained many of them to the sea from their childhood, took to the water in their light galleys with all the world before them. Under most circumstances society is protected against thieves by their inability to combine. But the pirates of the Mediterranean had learnt from the Romans the advantage of union, and had drifted into a vast confederation. Cilicia was their head-quarters. Servilius had checked them for a time, but the Roman Senate was too eager for a revenue, and the Roman governors and farmers of the taxes were too bent upon filling their private purses, to allow fleets to be maintained in the provincial harbors adequate to keep the peace. When Servilius retired, the pirates reoccupied their old haunts. The Cilician forests furnished them with ship timber. The mountain gorges provided inaccessible storehouses for plunder. Crete was completely in their hands also, and they had secret friends along the entire Mediterranean shores. They grew at last into a thousand sail, divided into squadrons under separate commanders. They were admirably armed. They roved over the waters at their pleasure, attacking islands or commercial ports, plundering temples and warehouses, arresting every trading vessel they encountered, till at last no Roman could go abroad on business save during the winter storms, when the sea was comparatively clear. They flaunted their sails in front of Ostia itself; they landed in their boats at the villas on the Italian coast, carrying off lords and ladies, and holding them to ransom. They levied black-mail at their pleasure. The wretched provincials had paid their taxes to Rome in exchange for promised defence, and no defence was provided.[4] The revenue which ought to have been spent on the protection of the Empire a few patricians were dividing among themselves. The pirates had even marts in different islands, where their prisoners were sold to the slave-dealers; and for fifteen years nothing was done or even attempted to put an end to so preposterous an enormity. The ease with which these buccaneers of the old world were eventually suppressed proved conclusively that they existed by connivance. It was discovered at last that large sums had been sent regularly from Crete to some of the most distinguished members of the aristocracy. The Senate was again the same body which it was found by Jugurtha, and the present generation were happier than their fathers in that larger and richer fields were now open to their operation.

While the pirates were at work on the extremities, the senators in the provinces were working systematically, squeezing the people as one might squeeze a sponge of all the wealth that could be drained out of them. After the failure of Lepidus the elections in Rome were wholly in the Senate's hands. Such independence as had not been crushed was corrupted. The aristocracy divided the consulships, praetorships, and quaestorships among themselves, and after the year of office the provincial prizes were then distributed. Of the nature of their government a picture has been left by Cicero, himself one of the senatorial party, and certainly not to be suspected of having represented it as worse than it was in the famous prosecution of Verres. There is nothing to show that Verres was worse than the rest of his order. Piso, Gabinius, and many others equalled or perhaps excelled him in villainy. But historical fate required a victim, and the unfortunate wretch has been selected out of the crowd individually to illustrate his class.

By family he was connected with Sylla. His father was noted as an election manager at the Comitia. The son had been attached to Carbo when the democrats were in power, but he had deserted them on Sylla's return. He had made himself useful in the proscriptions, and had scraped together a considerable fortune. He was employed afterward in Greece and Asia, where he distinguished himself by fresh rapacity and by the gross brutality with which he abused an innocent lady. With the wealth which he had extorted or stolen he bought his way into the praetorship, probably with his father's help; he then became a senator, and was sent to govern Sicily--a place which had already suffered, so the Senate said, from the malpractices of Lepidus, and needing, therefore, to be generously dealt with.

Verres held his province for three years. He was supreme judge in all civil and criminal cases. He negotiated with the parties to every suit which was brought before him, and then sold his decisions. He confiscated estates on fictitious accusations. The island was rich in works of art. Verres had a taste for such things, and seized without scruple the finest productions of Praxiteles or Zeuxis. If those who were wronged dared to complain, they were sent to forced labor at the quarries, or, as dead men tell no tales, were put out of the world. He had an understanding with the pirates, which throws light upon the secret of their impunity. A shipful of them were brought into Messina as prisoners, and were sentenced to be executed. A handsome bribe was paid to Verres, and a number of Sicilians whom he wished out of the way were brought out, veiled and gagged that they might not be recognized, and were hanged as the pirates' substitutes. By these methods Verres was accused of having gathered out of Sicily three quarters of a million of our money. Two thirds he calculated on having to spend in corrupting the consuls and the court before which he might be prosecuted. The rest he would be able to save, and with the help of it to follow his career of greatness through the highest offices of state. Thus he had gone on upon his way, secure, as he supposed, of impunity. One of the consuls for the year and the consuls for the year which was to come next were pledged to support him. The judges would be exclusively senators, each of whom might require assistance in a similar situation. The chance of justice on these occasions was so desperate that the provincials preferred usually to bear their wrongs in silence rather than expose themselves to expense and danger for almost certain failure. But, as Cicero said, the whole world inside the ocean was ringing with the infamy of the Roman senatorial tribunals.

Cicero, whose honest wish was to save the Senate from itself, determined to make use of Verres's conduct to shame the courts into honesty. Every difficulty was thrown in his way. He went in person to Sicily to procure evidence. He was browbeaten and threatened with violence. The witnesses were intimidated, and in some instances were murdered. The technical ingenuities of Roman law were exhausted to shield the culprit. The accident that the second consul had a conscience alone enabled Cicero to force the criminal to the bar. But the picture which Cicero drew and laid before the people, proved as it was to every detail, and admitting of no answer save that other governors had been equally iniquitous and had escaped unpunished, created a storm which the Senate dared not encounter. Verres dropped his defence and fled, and part of his spoils was recovered. There was no shame in the aristocracy to prevent them from committing crimes: there was enough to make them abandon a comrade who was so unfortunate as to be detected and brought to justice.

This was the state of the Roman dominion under the constitution as reformed by Sylla: the Spanish Peninsula recovered by murder to temporary submission; the sea abandoned to buccaneers; decent industrious people in the provinces given over to have their fortunes stolen from them, their daughters dishonored, and themselves beaten or killed if they complained, by a set of wolves calling themselves Roman senators--and these scenes not localized to any one unhappy district, but extending through the entire civilized part of mankind. There was no hope for these unhappy people, for they were under the tyranny of a dead hand. A bad king is like a bad season. The next may bring improvement, or if his rule is wholly intolerable he can be deposed. Under a bad constitution no such change is possible. It can be ended only by a revolution. Republican Rome had become an Imperial State-- she had taken upon herself the guardianship of every country in the world where the human race was industrious and prosperous, and she was discharging her great trust by sacrificing them to the luxury and ambition of a few hundred scandalous politicians.

[Sidenote: B.C. 74.] The nature of man is so constructed that a constitution so administered must collapse. It generates faction within, it invites enemies from without. While Sertorius was defying the Senate in Spain and the pirates were buying its connivance in the Mediterranean, Mithridates started into life again in Pontus. Sylla had beaten him into submission; but Sylla was gone, and no one was left to take Sylla's place. The watchful barbarian had his correspondents in Rome, and knew everything that was passing there. He saw that he had little to fear by trying the issue with the Romans once more. He made himself master of Armenia. In the corsair fleet he had an ally ready made. The Roman province in Asia Minor, driven to despair by the villainy of its governors, was ripe for revolt. Mithridates rose, and but for the young Caesar would a second time have driven the Romans out of Asia. Caesar, in the midst of his rhetorical studies at Rhodes, heard the mutterings of the coming storm. Deserting Apollonius's lecture-room, he crossed over to the continent, raised a corps of volunteers, and held Caria to its allegiance; but Mithridates possessed himself easily of the interior kingdoms and of the whole valley of the Euphrates to the Persian Gulf. The Black Sea was again covered with his ships. He defeated Cotta in a naval battle, drove him through the Bosphorus, and destroyed the Roman squadron. The Senate exerted itself at last. Lucullus, Sylla's friend, the only moderately able man that the aristocracy had among them, was sent to encounter him. Lucullus had been trained in a good school, and the superiority of the drilled Roman legions when tolerably led again easily asserted itself. Mithridates was forced back into the Armenian hills. The Black Sea was swept clear, and eight thousand of the buccaneers were killed at Sinope. Lucullus pursued the retreating prince across the Euphrates, won victories, took cities and pillaged them. He reached Lake Van, he marched round Mount Ararat and advanced to Artaxata. But Asia was a scene of dangerous temptation for a Roman commander. Cicero, though he did not name Lucullus, was transparently alluding to him when he told the assembly in the Forum that Rome had made herself abhorred throughout the world by the violence and avarice of her generals. No temple had been so sacred, no city so venerable, no houses so well protected, as to be secure from their voracity. Occasions of war had been caught at with rich communities where plunder was the only object. The proconsuls could win battles, but they could not keep their hands from off the treasures of their allies and subjects.[5]

Lucullus was splendid in his rapacity, and amidst his victories he had amassed the largest fortune which had yet belonged to patrician or commoner, except Crassus. Nothing came amiss to him. He had sold the commissions in his army. He had taken money out of the treasury for the expenses of the campaign. Part he had spent in bribing the administration to prolong his command beyond the usual time; the rest he had left in the city to accumulate for himself at interest.[6] He lived on the plunder of friend and foe, and the defeat of Mithridates was never more than a second object to him. The one steady purpose in which he never varied was to pile up gold and jewels.

An army so organized and so employed soon loses efficiency and coherence. The legions, perhaps considering that they were not allowed a fair share of the spoil, mutinied. The disaffection was headed by young Publius Clodius, whose sister Lucullus had married. The campaign which had opened brilliantly ended ignominiously. The Romans had to fall back behind Pontus, closely pursued by Mithridates. Lucullus stood on the defensive till he was recalled, and he then returned to Rome to lounge away the remainder of his days in voluptuous magnificence.

While Lucullus was making his fortune in the East, a spurt of insurrectionary fire had broken out in Italy. The agrarian laws and Sylla's proscriptions and confiscations had restored the numbers of the small proprietors, but the statesmen who had been so eager for their reinstatement were fighting against tendencies too strong for them. Life on the farm, like life in the city, was growing yearly more extravagant. [7] The small peasants fell into debt. Sylla's soldiers were expensive, and became embarrassed. Thus the small properties artificially re-established were falling rapidly again into the market. The great landowners bought them up, and Italy was once more lapsing to territorial magnates cultivating their estates by slaves.

Vast gangs of slave laborers were thus still dispersed over the peninsula, while others in large numbers were purchased and trained for the amusement of the metropolis. Society in Rome, enervated as it was by vicious pleasures, craved continually for new excitements. Sensuality is a near relation of cruelty; and the more savage the entertainments, the more delightful they were to the curled and scented patricians who had lost the taste for finer enjoyments. Combats of wild beasts were at first sufficient for them, but to see men kill each other gave a keener delight; and out of the thousands of youths who were sent over annually by the provincial governors, or were purchased from the pirates by the slave-dealers, the most promising were selected for the arena. Each great noble had his training establishment of gladiators, and was as vain of their prowess as of his race-horses. The schools of Capua were the most celebrated; and nothing so recommended a candidate for the consulship to the electors as the production of a few pairs of Capuan swords-men in the circus.

[Sidenote: B.C. 72-70.] These young men had hitherto performed their duties with more submissiveness than might have been expected, and had slaughtered one another in the most approved methods. But the horse knows by the hand on his rein whether he has a fool for his rider. The gladiators in the schools and the slaves on the plantations could not be kept wholly ignorant of the character of their rulers. They were aware that the seas were held by their friends the pirates, and that their masters were again being beaten out of Asia, from which many of themselves had been carried off. They began to ask themselves why men who could use their swords should be slaves when their comrades and kindred were up and fighting for freedom. They found a leader in a young Thracian robber chief, named Spartacus, who was destined for the amphitheatre, and who preferred meeting his masters in the field to killing his friends to make a Roman holiday. Spartacus, with two hundred of his companions, burst out from the Capuan "stable," seized their arms, and made their way into the crater of Vesuvius, which was then, after the long sleep of the volcano, a dense jungle of wild vines. The slaves from the adjoining plantations deserted and joined them. The fire spread, Spartacus proclaimed universal emancipation, and in a few weeks was at the head of an army with which he overran Italy to the foot of the Alps, defeated consuls and praetors, captured the eagles of the legions, wasted the farms of the noble lords, and for two years held his ground against all that Rome could do.

Of all the illustrations of the Senate's incapacity, the slave insurrection was perhaps the worst. It was put down at last after desperate exertions by Crassus and Pompey. Spartacus was killed, and six thousand of his followers were impaled at various points on the sides of the high-roads, that the slaves might have before their eyes examples of the effect of disobedience. The immediate peril was over; but another symptom had appeared of the social disease which would soon end in death unless some remedy could be found. The nation was still strong. There was power and worth in the undegenerate Italian race, which needed only to be organized and ruled. But what remedy was possible? The practical choice of politicians lay between the Senate and the democracy. Both were alike bloody and unscrupulous; and the rule of the Senate meant corruption and imbecility, and the rule of the democracy meant anarchy.

[1] "Unum hoc dico: nostri isti nobiles, nisi vigilantes et boni et fortes et misericordes erunt, iis hominibus in quibus haec erunt, ornamenta sua concedant necesse est."--Pro Roscio Amerino, sec. 48.

[2] "Sunt enim ista maledicta pervulgata in omnes, quorum in adolescenti?forma et species fuit liberalis."--Oratio pro Marca Caelio.

[3] Now Fermaco.

[4] "Videbat enim populum Romanum non locupletari quotannis pecuni?public?praeter paucos: neque eos quidquam aliud assequi classium nomine, nisi ut, detrimentis accipiendis majore affici turpitudine videremur."--Cicero, _Pro Lege Manili, 23.

[5] "Difficile est dictu, Quirites, quanto in odio simus apud exteras nationes, propter eorum, quos ad eas per hos annos cum imperio misimus, injurias ac libidines. Quod enim fanum putatis in illis terris nostris magistratibus religiosum, quam civitatem sanctam, quam domum satis clausam ac munitam fuisse? Urbes jam locupletes ac copiosae requiruntur, quibus causa belli

propter diripiendi cupiditatem inferatur.... Quare etiamsi quem habetis, qui collatis signis exercitus regios superare posse videatur, tamen, nisi erit idem, qui se a pecuniis sociorum, qui ab eorum conjugibus ac liberis, qui ab ornamentis fanorum atque oppidorum, qui ab auro gazaque regio?manus, oculos, animum cohibere possit, non erit idoneus, qui ad bellum Asiaticum regiumque mittatur."--_Pro Lege Manili, 22, 23.

[6] "Quem possumus imperatorem aliquo in numero putare, cujus in exercitu veneant centuriatus atque venierint? Quid hunc hominem magnum aut amplum de republic?cogitare, qui pecuniam ex aerario depromtam ad bellum administrandum, aut propter cupiditatem provinciae magistratibus diviserit aut propter avaritiam Romae in quaestu reliquerit? Vestra admurmuratio facit, Quirites, ut agnoscere videamini qui haec fecerint: ego autem neminem nomino."--_Pro Lege Manili_, 13.

[7] Varro mentions curious instances of the change in country manners. He makes an old man say that when he was a boy, a farmer's wife used to be content with a jaunt in a cart once or twice a year, the farmer not taking out the covered wagon (the more luxurious vehicle) at all unless he pleased. The farmer used to shave only once a week, etc.--_M. Ter. Varronis Reliquiae_, ed. Alexander Riese, pp. 139, 140.

CHAPTER X.

Caesar, having done his small piece of independent service in Caria, and having finished his course with Apollonius, now came again to Rome and re-entered practical life. He lived with his wife and his mother Aurelia in a modest house, attracting no particular notice. But his defiance of Sylla, his prosecution of Dolabella, and his known political sympathies made him early a favorite with the people. The growing disorders at home and abroad, with the exposures on the trial of Verres, were weakening daily the influence of the Senate. Caesar was elected military tribune as a reward for his services in Asia, and he assisted in recovering part of the privileges so dear to the citizens which Sylla had taken from the tribunes of the people. They were again enabled to call the assembly together, and though they were still unable to propose laws without the Senate's sanction, yet they regained the privilege of consulting directly with the nation on public affairs. Caesar now spoke well enough to command the admiration of even Cicero--without ornament, but directly to the purpose. Among the first uses to which he addressed his influence was to obtain the pardon of his brother-in-law, the younger Cinna, who had been exiled since the failure of the attempt of Lepidus. In B.C. 68, being then thirty-two, he gained his first step on the ladder of high office. He was made quaestor, which gave him a place in the Senate.

Soon after his election, his aunt Julia, the widow of Marius, died. It was usual on the death of eminent persons for a near relation to make an oration at the funeral. Caesar spoke on this occasion. It was observed that he dwelt with some pride on the lady's ancestry, descending on one side from the gods, on another from the kings of Rome. More noticeably he introduced into the burial procession the insignia and images of Marius himself, whose name for some years it had been unsafe to mention.[1]

Pompey, after Sertorius's death, had pacified Spain. He had assisted Crassus in extinguishing Spartacus. The Senate had employed him, but had never liked him or trusted him. The Senate, however, was no longer omnipotent, and in the year 70 he and Crassus had been consuls. Pompey was no politician, but he was honorable and straightforward. Like every true Roman, he was awake to the dangers and disgrace of the existing mal-administration, and he and Caesar began to know each other, and to find their interest in working together. Pompey was the elder of the two by six years. He was already a great man, covered with distinctions, and perhaps he supposed that he was finding in Caesar a useful subordinate. Caesar naturally liked Pompey, as a really distinguished soldier and an upright disinterested man. They became connected by marriage. Cornelia dying, Caesar took for his second wife Pompey's cousin, Pompeia; and, no doubt at Pompey's instance, he was sent into Spain to complete Pompey's work and settle the finances of that distracted country. His reputation as belonging to the party of Marius and Sertorius secured him the confidence of Sertorius's friends. He accomplished his mission completely and easily. On his way back he passed through northern Italy, and took occasion to say there that he considered the time to have come for the franchise, which now stopped at the Po, to be extended to the foot of the Alps.

The consulship of Pompey and Crassus had brought many changes with it, all tending in the same direction. The tribunes were restored to their old functions, the censorship was re-established, and the Senate was at once weeded of many of its disreputable members. Cicero, conservative as he was, had looked upon these measures if not approvingly yet without active opposition. To another change he had himself contributed by his speeches on the Verres prosecution. The exclusive judicial powers which the Senate had abused so scandalously were again taken from them. The courts of the equites were remembered in contrast, and a law was passed that for the future the courts were to be composed two thirds of knights and one third only of senators. Cicero's hope of resisting democracy lay in the fusion of the great commoners with the Senate. It was no longer possible for the aristocracy to rule alone. The few equites who, since Sylla's time, had made their way into the Senate had yielded to patrician ascendency. Cicero aimed at a reunion of the orders; and the consulship of Crassus, little as Cicero liked Crassus personally, was a sign of a growing tendency in this direction. At all costs the knights must be prevented from identifying themselves with the democrats, and therefore all possible compliments and all possible concessions to their interests were made to them.

They recovered their position in the law-courts; and, which was of more importance to them, the system of farming the taxes, in which so many of them had made their fortunes, and which Sylla had abolished, was once again reverted to. It was not a good system, but it was better than a state of things in which little of the revenue had reached the public treasury at all, but had been intercepted and parcelled out among the oligarchy.

[Sidenote: B.C. 67.] With recovered vitality a keener apprehension began to be felt of the pirate scandal. The buccaneers, encouraged by the Senate's connivance, were more daring than ever. They had become a sea community, led by high-born adventurers, who maintained out of their plunder a show of wild magnificence. The oars of the galleys of their commanders were plated with silver; their cabins were hung with gorgeous tapestry. They had bands of music to play at their triumphs. They had a religion of their own, an oriental medley called the Mysteries of Mithras. They had captured and pillaged four hundred considerable towns, and had spoiled the temples of the Grecian gods. They had maintained and extended their depots where they disposed of their prisoners to the slave-dealers. Roman citizens who could not ransom themselves, and could not conveniently be sold, were informed that they might go where they pleased; they were led to a plank projecting over some vessel's side, and were bidden depart--into the sea. Not contented with insulting Ostia by their presence outside, they had ventured into the harbor itself, and had burnt the ships there. They held complete possession of the Italian waters. Rome, depending on Sicily and Sardinia and Africa for her supplies of corn, was starving for want of food, and the foreign trade on which so many of the middle classes were engaged was totally destroyed. The return of the commoners to power was a signal for an active movement to put an end to the disgrace. No one questioned that it could be done if there was a will to do it. But the work could be accomplished only by persons who would be proof against corruption. There was but one man in high position who could be trusted, and that was Pompey. The general to be selected must have unrestricted and therefore unconstitutional authority. But Pompey was at once capable and honest. Pompey could not be bribed by the pirates, and Pompey could be depended on not to abuse his opportunities to the prejudice of the Commonwealth.

[Sidenote: B.C. 67.] The natural course, therefore, would have been to declare Pompey dictator; but Sylla had made the name unpopular; the right to appoint a dictator lay with the Senate, with whom Pompey had never been a favorite, and the aristocracy had disliked and feared him more than ever since his consulship. From that quarter no help was to be looked for, and a method was devised to give him the reality of power without the title. Unity of command was the one essential--command untrammelled by orders from committees of weak and treacherous noblemen, who cared only for the interest of their class. The established forms were scrupulously observed, and the plan designed was brought forward first, according to rule, in the Senate. A tribune, Aulus Gabinius, introduced a proposition there that one person of consular rank should have absolute jurisdiction during three years over the whole Mediterranean, and over all Roman territory for fifty miles inland from the coast; that the money in the treasury should be at his disposition; that he should have power to raise 500 ships of war and to collect and organize 130,000 men. No such command for such a time had ever been committed to any one man since the abolition of the monarchy. It was equivalent to a suspension of the Senate itself, and of all constitutional government. The proposal was received with a burst of fury. Every one knew that the person intended was Pompey. The decorum of the old days was forgotten. The noble lords started from their seats, flew at Gabinius, and almost strangled him: but he had friends outside the house ready to defend their champion; the country people had flocked in for the occasion; the city was thronged with multitudes such as had not been seen there since the days of the Gracchi. The tribune freed himself from the hands that were at his throat; he rushed out into the Forum, closely pursued by the consul Piso, who would have been torn in pieces in turn had not Gabinius interposed to save him. Senate or no Senate, it was decided that Gabinius's proposition should be submitted to the assembly, and the aristocrats were driven to their old remedy of bribing other members of the college of tribunes to interfere. Two renegades were thus secured, and when the voting-day came, Trebellius, who was one of them, put in a veto; the other, Roscius, said that the power intended for Pompey was too considerable to be trusted to a single person, and proposed two commanders instead of one. The mob was packed so thick that the house-tops were covered. A yell rose from tens of thousands of throats so piercing that it was said a crow flying over the Forum dropped dead at the sound of it. The old patrician Catulus tried to speak, but the people would not hear him. The vote passed by acclamation, and Pompey was for three years sovereign of the Roman world.

It now appeared how strong the Romans were when a fair chance was allowed them. Pompey had no extraordinary talents, but not in three years, but in three months, the pirates were extinguished. He divided the Mediterranean into thirteen districts, and allotted a squadron to each, under officers on whom he could thoroughly rely. Ships and seamen were found in abundance lying idle from the suspension of trade. In forty days he had cleared the seas between Gibraltar and Italy. He had captured entire corsair fleets, and had sent the rest flying into the Cilician creeks. There, in defence of their plunder and their families, they fought one desperate engagement, and when defeated, they surrendered without a further blow. Of real strength they had possessed none from the first. They had subsisted only through the guilty complicity of the Roman authorities, and they fell at the first stroke which was aimed at them in earnest. Thirteen hundred pirate ships were burnt. Their docks and arsenals were destroyed, and their fortresses were razed. Twenty-two thousand prisoners fell into the hands of Pompey. To the astonishment of mankind, Pompey neither impaled them, as the Senate had impaled the followers of Spartacus, nor even sold them for slaves. He was contented to scatter them among inland colonies, where they could no longer be dangerous.

The suppression of the buccaneers was really a brilliant piece of work, and the ease with which it was accomplished brought fresh disgrace on the Senate and fresh glory on the hero of the hour. Cicero, with his thoughts fixed on saving the constitution, considered that Pompey might be the man to save it; or, at all events, that it would be unsafe to leave him to the democrats who had given him power and were triumphing in his success. On political grounds Cicero thought that Pompey ought to be recognized by the moderate party which he intended to form; and a person like himself who hoped to rise by the popular votes could not otherwise afford to seem cold amidst the universal enthusiasm. The pirates were abolished. Mithridates was still undisposed of. Lucullus, the hope of the aristocracy, was lying helpless within the Roman frontier, with a disorganized and mutinous army. His victories were forgotten. He was regarded as the impersonation of every fault which had made the rule of the Senate so hateful. Pompey, the people's general, after a splendid success, had come home with clean hands; Lucullus had sacrificed his country to his avarice. The contrast set off his failures in colors perhaps darker than really belonged to them, and the cry naturally rose that Lucullus must be called back, and the all-victorious Pompey must be sent for the reconquest of Asia. Another tribune, Manilius, brought the question forward, this time directly before the assembly, the Senate's consent not being any more asked for. Caesar again brought his influence to bear on Pompey's side; but Caesar found support in a quarter where it might not have been looked for. The Senate was furious as before, but by far the most gifted person in the conservative party now openly turned against them. Cicero was praetor this year, and was thus himself a senator. A seat in the Senate had been the supreme object of his ambition. He was vain of the honor which he had won, and delighted with the high company into which he had been received; but he was too shrewd to go along with them upon a road which could lead only to their overthrow; and for their own sake, and for the sake of the institution itself of which he meant to be an illustrious ornament, he not only supported the Manilian proposition, but supported it in a speech more effective than the wildest outpourings of democratic rhetoric.

Asia Minor, he said, was of all the Roman provinces the most important, because it was the most wealthy.[2] So rich it was and fertile that, for the productiveness of its soil, the variety of its fruits, the extent of its pastures, and the multitude of its exports, there was no country in the world to be compared with it; yet Asia was in danger of being utterly lost through the worthlessnesss of the governors and military commanders charged with the care of it. "Who does not know," Cicero asked, "that the avarice of our generals has been the cause of the misfortunes of our armies? You can see for yourselves how they act here at home in Italy; and what will they not venture far away in distant countries? Officers who cannot restrain their own appetites can never maintain discipline in their troops. Pompey has been victorious because he does not loiter about the towns for plunder or pleasure, or making collections of statues and pictures. Asia is a land of temptations. Send no one thither who cannot resist gold and jewels and shrines and pretty women. Pompey is upright and pure-sighted. Pompey knows that the State has been impoverished because the revenue flows into the coffers of a few individuals. Our fleets and armies have availed only to bring the more disgrace upon us through our defeats and losses." [3]

After passing a deserved panegyric on the suppression of the pirates, Cicero urged with all the power of his oratory that Manilius's measures should be adopted, and that the same general who had done so well already should be sent against Mithridates.

This was perhaps the only occasion on which Cicero ever addressed the assembly in favor of the proposals of a popular tribune. Well would it have been for him and well for Rome if he could have held on upon a course into which he had been led by real patriotism. He was now in his proper place, where his better mind must have told him that he ought to have continued, working by the side of Caesar and Pompey. It was observed that more than once in his speech he mentioned with high honor the name of Marius. He appeared to have seen clearly that the Senate was bringing the State to perdition; and that unless the Republic was to end in dissolution, or in mob rule and despotism, the wise course was to recognize the legitimate tendencies of popular sentiment, and to lend the constant weight of his authority to those who were acting in harmony with it. But Cicero could never wholly forget his own consequence, or bring himself to persist in any policy where he could play but a secondary part.

[Sidenote: B.C. 66-63.] The Manilian law was carried. In addition to his present extraordinary command, Pompey was entrusted with the conduct of the war in Asia, and he was left unfettered to act at his own discretion. He crossed the Bosphorus with fifty thousand men; he invaded Pontus; he inflicted a decisive defeat on Mithridates, and broke up his army; he drove the Armenians back into their own mountains, and extorted out of them a heavy war indemnity. The barbarian king who had so long defied the Roman power was beaten down at last, and fled across the Black Sea to Kertch, where his sons turned against him. He was sixty-eight years old, and could not wait till the wheel should make another turn. Broken down at last, he took leave of a world in which for him there was no longer a place. His women poisoned themselves successfully. He, too fortified by antidotes to end as they ended, sought a surer death, and fell like Saul by the sword of a slave. Rome had put out her real strength, and at once, as before, all opposition went down before her. Asia was completely conquered up to the line of the Euphrates. The Black Sea was held securely by a Roman fleet. Pompey passed down into Syria. Antioch surrendered without resistance. Tyre and Damascus followed. Jerusalem was taken by storm, and the Roman general entered the Holy of Holies. Of all the countries bordering on the Mediterranean Egypt only was left independent, and of all the islands only Cyprus. A triumphal inscription in Rome declared that Pompey, the people's general, had in three years captured fifteen hundred cities, and had slain, taken, or reduced to submission twelve million human beings. He justified what Cicero had foretold of his moral uprightness. In the midst of opportunities such as had fallen to no commander since Alexander, he outraged no woman's honor, and he kept his hands clean from "the accursed thing." When he returned to Rome, he returned, as he went, personally poor, but he filled the treasury to overflowing. His campaign was not a marauding raid, like the march of Lucullus on Artaxata. His conquests were permanent. The East, which was then thickly inhabited by an industrious civilized Graeco-Oriental race, became incorporated in the Roman dominion, and the annual revenue of the State rose to twice what it had been. Pompey's success had been dazzlingly rapid. Envy and hatred, as he well knew, were waiting for him at home, and he was in no haste to present himself there. He lingered in Asia, organizing the administration and consolidating his work, while at Rome the constitution was rushing on upon its old courses among the broken waters, with the roar of the not distant cataract growing every moment louder.

[1] The name of Marius, it is to be observed, remained so popular in Rome that Cicero after this always spoke of him with respect.

[2] "Asia vero tam opima est et fertilis, ut et ubertate agrorum et varietate

fructuum et magnitudine pastionis, et multitudine earum rerum, quae exportentur, facile omnibus terris antecellat."--_Pro Lege Manili. Cicero's expressions are worth notice at a time when Asia Minor has become of importance to England.

[3] _Pro Lege Manili. abridged.

CHAPTER XI.

[Sidenote: B.C. 64.] Among the patricians who were rising through the lower magistracies and were aspiring to the consulship was Lucius Sergius Catiline. Catiline, now in middle life, had when young been a fervent admirer of Sylla, and, as has been already said, had been an active agent in the proscription. He had murdered his brother-in-law, and perhaps his brother, under political pretences. In an age when licentiousness of the grossest kind was too common to attract attention, Catiline had achieved a notoriety for infamy. Ho had intrigued with a Vestal virgin, the sister of Cicero's wife, Terentia. If Cicero is to be believed, he had made away with his own wife, that he might marry Aurelia Orestilla, a woman as wicked as she was beautiful, and he had killed his child also because Aurelia had objected to be encumbered with a step-son. But this, too, was common in high society in those days. Adultery and incest had become familiar excitements. Boys of ten years old had learnt the art of poisoning their fathers,[1] and the story of Aurelia Orestilla and Catiline had been rehearsed a few years before by Sassia and Oppianicus at Larino.[2] Other enormities Catiline had been guilty of which Cicero declined to mention, lest he should show too openly what crimes might go unpunished under the senatorial administration. But villainy, however notorious, did not interfere with advancement in the public service. Catiline was adroit, bold, and even captivating. He made his way into high office along the usual gradations. He was praetor in B.C. 68. He went as governor to Africa in the year following, and he returned with money enough, as he reasonably hoped, to purchase the last step to the consulship. He was impeached when he came back for extortion and oppression, under one of the many laws which were made to be laughed at. Till his trial was over he was disqualified from presenting himself as a candidate, and the election for the year 65 was carried by Autronius Paetus and Cornelius Sylla. Two other patricians, Aurelius Cotta and Manlius Torquatus, had stood against them. The successful competitors were unseated for bribery; Cotta and Torquatus took their places, and, apparently as a natural resource in the existing contempt into which the constitution had fallen, the disappointed candidates formed a plot to kill their rivals and their rivals' friends in the Senate, and to make a revolution. Cneius Piso, a young nobleman of the bluest blood, joined in the conspiracy. Catiline threw himself into it as his natural element, and aristocratic tradition said in later years that Caesar and Crassus were implicated also. Some desperate scheme there certainly was, but the accounts of it are confused: one authority says that it failed because Catiline gave the signal prematurely; others that Caesar was to have given the signal, and did not do it; others that Crassus's heart failed him; others that the consuls had secret notice given to them and took precautions. Cicero, who was in Rome at the time, declares that he never heard of the conspiracy.[3] When evidence is inconclusive, probability becomes argument. Nothing can be less likely than that a cautious capitalist of vast wealth like Crassus should have connected himself with a party of dissolute adventurers. Had Caesar committed himself, jealously watched as he was by the aristocrats, some proofs of his complicity would have been forthcoming. The aristocracy under the empire revenged themselves for their ruin by charging Caesar with a share in every combination that had been formed against them, from Sylla's time downwards. Be the truth what it may, nothing came of this project. Piso went to Spain, where he was killed. The prosecution of Catiline for his African misgovernment was continued, and, strange to say, Cicero undertook his defence. He was under no uncertainty as to Catiline's general character, or his particular guilt in the charge brought against him. It was plain as the sun at midday.[4] But Cicero was about to stand himself for the consulship, the object of his most passionate desire. He had several competitors; and as he thought well of Catiline's prospects, he intended to coalesce with him.[5] Catiline was acquitted, apparently through a special selection of the judges, with the connivance of the prosecutor. The canvass was violent, and the corruption flagrant. [6]Cicero did not bribe himself, but if Catiline's voters would give him a help, he was not so scrupulous as to be above taking advantage of it. Catiline's humor or the circumstances of the time provided him with a more honorable support. He required a more manageable colleague than he could have found in Cicero. Among the candidates was one of Sylla's officers, Caius Antonius, the uncle of Marc Antony, the triumvir. This Antonius had been prosecuted by Caesar for ill-usage of the Macedonians. He had been expelled by the censors from the Senate for general worthlessness; but public disgrace seems to have had no effect whatever on the chances of a candidate for the consulship in this singular age. Antonius was weak and vicious, and Catiline could mould him as he pleased. He had made himself popular by his profusion when aedile in providing shows for the mob. The feeling against the Senate was so bitter that the aristocracy had no chance of carrying a candidate of their own, and the competition was reduced at last to Catiline, Antonius and Cicero. Antonius was certain of his election, and the contest lay between Catiline and Cicero. Each of them tried to gain the support of Antonius and his friends. Catiline promised Antonius a revolution, in which they were to share the world between them. Cicero promised his influence to obtain some lucrative province for Antonius to misgovern. Catiline would probably have succeeded, when the aristocracy, knowing what to expect if so scandalous a pair came into office, threw their weight on Cicero's side and turned the scale. Cicero was liked among the people for his prosecution of Verres, for his support of the Manilian law, and for the boldness with which he had exposed patrician delinquencies. With the Senate for him also, he was returned at the head of the poll. The proud Roman nobility had selected a self-made lawyer as their representative. Cicero was consul, and Antonius with him. Catiline had failed. It was the turning-point of Cicero's life. Before his consulship he had not irrevocably taken a side. No public speaker had more eloquently shown the necessity for reform; no one had denounced with keener sarcasm the infamies and follies of senatorial favorites. Conscience and patriotism should have alike held him to the reforming party; and political instinct, if vanity had left him the use of his perception, would have led him in the same direction. Possibly before he received the votes of the patricians and their clients he had bound himself with certain engagements to them. Possibly he held the Senate's intellect cheap, and saw the position which he could arrive at among the aristocracy if he offered them his services. The strongest intellect was with the reformers, and first on that side he could never be. First among the Conservatives[7] he could easily be; and he might prefer being at the head of a party which at heart he despised, to working at the side of persons who must stand inevitably above him. We may regret that gifted men should be influenced by personal considerations, but under party government it is a fact that they are so influenced, and will be as long as it continues. Caesar and Pompey were soldiers. The army was democratic, and the triumph of the democracy meant the rule of a popular general. Cicero was a civilian, and a man of speech. In the forum and in the Curia he knew that he could reign supreme.

Cicero had thus reached the highest step in the scale of promotion by trimming between the rival factions. Caesar was rising simultaneously behind him on lines of his own. In the year B.C. 65 he had been aedile, having for his colleague Bibulus, his future companion on the successive grades of ascent. Bibulus was a rich plebeian, whose delight in office was the introduction which it gave him into the society of the great; and in his politics he outdid his aristocratic patrons. The aediles had charge of the public buildings and the games and exhibitions in the capital. The aedileship was a magistracy through which it was ordinarily necessary to pass in order to reach the consulship; and as the aediles were expected to bear their own expenses, the consulship was thus restricted to those who could afford an extravagant outlay. They were expected to decorate the city with new ornaments, and to entertain the people with magnificent spectacles. If they fell short of public expectation, they need look no further for the suffrages of their many-headed master. Cicero had slipped through the aedileship, without ruin to himself. He was a self-raised man, known to be dependent upon his own exertions, and liked from the willingness with which he gave his help to accused persons on their trials. Thus no great demands had been made upon him. Caesar, either more ambitious or less confident in his services, raised a new and costly row of columns in front of the Capitol. He built a temple to the Dioscuri, and he charmed the populace with a show of gladiators unusually extensive. Personally he cared nothing for these sanguinary exhibitions, and he displayed his indifference ostentatiously by reading or writing while the butchery was going forward.[8] But he required the favor of the multitude, and then, as always, took the road which led most directly to his end. The noble lords watched him suspiciously, and their uneasiness was not diminished when, not content with having produced the insignia of Marius at his aunt's funeral, he restored the trophies for the victories over the Cimbri and Teutons, which had been removed by Sylla. The name of Marius was growing every day more dear to the popular party. They forgave, if they had ever resented, his credulities. His veterans who had fought with him through his campaigns came forward in tears to salute the honored relics of their once glorious commander.

As he felt the ground stronger under his feet, Caesar now began to assume an attitude more peremptorily marked. He had won a reputation in the Forum; he had spoken in the Senate; he had warmly advocated the appointment of Pompey to his high commands; and he was regarded as a prominent democratic leader. But he had not aspired to the tribunate; he had not thrown himself into politics with any absorbing passion. His exertions had been intermittent, and he was chiefly known as a brilliant member of fashionable society, a peculiar favorite with women, and remarkable for his abstinence from the coarse debauchery which disgraced his patrician contemporaries. He was now playing for a higher stake, and the oligarchy had occasion to be reminded of Sylla's prophecy. In carrying out the proscription, Sylla had employed professional assassins, and payments had been made out of the treasury to wretches who came to him with bloody trophies in their hands to demand the promised fees. The time had come when these doings were to be looked into; hundreds of men had been murdered, their estates confiscated, and their families ruined, who had not been even ostensibly guilty of any public crime. At Caesar's instance an inquiry was ordered. He himself was appointed Judex Quaestionis, or chairman of a committee of investigation; and Catiline, among others, was called to answer for himself--a curious commentary on Caesar's supposed connection with him.

[Sidenote: B.C. 63.] Nor did the inquisition stop with Sylla. Titus Labienus, afterward so famous and so infamous, was then tribune of the people. His father had been killed at the side of Saturninus and Glaucia thirty-seven years before, when the young lords of Rome had unroofed the senate-house, and had pelted them and their companions to death with tiles. One of the actors in the scene, Caius Rabirius, now a very old man, was still alive. Labienus prosecuted him before Caesar. Rabirius was condemned, and appealed to the people; and Cicero, who had just been made consul, spoke in his defence. On this occasion Cicero for the first time came actively in collision with Caesar. His language contrasted remarkably with the tone of his speeches against Verres and for the Manilian law. It was adroit, for he charged Marius with having shared the guilt, if guilt there had been, in the death of those men; but the burden of what he said was to defend enthusiastically the conservative aristocracy, and to censure with all his bitterness the democratic reformers. Rabirius was acquitted, perhaps justly. It was a hard thing to revive the memory of a political crime which had been shared by the whole patrician order after so long an interval. But Cicero had shown his new colors; no help, it was evident, was thenceforward to be expected from him in the direction of reform. The popular party replied in a singular manner. The office of Pontifex Maximus was the most coveted of all the honors to which a Roman citizen could aspire. It was held for life, it was splendidly endowed, and there still hung about the pontificate the traditionary dignity attaching to the chief of the once sincerely believed Roman religion. Like other objects of ambition, the nomination had fallen, with the growth of democracy, to the people, but the position had always been held by some member of the old aristocracy; and Sylla, to secure them in the possession of it, had reverted to the ancient constitution, and had restored to the Sacred College the privilege of choosing their head. Under the impulse which the popular party had received from Pompey's successes, Labienus carried a vote in the assembly, by which the people resumed the nomination to the pontificate themselves. In the same year it fell vacant by the death of the aged Metullus Pius. Two patricians, Quintus Catulus and Caesar's old general Servilius Isauricus, were the Senate's candidates, and vast sums were subscribed and spent to secure the success of one or other of the two. Caesar came forward to oppose them. Caesar aspired to be Pontifex Maximus--Pope of Rome--he who of all men living was the least given to illusion; he who was the most frank in his confession of entire disbelief in the legends which, though few credited them any more, yet almost all thought it decent to pretend to credit. Among the phenomena of the time this was surely the most singular. Yet Caesar had been a priest from his boyhood, and why should he not be Pope? He offered himself to the Comitia. Committed as he was to a contest with the richest men in Rome, he spent money freely. He was in debt already for his expenses as aedile. He engaged his credit still deeper for this new competition. The story ran that when his mother kissed him as he was leaving his home for the Forum on the morning of the election, he told her that he would return as pontiff, or she would never see him more. He was chosen by an overwhelming majority, the votes given for him being larger than the collective numbers of the votes entered for his opponents.

[Sidenote: B.C. 63.] The election for the pontificate was on the 6th of March, and soon after Caesar received a further evidence of popular favor on being chosen praetor for the next year. As the liberal party was growing in courage and definiteness, Cicero showed himself more decidedly on the other side. Now was the time for him, highly placed as he was, to prevent a repetition of the scandals which he had so eloquently denounced, to pass laws which no future Verres or Lucullus could dare to defy. Now was his opportunity to take the wind out of the reformers' sails, and to grapple himself with the thousand forms of patrician villainy which he well knew to be destroying the Commonwealth. Not one such measure, save an ineffectual attempt to check election bribery, distinguished the consulship of Cicero. His entire efforts were directed to the combination in a solid phalanx of the equestrian and patrician orders. The danger to society, he had come to think, was an approaching war against property, and his hope was to unite the rich of both classes in defence against the landless and moneyless multitudes.[9] The land question had become again as pressing as in the time of the Gracchi. The peasant proprietors were melting away as fast as ever, and Rome was becoming choked with impoverished citizens, who ought to have been farmers and fathers of families, but were degenerating into a rabble fed upon the corn grants, and occupied with nothing but spectacles and politics. The agrarian laws in the past had been violent, and might reasonably be complained of; but a remedy could now be found for this fast-increasing mischief without injury to anyone. Pompey's victories had filled the public treasury. Vast territories abroad had lapsed to the possession of the State; and Rullus, one of the tribunes, proposed that part of these territories should be sold, and that out of the proceeds, and out of the money which Pompey had sent home, farms should be purchased in Italy and poor citizens settled upon them. Rullus's scheme might have been crude, and the details of it objectionable; but to attempt the problem was better than to sit still and let the evil go unchecked. If the bill was impracticable in its existing form, it might have been amended; and so far as the immediate effect of such a law was concerned, it was against the interests of the democrats. The popular vote depended for its strength on the masses of poor who were crowded into Rome; and the tribune was proposing to weaken his own army. But the very name of an agrarian law set patrician households in a flutter, and Cicero stooped to be their advocate. He attacked Rullus with brutal sarcasm. He insulted his appearance; he ridiculed his dress, his hair, and his beard. He mocked at his bad enunciation and bad grammar. No one more despised the mob than Cicero; but because Rullus had said that the city rabble was dangerously powerful, and ought to be "drawn off" to some wholesome employment, the eloquent consul condescended to quote the words, to score a point against his opponent; and he told the crowd that their tribune had described a number of excellent citizens to the Senate as no better than the contents of a cesspool.[10]

By these methods Cicero caught the people's voices. The plan came to nothing, and his consulship would have waned away, undistinguished by any act which his country would have cared to remember, but for an accident which raised him for a moment into a position of real consequence, and impressed on his own mind a conviction that he was a second Romulus.

Revolutionary conspiracies are only formidable when the government against which they are directed is already despised and detested. As long as an administration is endurable the majority of citizens prefer to bear with it, and will assist in repressing violent attempts at its overthrow. Their patience, however, may be exhausted, and the disgust may rise to a point when any change may seem an improvement. Authority is no longer shielded by the majesty with which it ought to be surrounded. It has made public its own degradation; and the most worthless adventurer knows that he has no moral indignation to fear if he tries to snatch the reins out of hands which are at least no more pure than his own. If he can dress his endeavors in the livery of patriotism, if he can put himself forward as the champion of an injured people, he can cover the scandals of his own character and appear as a hero and a liberator. Catiline had missed the consulship, and was a ruined man. He had calculated on succeeding to a province where he might gather a golden harvest and come home to live in splendor, like Lucullus. He had failed, defeated by a mere plebeian whom his brother-patricians had stooped to prefer to him. Were the secret history known of the contest for the consulship, much might be discovered there to explain Cicero's and Catiline's hatred of each other. Cicero had once thought of coalescing with Catiline, notwithstanding his knowledge of his previous crimes: Catiline had perhaps hoped to dupe Cicero, and had been himself outwitted. He intended to stand again for the year 62, but evidently on a different footing from that on which he had presented himself before. That such a man should have been able to offer himself at all, and that such a person as Cicero should have entered into any kind of amicable relations with him, was a sign by itself that the Commonwealth was already sickening for death.

Catiline was surrounded by men of high birth, whose fortunes were desperate as his own. There was Lentulus, who had been consul a few years before, and had been expelled from the Senate by the censors. There was Cethegus, staggering under a mountain of debts. There was Autronius, who had been unseated for bribery when chosen consul in 65. There was Manlius, once a distinguished officer in Sylla's army, and now a beggar. Besides these were a number of senators, knights, gentlemen, and dissolute young patricians, whose theory of the world was that it had been created for them to take their pleasure in, and who found their pleasures shortened by emptiness of purse. To them, as to their betters, the Empire was but a large dish out of which they considered that they had a right to feed themselves. They were defrauded of their proper share, and Catiline was the person who would help them to it.

Etruria was full of Sylla's disbanded soldiers, who had squandered their allotments, and were hanging about, unoccupied and starving. Catiline sent down Manlius, their old officer, to collect as many as he could of them without attracting notice. He himself, as the election day approached, and Cicero's year of office was drawing to an end, took up the character of an aristocratic demagogue, and asked for the suffrages of the people as the champion of the poor against the rich, as the friend of the wretched and oppressed; and those who thought themselves wretched and oppressed in Rome were so large a body, and so bitterly hostile were they all to the prosperous classes, that his election was anticipated as a certainty. In the Senate the consulship of Catiline was regarded as no less than an impending national calamity. Marcus Cato, great-grandson of the censor, then growing into fame by his acrid tongue and narrow republican fanaticism, who had sneered at Pompey's victories as triumphs over women, and had not spared even Cicero himself, threatened Catiline in the Curia. Catiline answered, in a fully attended house, that if any agitation was kindled against him he would put it out, not with water, but with revolution. His language became so audacious that, on the eve of the election day, Cicero moved for a postponement, that the Senate might take his language into consideration. Catiline's conduct was brought on for debate, and the consul called on him to explain himself. There was no concealment in Catiline. Then and always Cicero admits he was perfectly frank. He made no excuses. He admitted the truth of what had been reported of him. The State, he said, had two bodies, one weak (the aristocracy), with a weak leader (Cicero); the other, the great mass of the citizens-- strong in themselves, but without a head, and he himself intended to be that head.[11] A groan was heard in the house, but less loud than in Cicero's opinion it ought to have been; and Catiline sailed out in triumph, leaving the noble lords looking in each other's faces.

[Sidenote: October, B.C. 63.] Both Cicero and the Senate were evidently in the greatest alarm that Catiline would succeed constitutionally in being chosen consul, and they strained every sinew to prevent so terrible a catastrophe. When the Comitia came on, Cicero admits that he occupied the voting place in the Campus Martius with a guard of men who could be depended on. He was violating the law, which forbade the presence of an armed force on those occasions. He excused himself by pretending that Catiline's party intended violence, and he appeared ostentatiously in a breastplate as if his own life was aimed at. The result was that Catiline failed once more, and was rejected by a small majority. Cicero attributes his defeat to the moral effect produced by the breastplate. But from the time of the Gracchi downwards the aristocracy had not hesitated to lay pressure on the elections when they could safely do it; and the story must be taken with reservation, in the absence of a more impartial account than we possess of the purpose to which Cicero's guard was applied. Undoubtedly it was desirable to strain the usual rules to keep a wretch like Catiline from the consulship; but as certainly, both before the election and after it, Catiline had the sympathies of a very large part of the resident inhabitants of the city, and these sympathies must be taken into account if we are to understand the long train of incidents of which this occasion was the beginning.

Two strict aristocrats, Decimus Silanus and Lucius Murena,[12] were declared elected. Pompey was on his way home, but had not yet reached Italy. There were no regular troops in the whole peninsula, and the nearest approach to an army was the body of Syllans, whom Manlius had quietly collected at Fiesole. Cicero's colleague Antonius was secretly in communication with Catiline, evidently thinking it likely that he would succeed. Catiline determined to wait no longer, and to raise an insurrection in the capital, with slave emancipation and a cancelling of debt for a cry. Manlius was to march on Rome, and the Senate, it was expected, would fall without a blow. Caesar and Crassus sent a warning to Cicero to be on his guard. Caesar had called Catiline to account for his doings at the time of the proscription, and knew his nature too well to expect benefit to the people from a revolution conducted under the auspices of bankrupt patrician adventurers. No citizen had more to lose than Crassus from a crusade of the poor against the rich. But they had both been suspected two years before, and in the excited temper of men's minds they took precautions for their own reputation's sake, as well as for the safety of the State. Quintus Curius, a senator, who was one of the conspirators, was meanwhile betraying his accomplices, and gave daily notice to the consuls of each step which was contemplated. But so weak was authority and so dangerous the temper of the people that the difficulty was to know what to do. Secret information was scarcely needed. Catiline, as Cicero said, was "apertissimus," most frank in the declaration of his intentions. Manlius's army at Fiesole was an open fact, and any day might bring news that he was on the march to Rome. The Senate, as usual in extreme emergencies, declared the State in danger, and gave the consuls unlimited powers to provide for public security. So scornfully confident was Catiline that he offered to place himself under surveillance at the house of any senator whom Cicero might name, or to reside with Cicero himself, if the consul preferred to keep a personal eye upon him. Cicero answered that he dared not trust himself with so perilous a guest.

[Sidenote: November, B.C. 63.] So for a few days matters hung in suspense, Manlius expecting an order to advance, Catiline waiting apparently for a spontaneous insurrection in the city before he gave the word. Intended attempts at various points had been baffled by Cicero's precautions. At last, finding that the people remained quiet, Catiline called a meeting of his friends one stormy night at the beginning of November, and it was agreed that two of the party should go the next morning at dawn to Cicero's house, demand to see him on important business, and kill him in his bed. Curius, who was present, immediately furnished Cicero with an account of what had passed. When his morning visitors arrived they were told that they could not be admitted; and a summons was sent round to the senators to assemble immediately at the Temple of Jupiter Stator, one of the strongest positions in the city.[13] The audacious Catiline attended, and took his usual seat; every one shrank from him, and he was left alone on the bench. Then Cicero rose. In the Senate, where to speak was the first duty of man, he was in his proper element, and had abundant courage. He addressed himself personally to the principal conspirator. He exposed, if exposure be the fitting word when half the persons present knew as much as he could tell them, the history of Catiline's proceedings. He described in detail the meeting of the past evening, looking round perhaps in the faces of the senators who he was aware had been present at it. He spoke of the visit designed to himself in the morning, which had been baffled by his precautions. He went back over the history of the preceding half-century. Fresh from the defence of Rabirius, he showed how dangerous citizens, the Gracchi, Saturninus, Glaucia, had been satisfactorily killed when they were meditating mischief. He did not see that a constitution was already doomed when the ruling powers were driven to assassinate their opponents, because a trial with the forms of law would have ended in their acquittal. He told Catiline that under the powers which the Senate had conferred on him he might order his instant execution. He detailed Catiline's past enormities, which he had forgotten when he sought his friendship, and he ended in bidding him leave the city, go and join Manlius and his army.

Never had Cicero been greater, and never did oratory end in a more absurd conclusion. He dared not arrest Catiline. He confessed that he dared not. There was not a doubt that Catiline was meditating a revolution--but a revolution was precisely what half the world was wishing for. Rightly read, those sounding paragraphs, those moral denunciations, those appeals to history and patriotic sentiment, were the funeral knell of the Roman Commonwealth.

Let Catiline go into open war, Cicero said, and then there would no longer be a doubt. Then all the world would admit his treason. Catiline went; and what was to follow next? Antonius, the second consul, was notoriously not to be relied on. The other conspirators, senators who sat listening while Cicero poured out his eloquent indignation, remained still in the city with the threads of insurrection in their hands, and were encouraged to persevere by the evident helplessness of the government. The imperfect record of history retains for us only the actions of a few individuals whom special talent or special circumstances distinguished, and such information is only fragmentary. We lose sight of the unnamed seething multitudes by whose desires and by whose hatreds the stream of events was truly guided. The party of revolution was as various as it was wide. Powerful wealthy men belonged to it, who were politically dissatisfied; ambitious men of rank, whose money embarrassments weighted them in the race against their competitors; old officers and soldiers of Sylla, who had spent the fortunes which they had won by violence, and were now trying to bring him back from the dead to renew their lease of plunder; ruined wretches without number, broken down with fines and proscriptions, and debts and the accumulation of usurious interest. Add to these "the dangerous classes," the natural enemies of all governments--parricides, adulterers, thieves, forgers, escaped slaves, brigands, and pirates who had lost their occupation; and, finally, Catiline's own chosen comrades, the smooth-faced patrician youths with curled hair and redolent with perfumes, as yet beardless or with the first down upon their chins, wearing scarves and veils and sleeved tunics reaching to their ankles, industrious but only with the dice-box, night-watchers but in the supper- rooms, in the small hours before dawn, immodest, dissolute boys, whose education had been in learning to love and to be loved, to sing and to dance naked at the midnight orgies, and along with it to handle poniards and mix poisoned bowls.[14]

[Sidenote: November, B.C. 64.] Well might Cicero be alarmed at such a combination; well might he say that if a generation of such youths lived to manhood there would be a commonwealth of Catilines. But what was to be thought of the prospects of a society in which such phenomena were developing themselves? Cicero bade them all go--follow their chief into the war, and perish in the snow of the Apennines. But how if they would not go? How if from the soil of Rome, under the rule of his friends the Senate, fresh crops of such youths would rise perennially? The Commonwealth needed more drastic medicine than eloquent exhortations, however true the picture might be.

[Sidenote: November, B.C. 63.] None of the promising young gentlemen took Cicero's advice. Catiline went alone and joined Manlius, and had he come on at once he might perhaps have taken Rome. The army was to support an insurrection, and the insurrection was to support the army. Catiline waited for a signal from his friends in the city, and Lentulus, Cethegus, Autronius, and the rest of the leaders waited for Catiline to arrive. Conspirators never think that they have taken precautions enough or have gained allies enough; and in endeavoring to secure fresh support they made a fatal mistake. An embassy of Allobroges was in the city, a frontier tribe on the borders of the Roman province in Gaul, who were allies of Rome, though not as yet subjects. The Gauls were the one foreign nation whom the Romans really feared. The passes of the Alps alone protected Italy from the hordes of German or Gallic barbarians, whose numbers being unknown were supposed to be exhaustless. Middle-aged men could still remember the panic at the invasion of the Cimbri and Teutons, and it was the chief pride of the democrats that the State had then been saved by their own Marius. At the critical moment it was discovered that the conspirators had entered into a correspondence with these Allobroges, and had actually proposed to them to make a fresh inroad over the Alps. The suspicion of such an intention at once alienated from Catiline the respectable part of the democratic party. The fact of the communication was betrayed to Cicero. He intercepted the letters; he produced them in the Senate with the seals unbroken, that no suspicion might rest upon himself. Lentulus and Cethegus were sent for, and could not deny their hands. The letters were then opened and read, and no shadow of uncertainty any longer remained that they had really designed to bring in an army of Gauls. Such of the conspirators as were known and were still within reach were instantly seized.

[Sidenote: December 5, B.C. 63.] Cicero, with a pardonable laudation of himself and of the Divine Providence of which he professed to regard himself as the minister, congratulated his country on its escape from so genuine a danger; and he then invited the Senate to say what was to be done with these apostates from their order, whose treason was now demonstrated. A plot for a mere change of government, for the deposition of the aristocrats and the return to power of the popular party, it might be impolitic, perhaps impossible, severely to punish; but Catiline and his friends had planned the betrayal of the State to the barbarians; and with persons who had committed themselves to national treason there was no occasion to hesitate. Cicero produced the list of those whom he considered guilty, and there were some among his friends who thought the opportunity might be used to get rid of dangerous enemies, after the fashion of Sylla, especially of Crassus and Caesar. The name of Crassus was first mentioned, some said by secret friends of Catiline, who hoped to alarm the Senate into inaction by showing with whom they would have to deal. Crassus, it is possible, knew more than he had told the consul. Catiline's success had, at one moment, seemed assured; and great capitalists are apt to insure against contingencies. But Cicero moved and carried a resolution that the charge against him was a wicked invention. The attempt against Caesar was more determined. Old Catulus, whom Caesar had defeated in the contest for the pontificate, and Caius Calpurnius Piso,[15] a bitter aristocrat, whom Caesar had prosecuted for misgovernment in Gaul, urged Cicero to include his name. But Cicero was too honorable to lend himself to an accusation which he knew to be false. Some of the young lords in their disappointment threatened Caesar at the senate-house door with their swords; but the attack missed its mark, and served only to show how dreaded Caesar already was, and how eager a desire there was to make an end of him.

The list submitted for judgment contained the names of none but those who were indisputably guilty. The Senate voted at once that they were traitors to the State. The next question was of the nature of their punishment. In the first place the persons of public officers were sacred, and Lentulus was at the time a praetor. And next the Sempronian law forbade distinctly that any Roman citizen should be put to death without a trial, and without the right of appeal to the assembly.[16] It did not mean simply that Roman citizens were not to be murdered, or that at any time it had been supposed that they might. The object was to restrain the extraordinary power claimed by the Senate of setting the laws aside on exceptional occasions. Silanus, the consul-elect for the following year, was, according to usage, asked to give his opinion first. He voted for immediate death. One after the other the voices were the same, till the turn came of Tiberius Nero, the great-grandfather of Nero the Emperor. Tiberius was against haste. He advised that the prisoners should be kept in confinement till Catiline was taken or killed, and that the whole affair should then be carefully investigated. Investigation was perhaps what many senators were most anxious to avoid. When Tiberius had done, Caesar rose. The speech which Sallust places in his mouth was not an imaginary sketch of what Sallust supposed him likely to have said, but the version generally received of what he actually did say, and the most important passages of it are certainly authentic. For the first time we see through the surface of Caesar's outward actions into his real mind. During the three quarters of a century which had passed since the death of the elder Gracchus one political murder had followed upon another. Every conspicuous democrat had been killed by the aristocrats in some convenient disturbance. No constitution could survive when the law was habitually set aside by violence; and disdaining the suspicion with which he knew that his words would be regarded, Caesar warned the Senate against another act of precipitate anger which would be unlawful in itself, unworthy of their dignity, and likely in the future to throw a doubt upon the guilt of the men upon whose fate they were deliberating. He did not extenuate, he rather emphasized, the criminality of Catiline and his confederates; but for that reason and because for the present no reasonable person felt the slightest uncertainty about it, he advised them to keep within the lines which the law had marked out for them. He spoke with respect of Silanus. He did not suppose him to be influenced by feelings of party animosity. Silanus had recommended the execution of the prisoners, either because he thought their lives incompatible with the safety of the State, or because no milder punishment seemed adequate to the enormity of their conduct. But the safety of the State, he said, with a compliment to Ciceror, had been sufficiently provided for by the diligence of the consul. As to punishment, none could be too severe; but with that remarkable adherence to fact, which always distinguished Caesar, that repudiation of illusion and sincere utterance of his real belief, whatever that might be, he contended that death was not a punishment at all. Death was the end of human suffering. In the grave there was neither joy nor sorrow. When a man was dead he ceased to be.[17] He became as he had been before he was born. Probably almost every one in the Senate thought like Caesar on this subject. Cicero certainly did. The only difference was that plausible statesmen affected a respect for the popular superstition, and pretended to believe what they did not believe. Caesar spoke his convictions out. There was no longer any solemnity in an execution. It was merely the removal out of the way of troublesome persons; and convenient as such a method might be, it was of graver consequence that the Senate of Rome, the guardians of the law, should not set an example of violating the law. Illegality, Caesar told them, would be followed by greater illegalities. He reminded them how they had applauded Sylla, how they had rejoiced when they saw their political enemies summarily despatched; and yet the proscription, as they well knew, had been perverted to the license of avarice and private revenge. They might feel sure that no such consequence need be feared under their present consul: but times might change. The worst crimes which had been committed in Rome in the past century had risen out of the imitation of precedents, which at the moment seemed defensible. The laws had prescribed a definite punishment for treason. Those laws had been gravely considered; they had been enacted by the great men who had built up the Roman dominion, and were not to be set aside in impatient haste. Caesar therefore recommended that the estates of the conspirators should be confiscated, that they themselves should be kept in strict and solitary confinement dispersed in various places, and that a resolution should be passed forbidding an application for their pardon either to Senate or people.

The speech was weighty in substance and weightily delivered, and it produced its effect.[18] Silanus withdrew his opinion. Quintus Cicero, the consul's brother, followed, and a clear majority of the Senate went with them, till it came to the turn of a young man who in that year had taken his place in the house for the first time, who was destined to make a reputation which could be set in competition with that of the gods themselves, and whose moral opinion could be held superior to that of the gods.[19]

Marcus Porcius Cato was born in the year 95, and was thus five years younger than Caesar and eleven years younger than Cicero. He was the great-grandson, as was said above, of the stern rugged censor who hated Greek, preferred the teaching of the plough-tail and the Twelve Tables to the philosophy of Aristotle, disbelieved in progress, and held by the maxims of his father--the last, he of the Romans of the old type. The young Marcus affected to take his ancestor for a pattern. He resembled him as nearly as a modern Anglican monk resembles St. Francis or St. Bernard. He could reproduce the form, but it was the form with the life gone out of it. He was immeasurably superior to the men around him. He was virtuous, if it be virtue to abstain from sin. He never lied. No one ever suspected him of dishonesty or corruption. But his excellences were not of the retiring sort. He carried them written upon him in letters for all to read, as a testimony to a wicked generation. His opinions were as pedantic as his life was abstemious, and no one was permitted to differ from him without being held guilty rather of a crime than of a mistake. He was an aristocratic pedant, to whom the living forces of humanity seemed but irrational impulses of which he and such as he were the appointed school-masters. To such a temperament a man of genius is instinctively hateful. Cato had spoken often in the Senate, though so young a member of it, denouncing the immoral habits of the age. He now rose to match himself against Caesar; and with passionate vehemence he insisted that the wretches who had plotted the overthrow of the State should be immediately killed. He noticed Caesar's objections only to irritate the suspicion in which he probably shared, that Caesar himself was one of Catiline's accomplices. That Caesar had urged as a reason for moderation the absence of immediate danger, was in Cato's opinion an argument the more for anxiety. Naturally, too, he did not miss the opportunity of striking at the scepticism which questioned future retribution. Whether Cato believed himself in a future life mattered little, if Caesar's frank avowal could be turned to his prejudice.

Cato spoke to an audience well disposed to go with him. Silanus went round to his first view, and the mass of senators followed him. Caesar attempted to reply; but so fierce were the passions that had been roused, that again he was in danger of violence. The young knights who were present as a senatorial guard rushed at him with their drawn swords. A few friends protected him with their cloaks, and he left the Curia not to enter it again for the rest of the year. When Caesar was gone, Cicero rose to finish the debate.

He too glanced at Caesar's infidelity, and as Caesar had spoken of the wisdom of past generations, he observed that in the same generations there had been a pious belief that the grave was not the end of human existence. With an ironical compliment to the prudence of Caesar's advice, he said that his own interest would lead him to follow it; he would have the less to fear from the irritation of the people. The Senate, he observed, must have heard with pleasure that Caesar condemned the conspiracy. Caesar was the leader of the popular party, and from him at least they now knew that they had nothing to fear. The punishment which Caesar recommended was, in fact, Cicero admitted, more severe than death. He trusted, therefore, that if the conspirators were executed, and he had to answer to the people for the sentence to be passed upon them, Caesar himself would defend him against the charge of cruelty. Meanwhile he said that he had the ineffable satisfaction of knowing that he had saved the State. The Senate might adopt such resolutions as might seem good to them without alarm for the consequences. The conspiracy was disarmed. He had made enemies among the bad citizens; but he had deserved and he had won the gratitude of the good, and he stood secure behind the impregnable bulwark of his country's love.

So Cicero, in the first effusion of self-admiration with which he never ceased to regard his conduct on this occasion. No doubt he had acted bravely, and he had shown as much adroitness as courage. But the whole truth was never told. The Senate's anxiety to execute the prisoners arose from a fear that the people would be against them if an appeal to the assembly was allowed. The Senate was contending for the privilege of suspending the laws by its own independent will; and the privilege, if it was ever constitutional, had become so odious by the abuse of it, that to a large section of Roman citizens a conspiracy against the oligarchy had ceased to be looked on as treason at all. Cicero and Cato had their way. Lentulus, Cethegus, Autronius and their companions were strangled in their cells, on the afternoon of the debate upon their fate. A few weeks later Catiline's army was cut to pieces, and he himself was killed. So desperately his haggard bands had fought that they fell in their ranks where they stood, and never Roman commander gained a victory that cost him more dear. So furious a resistance implied a motive and a purpose beyond any which Cicero or Sallust records, and the commission of inquiry suggested by Tiberius Nero in the Senate might have led to curious revelations. The Senate perhaps had its own reasons for fearing such revelations, and for wishing the voices closed which could have made them.

[1] "Nunc quis patrem decem annorum natus non modo aufert sed tollit nisi veneno?"--Varronis Fragmenta, ed. Alexander Riese, p. 216.

[2] See the story in Cicero, Pro Cluentio.

[3] _Pro P. Sull, 4.

[4] "Catilina, si judicatum erit, meridie non lucere, certus erit competitor."--_Epist. ad Atticum_, i. 1.

[5] "Hoc tempore Catilinam, competitorem nostrum, defendere cogitamus. Judices habemus, quos volumus, summa accusatoris voluntate. Spero, si absolutus erit, conjunctiorem illum nobis fore in ratione petitionis."--Ib., i. 2.

[6] "Scito nihil tam exercitum nunc esse Romae quam candidatos omnibus iniquitatibus."--Ib., i. 11.

[7] I use a word apparently modern, but Cicero himself gave the name of Conservatores Reipublicae to the party to which he belonged.

[8] Suetonius, speaking of Augustus, says: "Quoties adesset, nihil praeterea agebat, seu vitandi rumoris caus? quo patrem Caesarem vulgo reprehensum commemorabat, quod inter spectandum epistolis libellisque legendis aut rescribendis vacaret; seu studio spectandi et voluptate," etc.--Vita Octavii, 45.

[9] Writing three years later to Atticus, he says: "Confirmabam omnium privatorum possessiones, is enim est noster exercitus, ut tute scis locupletium."--To Atticus, i. 19. Pomponius Atticus, Cicero's most intimate correspondent, was a Roman knight, who inheriting a large estate from his father, increased it by contracts, banking, money-lending, and slave-dealing, in which he was deeply engaged. He was an accomplished, cultivated man, a shrewd observer of the times, and careful of committing himself on any side. His acquaintance with Cicero rested on similarity of temperament, with a solid financial basis at the bottom of it. They were mutually useful to each other.

[10] "Et nimium istud est, quod ab hoc tribuno plebis dictum est in senatu: urbanam plebem nimium in republic?posse: exhauriendam esse: hoc enim verbo est usus; quasi de aliqu?sentin? ac non de optimorum civium genere loqueretur."--Contra Rullum, ii. 26.

[11] Cicero, _Pro Muren, 25.

[12] Murena was afterward prosecuted for bribery at this election. Cicero defended him; but even Cato, aristocrat as he was, affected to be shocked at the virtuous consul's undertaking so bad a case. It is observable that in his speech for Murena, Cicero found as many virtues in Lucullus as in his speech on the Manilian law he had found vices. It was another symptom of his change of attitude.

[13] "In loco munitissimo."

[14] This description of the young Roman aristocracy is given by Cicero in his most powerful vein: "Postremum autem genus est, non solum numero, verum etiam genere ipso atque vita, quod proprium est Catilinae, de ejus delectu, immo vero de complexu ejus ac sinu: quos pexo capillo, nitidos, aut imberbes, aut bene barbatos, videtis, manicatis et talaribus tunicis; velis amictos, non togis: quorum omnis industria vitae et vigilandi labor in antelucanis coenis expromitur. In his gregibus omnes aleatores, omnes adulteri, omnes impuri impudicique versantur. Hi pueri tam lepidi ac delicati non solum amare et amari neque cantare et saltare, sed etiam sicas vibrare et spargere venena didicerunt.... Nudi in conviviis saltare didicerunt."--In Catilinam, ii. 10. Compare In Pisonem, 10.

The Romans shaved their beards at full maturity, and therefore "benebarbatos" does not mean grown men, but youths on the edge of manhood.

[15] Not to be confounded with Lucius Calpurnius Piso, who was Caesar's father-in-law.

[16] "Injussu populi."

[17] The real opinion of educated Romans on this subject was expressed in

the well-known lines of Lucretius, which were probably written near this very time:

"Nil igitur mors est, ad nos neque pertinet hilum, Quandoquidem natura animi mortalis habetur: Et, velut ante acto nil tempore sensimus aegri, Ad confligendum venientibus undique Poenis; Omnia cum belli trepido concussa tumultu, Horrida, contremuere sub altis aetheris auris; In dubioque fuit sub utrorum regna cadendum Omnibus humanis esset, terrâque ue, marique: Sic, ubi non erimus, cum corporis atque animai Discidium fuerit, quibus e sumus uniter apti, Scilicet haud nobis quicquam, qui non erimus tum, Accidere omnino poterit, sensumque movere: Non, si terra mari miscebitur, et mare coelo."

LUCRETIUS, lib. iii. 11. 842-854.

[18] In the following century when Caesar's life had become mythic, a story was current that when Caesar was speaking on this occasion a note was brought in to him, and Cato, suspecting that it referred to the conspiracy, insisted that it should be read. Caesar handed it to Cato, and it proved to be a love letter from Cato's sister, Servilia, the mother of Brutus. More will be said of the supposed liaison between Caesar and Servilia hereafter. For the present it is enough to say that there is no contemporary evidence for the story at all; and that if it be true that a note of some kind from Servilia was given to Caesar, it is more consistent with probability and the other circumstances of the case, that it was an innocent note of business. Ladies do not send in compromising letters to their lovers when they are on their feet in Parliament; nor, if such an accident should happen, do the lovers pass them over to be read by the ladies' brothers.

[19] "Victrix causa Deis placuit, sed victa Catoni."--LUCAN.

CHAPTER XII.

[Sidenote: B.C. 62.] The execution of Lentulus and Cethegus was received in Rome with the feeling which Caesar had anticipated. There was no active sympathy with the conspiracy, but the conspiracy was forgotten in indignation at the lawless action of the consul and the Senate. It was still violence--always violence. Was law, men asked, never to resume its authority?-

-was the Senate to deal at its pleasure with the lives and properties of citizens?--criminals though they might be, what right had Cicero to strangle citizens in dungeons without trial? If this was to be allowed, the constitution was at an end; Rome was no longer a republic, but an arbitrary oligarchy. Pompey's name was on every tongue. When would Pompey come? Pompey, the friend of the people, the terror of the aristocracy! Pompey, who had cleared the sea of pirates, and doubled the area of the Roman dominions! Let Pompey return and bring his army with him, and give to Rome the same peace and order which he had already given to the world.

A Roman commander, on landing in Italy after foreign service, was expected to disband his legions, and relapse into the position of a private person. A popular and successful general was an object of instinctive fear to the politicians who held the reins of government. The Senate was never pleased to see any individual too much an object of popular idolatry; and in the case of Pompey their suspicion was the greater on account of the greatness of his achievements, and because his command had been forced upon them by the people, against their will. In the absence of a garrison, the city was at the mercy of the patricians and their clients. That the noble lords were unscrupulous in removing persons whom they disliked they had shown in a hundred instances, and Pompey naturally enough hesitated to trust himself among them without security. He required the protection of office, and he had sent forward one of his most distinguished officers, Metellus Nepos, to prepare the way and demand the consulship for him. Metellus, to strengthen his hands, had stood for the tribuneship; and, in spite of the utmost efforts of the aristocracy, had been elected. It fell to Metellus to be the first to give expression to the general indignation in a way peculiarly wounding to the illustrious consul. Cicero imagined that the world looked upon him as its saviour. In his own eyes he was another Romulus, a second founder of Rome. The world, unfortunately, had formed an entirely different estimate of him. The prisoners had been killed on the 5th of December. On the last day of the year it was usual for the outgoing consuls to review the events of their term of office before the Senate; and Cicero had prepared a speech in which he had gilded his own performances with all his eloquence. Metellus commenced his tribunate with forbidding Cicero to deliver his oration, and forbidding him on the special ground that a man who had put Roman citizens to death without allowing them a hearing did not himself deserve to be heard. In the midst of the confusion and uproar which followed, Cicero could only shriek that he had saved his country: a declaration which could have been dispensed with, since he had so often insisted upon it already without producing the assent which he desired.

Notwithstanding his many fine qualities, Cicero was wanting in dignity. His vanity was wounded in its tenderest point, and he attacked Metellus a day or two after, in one of those violently abusive outpourings of which so many specimens of his own survive, and which happily so few other statesmen attempted to imitate. Metellus retorted with a threat of impeaching Cicero, and the grave Roman Curia became no better than a kennel of mad dogs. For days the storm raged on with no symptom of abatement. At last Metellus turned to the people and proposed in the assembly that Pompey should be recalled with his army to restore law and order.

Caesar, who was now praetor, warmly supported Metellus. To him, if to no one else, it was clear as the sun at noonday, that unless some better government could be provided than could be furnished by five hundred such gentlemen as the Roman senators, the State was drifting on to destruction. Resolutions to be submitted to the people were generally first drawn in writing, and were read from the Rostra. When Metellus produced his proposal, Cato, who was a tribune also, sprang to his side, ordered him to be silent, and snatched the scroll out of his hands. Metellus went on, speaking from memory Cato's friends shut his mouth by force. The patricians present drew their swords and cleared the Forum; and the Senate, in the exercise of another right to which they pretended, declared Caesar and Metellus degraded from their offices. Metullus, probably at Caesar's advice, withdrew and went off to Asia, to describe what had passed to Pompey. Caesar remained, and, quietly disregarding the Senate's sentence, continued to sit and hear cases as praetor. His court was forcibly closed. He yielded to violence and retired under protest, being escorted to the door of his house by an enormous multitude. There he dismissed his lictors and laid aside his official dress, that he might furnish no excuse for a charge against him of resisting the established authorities. The mob refused to be comforted. They gathered day after day. They clustered about the pontifical palace. They cried to Caesar to place himself at their head, that they might tear down the senate-house, and turn the caitiffs into the street. Caesar neither then nor ever lent himself to popular excesses. He reminded the citizens that if others broke the law, they must themselves set an example of obeying it, and he bade them return to their homes.

Terrified at the state of the city, and penitent for their injustice to Caesar, the Senate hurriedly revoked their decree of deposition, sent a deputation to him to apologize, and invited him to resume his place among them. The extreme patrician section remained irreconcilable. Caesar complied, but only to find himself denounced again with passionate pertinacity as having been an accomplice of Catiline. Witnesses were produced, who swore to having seen his signature to a treasonable bond. Curius, Cicero's spy, declared that Catiline himself had told him that Caesar was one of the conspirators. Caesar treated the charge with indignant disdain. He appealed to Cicero's conscience, and Cicero was obliged to say that he had derived his earliest and most important information from Caesar himself. The most violent of his accusers were placed under arrest. The informers, after a near escape from being massacred by the crowd, were thrown into prison, and for the moment the furious heats were able to cool.

All eyes were now turned to Pompey. The war in Asia was over. Pompey, it was clear, must now return to receive the thanks of his countrymen; and as he had triumphed in spite of the aristocracy, and as his victories could neither be denied nor undone, the best hope of the Senate was to win him over from the people, and to prevent a union between him and Caesar. Through all the recent dissensions Caesar had thrown his weight on Pompey's side. He, with Cicero, had urged Pompey's appointment to his successive commands. When Cicero went over to the patricians, Caesar had stood by Pompey's officers against the fury of the Senate. Caesar had the people behind him, and Pompey the army. Unless in some way an apple of discord could be thrown between them, the two favorites would overshadow the State, and the Senate's authority would be gone. Nothing could be done for the moment politically. Pompey owed his position to the democracy, and he was too great as yet to fear Caesar as a rival in the Commonwealth. On the personal side there was better hope. Caesar was as much admired in the world of fashion as he was detested in the Curia. He had no taste for the brutal entertainments and more brutal vices of male patrician society. He preferred the companionship of cultivated women, and the noble lords had the fresh provocation of finding their hated antagonist an object of adoration to their wives and daughters. Here, at any rate, scandal had the field to itself. Caesar was accused of criminal intimacy with many ladies of the highest rank, and

Pompey was privately informed that his friend had taken advantage of his absence to seduce his wife, Mucia. Pompey was Agamemnon; Caesar had been Aegisthus; and Pompey was so far persuaded that Mucia had been unfaithful to him, that he divorced her before his return.

Charges of this kind have the peculiar advantage that even when disproved or shown to be manifestly absurd, they leave a stain behind them. Careless equally of probability and decency, the leaders of the Senate sacrificed without scruple the reputation of their own relatives if only they could make Caesar odious. The name of Servilia has been mentioned already. Servilia was the sister of Marcus Cato and the mother of Marcus Brutus. She was a woman of remarkable ability and character, and between her and Caesar there was undoubtedly a close acquaintance and a strong mutual affection. The world discovered that she was Caesar's mistress, and that Brutus was his son. It might be enough to say that when Brutus was born Caesar was scarcely fifteen years old, and that, if a later intimacy existed between them, Brutus knew nothing of it or cared nothing for it. When he stabbed Caesar at last it was not as a Hamlet or an Orestes, but as a patriot sacrificing his dearest friend to his country. The same doubt extends to the other supposed victims of Caesar's seductiveness. Names were mentioned in the following century, but no particulars were given. For the most part his alleged mistresses were the wives of men who remained closely attached to him notwithstanding. The report of his intrigue with Mucia answered its immediate purpose, in producing a temporary coldness on Pompey's part toward Caesar; but Pompey must either have discovered the story to be false or else have condoned it, for soon afterward he married Caesar's daughter. Two points may be remarked about these legends: first, that on no single occasion does Caesar appear to have been involved in any trouble or quarrel on account of his love affairs; and secondly, that, with the exception of Brutus and of Cleopatra's Caesarion, whose claims to be Caesar's son were denied and disproved, there is no record of any illegitimate children as the result of these amours--a strange thing if Caesar was as liberal of his favors as popular scandal pretended. It would be idle to affect a belief that Caesar was particularly virtuous. He was a man of the world, living in an age as corrupt as has been ever known. It would be equally idle to assume that all the ink blots thrown upon him were certainly deserved, because we find them in books which we call classical. Proof deserving to be called proof there is none; and the only real evidence is the town talk of a society which feared and hated

Caesar, and was glad of every pretext to injure him when alive, or to discredit him after his death. Similar stories have been spread, are spread, and will be spread of every man who raises himself a few inches above the level of his fellows. We know how it is with our contemporaries. A single seed of fact will produce in a season or two a harvest of calumnies, and sensible men pass such things by, and pay no attention to them. With history we are less careful or less charitable. An accusation of immorality is accepted without examination when brought against eminent persons who can no longer defend themselves, and to raise a doubt of its truth passes as a sign of a weak understanding. So let it be. It is certain that Caesar's contemporaries spread rumors of a variety of intrigues, in which they said that he was concerned. It is probable that some were well founded. It is possible that all were well founded. But it is no less indubitable that they rest on evidence which is not evidence at all, and that the most innocent intimacies would not have escaped misrepresentation from the venomous tongues of Roman society. Caesar comes into court with a fairer character than those whose virtues are thought to overshadow him. Marriage, which under the ancient Romans was the most sacred of ties, had become the lightest and the loosest. Cicero divorced Tereutia when she was old and ill-tempered, and married a young woman. Cato made over his Marcia, the mother of his children, to his friend Hortensius, and took her back as a wealthy widow when Hortensius died. Pompey put away his first wife at Sylla's bidding, and took a second who was already the wife of another man. Caesar, when little more than a boy, dared the Dictator's displeasure rather than condescend to a similar compliance. His worst enemies admitted that from the gluttony, the drunkenness, and the viler forms of sensuality, which were then so common, he was totally free. For the rest, it is certain that no friend ever permanently quarrelled with him on any question of domestic injury; and either there was a general indifference on such subjects, which lightens the character of the sin, or popular scandals in old Rome were of no sounder material than we find them composed of in other countries and in other times.

Turning from scandal to reality, we come now to a curious incident, which occasioned a fresh political convulsion, where Caesar appears, not as an actor in an affair of gallantry, but as a sufferer.

Pompey was still absent. Caesar had resumed his duties as praetor, and was living in the official house of the Pontifex Maximus, with his mother Aurelia and his wife Pompeia. The age was fertile of new religions. The worship of the Bona Dea, a foreign goddess of unknown origin, had recently been introduced into Rome, and an annual festival was held in her honor in the house of one or other of the principal magistrates. The Vestal virgins officiated at the ceremonies, and women only were permitted to be present. This year the pontifical palace was selected for the occasion, and Caesar's wife Pompeia was to preside.

The reader may remember a certain youth named Clodius, who had been with Lucullus in Asia, and had been a chief instigator of the mutiny in his army. He was Lucullus's brother-in-law, a member of the Claudian family, a patrician of the patricians, and connected by blood and marriage with the proudest members of the Senate. If Cicero is to be believed, he had graduated even while a boy in every form of vice, natural and unnatural. He was bold, clever, unprincipled, and unscrupulous, with a slender diminutive figure and a delicate woman's face. His name was Clodius Pulcher. Cicero played upon it and called him Pulchellus Puer, "the pretty boy." Between this promising young man and Caesar's wife Pompeia there had sprung up an acquaintance, which Clodius was anxious to press to further extremes. Pompeia was difficult of access, her mother-in-law Aurelia keeping a strict watch over her; and Clodius, who was afraid of nothing, took advantage of the Bona Dea festival to make his way into Caesar's house dressed as a woman. Unfortunately for him, his disguise was detected. The insulted Vestals and the other ladies who were present flew upon him like the dogs of Actaeon, tore his borrowed garments from him, and drove him into the street naked and wounded. The adventure became known. It was mentioned in the Senate, and the College of Priests was ordered to hold an inquiry. The college found that Clodius had committed sacrilege, and the regular course in such cases was to send the offender to trial. There was general unwillingness, however, to treat this matter seriously. Clodius had many friends in the house, and even Cicero, who was inclined at first to be severe, took on reflection a more lenient view. Clodius had a sister, a light lady who, weary of her conquests over her fashionable admirers, had tried her fascinations on the great orator. He had escaped complete subjugation, but he had been flattered by the attention of the seductive beauty, and was ready to help her brother out of his difficulty. Clodius was not yet the dangerous desperado which he afterward became; and immorality, though seasoned with impiety, might easily, it was thought, be made too much of. Caesar himself did not press for punishment. As president of the college, he had acquiesced in their decision, and he divorced the unfortunate Pompeia; but he expressed no opinion as to the extent of her criminality, and he gave as his reason for separating from her, not that she was guilty, but that Caesar's wife must be above suspicion.

Cato, however, insisted on a prosecution. Messala, one of the consuls, was equally peremptory. The hesitation was regarded by the stricter senators as a scandal to the order; and in spite of the efforts of the second consul Piso, who was a friend of Clodius, it was decided that a bill for his indictment should be submitted to the assembly in the Forum. Clodius, it seems, was generally popular. No political question was raised by the proceedings against him; for the present his offence was merely a personal one; the wreck of Catiline's companions, the dissolute young aristocrats, the loose members of all ranks and classes, took up the cause, and gathered to support their favorite, with young Curio, whom Cicero called in mockery Filiola, at their head. The approaches to the Forum were occupied by them. Piso, by whom the bill was introduced, himself advised the people to reject it. Cato flew to the Rostra and railed at the consul. Hortensius, the orator, and many others spoke on the same side. It appeared at last that the people were divided, and would consent to the bill being passed, if it was recommended to them by both the consuls. Again, therefore, the matter was referred to the Senate. One of the tribunes introduced Clodius, that he might speak for himself. Cicero had now altered his mind, and was in favor of the prosecution.

[Sidenote: February, B.C. 61.] The "pretty youth" was alternately humble and violent, begging pardon, and then bursting into abuse of his brother-in-law, Lucullus, and more particularly of Cicero, whom he suspected of being the chief promoter of the proceedings against him. When it came to a division, the Senate voted by a majority of four hundred to fifteen that the consuls must recommend the bill. Piso gave way, and the tribune also who had been in Clodius's favor. The people were satisfied, and a court of fifty-six judges was appointed, before whom the trial was to take place. It seemed that a conviction must necessarily follow, for there was no question about the facts, which were all admitted. There was some manoeuvring, however, in the constitution of the court, which raised Cicero's suspicions. The judges, instead of being selected by the praetor, were chosen by lot, and the prisoner was allowed to challenge as many names as he pleased. The result was that in

Cicero's opinion a more scandalous set of persons than those who were finally sworn were never collected round a gaming table-- "disgraced senators, bankrupt knights, disreputable tribunes of the treasury, the few honest men that were left appearing to be ashamed of their company"--and Cicero considered that it would have been better if Hortensius, who was prosecuting, had withdrawn, and had left Clodius to be condemned by the general sense of respectable people, rather than risk the credit of Roman justice before so scandalous a tribunal.[1] Still the case as it proceeded appeared so clear as to leave no hope of an acquittal. Clodius's friends were in despair, and were meditating an appeal to the mob. The judges, on the evening of the first day of the trial, as if they had already decided on a verdict of guilty, applied for a guard to protect them while they delivered it. The Senate complimented them in giving their consent. With a firm expectation present in all men's minds the second morning dawned. Even in Rome, accustomed as it was to mockeries of justice, public opinion was shocked when the confident anticipation was disappointed. According to Cicero, Marcus Crassus, for reasons known to himself, had been interested in Clodius. During the night he sent for the judges one by one. He gave them money. What else he either gave or promised them, must continue veiled in Cicero's Latin.[2] Before these influences the resolution of the judges melted away, and when the time came, thirty-one out of fifty-six high-born Roman peers and gentlemen declared Clodius innocent.

The original cause was nothing. That a profligate young man should escape punishment for a licentious frolic was comparatively of no consequence; but the trial acquired a notoriety of infamy which shook once more the already tottering constitution.

"Why did you ask for a guard?" old Catulus growled to the judges: "was it that the money you have received might not be taken from you?"

"Such is the history of this affair," Cicero wrote to his friend Atticus. "We thought that the foundation of the Commonwealth had been surely re-established in my consulship, all orders of good men being happily united. You gave the praise to me and I to the gods; and now unless some god looks favorably on us, all is lost in this single judgment. Thirty Romans have been found to trample justice under foot for a bribe, and to declare an act not to have been committed, about which not only not a man, but not a beast of the field, can entertain the smallest doubt."

Cato threatened the judges with impeachment; Cicero stormed in the Senate, rebuked the consul Piso, and lectured Clodius in a speech which he himself admired exceedingly. The "pretty boy" in reply taunted Cicero with wishing to make himself a king. Cicero rejoined with asking Clodius about a man named "King," whose estates he had appropriated, and reminded him of a misadventure among the pirates, from which he had come off with nameless ignominy. Neither antagonist very honorably distinguished himself in this encounter of wit. The Senate voted at last for an inquiry into the judges' conduct; but an inquiry only added to Cicero's vexation, for his special triumph had been, as he conceived, the union of the Senate with the equites; and the equites took the resolution as directed against themselves, and refused to be consoled.[3]

Caesar had been absent during these scenes. His term of office having expired, he had been despatched as propraetor to Spain, where the ashes of the Sertorian rebellion were still smouldering; and he had started for his province while the question of Clodius's trial was still pending. Portugal and Gallicia were still unsubdued. Bands of robbers lay everywhere in the fastnesses of the mountain ranges. Caesar was already favorably known in Spain for his service as quaestor. He now completed the conquest of the peninsula. He put down the banditti. He reorganized the administration with the rapid skill which always so remarkably distinguished him. He sent home large sums of money to the treasury. His work was done quickly, but it was done completely. He nowhere left an unsound spot unprobed. He never contented himself with the superficial healing of a wound which would break out again when he was gone. What he began he finished, and left it in need of no further surgery. As his reward, he looked for a triumph, and the consulship, one or both; and the consulship he knew could not well be refused to him, unwelcome as it would be to the Senate.

Pompey meanwhile was at last coming back. All lesser luminaries shone faint before the sun of Pompey, the subduer of the pirates, the conqueror of Asia, the glory of the Roman name. Even Cicero had feared that the fame of the saviour of his country might pale before the lustre of the great Pompey. "I used to be in alarm," he confessed with naive simplicity, "that six hundred years hence the merits of Sampsiceramus[4] might seem to have been more than mine." [5] But how would Pompey appear? Would he come at the head of his army, like Sylla, the armed soldier of the democracy, to avenge the affront upon his officers, to reform the State, to punish the Senate for the murder of the Catiline conspirators? Pompey had no such views, and no capacity for such ambitious operations. The ground had been prepared beforehand. The Mucia story had perhaps done its work, and the Senate and the great commander were willing to meet each other, at least with outward friendliness.

His successes had been brilliant; but they were due rather to his honesty than to his military genius. He had encountered no real resistance, and Cato had sneered at his exploits as victories over women. He had put down the buccaneers, because he had refused to be bribed by them. He had overthrown Mithridates and had annexed Asia Minor and Syria to the Roman dominions. Lucullus could have done it as easily as his successor, if he could have turned his back upon temptations to increase his own fortune or gratify his own passions. The wealth of the East had lain at Pompey's feet, and he had not touched it. He had brought millions into the treasury. He returned, as he had gone out, himself moderately provided for, and had added nothing to his private income. He understood, and practised strictly, the common rules of morality. He detested dishonesty and injustice. But he had no political insight; and if he was ambitious, it was with the innocent vanity which desires, and is content with, admiration. In the time of the Scipios he would have lived in an atmosphere of universal applause, and would have died in honor with an unblemished name. In the age of Clodius and Catiline he was the easy dupe of men of stronger intellect than his own, who played upon his unsuspicious integrity. His delay in coming back had arisen chiefly from anxiety for his personal safety. He was eager to be reconciled to the Senate, yet without deserting the people. While in Asia, he had reassured Cicero that nothing was to be feared from him.[6] His hope was to find friends on all sides and in all parties, and he thought that he had deserved their friendship.

[Sidenote: December, B.C. 62.] Thus when Pompey landed at Brindisi his dreaded legions were disbanded, and he proceeded to the Capitol, with a train of captive princes, as the symbols of his victories, and wagons loaded with treasure as an offering to his country. He was received as he advanced with the shouts of applauding multitudes. He entered Rome in a galaxy of glory. A splendid column commemorated the cities which he had taken, the twelve million human beings whom he had slain or subjected. His triumph was the most magnificent which the Roman citizens had ever witnessed, and by special vote he was permitted to wear his triumphal robe in the Senate as often and as long as might please him. The fireworks over, and with the aureole of glory about his brow, the great Pompey, like another Samson shorn of his locks, dropped into impotence and insignificance. In February, 61, during the debate on the Clodius affair, he made his first speech in the Senate. Cicero, listening with malicious satisfaction, reported that "Pompey gave no pleasure to the wretched; to the bad he seemed without backbone; he was not agreeable to the well-to-do; the wise and good found him wanting in substance;" [7] in short, the speech was a failure. Pompey applied for a second consulship. He was reminded that he had been consul eight years previously, and that the ten years' interval prescribed by Sylla, between the first and the second term, had not expired. He asked for lands for his soldiers, and for the ratification of his acts in Asia. Cato opposed the first request, as likely to lead to another agrarian law. Lucullus, who was jealous of him, raised difficulties about the second, and thwarted him with continual delays.

[Sidenote: February 1, B.C. 60.] Pompey, being a poor speaker, thus found himself entirely helpless in the new field. Cicero, being relieved of fear from him as a rival, was wise enough to see that the collapse might not continue, and that his real qualities might again bring him to the front. The Clodius business had been a frightful scandal, and, smooth as the surface might seem, ugly cracks were opening all round the constitution. The disbanded legions were impatient for their farms. The knights, who were already offended with the Senate for having thrown the disgrace of the Clodius trial upon them, had a fresh and more substantial grievance. The leaders of the order had contracted to farm the revenues in Asia. They found that the terms which they had offered were too high, and they claimed an abatement, which the Senate refused to allow. The Catiline conspiracy should have taught the necessity of a vigorous administration. Caecilius Metellus and Lucius Afranius, who had been chosen consuls for the year 60, were mere nothings. Metellus was a vacant aristocrat,[8] to be depended on for resisting popular demands, but without insight otherwise; the second, Afranius, was a person "on whom only a philosopher could look without a groan;" [9] and one year more might witness the consulship of Caesar. "I have not a friend," Cicero wrote, "to whom I can express my real thoughts. Things cannot long stand as they are. I have been vehement: I have put out all my strength in the hope of mending matters and healing our disorders, but we will not endure the necessary medicine. The seat of justice has been publicly debauched. Resolutions are introduced against corruption, but no law can be carried. The knights are alienated. The Senate has lost its authority. The concord of the orders is gone, and the pillars of the Commonwealth which I set up are overthrown. We have not a statesman, or the shadow of one. My friend Pompey, who might have done something, sits silent, admiring his fine clothes.[10] Crassus will say nothing to make himself unpopular, and the rest are such idiots as to hope that although the constitution fall they will save their own fish-ponds.[11] Cato, the best man that we have, is more honest than wise. For these three months he has been worrying the revenue farmers, and will not let the Senate satisfy them." [12]

It was time for Cicero to look about him. The Catiline affair was not forgotten. He might still be called to answer for the executions, and he felt that he required some stronger support than an aristocracy, who would learn nothing and seemed to be bent on destroying themselves. In letter after letter he pours out his contempt for his friends "of the fish- ponds," as he called them, who would neither mend their ways nor let others mend them. He would not desert them altogether, but he provided for contingencies. The tribunes had taken up the cause of Pompey's legionaries. Agrarian laws were threatened, and Pompey himself was most eager to see his soldiers satisfied. Cicero, who had hitherto opposed an agrarian law with all his violence, discovered now that something might be said in favor of draining "the sink of the city" [13] and repeopling Italy. Besides the public advantage, he felt that he would please the mortified but still popular Pompey; and he lent his help in the Senate to improving a bill introduced by the tribunes, and endeavoring, though unsuccessfully, to push it through.

[Sidenote: July, B.C. 60.] So grateful was Pompey for Cicero's support that he called him, in the Senate, "the saviour of the world." [14]Cicero was delighted with the phrase, and began to look to Pompey as a convenient ally. He thought that he could control and guide him and use his popularity for moderate measures. Nay, even in his despair of the aristocracy, he began to regard as not impossible a coalition with Caesar. "You caution me about Pompey," he wrote to Atticus in the following July. "Do not suppose that I am attaching myself to him for my own protection; but the state of things is such, that if we two disagree the worst misfortunes may be feared. I make no concessions to him, I seek to make him better, and to cure him of his popular levity; and now he speaks more highly by far of my actions than of his own. He has merely done well, he says, while I have saved the State. However this may affect me, it is certainly good for the Commonwealth. What if I can make Caesar better also, who is now coming on with wind and tide? Will that be so bad a thing? Even if I had no enemies, if I was supported as universally as I ought to be, still a medicine which will cure the diseased parts of the State is better than the surgery which would amputate them. The knights have fallen off from the Senate. The noble lords think they are in heaven when they have barbel in their ponds that will eat out of their hands, and they leave the rest to fate. You cannot love Cato more than I love him, but he does harm with the best intentions. He speaks as if he was in Plato's Republic, instead of being in the dregs of that of Romulus. Most true that corrupt judges ought to be punished! Cato proposed it, the Senate agreed; but the knights have declared war upon the Senate. Most insolent of the revenue farmers to throw up their contract! Cato resisted them, and carried his point; but now when seditions break out, the knights will not lift a finger to repress them. Are we to hire mercenaries? Are we to depend on our slaves and freedmen?.... But enough."[15]

[Sidenote: October, B.C. 60.] [Sidenote: November, B.C. 60.] Cicero might well despair of a Senate who had taken Cato to lead them. Pompey had come home in the best of dispositions. The Senate had offended Pompey, and, more than that, had offended his legionaries. They had quarrelled with the knights. They had quarrelled with the moneyed interests. They now added an entirely gratuitous affront to Caesar. His Spanish administration was admitted by every one to have been admirable. He was coming to stand for the consulship, which could not be refused; but he asked for a triumph also, and as the rule stood there was a difficulty, for if he was to have a triumph, he must remain outside the walls till the day fixed for it, and if he was a candidate for office, he must be present in person on the day of the election. The custom, though convenient in itself, had been more than once set aside. Caesar applied to the Senate for a dispensation, which would enable him to be a candidate in his absence; and Cato, either from mere dislike of Caesar or from a hope that he might prefer vanity to ambition, and that the dreaded consulship might be escaped, persuaded the Senate to refuse. If this was the expectation, it was disappointed. Caesar dropped his triumph, came home, and went through the usual forms, and it at once appeared that his election was certain, and that every powerful influence in the State was combined in his favor. From Pompey he met the warmest reception. The Mucia bubble had burst. Pompey saw in Caesar only the friend who had stood by him in every step of his later career, and had braved the fury of the Senate at the side of his officer Metellus Nepos. Equally certain it was that Caesar, as a soldier, would interest himself for Pompey's legionaries, and that they could be mutually useful to each other. Caesar had the people at his back, and Pompey had the army. The third great power in Rome was that of the capitalists, and about the attitude of these there was at first some uncertainty. Crassus, who was the impersonation of them, was a friend of Caesar, but had been on bad terms with Pompey. Caesar, however, contrived to reconcile them; and thus all parties outside the patrician circle were combined for a common purpose. Could Cicero have taken his place frankly at their side, as his better knowledge told him to do, the inevitable revolution might have been accomplished without bloodshed, and the course of history have been different. Caesar wished it. But it was not so to be. Cicero perhaps found that he would have to be content with a humbler position than he had anticipated, that in such a combination he would have to follow rather than to lead. He was tempted. He saw a promise of peace, safety, influence, if not absolute, yet considerable. But he could not bring himself to sacrifice the proud position which he had won for himself in his consulship, as leader of the Conservatives; and he still hoped to reign in the Senate, while using the protection of the popular chiefs as a shelter in time of storms. Caesar was chosen consul without opposition. His party was so powerful that it seemed at one time as if he could name his colleague, but the Senate succeeded with desperate efforts in securing the second place. They subscribed money profusely, the immaculate Cato prominent among them. The machinery of corruption was well in order. The great nobles commanded the votes of their _clientele_, and they succeeded in giving Caesar the same companion who had accompanied him through the aedileship and the praetorship, Marcus Bibulus, a dull, obstinate fool, who could be relied on, if for nothing else, yet for dogged resistance to every step which the Senate disapproved. For the moment they appeared to have thought that with Bibulus's help they might defy Caesar and reduce his office to a nullity. Immediately on the election of the consuls, it was usual to determine the provinces to which they were to be appointed when their consulate should expire. The regulation lay with the Senate, and, either in mere spleen or to prevent Caesar from having the command of an army, they allotted him the department of the "Woods and

Forests." [16] A very few weeks had to pass before they discovered that they had to do with a man who was not to be turned aside so slightingly.

Hitherto Caesar had been feared and hated, but his powers were rather suspected than understood. As the nephew of Marius and the son-in-law of Cinna, he was the natural chief of the party which had once governed Rome and had been trampled under the hoof of Sylla. He had shown on many occasions that he had inherited his uncle's principles, and could be daring and skilful in asserting them. But he had held carefully within the constitutional lines; he had kept himself clear of conspiracies; he had never, like the Gracchi, put himself forward as a tribune or attempted the part of a popular agitator. When he had exerted himself in the political world of Rome, it had been to maintain the law against violence, to resist and punish encroachments of arbitrary power, or to rescue the Empire from being gambled away by incapable or profligate aristocrats. Thus he had gathered for himself the animosity of the fashionable upper classes and the confidence of the body of the people. But what he would do in power, or what it was in him to do, was as yet merely conjectural.

[Sidenote: B.C. 50.] At all events, after an interval of a generation there was again a popular consul, and on every side there was a harvest of iniquities ready for the sickle. Sixty years had passed since the death of the younger Gracchus; revolution after revolution had swept over the Commonwealth, and Italy was still as Tiberius Gracchus had found it. The Gracchan colonists had disappeared. The Syllan military proprietors had disappeared--one by one they had fallen to beggary, and had sold their holdings, and again the country was parcelled into enormous estates cultivated by slave-gangs. The Italians had been emancipated, but the process had gone no further. The libertini, the sons of the freedmen, still waited for equality of rights. The rich and prosperous provinces beyond the Po remained unenfranchised, while the value of the franchise itself was daily diminishing as the Senate resumed its control over the initiative of legislation. Each year the elections became more corrupt. The Clodius judgment had been the most frightful instance which had yet occurred of the depravity of the law courts; while, by Cicero's own admission, not a single measure could pass beyond discussion into act which threatened the interests of the oligarchy. The consulship of Caesar was looked to with hope from the respectable part of the citizens, with alarm from the high-born delinquents as a period of genuine reform. The new consuls were to enter office on the 1st of January. In December it was known that an agrarian law would be at once proposed under plea of providing for Pompey's troops; and Cicero had to decide whether he would act in earnest in the spirit which he had begun to show when the tribunes' bill was under discussion, or would fall back upon resistance with the rest of his party, or evade the difficult dilemma by going on foreign service, or else would simply absent himself from Rome while the struggle was going on. "I may either resist," he said, "and there will be an honorable fight; or I may do nothing, and withdraw into the country, which will be honorable also; or I may give active help, which I am told Caesar expects of me. His friend, Cornelius Balbus, who was with me lately, affirms that Caesar will be guided in everything by my advice and Pompey's, and will use his endeavor to bring Pompey and Crassus together. Such a course has its advantages; it will draw me closely to Pompey and, if I please, to Caesar. I shall have no more to fear from my enemies. I shall be at peace with the people. I can look to quiet in my old age. But the lines still move me which conclude the third book (of my Poem on my consulship): 'Hold to the track on which thou enteredst in thy early youth, which thou pursuedst as consul so valorously and bravely. Increase thy fame, and seek the praise of the good.'" [17]

It had been proposed to send Cicero on a mission to Egypt. "I should like well, and I have long wished," he said, "to see Alexandria and the rest of that country. They have had enough of me here at present, and they may wish for me when I am away. But to go now, and to go on a commission from Caesar and Pompey!

I should blush To face the men and long-robed dames of Troy.[18]

What will our optimates say, if we have any optimates left? Polydamas will throw in my teeth that I have been bribed by the opposition--I mean Cato, who is one out of a hundred thousand to me. What will history say of me six hundred years hence? I am more afraid of that than of the chatter of my contemporaries."[19]

So Cicero meditated, thinking as usual of himself first and of his duty afterward--the fatalest of all courses then and always.

[1] "Si causam quaeris absolutionis, egestas judicum fuit et turpitudo.... Non

vidit (Hortensius) satius esse illum in infami?relinqui ac sordibus quam infirmo judicio committi."--To Atticus, i. 16.

[2] "Jam vero, oh Dii Boni! rem perditam! etiam noctes certarum mulierum, atque adolescentulorum nobilium introductiones nonnullis judicibus pro mercedis cumulo fuerunt."--Ad Atticum, i. 16.

[3] "Nos hic in republic?infirm? miser?commutabilique versamur. Credo enim te audisse, nostros equites paene a senatu esse disjunctos; qui primum illud valde graviter tulerund, promulgatum ex senatus consulto fuisse, ut de iis, qui ob judicaudum pecuniam accepissent queareretur. Qu?in re decernend?cum ego casu non affuissem, sensissemque id equestrem ordinem ferre moleste, neque aperte dicere: objurgavi senatum, ut mihi visus sum, summ?cum auctoritate, et in caus?non verecund?admodum gravis et copiosus fui."--To Atticus, i. 17.

[4] A nickname under which Cicero often speaks of Pompey.

[5] "Solebat enim me pungere, ne Sampsicerami merita in patriam ad annos DC majora viderentur, quam nostra."--To Atticus, ii. 17.

[6] "Pompeius nobis amicissimus esse constat."--To Atticus, i. 13.

[7] "Non jucunda miseris, inanis improbis, beatis non grata, bonis non gravis. Itaque frigebat."--To Atticus, i. 14.

[8] "Metellus non homo, sed litus atque aer, et solitudo mera."--To Atticus, i. 18.

[9] "Consul est impositus is nobis, quem nemo, praeter nos philosophos, aspicere sine suspiratu potest."--Ib. i. 18.

[10] "Pompeius togulam illam pictam silentio tuetur suam."--Ib. The "picta togula" means the triumphal robe which Pompey was allowed to wear.

[11] "Ceteros jam nosti; qui ita sunt stulti, ut amiss?republic?piscinas suas fore salvas sperare videantur."--Ib.

[12] Ib., abridged.

[13] "Sentinam urbis," a worse word than he had blamed in Rullus three years before.--To Atticus, i. 19.

[14] "Pompeium adduxi in eam voluntatem, ut in Senatu non semel, sed saepe, multisque verbis, hujus mihi salutem imperii atque orbis terrarum adjudicarit."--ib.

[15] To Atticus, ii. 1, abridged.

[16] _Silvae Callesque_--to which "woods and forests" is a near equivalent.

[17] "Interea cursus, quos prim?a parte juventae, Quosque ideo consul virtute animoque petisti, Hos retine atquae auge famam laudesque bonorum." To Atticus, ii. 3.

[18] Iliad, vi. 442. Lord Derby's translation.

[19] To Atticus, ii. 5.

CHAPTER XIII.

The consulship of Caesar was the last chance for the Roman aristocracy. He was not a revolutionist. Revolutions are the last desperate remedy when all else has failed. They may create as many evils as they cure, and wise men always hate them. But if revolution was to be escaped, reform was inevitable, and it was for the Senate to choose between the alternatives. Could the noble lords have known then, in that their day, the things that belonged to their peace--could they have forgotten their fish-ponds and their game-preserves, and have remembered that, as the rulers of the civilized world, they had duties which the eternal order of nature would exact at their hands--the shaken constitution might again have regained its stability, and the forms and even the reality of the Republic might have continued for another century. It was not to be. Had the Senate been capable of using the opportunity, they would long before have undertaken a reformation for themselves. Even had their eyes been opened, there were disintegrating forces at work which the highest political wisdom could do no more than arrest; and little good is really effected by prolonging artificially the lives of either constitutions or individuals beyond their natural period. From the time when Rome became an empire, mistress of provinces to which she was unable to extend her own liberties, the days of her self-government were numbered. A homogeneous and vigorous people may manage their own affairs under a popular constitution so long as their personal characters remain undegenerate. Parliaments and Senates may represent the general will of the community, and may pass laws and administer them as public sentiment approves. But such bodies can preside successfully only among subjects who are directly represented in them. They are too ignorant, too selfish, too divided, to govern others; and imperial aspirations draw after them, by obvious necessity, an imperial rule. Caesar may have known this in his heart, yet the most far-seeing statesman will not so trust his own misgivings as to refuse to hope for the regeneration of the institutions into which he is born. He will determine that justice shall be done. Justice is the essence of government, and without justice all forms, democratic or monarchic, are tyrannies alike. But he will work with the existing methods till the inadequacy of them has been proved beyond dispute. Constitutions are never overthrown till they have pronounced sentence on themselves.

Caesar accordingly commenced office by an endeavor to conciliate. The army and the moneyed interests, represented by Pompey and Crassus, were already with him; and he used his endeavors, as has been seen, to gain Cicero, who might bring with him such part of the landed aristocracy as were not hopelessly incorrigible. With Cicero he but partially succeeded. The great orator solved the problem of the situation by going away into the country and remaining there for the greater part of the year, and Caesar had to do without an assistance which, in the speaking department, would have been invaluable to him. His first step was to order the publication of the "Acta Diurna," a daily journal of the doings of the Senate. The light of day being thrown in upon that august body might prevent honorable members from laying hands on each other as they had lately done, and might enable the people to know what was going on among them--on a better authority than rumor. He then introduced his agrarian law, the rough draft of which had been already discussed, and had been supported by Cicero in the preceding year. Had he meant to be defiant, like the Gracchi, he might have offered it at once to the people. Instead of doing so, he laid it before the Senate, inviting them to amend his suggestions, and promising any reasonable concessions if they would co-operate. No wrong was to be done to any existing occupiers. No right of property was to be violated which was any real right at all. Large tracts in Campania which belonged to the State were now held on the usual easy terms by great landed patricians. These Caesar proposed to buy out, and to settle on the ground twenty thousand of Pompey's veterans. There was money enough and to spare in the treasury, which they had themselves brought home. Out of the large funds which would still remain land might be purchased in other parts of Italy for the rest, and for a few thousand of the unemployed population which was crowded into Rome. The measure in itself was admitted to be a moderate one. Every pains had been taken to spare the interests and to avoid hurting the susceptibilities of the aristocrats. But, as Cicero said, the very name of an agrarian law was intolerable to them. It meant in the end spoliation and division of property, and the first step would bring others after it. The public lands they had shared conveniently among themselves from immemorial time. The public treasure was their treasure, to be laid out as they might think proper. Cato headed the opposition. He stormed for an entire day, and was so violent that Caesar threatened him with arrest. The Senate groaned and foamed; no progress was made or was likely to be made; and Caesar, as much in earnest as they were, had to tell them that if they would not help him he must appeal to the assembly. "I invited you to revise the law," he said; "I was willing that if any clause displeased you it should be expunged. You will not touch it. Well, then, the people must decide."

The Senate had made up their minds to fight the battle. If Caesar went to the assembly, Bibulus, their second consul, might stop the proceedings. If this seemed too extreme a step, custom provided other impediments to which recourse might be had. Bibulus might survey the heavens, watch the birds, or the clouds, or the direction of the wind, and declare the aspects unfavorable; or he might proclaim day after day to be holy, and on holy days no legislation was permitted. Should these religious cobwebs be brushed away, the Senate had provided a further resource in three of the tribunes whom they had bribed. Thus they held themselves secure, and dared Caesar to do his worst. Caesar on his side was equally determined. The assembly was convoked. The Forum was choked to overflowing. Caesar and Pompey stood on the steps of the Temple of Castor, and Bibulus and his tribunes were at hand ready with their interpellations. Such passions had not been roused in Rome since the days of Cinna and Octavius, and many a young lord was doubtless hoping that the day would not close without another lesson to ambitious demagogues and howling mobs. In their eyes the one reform which Rome needed was another Sylla.

Caesar read his law from the tablet on which it was inscribed; and, still courteous to his antagonist, he turned to Bibulus and asked him if he had any fault to find. Bibulus said sullenly that he wanted no revolutions, and that while he was consul there should be none. The people hissed; and he then added in a rage, "You shall not have your law this year though every man of you demand it." Caesar answered nothing, but Pompey and Crassus stood forward. They were not officials, but they were real forces. Pompey was the idol of every soldier in the State, and at Caesar's invitation he addressed the assembly. He spoke for his veterans. He spoke for the poor citizens. He said that he approved the law to the last letter of it.

"Will you then," asked Caesar, "support the law if it be illegally opposed?" "Since," replied Pompey, "you consul, and you my fellow- citizens, ask aid of me, a poor individual without office and without authority, who nevertheless has done some service to the State, I say that I will bear the shield if others draw the sword." Applause rang out from a hundred thousand throats. Crassus followed to the same purpose, and was received with the same wild delight. A few senators, who retained their senses, saw the uselessness of the opposition, and retired. Bibulus was of duller and tougher metal. As the vote was about to be taken, he and his tribunes rushed to the rostra. The tribunes pronounced their veto. Bibulus said that he had consulted the sky; the gods forbade further action being taken that day, and he declared the assembly dissolved. Nay, as if a man like Caesar could be stopped by a shadow, he proposed to sanctify the whole remainder of the year, that no further business might be transacted in it. Yells drowned his voice. The mob rushed upon the steps; Bibulus was thrown down, and the rods of the lictors were broken; the tribunes who had betrayed their order were beaten. Cato held his ground, and stormed at Caesar till he was led off by the police, raving and gesticulating. The law was then passed, and a resolution besides that every senator should take an oath to obey it.

So in ignominy the Senate's resistance collapsed: the Caesar whom they had thought to put off with their "woods and forests" had proved stronger than the whole of them; and, prostrate at the first round of the battle, they did not attempt another. They met the following morning. Bibulus told his story and appealed for support. Had the Senate complied, they would probably have ceased to exist. The oath was unpalatable, but they made the best of it. Metellus Celer, Cato, and Favonius, a senator whom men called Cato's ape, struggled against their fate, but, "swearing they would ne'er consent, consented." The unwelcome formula was swallowed by the whole of them; and Bibulus, who had done his part and had been beaten and kicked and trampled upon, and now found his employers afraid to stand by him, went off sulkily to his house, shut himself up there, and refused to act as consul further during the remainder of the year.

There was no further active opposition. A commission was appointed by Caesar to carry out the land act, composed of twenty of the best men that could be found, one of them being Atius Balbus, the husband of Caesar's only sister, and grandfather of a little child now three years old, who was known afterward to the world as Augustus. Cicero was offered a place, but declined. The land question having been disposed of, Caesar then proceeded with the remaining measures by which his consulship was immortalized. He had redeemed his promise to Pompey by providing for his soldiers. He gratified Crassus by giving the desired relief to the farmers of the taxes. He confirmed Pompey's arrangements for the government of Asia, which the Senate had left in suspense. The Senate was now itself suspended. The consul acted directly with the assembly, without obstruction and without remonstrance, Bibulus only from time to time sending out monotonous admonitions from within doors that the season was consecrated, and that Caesar's acts had no validity. Still more remarkably, and as the distinguishing feature of his term of office, Caesar carried, with the help of the people, the body of admirable laws which are known to jurists as the "Leges Juliae," and mark an epoch in Roman history. They were laws as unwelcome to the aristocracy as they were essential to the continued existence of the Roman State, laws which had been talked of in the Senate, but which could never pass through the preliminary stage of resolutions, and were now enacted over the Senate's head by the will of Caesar and the sovereign power of the nation. A mere outline can alone be attempted here. There was a law declaring the inviolability of the persons of magistrates during their term of authority, reflecting back on the murder of Saturninus, and touching by implication the killing of Lentulus and his companions. There was a law for the punishment of adultery, most disinterestedly singular if the popular accounts of Caesar's habits had any grain of truth in them. There were laws for the protection of the subject from violence, public or private; and laws disabling persons who had laid hands illegally on Roman citizens from holding office in the Commonwealth. There was a law, intended at last to be effective, to deal with judges who allowed themselves to be bribed. There were laws against defrauders of the revenue; laws against debasing the coin; laws against sacrilege; laws against corrupt State contracts; laws against bribery at elections. Finally, there was a law, carefully framed, De repetundis, to exact retribution from proconsuls or propraetors of the type of Verres who had plundered the provinces. All governors were required, on relinquishing office, to make a double return of their accounts, one to remain for inspection among the archives of the province, and one to be sent to Rome; and where peculation or injustice could be proved, the offender's estate was made answerable to the last sesterce.[1]

Such laws were words only without the will to execute them; but they affirmed the principles on which Roman or any other society could alone continue. It was for the officials of the constitution to adopt them, and save themselves and the Republic, or to ignore them as they had ignored the laws which already existed, and see it perish as it deserved. All that man could do for the preservation of his country from revolution Caesar had accomplished. Sylla had re-established the rule of the aristocracy, and it had failed grossly and disgracefully. Cinna and Marius had tried democracy, and that had failed. Caesar was trying what law would do, and the result remained to be seen. Bibulus, as each measure was passed, croaked that it was null and void. The leaders of the Senate threatened between their teeth that all should be undone when Caesar's term was over. Cato, when he mentioned the "Leges Juliae," spoke of them as enactments, but refused them their author's name. But the excellence of these laws was so clearly recognized that they survived the irregularity of their introduction; and the "Lex de Repetundis" especially remained a terror to evil-doers, with a promise of better days to the miserable and pillaged subjects of the Roman Empire.

So the year of Caesar's consulship passed away. What was to happen when it had expired? The Senate had provided "the woods and forests" for him. But the Senate's provision in such a matter could not be expected to hold. He asked for nothing, but he was known to desire an opportunity of distinguished service. Caesar was now forty-three. His life was ebbing away, and, with the exception of his two years in Spain, it had been spent in struggling with the base elements of Roman faction. Great men will bear such sordid work when it is laid on them, but they loathe it notwithstanding, and for the present there was nothing more to be done. A new point of departure had been taken. Principles had been laid down for the Senate and people to act on, if they could and would. Caesar could only wish for a long absence in some new sphere of usefulness, where he could achieve something really great which his country would remember.

And on one side only was such a sphere open to him. The East was Roman to the Euphrates. No second Mithridates could loosen the grasp with which the legions now held the civilized parts of Asia. Parthians might disturb the frontier, but could not seriously threaten the Eastern dominions; and no advantage was promised by following on the steps of Alexander and annexing countries too poor to bear the cost of their maintenance. To the west it was different. Beyond the Alps there was still a territory of unknown extent, stretching away to the undefined ocean, a territory peopled with warlike races, some of whom in ages long past had swept over Italy and taken Rome, and had left their descendants and their name in the northern province, which was now called Cisalpine Gaul. With these races the Romans had as yet no clear relations, and from them alone could any serious danger threaten the State. The Gauls had for some centuries ceased their wanderings, had settled down in fixed localities. They had built towns and bridges; they had cultivated the soil, and had become wealthy and partly civilized. With the tribes adjoining Provence the Romans had alliances more or less precarious, and had established a kind of protectorate over them. But even here the inhabitants were uneasy for their independence, and troubles were continually arising with them; while into these districts and into the rest of Gaul a fresh and stormy element was now being introduced. In earlier times the Gauls had been stronger than the Germans, and not only could they protect their own frontier, but they had formed settlements beyond the Rhine. These relations were being changed. The Gauls, as they grew in wealth, declined in vigor. The Germans, still roving and migratory, were throwing covetous eyes out of their forests on the fields and vineyards of their neighbors, and enormous numbers of them were crossing the Rhine and Danube, looking for new homes. How feeble a barrier either the Alps or the Gauls themselves might prove against such invaders had been but too recently experienced. Men who were of middle age at the time of Caesar's consulship could still remember the terrors which had been caused by the invasion of the Cimbri and Teutons. Marius had saved Italy then from destruction, as it were, by the hair of its head. The annihilation of those hordes had given Rome a passing respite. But fresh generations had grown up. Fresh multitudes were streaming out of the North. Germans in hundreds of thousands were again passing the Upper Rhine, rooting themselves in Burgundy, and coming in collision with tribes which Rome protected. There were uneasy movements among the Gauls themselves, whole nations of them breaking up from their homes and again adrift upon the world. Gaul and Germany were like a volcano giving signs of approaching eruption; and at any moment, and hardly with warning, another lava-stream might be pouring down into Venetia and Lombardy.

To deal with this danger was the work marked out for Caesar. It is the fashion to say that he sought a military command that he might have an army behind him to overthrow the constitution. If this was his object, ambition never chose a more dangerous or less promising route for itself. Men of genius who accomplish great things in this world do not trouble themselves with remote and visionary aims. They encounter emergencies as they rise, and leave the future to shape itself as it may. It would seem that at first the defence of Italy was all that was thought of. "The woods and forests" were set aside, and Caesar, by a vote of the people, was given the command of Cisalpine Gaul and Illyria for five years; but either he himself desired, or especial circumstances which were taking place beyond the mountains recommended, that a wider scope should be allowed him. The Senate, finding that the people would act without them if they hesitated, gave him in addition Gallia Comata, the land of the Gauls with the long hair, the governorship of the Roman province beyond the Alps, with untrammelled liberty to act as he might think good throughout the country which is now known as France and Switzerland and the Rhine provinces of Germany.

He was to start early in the approaching year. It was necessary before he went to make some provision for the quiet government of the capital. The alliance with Pompey and Crassus gave temporary security. Pompey had less stability of character than could have been wished, but he became attached to Caesar's daughter Julia; and a fresh link of marriage was formed to hold them together. Caesar himself married Calpurnia, the daughter of Calpurnius Piso. The Senate having temporarily abdicated, he was able to guide the elections; and Piso and Pompey's friend Gabinius, who had obtained the command of the pirate war for him, were chosen consuls for the year 58. Neither of them, if we can believe a tithe of Cicero's invective, was good for much; but they were stanch partisans, and were to be relied on to resist any efforts which might be made to repeal the "Leges Juliae." These matters being arranged, and his own term having expired, Caesar withdrew, according to custom, to the suburbs beyond the walls to collect troops and prepare for his departure. Strange things, however, had yet to happen before he was gone.

[Sidenote: B. C. 58.] It is easy to conceive how the Senate felt at these transactions, how ill they bore to find themselves superseded and the State managed over their heads. Fashionable society was equally furious, and the three allies went by the name of Dynasts, or "Reges Superbi." After resistance had been abandoned, Cicero came back to Rome to make cynical remarks from which all parties suffered equally. His special grievance was the want of consideration which he conceived to have been shown for himself. He mocked at the Senate; he mocked at Bibulus, whom he particularly abominated; he mocked at Pompey and the agrarian law. Mockery turned to indignation when he thought of the ingratitude of the Senate, and his chief consolation in their discomfiture was that it had fallen on them through the neglect of their most distinguished member. "I could have saved them if they would have let me," he said. "I could save them still if I were to try; but I will go study philosophy in my own family." [2] "Freedom is gone," he wrote to Atticus; "and if we are to be worse enslaved, we shall bear it. Our lives and properties are more to us than liberty. We sigh, and we do not even remonstrate." [3]

Cato, in the desperation of passion, called Pompey a dictator in the assembly, and barely escaped being killed for his pains.[4] The patricians revenged themselves in private by savage speeches and plots and purposes. Fashionable society gathered in the theatres and hissed the popular leaders. Lines were introduced into the plays reflecting on Pompey, and were encored a thousand times. Bibulus from his closet continued to issue venomous placards, reporting scandals about Caesar's life, and now for the first time bringing up the story of Nicomedes. The streets were impassable where these papers were pasted up, from the crowds of loungers which were gathered to read them, and Bibulus for the moment was the hero of patrician saloons.

Some malicious comfort Cicero gathered out of these manifestations of feeling. He had no belief in the noble lords, and small expectations from them. Bibulus was, on the whole, a fit representative for the gentry of the fish-ponds. But the Dynasts were at least heartily detested in quarters which had once been powerful, and might be powerful again; and he flattered himself, though he affected to regret it, that the animosity against them was spreading. To all parties there is attached a draggled trail of disreputables, who hold themselves entitled to benefits when their side is in power, and are angry when they are passed over.

"The State," Cicero wrote in the autumn of 59 to Atticus, "is in a worse condition than when you left us; then we thought that we had fallen under a power which pleased the people, and which, though abhorrent to the good, yet was not totally destructive to them. Now all hate it equally, and we are in terror as to where the exasperation may break out. We had experienced the ill-temper and irritation of those who in their anger with Cato had brought ruin on us; but the poison worked so slowly that it seemed we might die without pain. I hoped, as I often told you, that the wheel of the constitution was so turning that we should scarcely hear a sound or see any visible track; and so it would have been could men have waited for the tempest to pass over them. But the secret sighs turned to groans, and the groans to universal clamor; and thus our friend Pompey, who so lately swam in glory and never heard an evil word of himself, is broken-hearted and knows not whither to turn. A precipice is before him, and to retreat is dangerous. The good are against him; the bad are not his friends. I could scarce help weeping the other day when I heard him complaining in the Forum of the publication of Bibulus. He who but a short time since bore himself so proudly there, with the people in raptures with him, and with the world on his side, was now so humble and abject as to disgust even himself, not to say his hearers. Crassus enjoyed the scene, but no one else. Pompey had fallen down out of the stars--not by a gradual descent, but in a single plunge; and as Apelles if he had seen his Venus, or Protogenes his Ialysus, all daubed with mud, would have been vexed and annoyed, so was I grieved to the very heart to see one whom I had painted out in the choicest colors of art thus suddenly defaced.[5] Pompey is sick with irritation at the placards of Bibulus. I am sorry about them. They give such excessive annoyance to a man whom I have always liked; and Pompey is so prompt with his sword, and so unaccustomed to insult, that I fear what he may do. What the future may have in store for Bibulus I know not. At present he is the admired of all." [6]

"Sampsiceramus," Cicero wrote a few days later, "is greatly penitent. He would gladly be restored to the eminence from which he has fallen. Sometimes he imparts his griefs to me, and asks me what he should do, which I cannot tell him." [7]

Unfortunate Cicero, who knew what was right, but was too proud to do it! Unfortunate Pompey, who still did what was right, but was too sensitive to bear the reproach of it, who would so gladly not leave his duty unperformed, and yet keep the "sweet voices" whose applause had grown so delicious to him! Bibulus was in no danger. Pompey was too good-natured to hurt him; and Caesar let fools say what they pleased, as long as they were fools without teeth, who would bark but could not bite. The risk was to Cicero himself, little as he seemed to be aware of it. Caesar was to be long absent from Rome, and he knew that as soon as he was engaged in Gaul the extreme oligarchic faction would make an effort to set aside his land commission and undo his legislation. When he had a clear purpose in view, and was satisfied that it was a good purpose, he was never scrupulous about his instruments. It was said of him that when he wanted any work done he chose the persons best able to do it, let their general character be what it might. The rank and file of the patricians, proud, idle, vicious, and self-indulgent, might be left to their mistresses and their gaming-tables. They could do no mischief unless they had leaders at their head who could use their resources more effectively than they could do themselves. There were two men only in Rome with whose help they could be really dangerous--Cato, because he was a fanatic, impregnable to argument, and not to be influenced by temptation of advantage to himself; Cicero, on account of his extreme ability, his personal ambition, and his total want of political principle. Cato he knew to be impracticable. Cicero he had tried to gain; but Cicero, who had played a first part as consul, could not bring himself to play a second, and, if the chance offered, had both power and will to be troublesome. Some means had to be found to get rid of these two, or at least to tie their hands and to keep them in order. There would be Pompey and Crassus still at hand. But Pompey was weak, and Crassus understood nothing beyond the art of manipulating money. Gabinius and Piso, the next consuls, had an indifferent reputation and narrow abilities, and at best they would have but their one year of authority. Politics, like love, makes strange bedfellows. In this difficulty accident threw in Cesar's way a convenient but most unexpected ally.

Young Clodius, after his escape from prosecution by the marvellous methods which Crassus had provided for him, was more popular than ever. He had been the occasion of a scandal which had brought infamy on the detested Senate. His offence in itself seemed slight in so loose an age, and was as nothing compared with the enormity of his judges. He had come out of his trial with a determination to be revenged on the persons from whose tongues he had suffered most severely in the senatorial debates. Of these Cato had been the most savage; but Cicero had been the most exasperating, from his sarcasms, his airs of patronage, and perhaps his intimacy with his sister. The noble youth had exhausted the common forms of pleasure. He wanted a new excitement, and politics and vengeance might be combined. He was as clever as he was dissolute, and, as clever men are fortunately rare in the licentious part, of society, they are always idolized, because they make vice respectable by connecting it with intellect. Clodius was a second, an abler Catiline, equally unprincipled and far more dexterous and prudent. In times of revolution there is always a disreputable wing to the radical party, composed of men who are the natural enemies of established authority, and these all rallied about their new leader with devout enthusiasm. Clodius was not without political experience. His first public appearance had been as leader of a mutiny. He was already quaestor, and so a senator; but he was too young to aspire to the higher magistracies which were open to him as a patrician. He declared his intention of renouncing his order, becoming a plebeian, and standing for the tribuneship of the people. There were precedents for such a step, but they were rare. The abdicating noble had to be adopted into a plebeian family, and the consent was required of the consuls and of the Pontifical College. With the growth of political equality the aristocracy had become more insistent upon the privilege of birth, which could not be taken from them; and for a Claudius to descend among the canaille was as if a Howard were to seek adoption from a shopkeeper in the Strand.

At first there was universal amazement. Cicero had used the intrigue with Pompeia as a text for a sermon on the immoralities of the age. The aspirations of Clodius to be a tribune he ridiculed as an illustration of its follies, and after scourging him in the Senate, he laughed at him and jested with him in private.[8] Cicero did not understand with how venomous a snake he was playing. He even thought Clodius likely to turn against the Dynasts, and to become a serviceable member of the conservative party. Gradually he was forced to open his eyes. Speeches were reported to him as coming from Clodius or his allies threatening an inquiry into the death of the Catilinarians. At first he pushed his alarms aside, as unworthy of him. What had so great a man as he to fear from a young reprobate like "the pretty boy"? The "pretty boy," however, found favor where it was least looked for. Pompey supported his adventure for the tribuneship. Caesar, though it was Caesar's house which he had violated, did not oppose. Bibulus refused consent, but Bibulus had virtually abdicated and went for nothing. The legal forms were complied with. Clodius found a commoner younger than himself who was willing to adopt him, and who, the day after the ceremony, released him from the new paternal authority. He was now a plebeian, and free. He remained a senator in virtue of his quaestorship, and he was chosen tribune of the people for the year 58.

Cicero was at last startled out of his security. So long as the consuls, or one of them, could be depended on, a tribune's power was insignificant. When the consuls were of his own way of thinking, a tribune was a very important personage indeed. Atticus was alarmed for his friend, and cautioned him to look to himself. Warnings came from all quarters that mischief was in the wind. Still it was impossible to believe the peril to be a real one. Cicero, to whom Rome owed its existence, to be struck at by a Clodius! It could not be. As little could a wasp hurt an elephant.

There can be little doubt that Caesar knew what Clodius had in his mind; or that, if the design was not his own, he had purposely allowed it to go forward. Caesar did not wish to hurt Cicero. He wished well to him, and admired him; but he did not mean to leave him free in Rome to lead a senatorial reaction. A prosecution for the execution of the prisoners was now distinctly announced. Cicero as consul had put to death Roman citizens without a trial. Cicero was to be called to answer for the illegality before the sovereign people. The danger was unmistakable; and Caesar, who was still in the suburbs making his preparations, invited Cicero to avoid it, by accompanying him as second in command into Gaul. The offer was made in unquestionable sincerity. Caesar may himself have created the situation to lay Cicero under a pressure, but he desired nothing so much as to take him as his companion, and to attach him to himself. Cicero felt the compliment and hesitated to refuse, but his pride again came in his way. Pompey assured him that not a hair of his head should be touched. Why Pompey gave him this encouragement Cicero could never afterwards understand. The scenes in the theatres had also combined to mislead him, and he misread the disposition of the great body of citizens. He imagined that they would all start up in his defence, Senate, aristocracy, knights, commoners, and tradesmen. The world, he thought, looked back upon his consulship with as much admiration as he did himself, and was always contrasting him with his successors. Never was mistake more profound. The Senate, who had envied his talents and resented his assumption, now despised him as a trimmer. His sarcasms had made him enemies among those who acted with him politically. He had held aloof at the crisis of Caesar's election and in the debates which followed, and therefore all sides distrusted him; while throughout the body of the people there was, as Caesar had foretold, a real and sustained resentment at the conduct of the Catiline affair. The final opinion of Rome was that the prisoners ought to have been tried; and that they were not tried was attributed not unnaturally to a desire, on the part of the Senate, to silence an inquiry which might have proved inconvenient.

Thus suddenly out of a clear sky the thunder-clouds gathered over Cicero's head. "Clodius," says Dion Cassius, "had discovered that among the senators Cicero was more feared than loved. There were few of them who had not been hit by his irony, or irritated by his presumption." Those who most agreed in what he had done were not ashamed to shuffle off upon him their responsibilities. Clodius, now omnipotent with the assembly at his back, cleared the way by a really useful step; he carried a law abolishing the impious form of declaring the heavens unfavorable when an inconvenient measure was to be stopped or delayed. Probably it formed a part of his engagement with Caesar. The law may have been meant to act retrospectively, to prevent a question being raised on the interpellations of Bibulus. This done, and without paying the Senate the respect of first consulting it, he gave notice that he would propose a vote to the assembly, to the effect that any person who had put to death a Roman citizen without trial, and without allowing him an appeal to the people, had violated the constitution of the State. Cicero was not named directly; every senator who had voted for the execution of Cethegus and Lentulus and their companions was as guilty as he; but it was known immediately that Cicero was the mark that was being aimed at; and Caesar at once renewed the offer, which he made before, to take Cicero with him. Cicero, now frightened in earnest, still could not bring himself to owe his escape to Caesar. The Senate, ungrateful as they had been, put on mourning with an affectation of dismay. The knights petitioned the consuls to interfere for Cicero's protection. The consuls declined to receive their request. Caesar outside the city gave no further sign. A meeting of the citizens was held in the camp. Caesar's opinion was invited. He said that he had not changed his sentiments. He had remonstrated at the time against the execution. He disapproved of it still, but he did not directly advise legislation upon acts that were past. Yet, though he did not encourage Clodius, he did not interfere. He left the matter to the consuls, and one of them was his own father-in-law, and the other was Gabinius, once Pompey's favorite officer. Gabinius, Cicero thought, would respect Pompey's promise to him. To Piso he made a personal appeal. He found him, he said afterwards,[9] at eleven in the morning, in his slippers, at a low tavern. Piso came out, reeking with wine, and excused himself by saying that his health required a morning draught. Cicero attempted to receive his apology, and he stood for a while at the tavern door, till he could no longer bear the smell and the foul language and expectorations of the consul. Hope in that quarter there was none. Two days later the assembly was called to consider Clodius's proposal. Piso was asked to say what he thought of the treatment of the conspirators; he answered gravely, and, as Cicero described him, with one eye in his forehead, that he disapproved of cruelty. Neither Pompey nor his friends came to help. What was Cicero to do? Resist by force? The young knights rallied about him eager for a fight, if he would but give the word. Sometimes as he looked back in after-years he blamed himself for declining their services, sometimes he took credit to himself for refusing to be the occasion of bloodshed.[10]

"I was too timid," he said once; "I had the country with me, and I should have stood firm. I had to do with a band of villains only, with two monsters of consuls, and with the male harlot of rich buffoons, the seducer of his sister, the high-priest of adultery, a poisoner, a forger, an assassin, a thief. The best and bravest citizens implored me to stand up to him. But I reflected that this Fury asserted that he was supported by Pompey and Crassus and Caesar. Caesar had an army at the gates. The other two could raise another army when they pleased; and when they knew that their names were thus made use of, they remained silent. They were alarmed perhaps, because the laws which they had carried in the preceding year were challenged by the new praetors, and were held by the Senate to be invalid; and they were unwilling to alienate a popular tribune."[11]

And again elsewhere: "When I saw that the faction of Catiline was in power, that the party which I had led, some from envy of myself, some from fear for their own lives, had betrayed and deserted me; when the two consuls had been purchased by promises of provinces, and had gone over to my enemies, and the condition of the bargain was that I was to be delivered over, tied and bound, to my enemies; when the Senate and knights were in mourning, but were not allowed to bring my cause before the people; when my blood had been made the seal of the arrangement under which the State had been disposed of; when I saw all this, although 'the good' were ready to fight for me, and were willing to die for me, I would not consent, because I saw that victory or defeat would alike bring ruin to the Commonwealth. The Senate was powerless. The Forum was ruled by violence. In such a city there was no place for me." [12]

So Cicero, as he looked back afterwards, described the struggle in his own mind. His friends had then rallied; Caesar was far away; and he could tell his own story, and could pile his invectives on those who had injured him. His matchless literary power has given him exclusive command over the history of his time. His enemies' characters have been accepted from his pen as correct portraits. If we allow his description of Clodius and the two consuls to be true to the facts, what harder condemnation can be pronounced against a political condition in which such men as these could be raised to the first position in the State?[13] Dion says that Cicero's resolution to yield did not wholly proceed from his own prudence, but was assisted by advice from Cato and Hortensius the orator. Anyway, the blow fell, and he went down before the stroke. His immortal consulship, in praise of which he had written a poem, brought after it the swift retribution which Caesar had foretold. When the vote proposed by Clodius was carried, he fled to Sicily, with a tacit confession that he dared not abide his trial, which would immediately have followed. Sentence was pronounced upon him in his absence. His property was confiscated. His houses in town and country were razed. The site of his palace in Rome was dedicated to the Goddess of Liberty, and he himself was exiled. He was forbidden to reside within four hundred miles of Rome, with a threat of death if he returned; and he retired to Macedonia, to pour out his sorrows and his resentments in lamentations unworthy of a woman.

[1] See a list of the Leges Juliae in the 48th Book of the Corpus Juris Civilis.

[2] To Atticus, ii. 16.

[3] "Tenemur undique, neque jam, quo minus serviamus, recusamus, sed mortem et ejectionem quasi majora timemus, quae multo sunt minora. Atque hic status, qui una voce omnium gemitur neque verbo cujusdam sublevatur."--To Atticus, ii. 18.

[4] "In concionem ascendit et Pompeium privatus dictatorem appellavit. Propius nihil est factum quam ut occideretur."--Cicero, Ad Quintum Fratrem, i. 2.

[5] To Athens, ii, 21. In this comparison Cicero betrays his naive conviction that Pompey was indebted to him and to his praises for his reputation. Here, as always, Cicero was himself the centre round which all else revolved or ought to revolve.

[6] Ib.

[7] To Atticus, ii. 22.

[8] "Jam familiariter cum illo etiam cavillor ac jocor."--To Atticus, ii. 1.

[9] _Oratio in L. Pisonem_.

[10] He seems to have even thought of suicide.--To Atticus, iii. 9.

[11] Abridged from the _Oratio pro P. Sextio_.

[12] Oratio post reditum ad Quirites.

[13] In a letter to his brother Quintus, written at a time when he did not know the real feelings of Caesar and Pompey, and had supposed that he had only to deal with Clodius, Cicero announced a distinct intention of resisting by force. He expected that the whole of Italy would be at his side. He said: "Si diem nobis Clodius dixerit, tota Italia concurret, ut

multiplicat?glori?discedamus. Sin autem vi agere conabitur, spero fore, studiis non solum amicorum, sedetiam alienorum, ut vi resistamus. Omnes et se et suos liberos, amicos, clientes, libertos, servos, pecunias denique suas pollicentur. Nostra antiqua manus bonorum ardet studio nostri atque amore. Si qui antea aut alieniores fuerant, ant languidiores, nunc horum regum odio se cum bonis conjungunt. Pompeius omnia pollicetur et Caesar, do quibus ita credo, ut nihil de me?comparatione deminuam."--Ad Quintum Fratrem, i. 2.

CHAPTER XIV.

From the fermentation of Roman politics, the passions of the Forum and Senate, the corrupt tribunals, the poisoned centre of the Empire, the story passes beyond the frontier of Italy. We no longer depend for our account of Caesar on the caricatures of rival statesmen. He now becomes himself our guide. We see him in his actions and in the picture of his personal character which he has unconsciously drawn. Like all real great men, he rarely speaks of himself. He tells us little or nothing of, his own feelings or his own purposes. Cicero never forgets his individuality. In every line that he wrote Cicero was attitudinizing for posterity, or reflecting on the effect of his conduct upon his interests or his reputation. Caesar is lost in his work; his personality is scarcely more visible than Shakespeare's. He was now forty-three years old. His abstemious habits had left his health unshaken. He was in the fullest vigor of mind and body, and it was well for him that his strength had not been undermined. He was going on an expedition which would make extraordinary demands upon his energies. That he had not contemplated operations so extended as those which were forced upon him is evident from the nature of his preparations. His command in Further Gaul had been an afterthought, occasioned probably by news which had been received of movements in progress there during his consulship. Of the four legions which were allowed to him, one only was beyond the Alps; three were at Aquileia. It was late in life for him to begin the trade of a soldier; and as yet, with the exception of his early service in Asia and a brief and limited campaign in Spain when propraetor, he had no military experience at all. His ambition hitherto had not pointed in that direction; nor is it likely that a person of so strong an understanding would have contemplated beforehand the deliberate undertaking of the gigantic war into which circumstances immediately forced him. Yet he must have known that he had to deal with a problem of growing difficulty. The danger to Italy from inroads across the Alps was perpetually before the minds of thoughtful Roman statesmen. Events were at that moment taking place among the Gallic tribes which gave point to the general uneasiness. And unwilling as the Romans were to extend their frontiers and their responsibilities in a direction so unknown and so unpromising, yet some interference either by arms or by authority beyond those existing limits was being pressed upon them in self-defence.

The Transalpine Gaul of Caesar was the country included between the Rhine, the ocean, the Pyrenees, the Mediterranean, and the Alps. Within these limits, including Switzerland, there was at this time a population vaguely estimated at six or seven millions. The Roman Province stretched along the coast to the Spanish border; it was bounded on the north by the Cevennes mountains, and for some generations by the Isle; but it had been found necessary lately[1] to annex the territory of the Allobroges (Dauphine and Savoy), and the proconsular authority was now extended to within a few miles of Geneva. The rest was divided into three sections, inhabited by races which, if allied, were distinctly different in language, laws, and institutions. The Aquitani, who were connected with the Spaniards or perhaps the Basques, held the country between the Pyrenees and the Garonne. The Belgae, whom Caesar believed to have been originally Germans, extended from the mouth of the Seine to the mouth of the Rhine, and inland to the Marne and Moselle. The people whom the Romans meant especially when they spoke of Gauls occupied all the remainder. At one time the Celts had probably been masters of the whole of France, but had gradually yielded to encroachment. According to the Druids, they came out of darkness, _ab Dite Patre_; they called themselves Children of Night, counting time by nights instead of days, as we say fortnight and sennight. Comparison of language has taught us that they were a branch of the great Aryan race, one of the first which rolled westward into Europe, before Greeks or Latins had been heard of.

This once magnificent people was now in a state of change and decomposition. On Aquitaine and Belgium Roman civilization had as yet produced no effect. The severe habits of earlier generations remained unchanged. The Gauls proper had yielded to contact with the Province and to intercourse with Italian traders. They had built towns and villages. They had covered the land with farms and homesteads. They had made roads. They had bridged their rivers, even such rivers as the Rhone and the Loire. They had amassed wealth, and had adopted habits of comparative luxury, which, if it had not abated their disposition to fight, had diminished their capacity for fighting. Their political and perhaps their spiritual system was passing through analogous transformations. The ancient forms remained, but an altered spirit was working under them. From the earliest antiquity they had been divided into tribes and sub-tribes: each tribe and sub-tribe being practically independent, or united only by common objects and a common sentiment of race. The rule was the rule of the strong, under the rudest forms of tribal organization. The chief was either hereditary or elected, or won his command by the sword. The mass of the people were serfs. The best fighters were self-made nobles, under the chief's authority. Every man in the tribe was the chief's absolute subject; the chief, in turn, was bound to protect the meanest of them against injury from without. War, on a large scale or a small, had been the occupation of their lives. The son was not admitted into his father's presence till he was old enough to be a soldier. When the call to arms went out, every man of the required age was expected at the muster, and the last comer was tortured to death in the presence of his comrades as a lesson against backwardness.

As the secular side of things bore a rude resemblance to feudalism, so on the religious there was a similar anticipation of the mediaeval Catholic Church. The Druids were not a special family, like the Levites, or in any way born into the priesthood. They were an order composed of persons selected, when young, out of the higher ranks of the community, either for speciality of intellect, or from disposition, or by the will of their parents, or from a desire to avoid military service, from which the Druids were exempt. There were no tribal distinctions among them. Their head-quarters were in Britain, to which those who aspired to initiation in the more profound mysteries repaired for instruction; but they were spread universally over Gaul and the British Islands. They were the ministers of public worship, the depositaries of knowledge, and the guardians of public morality. Young men repaired to the Druids for education. They taught theology; they taught the movements of the stars. They presided in the civil courts and determined questions of disputed inheritance. They heard criminal cases and delivered judgment; and, as with the Church, their heaviest and most dreaded punishment was excommunication. The excommunicated person lost his civil rights. He became an outlaw from society, and he was excluded from participation in the sacrifices. In the religious services the victims most acceptable to the gods were human beings--criminals, if such could be had; if not, then innocent persons, who were burnt to death in huge towers of wicker. In the Quemadero at Seville, as in our own Smithfield, the prisoners of the Church were fastened to stakes, and the sticks with which they were consumed were tied into fagots, instead of being plaited into basket-work. So slight a difference does not materially affect the likeness.

The tribal chieftainship and the religious organization of the Druids were both of them inherited from antiquity. They were institutions descending from the time when the Gauls had been a great people; but both had outlived the age to which they were adapted, and one at least was approaching its end. To Caesar's eye, coming new upon them, the Druids were an established fact, presenting no sign of decay; but in Gaul, infected with Roman manners, they existed merely by habit, exercising no influence any longer over the hearts of the people. In the great struggle which was approaching we find no Druids among the national leaders, no spirit of religion inspiring and consecrating the efforts of patriotism. So far as can be seen, the Druids were on the Roman side, or the Romans had the skill to conciliate them. In half a century they were suppressed by Augustus, and they and their excommunications, and their flaming wicker-works, had to be sought for in distant Britain or in the still more distant Ireland. The active and secular leadership could not disappear so easily. Leaders of some kind were still required and inevitably found, but the method of selection in the times which had arrived was silently changing. While the Gallic nation retained, or desired to retain, a kind of unity, some one of the many tribes had always been allowed a hegemony. The first place had rested generally with the aedui, a considerable people who occupied the central parts of France, between the Upper Loire and the Saine. The Romans, anxious naturally to extend their influence in the country without direct interference, had taken the aedui under their protectorate. The aedui again had their clients in the inferior tribes; and a Romano-aeduan authority of a shadowy kind had thus penetrated through the whole nation.

But the aeduans had rivals and competitors in the Sequani, another powerful body in Burgundy and Franche-Comt? If the Romans feared, the Gauls, the Gauls in turn feared the Romans; and a national party had formed itself everywhere, especially among the younger men, who were proud of their independence, impatient of foreign control, and determined to maintain the liberties which had descended to them. To these the Sequani offered themselves as champions. Among the aedui too there were fiery spirits who cherished the old traditions, and saw in the Roman alliance a prelude to annexation. And thus it was that when Caesar was appointed to Gaul, in every tribe and every sub-tribe, in every village and every family, there were two factions,[2] each under its own captain, each struggling for supremacy, each conspiring and fighting among themselves, and each seeking or leaning upon external support. In many, if not in all, of the tribes there was a senate, or counsel of elders, and these appear almost everywhere to have been aeduan and Roman in their sympathies. The Sequani, as the representatives of nationalism, knowing that they could not stand alone, had looked for friends elsewhere.

The Germans had long turned covetous eyes upon the rich cornfields and pastures from which the Rhine divided them. The Cimbri and Teutons had been but the vanguard of a multitude who were eager to follow. The fate of these invaders had checked the impulse for half a century, but the lesson was now forgotten. Ariovistus, a Bavarian prince, who spoke Gaelic like a native, and had probably long meditated conquest, came over into Franche- Comt?at the invitation of the Sequani, bringing his people with him. The few thousand families which were first introduced had been followed by fresh detachments; they had attacked and beaten the aedui, out of whose territories they intended to carve a settlement for themselves. They had taken hostages from them, and had broken down their authority, and the faction of the Sequani was now everywhere in the ascendant. The aedui, three years before Caesar came, had appealed to Rome for assistance, and the Senate had promised that the Governor of Gaul should support them. The Romans, hoping to temporize with the danger, had endeavored to conciliate Ariovistus, and in the year of Caesar's consulship had declared him a friend of the Roman people. Ariovistus, in turn, had pressed the aedui still harder, and had forced them to renounce the Roman alliance. Among the aedui, and throughout the country, the patriots were in the ascendant, and Ariovistus and his Germans were welcomed as friends and deliverers. Thoughtful persons in Rome had heard of these doings with uneasiness; an old aeduan chief had gone in person thither, to awaken the Senate to the growing peril; but the Senate had been too much occupied with its fears of Caesar, and agrarian laws, and dangers to the fish-ponds, to attend; and now another great movement had begun, equally alarming and still closer to the Roman border.

The Helvetii were old enemies. They were a branch of the Celtic race, who occupied modern Switzerland, hardy, bold mountaineers, and seasoned in constant war with their German neighbors. On them, too, the tide of migration from the north had pressed continuously. They had hitherto defended themselves successfully, but they were growing weary of these constant efforts. Their numbers were increasing, and their narrow valleys were too strait for them. They also had heard of fertile, scantily peopled lands in other parts, of which they could possess themselves by force or treaty, and they had already shown signs of restlessness. Many thousands of them had broken out at the time of the Cimbrian invasion. They had defeated Cassius Longinus, who was then consul, near their own border, and had annihilated his army. They had carried fire and sword down the left bank of the Rhone. They had united themselves with the Teutons, and had intended to accompany them into Italy. Their first enterprise failed. They perished in the great battle at Aix, and the parent tribe had remained quiet for forty years till a new generation had grown to manhood. Once more their ambition had revived. Like the Germans, they had formed friendships among the Gallic factions. Their reputation as warriors made them welcome to the patriots. In a fight for independence they would form a valuable addition to the forces of their countrymen. They had allies among the Sequani; they had allies in the anti-Roman party which had risen among the Aedui; and a plan had been formed in concert with their friends for a migration to the shores of the Bay of Biscay between the mouths of the Garonne and the Loire. The Cimbri and Teutons had passed away, but the ease with which the Cimbri had made the circuit of these districts had shown how slight resistance could be expected from the inhabitants. Perhaps their coming had been anticipated and prepared for. The older men among the Helvetii had discouraged the project when it was first mooted, but they had yielded to eagerness and enthusiasm, and it had taken at last a practical form. Double harvests had been raised; provision had been made of food and transport for a long march; and a complete exodus of the entire tribe with their wives and families had been finally resolved on.

If the Helvetii deserted Switzerland, the cantons would be immediately occupied by Germans, and a road would be opened into the province for the enemy whom the Romans had most reason to dread. The distinction between Germans and Gauls was not accurately known at Rome. They were confounded under the common name of Celts[3] or Barbarians. But they formed together an ominous cloud charged with forces of uncertain magnitude, but of the reality of which Italy had already terrible experience. Divitiacus, chief of the Aedui, who had carried to Rome the news of the inroads of Ariovistus, brought again in person thither the account of this fresh peril. Every large movement of population suggested the possibility of a fresh rush across the Alps. Little energy was to be expected from the Senate. But the body of the citizens were still sound at heart. Their lives and properties were at stake, and they could feel for the dignity of the Empire. The people had sent Pompey to crush the pirates and conquer Mithridates. The people now looked to Caesar, and instead of the "woods and forests" which the Senate designed for him, they had given him a five years' command on their western frontier.

The details of the problem before him Caesar had yet to learn, but with its general nature he must have intimately acquainted himself. Of course he had seen and spoken with Divitiacus. He was consul when Ariovistus was made "a friend of the Roman people." He must have been aware, therefore, of the introduction of the Germans over the Rhine. He could not tell what he might have first to do. There were other unpleasant symptoms on the side of Illyria and the Danube. From either quarter the storm might break upon him. No Roman general was ever sent upon an enterprise so fraught with complicated possibilities, and few with less experience of the realities of war.

The points in his favor were these. He was the ablest Roman then living, and he had the power of attracting and attaching the ablest men to his service. He had five years in which to look about him and to act at leisure--as much time as had been given to Pompey for the East. Like Pompey, too, he was left perfectly free. No senatorial officials could encumber him with orders from home. The people had given him his command, and to the people alone he was responsible. Lastly, and beyond everything, he could rely with certainty on the material with which he had to work. The Roman legionaries were no longer yeomen taken from the plough or shopkeepers from the street. They were men more completely trained in every variety of accomplishment than have perhaps ever followed a general into the field before or since. It was not enough that they could use sword and lance. The campaign on which Caesar was about to enter was fought with spade and pick and axe and hatchet. Corps of engineers he may have had; but if the engineers designed the work, the execution lay with the army. No limited department would have been equal to the tasks which every day demanded. On each evening after a march, a fortified camp was to be formed, with mound and trench, capable of resisting surprises, and demanding the labor of every single hand. Bridges had to be thrown over rivers. Ships and barges had to be built or repaired, capable of service against an enemy, on a scale equal to the requirements of an army, and in a haste which permitted no delay. A transport service there must have been organized to perfection; but there were no stores sent from Italy to supply the daily waste of material. The men had to mend and perhaps make their own clothes and shoes, and repair their own arms. Skill in the use of tools was not enough without the tools themselves. Had the spades and mattocks been supplied by contract, had the axes been of soft iron, fair to the eye and failing to the stroke, not a man in Caesar's army would have returned to Rome to tell the tale of its destruction. How the legionaries acquired these various arts, whether the Italian peasantry were generally educated in such occupations, or whether on this occasion there was a special selection of the best, of this we have no information. Certain only it was that men and instruments were as excellent in their kind as honesty and skill could make them; and, however degenerate the patricians and corrupt the legislature, there was sound stuff somewhere in the Roman constitution. No exertion, no forethought on the part of a commander could have extemporized such a variety of qualities. Universal practical accomplishments must have formed part of the training of the free Roman citizens. Admirable workmanship was still to be had in each department of manufacture, and every article with which Caesar was provided must have been the best of its kind.

The first quarter of the year 58 was consumed in preparations. Caesar's antagonists in the Senate were still raving against the acts of his consulship, threatening him with impeachment for neglecting Bibulus's interpellations, charging him with impiety for disregarding the weather, and clamoring for the suppression of his command. But Cicero's banishment damped the ardor of these gentlemen; after a few vicious efforts, they subsided into sullenness, and trusted to Ariovistus or the Helvetii to relieve them of their detested enemy. Caesar himself selected his officers. Cicero having declined to go as his lieutenant, he had chosen Labienus, who had acted with him, when tribune, in the prosecution of Rabirius, and had procured him the pontificate by giving the election to the people. Young men of rank in large numbers had forgotten party feeling, and had attached themselves to the expedition as volunteers to learn military experience. His own equipments were of the simplest. No common soldier was more careless of hardships than Caesar. His chief luxury was a favorite horse, which would allow no one but Caesar to mount him; a horse which had been bred in his own stables, and, from the peculiarity of a divided hoof, had led the augurs to foretell wonders for the rider of it. His arrangements were barely completed when news came in the middle of March that the Helvetii were burning their towns and villages, gathering their families into their wagons, and were upon the point of commencing their emigration. Their numbers, according to a register which was found afterward, were 368,000, of whom 92,000 were fighting men. They were bound for the West; and there were two roads, by one or other of which alone they could leave their country. One was on the right bank of the Rhone by the Pas de l'Ecluse, a pass between the Jura mountains and the river, so narrow that but two carts could go abreast along it; the other, and easier, was through Savoy, which was now Roman.

Under any aspect the transit of so vast a body through Roman territory could not but be dangerous. Savoy was the very ground on which Longinus had been destroyed. Yet it was in this direction that the Helvetii were preparing to pass, and would pass unless they were prevented; while in the whole Transalpine province there was but a single legion to oppose them. Caesar started on the instant. He reached Marseilles in a few days, joined his legion, collected a few levies in the Province, and hurried to Geneva. Where the river leaves the lake there was a bridge which the Helvetii had neglected to occupy. Caesar broke it, and thus secured a breathing time. The Helvetii, who were already on the move and were assembling in force a few miles off, sent to demand a passage. If it was refused, there was more than one spot between the lake and the Pas de l'Ecluse where the river could be forded. The Roman force was small, and Caesar postponed his reply.

It was the 1st of April; he promised an answer on the 15th. In the interval he threw up forts, dug trenches, and raised walls at every point where a passage could be attempted; and when the time was expired, he declined to permit them to enter the Province. They tried to ford; they tried boats; but at every point they were driven back. It remained for them to go by the Pas de l'Ecluse. For this route they required the consent of the Sequani; and, however willing the Sequani might be to see them in their neighbors' territories, they might object to the presence in their own of such a flight of devouring locusts.

Evidently, however, there was some general scheme, of which the entry of the Helvetii into Gaul was the essential part; and through the mediation of Dumnorix, an Aeduan and an ardent patriot, the Sequani were induced to agree.

The Province had been saved, but the exodus of the enormous multitude could no longer be prevented. If such waves of population were allowed to wander at pleasure, it was inevitable that sooner or later they would overflow the borders of the Empire. Caesar determined to show, at once and peremptorily, that these movements would not be permitted without the Romans' consent. Leaving Labienus to guard the forts on the Rhone, he hurried back to Italy, gathered up his three legions at Aquileia, raised two more at Turin with extreme rapidity, and returned with them by the shortest route over the Mont. The mountain tribes attacked him, but could not even delay his march. In seven days he had surmounted the passes, and was again with Labienus.

The Helvetii, meanwhile, had gone through the Pas de l'Ecluse, and were now among the Aedui, laying waste the country. It was early in the summer. The corn was green, the hay was still uncut, and the crops were being eaten off the ground. The Aedui threw themselves on the promised protection of Rome. Caesar crossed the Rhone above Lyons, and came up with the marauding hosts as they were leisurely passing in boats over the Saine. They had been twenty days upon the river, transporting their wagons and their families. Three quarters of them were on the other side. The Tigurini from Zurich, the most warlike of their tribes, were still on the left bank. The Tigurini had destroyed the army of Longinus, and on them the first retribution fell. Caesar cut them to pieces. A single day sufficed to throw a bridge over the Saine, and the Helvetii, who had looked for nothing less than to be pursued by six Roman legions, begged for peace. They were willing, they said, to go to any part of the country which Caesar would assign to them; and they reminded him that they might be dangerous if pushed to extremities. Caesar knew that they were dangerous. He had followed them because he knew it. He said that they must return the way that they had come. They must pay for the injuries which they had inflicted on the Aedui, and they must give him hostages for their obedience. The fierce mountaineers replied that they had been more used to demand hostages than to give them; and confident in their numbers, and in their secret allies among the Gauls, they marched on through the Aeduan territories up the level banks of the Saine, thence striking west toward Autun.

Caesar had no cavalry; but every Gaul could ride, and he raised a few thousand horse among his supposed allies. These he meant to employ to harass the Helvetian march; but they were secret traitors, under the influence of Dumnorix, and they fled at the first encounter. The Helvetii had thus the country at their mercy, and they laid it waste as they went, a day's march in advance of the Romans. So long as they kept by the river, Caesar's stores accompanied him in barges. He did not choose to let the Helvetii out of his sight, and when they left the Saine, and when he was obliged to follow, his provisions ran short. He applied to the Aeduan chiefs, who promised to furnish him, but they failed to do it. Ten days passed, and no supplies came in. He ascertained at last that there was treachery. Dumnorix and other Aeduan leaders were in correspondence with the enemy. The cavalry defeat and the other failures were thus explained. Caesar, who trusted much to gentleness and to personal influence, was unwilling to add the Aeduii to his open enemies. Dumnorix was the brother of Divitiacus, the reigning chief, whom Caesar had known in Rome. Divitiacus was sent for, confessed with tears his brother's misdeeds, and begged that he might be forgiven. Dumnorix was brought in. Caesar showed that he was aware of his conduct; but spoke kindly to him, and cautioned him for the future. The corn-carts, however, did not appear; supplies could not be dispensed with; and the Romans, leaving the Helvetii, struck off to Bibracte, on Mont Beauvray, the principal Aeduan town in the highlands of Nivernais. Unfortunately for themselves, the Helvetii thought the Romans were flying, and became in turn the pursuers. They gave Caesar an opportunity, and a single battle ended them and their migrations. The engagement lasted from noon till night. The Helvetii fought gallantly, and in numbers were enormously superior; but the contest was between skill and courage, sturdy discipline and wild valor; and it concluded as such contests always must. In these hand-to-hand engagements there were no wounded. Half the fighting men of the Swiss were killed; their camp was stormed; the survivors, with the remnant of the women and children, or such of them as were capable of moving (for thousands had perished, and little more than a third remained of those who had left Switzerland), straggled on to Langres, where they surrendered. Caesar treated the poor creatures with kindness and care. A few were settled in Gaul, where they afterward did valuable service. The rest were sent back to their own cantons, lest the Germans should take possession of their lands; and lest they should starve in the homes which they had desolated before their departure, they were provided with food out of the Province till their next crops were grown.

A victory so complete and so unexpected astonished the whole country. The peace party recovered the ascendency. Envoys came from all the Gaulish tribes to congratulate, and a diet of chiefs was held under Caesar's presidency, where Gaul and Roman seemed to promise one another eternal friendship. As yet, however, half the mischief only had been dealt with, and that the lighter part. The Helvetii were disposed of, but the Germans remained; and till Ariovistus was back across the Rhone, no permanent peace was possible. Hitherto Caesar had only received vague information about Ariovistus. When the diet was over, such of the chiefs as were sincere in their professions came to him privately and explained what the Germans were about. A hundred and twenty thousand of them were now settled near Belfort, and between the Vosges and the Rhine, with the connivance of the Sequani. More were coming, and in a short time Gaul would be full of them. They had made war on the Aedui; they were in correspondence with the anti-Roman factions; their object was the permanent occupation of the country.

Two months still remained of summer. Caesar was now conveniently near to the German positions. His army was in high spirits from its victory, and he himself was prompt in forming resolutions and swift in executing them. An injury to the Aedui could be treated as an injury to the Romans, which it would be dishonor to pass over. If the Germans were allowed to overrun Gaul, they might soon be seen again in Italy.

Ariovistus was a "friend of Rome." Caesar had been himself a party to the conferring this distinction upon him. As a friend, therefore, he was in the first instance to be approached. Caesar sent to invite him to a conference. Ariovistus, it seemed, set small value upon his honors. He replied that if he needed anything from Caesar, he would go to Caesar and ask for it. If Caesar required anything from him, Caesar might do the same. Meanwhile Caesar was approaching a part of Gaul which belonged to himself by right of conquest, and he wished to know the meaning of the presence of a Roman army there.

After such an answer, politeness ceased to be necessary. Caesar rejoined that since Ariovistus estimated so lightly his friendship with the Romans as to refuse an amicable meeting, he would inform him briefly of his demands upon him. The influx of Germans on the Rhine must cease: no more must come in. He must restore the hostages which he had taken from the Aedui, and do them no further hurt. If Ariovistus complied, the Romans would continue on good terms with him. If not, he said that by a decree of the Senate the Governor of Gaul was ordered to protect the Aedui, and he intended to do it.

Ariovistus answered that he had not interfered with the Romans; and the Romans had no right to interfere with him. Conquerors treated their subjects as they pleased. The Aedui had begun the quarrel with him. They had been defeated, and were now his vassals. If Caesar chose to come between him and his subjects, he would have an opportunity of seeing how Germans could fight who had not for fourteen years slept under a roof.

It was reported that a large body of Suevi were coming over the Rhine to swell Ariovistus's force, and that Ariovistus was on the point of advancing to seize Besanen. Besanen was a position naturally strong, being surrounded on three sides by the Doubs. It was full of military stores, and was otherwise important for the control of the Sequani. Caesar advanced swiftly and took possession of the place, and announced that he meant to go and look for Ariovistus.

The army so far had gained brilliant successes, but the men were not yet fully acquainted with the nature of their commander. They had never yet looked Germans in the face, and imagination magnifies the unknown. Roman merchants and the Gauls of the neighborhood brought stories of the gigantic size and strength of these northern warriors. The glare of their eyes was reported to be so fierce that it could not be borne. They were wild, wonderful, and dreadful. Young officers, patricians and knights, who had followed Caesar for a little mild experience, began to dislike the notion of these new enemies. Some applied for leave of absence; others, though ashamed to ask to be allowed to leave the army, cowered in their tents with sinking hearts, made their wills, and composed last messages for their friends. The centurions caught the alarm from their superiors, and the legionaries from the centurions. To conceal their fear of the Germans, the men discovered that, if they advanced farther, it would be through regions where provisions could not follow them, and that they would be starved in the forests. At length, Caesar was informed that if he gave the order to march, the army would refuse to move.

Confident in himself, Caesar had the power, so indispensable for a soldier, of inspiring confidence in others as soon as they came to know what he was. He called his officers together. He summoned the centurions, and rebuked them sharply for questioning his purposes. The German king, he said, had been received at his own request into alliance with the Romans, and there was no reason to suppose that he meant to break with them. Most likely he would do what was required of him. If not, was it to be conceived that they were afraid? Marius had beaten these same Germans. Even the Swiss had beaten them. They were no more formidable than other barbarians. They might trust their commander for the commissariat. The harvest was ripe, and the difficulties were nothing. As to the refusal to march, he did not believe in it. Romans never mutinied, save through the rapacity or incompetence of their general. His life was a witness that he was not rapacious, and his victory over the Helvetii that as yet he had made no mistake. He should order the advance on the next evening, and it would then be seen whether sense of duty or cowardice was the stronger. If others declined, Caesar said that he should go forward alone with the legion which he knew would follow him, the 10th, which was already his favorite.

The speech was received with enthusiasm. The 10th thanked Caesar for his compliment to them. The rest, officers and men, declared their willingness to follow wherever he might lead them. He started with Divitiacus for a guide; and, passing Belfort, came in seven days to Cernay or to some point near it. Ariovistus was now but four-and-twenty miles from him. Since Caesar had come so far, Ariovistus said that he was willing to meet him. Day and place were named, the conditions being that the armies should remain in their ranks, and that Caesar and he might each bring a guard of horse to the interview. He expected that Caesar would be contented with an escort of the Aeduan cavalry. Caesar, knowing better than to trust himself with Gauls, mounted his 10th legion, and with them proceeded to the spot which Ariovistus had chosen. It was a tumulus, in the centre of a large plain equidistant from the two camps. The guard on either side remained two hundred paces in the rear. The German prince and the Roman general met on horseback at the mound, each accompanied by ten of his followers. Caesar spoke first and fairly. He reminded Ariovistus of his obligations to the Romans. The Aedui, he said, had from immemorial time been the leading tribe in Gaul. The Romans had an alliance with them of old standing, and never deserted their friends. He required Ariovistas to desist from attacking them, and to return their hostages. He consented that the Germans already across the Rhine might remain in Gaul, but he demanded a promise that no more should be brought over.

Ariovistus haughtily answered that he was a great king; that he had come into Gaul by the invitation of the Gauls themselves; that the territory which he occupied was a gift from them; and that the hostages of which Caesar spoke had remained with him with their free consent. The Aedui, he said, had begun the war, and, being defeated, were made justly to pay forfeit. He had sought the friendship of the Romans, expecting to profit by it. If friendship meant the taking away his subjects from him, he desired no more of such friendship. The Romans had their Province. It was enough for them, and they might remain there unmolested. But Caesar's presence so far beyond his own borders was a menace to his own independence, and his independence he intended to maintain. Caesar must go away out of those parts, or he and his Germans would know how to deal with him.

Then, speaking perhaps more privately, he told Caesar that he knew something of Rome and of the Roman Senate, and had learnt how the great people there stood affected toward the Governor of Gaul. Certain members of the Roman aristocracy had sent him messages to say that if he killed Caesar they would hold it a good service done,[4] and would hold him their friend forever. He did not wish, he said, to bind himself to these noble persons. He would prefer Caesar rather; and would fight Caesar's battles for him anywhere in the world if Caesar would but retire and leave him. Ariovistus was misled, not unnaturally, by these strange communications from the sovereign rulers of the Empire. He did not know, he could not know, that the genius of Rome and the true chief of Rome were not in the treacherous Senate, but were before him there on the field in the persons of Caesar and his legions.

More might have passed between them; but Ariovistus thought to end the conference by a stroke of treachery. His German guard had stolen round to where the Romans stood, and, supposing that they had Gauls to deal with, were trying to surround and disarm them. The men of the 10th legion stood firm; Caesar fell back and joined them, and, contenting themselves with simply driving off the enemy, they rode back to the camp.

[Sidenote: B.C. 57.] The army was now passionate for an engagement. Ariovistus affected a desire for further communication, and two officers were despatched to hear what he had to say; but they were immediately seized and put in chains, and the Germans advanced to within a few miles of the Roman outposts. The Romans lay entrenched near Cernay. The Germans were at Colmar. Caesar offered battle, which Ariovistus declined. Cavalry fights happened daily which led to nothing. Caesar then formed a second camp, smaller but strongly fortified, within sight of the enemy, and threw two legions into it. Ariovistus attacked them, but he was beaten back with loss. The "wise women" advised him to try no more till the new moon. But Caesar would not wait for the moon, and forced an engagement. The wives and daughters of the Germans rushed about their camp, with streaming hair, adjuring their countrymen to save them from slavery. The Germans fought like heroes; but they could not stand against the short sword and hand-to-hand grapple of the legionaries. Better arms and better discipline again asserted the superiority; and in a few hours the invaders were flying wildly to the Rhine. Young Publius Crassus, the son of the millionaire, pursued with the cavalry. A few swam the river; a few, Ariovistus among them, escaped in boats; all the rest, men and women alike, were cut down and killed. The Suevi, who were already on the Rhine, preparing to cross, turned back into their forests; and the two immediate perils which threatened the peace of Gaul had been encountered and trampled out in a single summer. The first campaign was thus ended. The legions were distributed in winter quarters among the Sequani, the contrivers of the mischief; and Labienus was left in charge of them. Caesar went back over the Alps to the Cisalpine division of the Province to look into the administration and to communicate with his friends in Rome.

In Gaul there was outward quiet; but the news of the Roman victories penetrated the farthest tribes and agitated the most distant households on the shores of the North Sea. The wintering of the legions beyond the province was taken to indicate an intention of permanent conquest. The Gauls proper were divided and overawed; but the Belgians of the north were not prepared to part so easily with their liberty. The Belgians considered that they too were menaced, and that now or never was the time to strike for their independence. They had not been infected with Roman manners. They had kept the merchants from their borders with their foreign luxuries. The Nervii, the fiercest of them, as the abstemious Caesar marks with approbation, were water-drinkers, and forbade wine to be brought among them, as injurious to their sinews and their courage. Caesar learnt while in Italy from Labienus that the Belgae were mustering and combining. A second vast horde of Germans were in Flanders and Artois; men of the same race with the Belgae and in active confederacy with them. They might have been left in peace, far off as they were, had they sat still; but the notes of their preparations were sounding through the country and feeding the restless spirit which was stunned but not subdued.

Caesar, on his own responsibility, raised two more legions and sent them across the Alps in the spring. When the grass began to grow he followed himself. Suddenly, before any one looked for him, he was on the Marne with his army. The Remi (people of Rheims), startled by his unexpected appearance, sent envoys with their submission and offers of hostages. The other Belgian tribes, they said, were determined upon war, and were calling all their warriors under arms. Their united forces were reported to amount to 300,000. The Bellovaci from the mouth of the Seine had sent 60,000; the Suessiones from Soissons 50,000; the Nervii, between the Sambre and the Scheldt, 50,000; Arras and Amiens, 25,000; the coast tribes, 36,000; and the tribes between the Ardennes and the Rhine, called collectively Germani, 40,000 more. This irregular host was gathered in the forests between Laon and Soissons.

Caesar did not wait for them to move. He advanced at once to Rheims, where he called the Senate together and encouraged them to be constant to the Roman alliance. He sent a party of Aedui down the Seine to harass the territory of the Bellovaci and recall them to their own defence; and he went on himself to the Aisne, which he crossed by a bridge already existing at Berry-au-Bac. There, with the bridge and river at his back, he formed an entrenched camp of extraordinary strength, with a wall 12 feet high and a fosse 22 feet deep. Against an attack with modern artillery such defences would, of course, be idle. As the art of war then stood, they were impregnable. In this position Caesar waited, leaving six cohorts on the left bank to guard the other end of the bridge. The Belgae came forward and encamped in his front. Their watch-fires at night were seen stretching along a line eight miles wide. Caesar, after feeling his way with his cavalry, found a rounded ridge projecting like a promontory into the plain where the Belgian host was lying. On this he advanced his legions, protecting his flanks with continuous trenches and earthworks, on which were placed heavy cross-bows, the ancient predecessors of cannon. Between these lines, if he attacked the enemy and failed, he had a secure retreat. A marsh lay between the armies; and each waited for the other to cross. The Belgians, impatient of delay, flung themselves suddenly on one side and began to pour across the river, intending to destroy the cohorts on the other bank, to cut the bridge, and burn and plunder among the Remi. Caesar calmly sent back his cavalry and his archers and slingers. They caught the enemy in the water or struggling out of it in confusion; all who had got over were killed; multitudes were slaughtered in the river; others, trying to cross on the bodies of their comrades, were driven back. The confederates, shattered at a single defeat, broke up like an exploded shell. Their provisions had run short. They melted away and dispersed to their homes, Labienus pursuing and cutting down all that he could overtake.

The Roman loss was insignificant in this battle. The most remarkable feature in Caesar's campaigns, and that which indicates most clearly his greatness as a commander, was the smallness of the number of men that he ever lost, either by the sword or by wear and tear. No general was ever so careful of his soldiers' lives.

Soissons, a fortified Belgian town, surrendered the next day. From Soissons Caesar marched on Breteuil and thence on Amiens, which surrendered also. The Bellovaci sent in their submission, the leaders of the war party having fled to Britain. Caesar treated them all with scrupulous forbearance, demanding nothing but hostages for their future good behavior. His intention at this time was apparently not to annex any of these tribes to Rome, but to settle the country in a quasi-independence under an Aeduan hegemony.

But the strongest member of the confederacy was still unsubdued. The hardy, brave, and water-drinking Nervii remained defiant. The Nervii would send no envoys; they would listen to no terms of peace.[5] Caesar learnt that they were expecting to be joined by the Aduatuci, a tribe of pure Germans, who had been left behind near Liege at the time of the invasion of the

Teutons. Preferring to engage them separately, he marched from Amiens through Cambray, and sent forward some officers and pioneers to choose a spot for a camp on the Sambre. Certain Gauls, who had observed his habits on march, deserted to the Nervii, and informed them that usually a single legion went in advance, the baggage-wagons followed, and the rest of the army came in the rear. By a sudden attack in front they could overwhelm the advanced troops, plunder the carts, and escape before they could be overtaken. It happened that on this occasion the order was reversed. The country was enclosed with thick fences, which required to be cut through. Six legions marched in front, clearing a road; the carts came next, and two legions behind. The site selected by the officers was on the left bank of the Sambre at Maubeuge, fifty miles above Namur. The ground sloped easily down to the river, which was there about a yard in depth. There was a corresponding rise on the other side, which was densely covered with wood. In this wood the whole force of the Nervii lay concealed, a few only showing themselves on the water side. Caesar's light horse which had gone forward, seeing a mere handful of stragglers, rode through the stream and skirmished with them; but the enemy retired under cover; the horse did not pursue; the six legions came up, and, not dreaming of the nearness of the enemy, laid aside their arms and went to work intrenching with spade and mattock. The baggage-wagons began presently to appear at the crest of the hill, the signal for which the Nervii had waited; and in a moment all along the river sixty thousand of them rushed out of the forest, sent the cavalry flying, and came on so impetuously that, as Caesar said, they seemed to be in the wood, in the water, and up the opposite bank at sword's point with the legions at the same moment. The surprise was complete: the Roman army was in confusion. Many of the soldiers were scattered at a distance, cutting turf. None were in their ranks, and none were armed. Never in all his campaigns was Caesar in greater danger. He could himself give no general orders which there was time to observe. Two points only, he said, were in his favor. The men themselves were intelligent and experienced, and knew what they had to do; and the officers were all present, because he had directed that none of them should leave their companies till the camp was completed. The troops were spread loosely in their legions along the brow of the ridge. Caesar joined the 10th on his right wing, and had but time to tell the men to be cool and not to agitate themselves, when the enemy were upon them. So sudden was the onslaught that they could neither put their helmets on, nor strip the coverings from their shields, nor find their places in the ranks. They fought where they stood among thick hedges which obstructed the sight of what was passing elsewhere. Though the Aduatuci had not come up, the Nervii had allies with them from Arras and the Somme. The allies encountered the 8th, 9th, 10th, and 11th legions, and were driven rapidly back down the hill through the river. The Romans, led by Labienus, crossed in pursuit, followed them into the forest, and took their camp. The Nervii meanwhile flung themselves with all their force on the two legions on the left, the 12th and 7th, enveloped them with their numbers, penetrated behind them, and fell upon the baggage-wagons. The light troops and the camp-followers fled in all directions. The legionaries, crowded together in confusion, were fighting at disadvantage, and were falling thick and fast. A party of horse from Tries, who had come to treat with Caesar, thought that all was lost, and rode off to tell their countrymen that the Romans were destroyed.

Caesar, who was in the other wing, learning late what was going on, hurried to the scene. He found the standards huddled together, the men packed so close that they could not use their swords, almost all the officers killed or wounded, and one of the best of them, Sextius Baculus (Caesar always paused in his narrative to note any one who specially distinguished himself), scarce able to stand. Caesar had come up unarmed. He snatched a shield from a soldier, and, bareheaded, flew to the front. He was known; he addressed the centurions by their names. He bade them open their ranks and give the men room to strike. His presence and his calmness gave them back their confidence. In the worst extremities he observes that soldiers will fight well under their commander's eye. The cohorts formed into order. The enemy was checked. The two legions from the rear, who had learnt the danger from the flying camp-followers, came up. Labienus, from the opposite hill, saw what had happened, and sent the 10th legion back. All was now changed. The fugitives, ashamed of their cowardice, rallied, and were eager to atone for it. The Nervii fought with a courage which filled Caesar with admiration--men of greater spirit he said that he had never seen. As their first ranks fell, they piled the bodies of their comrades into heaps, and from the top of them hurled back the Roman javelins. They would not fly; they dropped where they stood; and the battle ended only with their extermination. Out of 600 senators there survived but three; out of 60,000 men able to bear arms, only 500. The aged of the tribe, and the women and children, who had been left in the morasses for security, sent in their surrender, their warriors being all dead. They professed to fear lest they might be destroyed by neighboring clans who were on bad terms with them. Caesar received them and protected them, and gave severe injunctions that they should suffer no injury.

By the victory over the Nervii the Belgian confederacy was almost extinguished. The German Aduatuci remained only to be brought to submission. They had been on their way to join their countrymen; they were too late for the battle, and returned and shut themselves up in Namur, the strongest position in the Low Countries. Caesar, after a short rest, pushed on and came under their walls. The Aduatuci were a race of giants, and were at first defiant. When they saw the Romans' siege-towers in preparation, they could not believe that men so small could move such vast machines. When the towers began to approach, they lost heart and sued for terms. Caesar promised to spare their lives and properties if they surrendered immediately, but he refused to grant conditions. They had prayed to be allowed to keep their arms; affecting to believe, like the Nervii, that they would be in danger from the Gauls if they were unable to defend themselves. Caesar undertook that they should have no hurt, but he insisted that their arms must be given up. They affected obedience. They flung their swords and lances over the walls till the ditch was filled with them. They opened their gates; the Romans occupied them, but were forbidden to enter, that there might be no plundering. It seems that there was a desperate faction among the Aduatuci who had been for fighting to extremity. A third part of the arms had been secretly reserved, and after midnight the tribe sallied with all their force, hoping to catch the Romans sleeping. Caesar was not to be surprised a second time. Expecting that some such attempt might be made, he had prepared piles of fagots in convenient places. These bonfires were set blazing in an instant. By their red light the legions formed; and, after a desperate but unequal combat, the Germans were driven into the town again, leaving 4,000 dead. In the morning the gates were broken down, and Namur was taken without more resistance. Caesar's usual practice was gentleness. He honored brave men, and never punished bold and open opposition. Of treachery he made a severe example. Namur was condemned. The Aduatuci within its walls were sold into slavery, and the contractors who followed the army returned the number of prisoners whom they had purchased at 53,000. Such captives were the most valuable form of spoil.

The Belgae were thus crushed as completely as the Gauls had been crushed in the previous year. Publius Crassus had meanwhile made a circuit of Brittany, and had received the surrender of the maritime tribes. So great was the impression made by these two campaigns, that the Germans beyond the Rhine sent envoys with offers of submission. The second season was over. Caesar left the legions in quarters about Chartres, Orleans, and Blois. He himself returned to Italy again, where his presence was imperatively required. The Senate, on the news of his successes, had been compelled, by public sentiment, to order an extraordinary thanksgiving; but there were men who were anxious to prevent Caesar from achieving any further victories since Ariovistus had failed to destroy him.

[1] Perhaps in consequence of the Catiline conspiracy.

[2] "In Galli?non solum in omnibus civitatibus atque in omnibus pagis partibusque sed paene etiam in singulis domibus factiones sunt, earumque factionum principes sunt qui summam auctoritatem eorum judicio habere existimantur.... Haec est ratio in summ?totius Galliae, namque omnes civitates in partes divisae sunt duas. Cum Caesar in Galliam venit, alterius factionis principes erant Haedui, alterius Sequani."--De Bello Gallico, lib. vi. capp. 11, 12.

[3] Even Dion Cassius speaks of the Germans as Keltoi.

[4] "Id se ab ipsis per eorum nuntios compertum habere, quorum omnium gratiam atque amicitiam ejus morte redimere posset."--_De Bell. Gall_., i. 44.

[5] Caesar thus records his admiration of the Nervian character: "Quorum de natur?moribusque Caesar cum quaereret sic reperiebat, nullum aditum esse ad eos mercatoribus; nihil pati vini reliquarumque rerum ad luxuriam pertinentium inferri, quod iis rebus relanguescere animos eorum et remitti virtutem existimarent: esse homines feros magnaeque virtutis; increpitare atque incusare reliquos Belgas qui se populo Romano dedidissent patriamque virtutem projecissent; confirmare sese neque legatos missuros neque ullam conditionem pacis accepturos."--_De Bell. Gall_., ii. 15.

CHAPTER XV.

[Sidenote B.C.58] Before his own catastrophe, and before he could believe that he was in danger, Cicero had discerned clearly the perils which threatened the State. The Empire was growing more extensive. The "Tritons of the fish-ponds" still held the reins; and believed their own supreme duty was to divide the spoils among themselves. The pyramid was standing on its point. The mass which rested on it was becoming more portentous and unwieldy. The Senate was the official power; the armies were the real power; and the imagination of the Senate was that after each conquest the soldiers would be dismissed back into humble life unrewarded, while the noble lords took possession of the new acquisitions, and added new millions to their fortunes. All this Cicero knew, and yet he had persuaded himself that it could continue without bringing on a catastrophe. He saw his fellow-senators openly bribed; he saw the elections become a mere matter of money. He saw adventurers pushing themselves into office by steeping themselves in debt, and paying their debts by robbing the provincials. He saw these high-born scoundrels coming home loaded with treasure, buying lands and building palaces, and, when brought to trial, purchasing the consciences of their judges. Yet he had considered such phenomena as the temporary accidents of a constitution which was still the best that could be conceived, and every one that doubted the excellence of it he had come to regard as an enemy of mankind. So long as there was free speech in Senate and platform for orators like himself, all would soon be well again. Had not he, a mere country gentleman's son, risen under it to wealth and consideration? and was not his own rise a sufficient evidence that there was no real injustice? Party struggles were over, or had no excuse for continuance. Sylla's constitution had been too narrowly aristocratic. But Sylla's invidious laws had been softened by compromise. The tribunes had recovered their old privileges. The highest offices of State were open to the meanest citizen who was qualified for them. Individuals of merit might have been kept back for a time by jealousy; the Senate had too long objected to the promotion of Pompey; but their opposition had been overcome by purely constitutional means. The great general had obtained his command by land and sea; he, Cicero, having by eloquent speech proved to the people that he ought to be nominated. What could any one wish for more? And yet Senate and Forum were still filled with faction, quarrel, and discontent! One interpretation only Cicero had been able to place on such a phenomenon. In Rome, as in all great communities, there were multitudes of dissolute, ruined wretches, the natural enemies of property and order. Bankrupt members of the aristocracy had lent themselves to these people as their leaders, and had been the cause of all the trouble of the past years. If such renegades to their order could be properly discouraged or extinguished, Cicero had thought that there would be nothing more to desire. Catiline he had himself made an end of to his own immortal glory, but now Catiline had revived in Clodius; and Clodius, so far from being discouraged, was petted and encouraged by responsible statesmen who ought to have known better. Caesar had employed him; Crassus had employed him; even Pompey had stooped to connect himself with the scandalous young incendiary, and had threatened to call in the army if the Senate attempted to repeal Caesar's iniquitous laws.[1] Still more inexplicable was the ingratitude of the aristocracy and their friends, the "boni" or good-- the "Conservatives of the State," [2] as Cicero still continued to call Caesar's opponents. He respected them; he loved them; he had done more for their cause than any single man in the Empire; and yet they had never recognized his services by word or deed. He had felt tempted to throw up public life in disgust, and retire to privacy and philosophy.

So Cicero had construed the situation before his exile, and he had construed it ill. If he had wished to retire he could not. He had been called to account for the part of his conduct for which he most admired himself. The ungracious Senate, as guilty as he, if guilt there had been, had left him to bear the blame of it, and he saw himself driven into banishment by an insolent reprobate, a patrician turned Radical and demagogue, Publius Clodius. Indignity could be carried no farther.

Clodius is the most extraordinary figure in this extraordinary period. He had no character. He had no distinguished talent save for speech; he had no policy; he was ready to adopt any cause or person which for the moment was convenient to him; and yet for five years this man was the omnipotent leader of the Roman mob. He could defy justice, insult the consuls, beat the tribunes, parade the streets with a gang of armed slaves, killing persons disagreeable to him; and in the Senate itself he had his high friends and connections who threw a shield over him when his audacity had gone beyond endurance. We know Clodius only from Cicero; and a picture of him from a second hand might have made his position more intelligible, if not more reputable. Even in Rome it is scarcely credible that the Clodius of Cicero could have played such a part, or that the death of such a man should have been regarded as a national calamity. Cicero says that Clodius revived Catiline's faction; but what was Catiline's faction? or how came Catiline to have a faction which survived him?

Be this as it may, Clodius had banished Cicero, and had driven him away over the seas to Greece, there, for sixteen months, to weary Heaven and his friends with his lamentations. Cicero had refused Caesar's offered friendship; Caesar had not cared to leave so powerful a person free to support the intended attacks on his legislation, and had permitted, perhaps had encouraged, the prosecution. Cicero out of the way, the second person whose presence in Rome Caesar thought might be inconvenient, Marcus Cato, had been got rid of by a process still more ingenious. The aristocracy pretended that the acts of Caesar's consulship had been invalid through disregard of the interdictions of Bibulus; and one of those acts had been the reduction of Clodius to the order of plebeians. If none of them were valid, Clodius was not legally tribune, and no commission which Clodius might confer through the people would have validity. A service was discovered by which Cato was tempted, and which he was induced to accept at Clodius's hands. Thus he was at once removed from the city, and it was no longer open to him to deny that Caesar's laws had been properly passed. The work on which he was sent deserves a few words. The kingdom of Cyprus had long been attached to the crown of Egypt. Ptolemy Alexander, dying in the year 80, had bequeathed both Egypt and Cyprus to Rome; but the Senate had delayed to enter on their bequest, preferring to share the fines which Ptolemy's natural heirs were required to pay for being spared. One of these heirs, Ptolemy Auletes, or "the Piper," father of the famous Cleopatra, was now reigning in Egypt, and was on the point of being expelled by his subjects. He had been driven to extortion to raise a subsidy for the senators, and he had made himself universally abhorred. Ptolemy of Cyprus had been a better sovereign, but a less prudent client. He had not overtaxed his people; he had kept his money. Clodius, if Cicero's story is true, had a private grudge against him. Clodius had fallen among Cyprian pirates. Ptolemy had not exerted himself for his release, and he had suffered unmentionable indignities. At all events, the unfortunate king was rich, and was unwilling to give what was expected of him. Clodius, on the plea that the King of Cyprus protected pirates, persuaded the Assembly to vote the annexation of the island; and Cato, of all men, was prevailed on by the mocking tribune to carry out the resolution. He was well pleased with his mission, though he wished it to appear to be forced upon him. Ptolemy poisoned himself; Cato earned the glory of adding a new province to the Empire, and did not return for two years, when he brought 7,000 talents--a million and a half of English money--to the Roman treasury.

Cicero and Cato being thus put out of the way--Caesar being absent in Gaul, and Pompey looking on without interfering--Clodius had amused himself with legislation. He gratified his corrupt friends in the Senate by again abolishing the censor's power to expel them. He restored cheap corn establishments in the city--the most demoralizing of all the measures which the democracy had introduced to swell their numbers. He re- established the political clubs, which were hot-beds of distinctive radicalism. He took away the right of separate magistrates to lay their vetoes on the votes of the sovereign people, and he took from the Senate such power as they still possessed of regulating the government of the provinces, and passed it over to the Assembly. These resolutions, which reduced the administration to a chaos, he induced the people to decree by irresistible majorities. One measure only he passed which deserved commendation, though Clodius deserved none for introducing it. He put an end to the impious pretence of "observing the heavens," of which conservative officials had availed themselves to obstruct unwelcome motions. Some means were, no doubt, necessary to check the precipitate passions of the mob; but not means which turned into mockery the slight surviving remnants of ancient Roman reverence.

In general politics the young tribune had no definite predilections. He had threatened at one time to repeal Caesar's laws himself. He attacked alternately the chiefs of the army and of the Senate, and the people let him do what he pleased without withdrawing their confidence from him. He went everywhere spreading terror with his body-guard of slaves. He quarrelled with the consuls, beat their lictors, and wounded Gabinius himself. Pompey professed to be in alarm for his life, and to be unable to appear in the streets. The state of Rome at this time has been well described by a modern historian as a "Walpurgis dance of political witches." [3]

Clodius was a licensed libertine; but license has its limits. He had been useful so far; but a rein was wanted for him, and Pompey decided at last that Cicero might now be recalled. Clodius's term of office ran out. The tribunes for the new year were well disposed to Cicero. The new consuls were Lentulus, a moderate aristocrat, and Cicero's personal friend, and Metellus Nepos, who would do what Pompey told him. Caesar had been consulted by letter and had given his assent. Cicero, it might be thought, had learnt his lesson, and there was no desire of protracting his penance. There were still difficulties, however. Cicero, smarting from wrath and mortification, was more angry with the aristocrats, who had deserted him, than with his open enemies. His most intimate companions, he bitterly said, had been false to him. He was looking regretfully on Caesar's offers,[4] and cursing his folly for having rejected them. The people, too, would not sacrifice their convictions at the first bidding for the convenience of their leaders; and had neither forgotten nor forgiven the killing of the Catiline conspirators; while Cicero, aware of the efforts which were being made, had looked for new allies in an imprudent quarter. His chosen friend on the conservative side was now Annius Milo, one of the new tribunes, a man as disreputable as Clodius himself; deep in debt and looking for a province to indemnify himself--famous hitherto in the schools of gladiators, in whose arts he was a proficient, and whose services were at his disposal for any lawless purpose.

[Sidenote: B.C. 57.] A decree of banishment could only be recalled by the people who had pronounced it. Clodius, though no longer in office, was still the idol of the mob; and two of the tribunes, who were at first well inclined to Cicero, had been gained over by him. As early as possible, on the first day of the new year, Lentulus Spinther brought Cicero's case before the Senate. A tribune reminded him of a clause, attached to the sentence of exile, that no citizen should in future move for its repeal. The Senate hesitated, perhaps catching at the excuse; but at length, after repeated adjournments, they voted that the question should be proposed to the Assembly. The day fixed was the 25th of January. In anticipation of a riot the temples on the Forum were occupied with guards. The Forum itself and the senate-house were in possession of Clodius and his gang. Clodius maintained that the proposal to be submitted to the people was itself illegal, and ought to be resisted by force. Fabricius, one of the tribunes, had been selected to introduce it. When Fabricius presented himself on the Rostra, there was a general rush to throw him down. The Forum was in theory still a sacred spot, where the carrying of arms was forbidden; but the new age had forgotten such obsolete superstitions. The guards issued out of the temples with drawn swords. The people were desperate and determined. Hundreds were killed on both sides; Quintus Cicero, who was present for his brother, narrowly escaping with life. The Tiber, Cicero says--perhaps with some exaggeration--was covered with floating bodies; the sewers were choked; the bloody area of the Forum had to be washed with sponges. Such a day had not been seen in Rome since the fight between Cinna and Octavius.[5] The mob remained masters of the field, and Cicero's cause had to wait for better times. Milo had been active in the combat, and Clodius led his victorious bands to Milo's house to destroy it. Milo brought an action against him for violence; but Clodius was charmed even against forms of law. There was no censor as yet chosen, and without a censor the praetors pretended that they could not entertain the prosecution. Finding law powerless, Milo imitated his antagonist. He, too, had his band of gladiators about him; and the streets of the Capital were entertained daily by fights between the factions of Clodius and Milo. The Commonwealth of the Scipios, the laws and institutions of the mistress of the civilized world, had become the football of ruffians. Time and reflection brought some repentance at last. Toward the summer "the cause of order" rallied. The consuls and Pompey exerted themselves to reconcile the more respectable citizens to Cicero's return; and, with the ground better prepared, the attempt was renewed with more success. In July the recall was again proposed in the Senate, and Clodius was alone in opposing it. When it was laid before the Assembly, Clodius made another effort; but voters had been brought up from other parts of Italy who outnumbered the city rabble; Milo and his gladiators were in force to prevent another burst of violence; and the great orator and statesman was given back to his country. Sixteen months he had been lamenting himself in Greece, bewailing his personal ill-treatment. He was the single object of his own reflections. In his own most sincere convictions he was the centre on which the destinies of Rome revolved. He landed at Brindisi on the 5th of August. His pardon had not yet been decreed, though he knew that it was coming. The happy news arrived in a day or two, and he set out in triumph for Rome. The citizens of Brindisi paid him their compliments; deputations came to congratulate from all parts of Italy. Outside the city every man of note of all the orders, save a few of his declared enemies, were waiting to receive him. The roofs and steps of the temples were thronged with spectators. Crowds attended him to the Capitol, where he went to pour out his gratitude to the gods, and welcomed him home with shouts of applause.

Had he been wise he would have seen that the rejoicing was from the lips outward; that fine words were not gold; that Rome and its factions were just where he had left them, or had descended one step lower. But Cicero was credulous of flattery when it echoed his own opinions about himself. The citizens, he persuaded himself, were penitent for their ingratitude to the most illustrious of their countrymen. The acclamations filled him with the delighted belief that he was to resume his place at the head of the State; and, as he could not forgive his disgrace, his first object in the midst of his triumph was to revenge himself on those who had caused it. Speeches of acknowledgment he had naturally to make both to the Senate and the Assembly. In addressing the people he was moderately prudent; he glanced at the treachery of his friends, but he did not make too much of it. He praised his own good qualities, but not extravagantly. He described Pompey as "the wisest, best, and greatest of all men that had been, were, or ever would be." Himself he compared to Marius returning also from undeserved exile, and he delicately spoke in honor of a name most dear to the Roman plebs, But he, he said, unlike Marius, had no enemies but the enemies of his country. He had no retaliation to demand for his own wrongs. If he punished bad citizens, it would be by doing well himself; if he punished false friends, it would be by never again trusting them. His first and his last object would be to show his gratitude to his fellow- citizens.[6]

Such language was rational and moderate. He understood his audience, and he kept his tongue under a bridle. But his heart was burning in him; and what he could not say in the Forum he thought he might venture on with impunity in the Senate, which might be called his own dunghill. His chief wrath was at the late consuls. They were both powerful men. Gabinius was Pompey's chief supporter. Calpurnius Piso was Caesar's father-in-law. Both had been named to the government of important provinces; and, if authority was not to be brought into contempt, they deserved at least a show of outward respect. Cicero lived to desire their friendship, to affect a value for them, and to regret his violence; but they had consented to his exile; and careless of decency, and oblivious of the chances of the future, he used his opportunity to burst out upon them in language in which the foulest ruffian in the streets would have scarcely spoken of the first magistrates of the Republic. Piso and Gabinius, he said, were thieves, not consuls. They had been friends of Catiline, and had been enemies to himself, because he had baffled the conspiracy. Piso could not pardon the death of Cethegus. Gabinius regretted in Catiline himself the loss of his lover.[7] Gabinius, he said, had been licentious in his youth; he had ruined his fortune; he had supplied his extravagance by pimping; and had escaped his creditors only by becoming tribune. "Behold him," Cicero said, "as he appeared when consul at a meeting called by the arch-thief Clodius, full of wine, and sleep, and fornication, his hair moist, his eyes heavy, his cheeks flaccid, and declaring, with a voice thick with drink, that he disapproved of putting citizens to death without trial." [8] As to Piso, his best recommendation was a cunning gravity of demeanor, concealing mere vacuity. Piso knew nothing--neither law, nor rhetoric, nor war, nor his fellow-men. "His face was the face of some half-human brute." "He was like a negro, a thing [_negotium_] without sense or savor, a Cappadocian picked out of a drove in the slave-market." [9]

Cicero was not taking the best means to regain his influence in the Senate by stooping to vulgar brutality. He cannot be excused by the manners of the age; his violence was the violence of a fluent orator whose temper ran away with him, and who never resisted the temptation to insult an opponent. It did not answer with him; he thought he was to be chief of the Senate, and the most honored person in the State again; he found that he had been allowed to return only to be surrounded by mosquitoes whose delight was to sting him, while the Senate listened with indifference or secret amusement. He had been promised the restoration of his property; but he had a suit to prosecute before he could get it. Clodius had thought to make sure of his Roman palace by dedicating it to "Liberty." Cicero challenged the consecration. It was referred to the College of Priests, and the College returned a judgment in Cicero's favor. The Senate voted for the restoration. They voted sums for the rebuilding both of the palace on the Palatine Hill and of the other villas, at the public expense. But the grant in Cicero's opinion was a stingy one. He saw too painfully that those "who had clipped his wings did not mean them to grow again." [10] Milo and his gladiators were not sufficient support, and if he meant to recover his old power he found that he must look for stronger allies. Pompey had not used him well; Pompey had promised to defend him from Clodius, and Pompey had left him to his fate. But by going with Pompey he could at least gall the Senate. An opportunity offered, and he caught at it. There was a corn famine in Rome. Clodius had promised the people cheap bread, but there was no bread to be had. The hungry mob howled about the senate-house, threatening fire and massacre. The great capitalists and contractors were believed to be at their old work. There was a cry, as in the "pirate" days, for some strong man to see to them and their misdoings. Pompey was needed again. He had been too much forgotten, and with Cicero's help a decree was carried which gave Pompey control over the whole corn trade of the Empire for five years.

This was something, and Pompey was gratified; but without an army Pompey could do little against the roughs in the streets, and Cicero's house became the next battle-ground. The Senate had voted it to its owner again, and the masons and carpenters were set to work; but the sovereign people had not been consulted. Clodius was now but a private citizen; but private citizens might resist sacrilege if the magistrates forgot their duty. He marched to the Palatine with his gang. He drove out the workmen, broke down the walls, and wrecked the adjoining house, which belonged to Cicero's brother Quintus. The next day he set on Cicero himself in the Via Sacra, and nearly murdered him, and he afterward tried to burn the house of Milo. Consuls and tribunes did not interfere. They were, perhaps, frightened. The Senate professed regret, and it was proposed to prosecute Clodius; but his friends were too strong, and it could not be done. Could Cicero have wrung his neck, as he had wrung the necks of Lentulus and Cethegus, Rome and he would have had a good deliverance. Failing this, he might wisely have waited for the law, which in time must have helped him. But he let himself down to Clodius's level. He railed at him in the Curia as he had railed at Gabinius and Piso. He ran over his history; he taunted him with incest with his sister, and with filthy relations with vulgar millionaires. He accused him of having sold himself to Catiline, of having forged wills, murdered the heirs of estates and stolen their property, of having murdered officers of the treasury and seized the public money, of having outraged gods and men, decency, equity, and law; of having suffered every abomination and committed every crime of which human nature was capable. So Cicero spoke in Clodius's own hearing and in the hearing of his friends. It never occurred to him that if half these crimes could be proved, a commonwealth in which such a monster could rise to consequence was not a commonwealth at all, but a frightful mockery which he and every honest man were called on to abhor. Instead of scolding and flinging impotent filth, he should have withdrawn out of public life when he could only remain in it among such companions, or should have attached himself with all his soul to those who had will and power to mend it.

Clodius was at this moment the popular candidate for the aedileship, the second step on the road to the consulship. He was the favorite of the mob. He was supported by his brother Appius Claudius, the praetor, and the _clientele_ of the great Claudian family; and Cicero's denunciations of him had not affected in the least his chances of success. If Clodius was to be defeated, other means were needed than a statement in the Senate that the aspirant to public honors was a wretch unfit to live. The election was fixed for the 18th of November, and was to be held in the Campus Martius. Milo and his gladiators took possession of the polling- place in the night, and the votes could not be taken. The Assembly met the next day in the Forum, but was broken up by violence, and Clodius had still to wait. The political witch-dance was at its height and Cicero was in his glory. "The elections," he wrote to Atticus, "will not, I think, be held; and Clodius will be prosecuted by Milo unless he is first killed. Milo will kill him if he falls in with him. He is not afraid to do it, and he says openly that he will do it. He is not frightened at the misfortune which fell on me. He is not the man to listen to traitorous friends or to trust indolent patricians." [11]

With recovered spirits the Senate began again to attack the laws of Caesar and Clodius as irregular; but they were met with the difficulty which Clodius had provided. Cato had come back from Cyprus, delighted with his exploit and with himself, and bringing a ship-load of money with him for the public treasury. If the laws were invalidated by the disregard of Bibulus and the signs of the sky, then the Cyprus mission had been invalid also, and Cato's fine performance void. Caesar's grand victories, the news of which was now coming in, made it inopportune to press the matter farther; and just then another subject rose, on which the optimates ran off like hounds upon a fresh scent.

Ptolemy of Cyprus had been disposed of. Ptolemy Auletes had been preserved on the throne of Egypt by subsidies to the chiefs of the Senate. But his subjects had been hardly taxed to raise the money. The Cyprus affair had further exasperated them, and when Ptolemy laid on fresh impositions the Alexandrians mutinied and drove him out. His misfortunes being due to his friends at Rome, he came thither to beg the Romans to replace him. The Senate agreed unanimously that he must be restored to his throne. But then the question rose, who should be the happy person who was to be the instrument of his reinstatement? Alexandria was rich. An enormous fine could be exacted for the rebellion, besides what might be demanded from Ptolemy's gratitude. No prize so splendid had yet been offered to Roman avarice, and the patricians quarrelled over it like jackals over a bone. Lentulus Spinther, the late consul, was now Governor of Cilicia; Gabinius was Governor of Syria; and each of these had their advocates. Cicero and the respectable conservatives were for Spinther; Pompey was for Gabinius. Others wished Pompey himself to go; others wished for Crassus.

[Sidenote: B.C. 56.] Meanwhile, the poor Egyptians themselves claimed a right to be heard in protest against the reimposition upon them of a sovereign who had made himself abhorred. Why was Ptolemy to be forced on them? A hundred of the principal Alexandrians came to Italy with a remonstrance; and had they brought money with them they might have had a respectful hearing. But they had brought none or not enough, and Ptolemy, secure of his patrons' support, hired a party of banditti, who set on the deputation when it landed, and killed the greater part of its members. Dion, the leader of the embassy, escaped for a time. There was still a small party among the aristocracy (Cato and Cato's followers) who had a conscience in such things; and Favonius, one of them, took up Dion's cause. Envoys and allied sovereigns or provinces, he said, were continually being murdered. Noble lords received hush-money, and there had been no inquiry. Such things happened too often, and ought to be stopped. The Senate voted decently to send for Dion and examine him. But Favonius was privately laughed at as "Cato's ape;" the unfortunate Dion was made away with, and Pompey took Ptolemy into his own house and openly entertained him there. Pompey would himself perhaps have undertaken the restoration, but the Senate was jealous. His own future was growing uncertain; and eventually, without asking for a consent which the Senate would have refused to give, he sent his guest to Syria with a charge to his friend Gabinius to take him back on his own responsibility.[12]

The killing of envoys and the taking of hush-money by senators were, as Favonius had said, too common to attract much notice; but the affair of Ptolemy, like that of Jugurtha, had obtained an infamous notoriety. The Senate was execrated. Pompey himself fell in public esteem. His overseership of the granaries had as yet brought in no corn. He had been too busy over the Egyptian matter to attend to it. Clearly enough there would now have been a revolution in Rome, but for the physical force of the upper classes with their bands of slaves and clients.

The year of Milo's tribunate being over, Clodius was chosen aedile without further trouble; and, instead of being the victim of a prosecution, he at once impeached Milo for the interruption of the Comitia on the 18th of November.

Milo appeared to answer on the 2d of February; but there was another riot, and the meeting was broken up. On the 6th the court was again held. The crowd was enormous. Cicero happily has left a minute account of the scene. The people were starving, the corn question was pressing. Milo presented himself, and Pompey came forward on the Rostra to speak. He was received with howls and curses from Clodius's hired ruffians, and his voice could not be heard for the noise. Pompey held on undaunted, and commanded occasional silence by the weight of his presence. Clodius rose when Pompey had done, and rival yells went up from the Milonians. Yells were not enough; filthy verses were sung in chorus about Clodius and Clodia, ribald bestiality, delightful to the ears of "Tully." Clodius, pale with anger, called out, "Who is murdering the people with famine?" A thousand throats answered, "Pompey!" "Who wants to go to Alexandria?" "Pompey!" they shouted again. "And whom do you want to go?" "Crassus!" they cried. Passion had risen too high for words. The Clodians began to spit on the Milonians. The Milonians drew swords and cut the heads of the Clodians. The working men, being unarmed, got the worst of the conflict; and Clodius was flung from the Rostra. The Senate was summoned to call Pompey to account. Cicero went off home, wishing to defend Pompey, but wishing also not to offend the "good" party, who were clamorous against him. That evening nothing could be done. Two days after the Senate met again; Cato abused Pompey, and praised Cicero much against Cicero's will, who was anxious to stand well with Pompey. Pompey accused Cato and Crassus of a conspiracy to murder him. In fact, as Cicero said, Pompey had just then no friend in any party. The mob was estranged from him, the noble lords hated him, the Senate did not like him, the patrician youth insulted him, and he was driven to bring up friends from the country to protect his life. All sides were mustering their forces in view of an impending fight.[13]

It would be wasted labor to trace minutely the particulars of so miserable a scene, or the motives of the principal actors in it--Pompey, bound to Caesar by engagement and conviction, yet jealous of his growing fame, without political conviction of his own, and only conscious that his weight in the State no longer corresponded to his own estimate of his merits--Clodius at the head of the starving mob, representing mere anarchy, and nourishing an implacable hate against Cicero--Cicero, anxious for his own safety, knowing now that he had made enemies of half the Senate, watching how the balance of factions would go, and dimly conscious that the sword would have to decide it, clinging, therefore, to Pompey, whose military abilities his civilian ignorance considered supereminent-- Cato, a virtuous fanatic, narrow, passionate, with a vein of vanity, regarding all ways as wrong but his own, and thinking all men who would not walk as he prescribed wicked as well as mistaken--the rest of the aristocracy scuffling for the plunder of Egypt, or engaged in other enterprises not more creditable--the streets given over to the factions-- the elections the alternate prize of bribery or violence, and consulates and praetorships falling to men more than half of whom, if Cicero can be but moderately believed, deserved to be crucified. Cicero's main affection was for Titus Annius Milo, to whom he clung as a woman will cling to a man whose strength she hopes will support her weakness. Milo, at least, would revenge his wrongs upon Clodius. Clodius, Cicero said even in the Senate, was Milo's predestined victim.[14] Titus Annius knew how an armed citizen who burnt temples and honest men's houses ought to be dealt with. Titus Annius was born to extinguish that pest of the Commonwealth.[15]

Still smarting over his exile, Cicero went one day with Milo and his gladiators to the Capitol when Clodius was absent, and carried off the brass tablet on which the decree of his exile had been engraved. It was some solace to his poor vanity to destroy the record of his misfortune. But it was in vain. All was going wrong. Caesar's growing glories came thick to trouble his peace. He, after all, then, was not to be the greatest man in Rome. How would these splendid successes affect parties? How would they affect Pompey? How would, they affect the Senate? What should he do himself?

The Senate distrusted him; the people distrusted him. In his perplexity he tried to rouse the aristocracy to a sense of their danger, and hinted that his was the name which yet might save them.

Sextius, who had been a tribune with Milo in the past year, was under prosecution for one of the innumerable acts of violence which had disgraced the city. Cicero defended him, and spoke at length on the state of affairs as he wished the world to believe that he regarded it.

"In the Commonwealth," he said, "there have always been two parties--the populares and the optimates. The populares say and do what will please the mob. The optimates say and do what will please the best men. And who are the best men? They are of all ranks and infinite in number--senators, municipals, farmers, men of business, even libertini. The type is distinct. They are the well-to-do, the sound, the honest, who do no wrong to any man. The object at which they aim is quiet with honor. [16] They are the conservatives of the State. Religion and good government, the Senate's authority, the laws and customs of our ancestors, public faith, integrity, sound administration-- these are the principles on which they rest, and these they will maintain with their lives. Their path is perilous. The foes of the State are stronger than its defenders; they are bold and desperate, and go with a will to the work of destruction; while the good, I know not why, are languid, and will not rouse themselves unless compelled. They would have quiet without honor, and so lose both quiet and honor. Some are triflers, some are timid, only a few stand firm. But it is not now as it was in the days of the Gracchi. There have been great reforms. The people are conservative at heart; the demagogues cannot rouse them, and are forced to pack the Assembly with hired gangs. Take away these gangs, stop corruption at the elections, and we shall be all of one mind. The people will be on our side. The citizens of Rome are not populares. They hate the populares, and prefer honorable men. How did they weep in the theatres where they heard the news that I was exiled! How did they cheer my name! 'Tully, the preserver of our liberties!' was repeated a thousand times. Attend to me," he said, turning paternally to the high- born youths who were listening to him, "attend to me when I bid you walk in the ways of your forefathers. Would you have praise and honor, would you have the esteem of the wise and good, value the constitution under which you live. Our ancestors, impatient of kings, appointed annual magistrates, and for the administration they nominated a Senate chosen from the whole people into which the road is open for the poorest citizen." [17]

So Cicero, trying to persuade others, and perhaps half persuading himself, that all might yet be well, and that the Roman Constitution would roll on upon its old lines in the face of the scandal of Ptolemy and the greater scandals of Clodius and Milo.

Cicero might make speeches; but events followed their inexorable course. The patricians had forgotten nothing and had learnt nothing. The Senate had voted thanksgivings for Caesar's victories; but in their hearts they hated him more for them, because they feared him more. Milo and his gladiators gave them courage. The bitterest of the aristocrats, Domitius Ahenobarbus, Cato's brother-in-law and praetor for the year, was a candidate for the consulship.

His enormous wealth made his success almost certain, and he announced in the Senate that he meant to recall Caesar and repeal his laws. In April a motion was introduced in the Senate to revise Caesar's land act. Suspicions had gone abroad that Cicero believed Caesar's star to be in the ascendant, and that he was again wavering. To clear himself he spoke as passionately as Domitius could himself have wished, and declared that he honored more the resistance of Bibulus than all the triumphs in the world. It was time to come to an end with these gentlemen. Pompey was deeply committed to Caesar's agrarian law, for it had been passed primarily to provide for his own disbanded soldiers. He was the only man in Rome who retained any real authority; and touched, as for a moment he might have been, with jealousy, he felt that honor, duty, every principle of prudence or patriotism, required him at so perilous a crisis to give Caesar his firm support. Clodius was made in some way to understand that, if he intended to retain his influence, he must conform to the wishes of the army. His brother, Appius, crossed the Alps to see Caesar himself; and Caesar, after the troops were in their winter quarters, came over to the north of Italy. Here an interview was arranged between the chiefs of the popular party. The place of meeting was Lucca, on the frontier of Caesar's province. Pompey, who had gone upon a tour along the coast and through the Mediterranean islands on his corn business, attended without concealment or mystery. Crassus was present, and more than a hundred senators. The talking power of the State was in Rome. The practical and real power was in the Lucca conference. Pompey, Caesar, and Crassus were irresistible when heartily united, and a complete scheme was arranged between them for the government of the Empire. There was to be no Domitius Ahenobarbus for a consul, or aristocratic _coups d'tat_. Pompey and Crassus were to be consuls for the ensuing year. The consulship over, Pompey was to have Spain for a province for five years, with an adequate army. Crassus, who was ambitious also of military distinction, was to have Syria. Caesar's command in Gaul was to be extended for five years further in addition to his present term. The consent of the Assembly was to be secured, if difficulty arose, by the votes of the army. The elections being in the winter, Caesar's soldiers were to be allowed to go to Rome on furlough.

In a personal interview Caesar easily asserted his ascendency. Pompey allowed himself to be guided, and the arrangement was probably dictated by Caesar's own prudence. He did not mean to leave Gaul half conquered, to see his work undone, and himself made into a plaything by men who had incited

Ariovistus to destroy him. The senators who were present at Lucca implied by their co-operation that they too were weary of anarchy, and would sustain the army in a remodelling of the State if milder measures failed.

Thus, for the moment, Domitius and Cato were baffled. Domitius was not to be consul. Caesar was not to be recalled, or his laws repealed. There was no hope for them or for the reaction, till Pompey and Caesar could be divided; and their alliance was closer now than ever. The aristocratic party could but chafe in impotent rage. The effect on Cicero was curious. He had expected that the conservative movement would succeed, and he had humiliated himself before the Senate, in the idle hope of winning back their favor. The conference at Lucca opened his eyes. For a time at least he perceived that Caesar's was the winning side, and he excused himself for going over to it by laying the blame on the Senate's folly and ingratitude to himself. Some private correspondence preceded his change of sides. He consulted Atticus, and had received characteristic and cautious advice from him. He described in reply his internal struggles, the resolution at which he had arrived, and the conclusion which he had formed upon his own past conduct.

"I am chewing what I have to swallow," he said. "Recantation does not seem very creditable; but adieu to straightforward, honest counsels. You would not believe the perfidy of these chiefs; as they wish to be, and what they might be if they had any faith in them. I had felt, I had known, that I was being led on by them, and then deserted and cast off; and yet I thought of making common cause with them. They were the same which they had always been. You made me see the truth at last. You will say you warned me. You advised what I should do, and you told me not to write to Caesar. By Hercules! I wished to put myself in a position where I should be obliged to enter into this new coalition, and where it would not be possible for me, even if I desired it, to go with those who ought to pity me, and, instead of pity, give me grudging and envy. I have been moderate in what I have written. I shall be more full if Caesar meets me graciously; and then those gentlemen who are so jealous that I should have a decent house to live in will make a wry face.... Enough of this. Since those who have no power will not be my friends, I must endeavor to make friends with those who have. You will say you wished this long ago. I know that you wished it, and that I have been a mere ass;[18] but it is time for me to be loved by myself, since I can get no love from them." [19]

Pompey, after leaving Lucca, sent Cicero a message, through his brother, complaining of his speech on the land act, but assuring him of his own and Caesar's friendship if he would now be true to them. In an apologetic letter to Lentulus Spinther, Cicero explained and justified what he meant to do.

"Pompey," he said, "did not let me know that he was offended. He went off to Sardinia, and on his way saw Caesar at Lucca. Caesar was angry with me; he had seen Crassus, and Crassus had prejudiced him. Pompey, too, was himself displeased. He met my brother a few days after, and told him to use his influence with me. He reminded him of his exertions in my behalf; he swore that those exertions had been made with Caesar's consent, and he begged particularly that, if I could not support Caesar, I would not go against him. I reflected. I debated the matter as if with the Commonwealth. I had suffered much and done much for the Commonwealth. I had now to think of myself. I had been a good citizen; I must now be a good man. Expressions came round to me that had been used by certain persons whom even you do not like. They were delighted to think that I had offended Pompey, and had made Caesar my mortal enemy. This was annoying enough. But the same persons embraced and kissed even in my presence my worst foe--the foe of law, order, peace, country, and every good man [20].... They meant to irritate me, but I had not spirit to be angry. I surveyed my situation. I cast up my accounts; and I came to a conclusion, which was briefly this. If the State was in the hands of bad men, as in my time I have known it to be, I would not join them though they loaded me with favors; but when the first person in the Commonwealth was Pompey, whose services had been so eminent, whose advancement I had myself furthered, and who stood by me in my difficulties, I was not inconsistent if I modified some of my opinions, and conformed to the wishes of one who has deserved so well of me. If I went with Pompey, I must go with Caesar too; and here the old friendship came to bear between Caesar, my brother, and myself, as well as Caesar's kindness to me, of which I had seen evidence in word and deed.... Public interest, too, moved me. A quarrel with these men would be most inexpedient, especially after what Caesar has done.... If the persons who assisted in bringing me back had been my friends afterward, they would have recovered their power when they had me to help them. The 'good' had gained heart when you were consul. Pompey was then won to the 'good' cause. Even Caesar, after being decorated by the Senate for his victories, might have been brought to a better judgment, and wicked citizens would have had no opening to make disturbances. But what happened? These very men protected Clodius, who cared no more for the Bona Dea than for the Three Sisters. They allowed my monument to be engraved with a hostile record....[21] The good party are not as you left them. Those who ought to have been staunch have fallen away. You see it in their faces. You see it in the words and votes of those whom we called 'optimates;' so that wise citizens, one of whom I wish to be and to be thought, must change their course. 'Persuade your countrymen, if you can,' said Plato; 'but use no violence.' Plato found that he could no longer persuade the Athenians, and therefore he withdrew from public life. Advice could not move them, and he held force to be unlawful. My case was different. I was not called on to undertake public responsibilities. I was content to further my own interests, and to defend honest men's causes. Caesar's goodness to me and to my brother would have bound me to him whatever had been his fortunes. Now after so much glory and victory I should speak nobly of him though I owed him nothing." [22]

Happy it would have been for Cicero, and happy for Rome, had he persevered in the course which he now seemed really to have chosen. Cicero and Caesar united might have restored the authority of the laws, punished corruption and misgovernment, made their country the mother as well as the mistress of the world; and the Republic, modified to suit the change of times, might have survived for many generations. But under such a modification, Cicero would have no longer been the first person in the Commonwealth. The talkers would have ceased to rule, and Cicero was a talker only. He could not bear to be subordinate. He was persuaded that he, and not Caesar, was the world's real great man; and so he held on, leaning now to one faction and now to another, waiting for the chance which was to put him at last in his true place. For the moment, however, he saved himself from the degradation into which the Senate precipitated itself. The arrangements at Lucca were the work of the army. The conservative majority refused to let the army dictate to them. Domitius intended still to be consul, let the army say what it pleased. Pompey and Crassus returned to Rome for the elections; the consuls for the year, Marcellinus and Philip, declined to take their names. The consuls and the Senate appealed to the Assembly, the Senate marching into the Forum in state, as if calling on the genius of the nation to defend the outraged constitution. In vain. The people would not listen. The consuls were groaned down. No genius of Rome presided in those meetings, but the genius of revolution in the person of Clodius. The senators were driven back into the

Curia, and Clodius followed them there. The officers forbade his entrance. Furious young aristocrats flew upon him, seized him, and would have murdered him in their rage. Clodius shrieked for help. His rascal followers rushed in with lighted torches, swearing to burn house and Senate if a hair of Clodius's head were hurt. They bore their idol off in triumph; and the wretched senators sat gazing at each other, or storming at Pompey, and inquiring scornfully if he and Crassus intended to appoint themselves consuls. Pompey answered that they had no desire for office, but anarchy must be brought to an end.

Still the consuls of the year stubbornly refused to take the names of the Lucca nominees. The year ran out, and no election had been held. In such a difficulty, the constitution had provided for the appointment of an Interrex till fresh consuls could be chosen. Pompey and Crassus were then nominated, with a foregone conclusion. Domitius still persisted in standing; and, had it been safe to try the usual methods, the patricians would have occupied the voting-places as before with their retinues, and returned him by force. But young Publius Crassus was in Rome with thousands of Caesar's soldiers, who had come up to vote from the north of Italy. With these it was not safe to venture on a conflict, and the consulships fell as the Lucca conference had ordered.

[Sidenote: B.C. 55.] The consent of the Assembly to the other arrangements remained to be obtained. Caesar was to have five additional years in Gaul; Pompey and Crassus were to have Spain and Syria, also for five years each, as soon as their year of office should be over. The defenders of the constitution fought to the last. Cato foamed on the Rostra. When the two hours allowed him to speak were expired, he refused to sit down, and was removed by a guard. The meeting was adjourned to the next day. Publius Gallus, another irreconcilable, passed the night in the senate-house, that he might be in his place at dawn. Cato and Favonius were again at their posts. The familiar cry was raised that the signs of the sky were unfavorable. The excuse had ceased to be legal. The tribunes ordered the voting to go forward. The last resource was then tried. A riot began, but to no purpose. The aristocrats and their clients were beaten back, and the several commands were ratified. As the people were dispersing, their opponents rallied back, filled the Forum, and were voting Caesar's recall, when Pompey came on them and swept them out. Gallus was carried off covered with blood; and, to prevent further question, the vote for Caesar was taken a second time.

The immediate future was thus assured. Time had been obtained for the completion of the work in Gaul. Pompey dedicated a new theatre, and delighted the mob with games and races. Five hundred lions were consumed in five days of combat. As a special novelty eighteen elephants were made to fight with soldiers; and, as a yet more extraordinary phenomenon, the sanguinary Roman spectators showed signs of compunction at their sufferings. The poor beasts were quiet and harmless. When wounded with the lances, they turned away, threw up their trunks, and trotted round the circus, crying, as if in protest against wanton cruelty. The story went that they were half human; that they had been seduced on board the African transports by a promise that they should not be ill-used, and they were supposed to be appealing to the gods.[23]Cicero alludes to the scene in a letter to one of his friends. Mentioning Pompey's exhibitions with evident contempt, he adds: "There remained the hunts, which lasted five days. All say that they were very fine. But what pleasure can a sensible person find in seeing a clumsy performer torn by a wild beast, or a noble animal pierced with a hunting-spear? The last day was given to the elephants; not interesting to me, however delightful to the rabble. A certain pity was felt for them, as if the elephants had some affinity with man." [24]

[1] _ To Atticus_, ii. 16.

[2] "Conservatores Reipublicae."--Pro Sextio.

[3] Mommsen.

[4] "Omnia sunt me?culp?commissa, qui ab his me amari putabam qui invidebant: eos non sequebar qui petebant."--Ad Familiares, xiv. 1. "Nullum est meum peccatum nisi quod iis credidi a quibus nefas putabam esse me decipi.... Intimus proximus familiarissimus quisque aut sibi pertimuit aut mihi invidit."--Ad Quintum Fratrem, i. 4.

[5] "Meministis tum, judices, corporibus civium Tiberim compleri, cloacas referciri, e foro spongiis effingi sanguinem.... Caedem tantam, tantos acervos corporum extruetos, nisi forte illo Cinnano atque Octaviano die, quis unquam in foro vidit?"--_Oratio prov P. Sextio_, xxxv. 36.

[6] Ad Quirites post Reditum.

[7] "Ejus vir Catilina."

[8] "Cum in Circo Flaminio non a tribuno plebis consul in concionem sed a latrone archipirata productus esset, primum processit qu?auctoritate vir. Vini, somni, stupri plenus, madenti com? gravibus oculis, fluentibus buccis, pressa voce et temulenta, quod in cives indemnatos esset animadversum, id sibi dixit gravis auctor vehementissime displicere."--Post Reditum in Senatu, 6.

[9] Cicero could never leave Gabinius and Piso alone. Again and again he returned upon them railing like a fishwife. In his oration for Sextius he scoffed at Gabinius's pomatum and curled hair, and taunted him with unmentionable sins; but he specially entertained himself with his description of Piso:

"For Piso!" he said: "O gods, how unwashed, how stern he looked--a pillar of antiquity, like one of the old bearded consuls; his dress plain plebeian purple, his hair tangled, his brow a very pledge for the Commonwealth! Such solemnity in his eye, such wrinkling of his forehead, that you would have said the State was resting on his head like the sky on Atlas. Here we thought we had a refuge. Here was the man to oppose the filth of Gabinius; his very face would be enough. People congratulated us on having one friend to save us from the tribune. Alas! I was deceived," etc. etc.

Piso afterward called Cicero to account in the Senate, and brought out a still more choice explosion of invectives. Beast, filth, polluted monster, and such like, were the lightest of the names which Cicero hurled back at one of the oldest members of the Roman aristocracy. A single specimen may serve to illustrate the cataract of nastiness which he poured alike on Piso and Clodius and Gabinius: "When all the good were hiding themselves in tears," he said to Piso, "when the temples were groaning and the very houses in the city were mourning (over my exile), you, heartless madman that you are, took up the cause of that pernicious animal, that clotted mass of incests and civil blood, of villanies intended and impurity of crimes committed[he was alluding to Clodius, who was in the Senate probably listening to him]. Need I speak of your feasting, your laughter, and handshakings--your drunken orgies with the filthy companions of your potations? Who in those days saw you ever sober, or doing anything that a citizen need not be ashamed of? While your colleague's house was sounding with songs and cymbals, and he himself was dancing naked at a supper-party ["cumque ipse nudus in convivio saltaret,"] you, you coarse glutton, with less taste for music, were lying in a stew of Greek boys and wine in a feast of the Centaurs and Lapithae, where one cannot say whether you drank most, or vomited most, or spilt most."--_In L. Pisonem_,10. The manners of the times do not excuse language of this kind, for there was probably not another member of the Senate who indulged in it. If Cicero was disliked and despised, he had his own tongue to thank for it.

[10] To Atticus, iv. 2.

[11] To Atticus, iv. 3.

[12] For the details of this story see Dion Cassius, lib. xxxix. capp. 12-16. Compare Cicero ad Familiares, lib. i. Epist. 1-2. Curious subterranean influences seem to have been at work to save the Senate from the infamy of restoring Ptolemy. Verses were discovered in the Sibylline Books directing that if an Egyptian king came to Rome as a suppliant, he was to be entertained hospitably, but was to have no active help. Perhaps Cicero was concerned in this.

[13] Ad Quintum Fratrem, ii. 3.

[14] "Tito Annio devota et constituta hostia esse videtur."--De Haruspicum responsis.

[15] Ibid.

[16] "Otium cum dignitate."

[17] Abridged from the Oratio pro Sextio.

[18] "Me germanum asinum fuisse." Perhaps "own brother to an ass" would be a more proper rendering.

[19] To Atticus, iv. 5.

[20] Clodius.

[21] Here follows much about himself and his own merits.

[22] To Lentulus Spinther, Ad Familiares, i. 9. The length of this remarkable letter obliges me to give but an imperfect summary of it. The letter itself should be studied carefully by those who would understand Cicero's conduct.

[23] Dion Cassius.

[24] Ad Familiares, vii. 1.

CHAPTER XVI.

[Sidenote: B.C. 56.] While Caesar was struggling with the Senate for leave to complete the conquest of Gaul, fresh work was preparing for him there. Young Publius Crassus, before he went to Italy, had wintered with the seventh legion in Brittany. The Breton tribes had nominally made their submission, and Crassus had desired them to supply his commissariat. They had given hostages for their good behavior, and most of them were ready to obey. The Veneti, the most important of the coast clans, refused. They induced the rest to join them. They seized the Roman officers whom Crassus had sent among them, and they then offered to exchange their prisoners for their countrymen whom the Romans held in pledge. The legions might be irresistible on land; but the Veneti believed that their position was impregnable to an attack on the land side. Their homes were on the Bay of Quiberon and on the creeks and estuaries between the mouth of the Loire and Brest. Their villages were built on promontories, cut off at high tide from the mainland, approachable only by water, and not by water except in shallow vessels of small draught which could be grounded safely on the mud. The population were sailors and fishermen. They were ingenious and industrious, and they carried on a considerable trade in the Bay of Biscay and in the British Channel. They had ships capable of facing the heavy seas which rolled in from the Atlantic, flat-bottomed, with high bow and stern, built solidly of oak, with timbers a foot thick, fastened with large iron nails. They had iron chains for cables. Their sails--either because sailcloth was scarce, or because they thought canvas too weak for the strain of the winter storms-- were manufactured out of leather. Such vessels were unwieldy, but had been found available for voyages even to Britain. Their crews were accustomed to handle them, and knew all the rocks and shoals and currents of the intricate and difficult harbors. They looked on the Romans as mere landsmen, and naturally enough they supposed that they had as little to fear from an attack by water as from the shore. At the worst they could take to their ships and find a refuge in the islands.

Crassus, when he went to Rome, carried the report to Caesar of the revolt of the Veneti, and Caesar felt that unless they were promptly punished, all Gaul might be again in flame. They had broken faith. They had imprisoned Roman officers who had gone on a peaceful mission among them. It was necessary to teach a people so restless, so hardly conquered, and so impatient of foreign dominion, that there was no situation which the Roman arm was unable to reach.

While the Lucca conference was going on, a fleet of Roman galleys was built by his order in the Loire. Rowers, seamen, and pilots were brought across from Marseilles. When the season was sufficiently advanced for active operations, Caesar came himself and rejoined his army. Titus Labienus was sent with three legions to check the Germans on the Rhine, and prevent disturbances among the Belgae. Titurius Sabinus, with three more, was stationed in Normandy. To Brittany Caesar went in person to reduce the rebellious Veneti. The weather was too unsettled for his fleet to be able as yet to join him. Without its help he found the problem as difficult as the Veneti expected. Each village required a siege; when it was reduced, the inhabitants took to their boats, and defied him again in a new position. Many weeks were thus fruitlessly wasted. The fine weather at length set in. The galleys from the Loire came out, accompanied by others from Rochelle and the mouth of the Garonne. The command at sea was given to Decimus Brutus, a cousin of the afterward famous Marcus, a clever, able, and so far loyal officer.

The Veneti had collected every ship that they or their allies possessed to defend themselves. They had 220 sail in all--a force, considering its character, extremely formidable. Their vessels were too strong to be run down. The galleys carried turrets; but the bows and sterns of the Veneti were still too lofty to be reached effectively by the Roman javelins. The Romans had the advantage in speed; but that was all. They too, however, had their ingenuities.

They had studied the construction of the Breton ships. They had provided sickles with long handles, with which they proposed to catch the halyards which held the weight of the heavy leather sails. It was not difficult to do, if, as is probable, the halyards were made fast, not to the mast, but to the gunwale. Sweeping rapidly alongside they could easily cut them; the sails would fall, and the vessels would be unmanageable.

A sea battle of this singular kind was thus fought off the eastern promontory of the Bay of Quiberon, Caesar and his army looking on from the shore. The sickles answered well; ship after ship was disabled; the galleys closed with them, and they were taken by boarding. The Veneti then tried to retreat; but a calm came on, and they could not move. The fight lasted from ten in the morning till sunset, when the entire Breton fleet was taken or sunk.

After this defeat the Veneti gave up the struggle. Their ships were all gone. Their best men were on board, and had been killed. They had no power of resistance left. Caesar was constitutionally lenient, and admired rather than resented a valiant fight for freedom. But the Veneti had been treacherous. They had laid hands on the sacred persons of Roman ambassadors, and he considered it expedient on this one occasion to use severity. The council who had contrived the insurrection were put to death. The rest of the tribe were treated as the Aduatuci had been, and were sold into slavery.

Sabinus, meanwhile, had been in difficulties in Normandy. The people there had risen and killed their chiefs, who tried to keep them quiet; vagabonds from other parts had joined them, and Sabinus, who wanted enterprise, allowed the disturbances to become dangerous. He ended them at last, however, successfully, and Caesar would not allow his caution to be blamed. During the same months, Publius Crassus had made a brilliant campaign in Aquitaine. The Aquitani had not long before overthrown two Roman armies. Determined not to submit to Caesar, they had allied themselves with the Spaniards of the Pyrenees, and had officers among them who had been trained by Sertorius. Crassus stormed their camp with a skill and courage which called out Caesar's highest approbation, and completely subdued the whole country.

In all France there now remained only a few unimportant tribes on the coast between Calais and the Scheldt which had not formally submitted. The summer being nearly over, Caesar contented himself with a hasty survey of their frontier. The weather broke up earlier than usual, and the troops were redistributed in their quarters. Again there had been a year of unbroken success. The Romans were masters of Gaul, and the admirable care of their commander had preserved the numbers in his legions almost undiminished. The smallness of the loss with which all these wonders were accomplished is perhaps the most extraordinary feature of the story. Not till a year later is there any notice of fresh recruits being brought from Italy.

The winter which followed brought with it another of the dangerous waves of German immigration. The powerful Suevi, a nation of warriors who cultivated no lands, who wore no clothes but a deer or sheep skin, who lived by hunting and pasture, despised the restraints of stationary life, and roved at pleasure into their neighbors' territories, were pressing on the weaker tribes and forcing them down into the Low Countries. The Belgians, hoping for their help against the Romans, had invited these tribes over the Rhine; and, untaught by the fate of Ariovistus, they were crossing over and collecting in enormous numbers above the junction of the Rhine and the Meuse. Into a half-peopled country, large portions of which are lying waste, it might be barbarous to forbid an immigration of harmless and persecuted strangers; but if these Germans were persecuted, they were certainly not harmless; they had come at the instance of the party in Gaul which was determined to resist the Roman conquest, and unless the conquest was to be abandoned, necessity required that the immigration must be prohibited. When the advance of spring allowed the troops to move, Caesar called a council of Gallic chiefs. He said nothing of the information which had reached him respecting their correspondence with these new invaders, but with his usual swiftness of decision he made up his mind to act without waiting for disaffection to show itself. He advanced at once to the Ardennes, where he was met by envoys from the German camp. They said that they had been expelled from their country, and had come to Gaul in search of a home; they did not wish to quarrel with the Romans; if Caesar would protect them and give them lands, they promised to be useful to him; if he refused their alliance, they declared that they would defend themselves. They had fled before the Sueves, for the Sueves were the first nation in the world; the immortal gods were not a match for the Sueves; but they were afraid of no one else, and Caesar might choose whether he would have them for friends or foes.

Caesar replied that they must not stay in Gaul. There were no unoccupied lands in Gaul which could receive so vast a multitude. The Ubii[1] on their own side of the Rhine were allies of the Romans; the Ubii, he was willing to undertake, would provide for them; meanwhile they must go back; he would listen to no other conditions. The envoys departed with their answer, begging Caesar to advance no farther till he had again heard from them. This could not be granted. The interval would be employed in communicating with the Gauls. Caesar pushed on, crossed the Meuse at Maestricht, and descended the river to Venloo, where he was but twelve miles distant from the German head-quarters. Again messengers came, asking for time--time, at least, till they could learn whether the Ubii would receive them. If the Ubii were favorable, they said that they were ready to go; but they could not decide without a knowledge of what was to become of them. They asked for a respite, if only for three days.

Three days meant only leisure to collect their scattered detachments, that they might make a better fight. Caesar gave them twenty-four hours.

The two armies were so near that their front lines were in sight of each other. Caesar had given orders to his officers not to meddle with the Germans. But the Germans, being undisciplined and hot-blooded, were less easy to be restrained. A large body of them flung themselves on the Roman advanced guard, and drove it in with considerable loss; seventy-four Roman knights fell, and two Aquitanian noblemen, brothers, serving under Caesar, were killed in defending each other.

Caesar was not sorry for an excuse to refuse further parley. The Germans were now scattered. In a day or two they would be united again. He knew the effect which would be produced on the restless minds of the Gauls by the news of a reverse however slight; and if he delayed longer, he feared that the country might be on fire in his rear. On the morning which followed the first action, the principal German chiefs appeared to apologize and to ask for a truce. They had come in of their own accord. They had not applied for a safe conduct, and war had been begun by their own people. They were detained as prisoners; and, marching rapidly over the short space which divided the camps, Caesar flung himself on the unfortunate people when they were entirely unprepared for the attack. Their chiefs were gone. They were lying about in confusion beside their wagons, women and children dispersed among the men; hundreds of thousands of human creatures, ignorant where to turn for orders, and uncertain whether to fight or fly. In this condition the legions burst in on them, furious at what they called the treachery of the previous day, and merciless in their vengeance. The poor Germans stood bravely defending themselves as they could; but the sight of their women flying in shrieking crowds, pursued by the Roman horse, was too much for them, and the whole host were soon rushing in despairing wreck down the narrowing isthmus between the Meuse and the Rhine. They came to the junction at last, and then they could go no further. Multitudes were slaughtered; multitudes threw themselves into the water and were drowned. Caesar, who was not given to exaggeration, says that their original number was 430,000. The only survivors, of whom any clear record remains, were the detachments who were absent from the battle, and the few chiefs who had come into Caesar's camp and continued with him at their own request from fear of being murdered by the Gauls.

This affair was much spoken of at the time, as well it might be. Questions were raised upon it in the Senate. Cato insisted that Caesar had massacred a defenceless people in a time of truce, that he had broken the law of nations, and that he ought to be given up to the Germans. The sweeping off the earth in such a manner of a quarter of a million human creatures, even in those unscrupulous times, could not be heard of without a shudder. The irritation in the Senate can hardly be taken as disinterested. Men who had intrigued with Ariovistus for Caesar's destruction, needed not to be credited with feelings of pure humanity when they made the most of the opportunity. But an opportunity had undoubtedly been offered them. The rights of war have their limits. No living man in ordinary circumstances recognized those limits more than Caesar did. No commander was more habitually merciful in victory. In this case the limits had been ruthlessly exceeded. The Germans were not indeed defending their own country; they were the invaders of another; but they were a fine brave race, overtaken by fate when doing no more than their forefathers had done for unknown generations. The excuse for their extermination was simply this: that Caesar had undertaken the conquest of Gaul for the defence of Italy. A powerful party among the Gauls themselves were content to be annexed to the Roman Empire. The patriots looked to the Germans to help them in driving out the Romans. The Germanizing of Gaul would lead with certainty to fresh invasions of Italy; and it seemed permissible, and even necessary, to put a stop to these immigrations once for all, and to show Gauls and Germans equally that they were not to be.

It was not enough to have driven the Germans out of Gaul. Caesar respected their character. He admired their abstinence from wine, their courage, their frugal habits, and their pure morality. But their virtues made them only more dangerous; and he desired to show them that the Roman arm was long and could reach them even in their own homes. Parties of the late invaders had returned over the Rhine, and were protected by the Sigambri in Westphalia. Caesar had demanded their surrender, and the Sigambri had answered that Roman authority did not reach across the river; if Caesar forbade Germans to cross into Gaul, the Germans would not allow the Romans to dictate to them in their own country. The Ubii were growing anxious. They were threatened by the Sueves for deserting the national cause. They begged Caesar to show himself among them, though his stay might be but short, as a proof that he had power and will to protect them; and they offered him boats and barges to carry his army over. Caesar decided to go, but to go with more ostentation. The object was to impress the German imagination; and boats and barges which might not always be obtainable would, if they seemed essential, diminish the effect. The legions were skilled workmen, able to turn their hand to anything. He determined to make a bridge, and he chose Bonn for the site of it. The river was broad, deep, and rapid. The materials were still standing in the forest; yet in ten days from the first stroke that was delivered by an axe, a bridge had been made standing firmly on rows of piles with a road over it forty feet wide. A strong guard was left at each end. Caesar marched across with the legions, and from all sides deputations from the astonished people poured in to beg for peace. The Sigambri had fled to their woods. The Suevi fell back into the Thuringian forests. He burnt the villages of the Sigambri, to leave the print of his presence. He paid the Ubii a long visit; and after remaining eighteen days beyond the river, he considered that his purpose had been gained, and he returned to Gaul, destroying the bridge behind him.

It was now about the beginning of August. A few weeks only of possible fine weather remained. Gaul was quiet, not a tribe was stirring. The people were stunned by Caesar's extraordinary performances. West of the channel which washed the shores of the Belgae lay an island where the enemies of Rome had found shelter, and from which help had been sent to the rebellious Bretons. Caesar, the most skilful and prudent of generals, was yet adventurous as a knight-errant. There was still time for a short expedition into Britain. As yet nothing was known of that country, save the white cliffs which could be seen from Calais; Roman merchants occasionally touched there, but they had never ventured into the interior; they could give no information as to the size of the island, the qualities of the harbors, the character or habits of the inhabitants. Complete ignorance of such near neighbors was undesirable and inconvenient; and Caesar wished to look at them with his own eyes. The fleet which had been used in the war with the Veneti was sent round into the channel. He directed Caius Volusenus, an officer whom he could trust, to take a galley and make a survey of the opposite coast, and he himself followed to Boulogne, where his vessels were waiting for him. The gathering of the flotilla and its object had been reported to Britain, and envoys from various tribes were waiting there with offers of hostages and humble protestations. Caesar received them graciously, and sent back with them a Gaul, named Commius, whom he had made chief of the Atrebates, to tell the people that he was coming over as a friend, and that they had nothing to fear.

Volusenus returned after five days' absence, having been unable to gather anything of importance. The ships which had come in were able only to take across two legions, probably at less than their full complement--or at most ten thousand men; but for Caesar's present purpose these were sufficient. Leaving Sabinus and Cotta in charge of the rest of the army, he sailed on a calm evening, and was off Dover in the morning. The cliffs were lined with painted warriors, and hung so close over the water that if he attempted to land there stones and lances could reach the boats from the edge of the precipice. He called his officers about him while his fleet collected, and said a few encouraging words to them; he then moved up the coast with the tide, apparently as far as Walmer or Deal. Here the beach was open and the water deep near the land. The Britons had followed by the brow of the cliff, scrambling along with their cars and horses. The shore was covered with them, and they evidently meant to fight. The transports anchored where the water was still up to the men's shoulders. They were encumbered with their arms, and did not like the look of what was before them. Seeing them hesitate, Caesar sent his armed galleys filled with archers and crossbow-men to clear the approach; and as the legionaries still hesitated, an officer who carried the eagle of the 10th leapt into the sea and bade his comrades follow if they wished to save their standard. They sprang overboard with a general cheer. The Britons rode their horses into the waves to meet them; and for a few minutes the Romans could make no progress. Boats came to their help, which kept back the most active of their opponents, and once on land they were in their own element. The Britons galloped off, and Caesar had no cavalry.

A camp was then formed. Some of the ships were left at anchor, others were brought on shore, and were hauled up to the usual high-water mark. Commius came in with deputations, and peace was satisfactorily arranged. All went well till the fourth day, when the full moon brought the spring tide, of which the Romans had no experience and had not provided for it. Heavy weather came up along with it. The galleys on the beach were floated off; the transports at anchor parted their cables; some were driven on shore, some out into the channel. Caesar was in real anxiety. He had no means of procuring a second fleet. He had made no preparations for wintering in Britain. The legions had come light, without tents or baggage, as he meant to stay no longer than he had done in Germany, two or three weeks at most. Skill and energy repaired the damage. The vessels which had gone astray were recovered. Those which were least injured were repaired with the materials of the rest. Twelve only were lost, the others were made seaworthy.

The Britons, as Caesar expected, had taken heart at the disaster. They broke their agreement, and fell upon his outposts. Seeing the small number of Romans, they collected in force, in the hope that if they could destroy the first comers no more such unwelcome visitors would ever arrive to trouble them. A sharp action taught them their mistake; and after many of the poor creatures had been killed, they brought in hostages, and again begged for peace. The equinox was now coming on. The weather was again threatening. Postponing, therefore, further inquiries into the nature of the British and their country, Caesar used the first favorable opportunity, and returned, without further adventure, to Boulogne. The legions were distributed among the Belgae; and Caesar himself, who could have no rest, hastened over the Alps, to deal with other disturbances which had broken out in Illyria.

[Sidenote: B.C. 54.] The bridge over the Rhine and the invasion of a country so remote that it was scarcely believed to exist, roused the enthusiasm at Rome beyond the point which it had hitherto reached. The Roman populace was accustomed to victories, but these were portents like the achievements of the old demigods. The humbled Senate voted twenty days of thanksgiving; and faction, controlled by Pompey, was obliged to be silent.

   The Illyrian troubles were composed without fighting, and the interval of winter was spent in preparations for a renewal of the expedition into Britain on a larger scale. Orders had been left with the officers in command to prepare as many transports as the time would allow, broader and lower in the side for greater convenience in loading and unloading. In April, Caesar returned. He visited the different stations, and he found that his expert legionaries, working incessantly, had built six hundred transports and twenty-eight armed galleys. All these were finished and ready to be launched. He directed that they should collect at Boulogne as before; and in the interval he paid a visit to the north of Gaul, where there were rumors of fresh correspondence with the Germans. Danger, if danger there was, was threatened by the Treveri, a powerful tribe still unbroken on the Moselle. Caesar, however, had contrived to attach the leading chiefs to the Roman interest. He found nothing to alarm him, and once more went down to the sea. In his first venture he had been embarrassed by want of cavalry. He was by this time personally acquainted with the most influential of the Gallic nobles. He had requested them to attend him into Britain with their mounted retinues, both for service in the field, and that he might keep these restless chiefs under his eye. Among the rest he had not overlooked the Aeduan prince, Dumnorix, whose intrigues had brought the Helvetii out of Switzerland, and whose treachery had created difficulty and nearly disaster in the first campaign. Dumnorix had not forgotten his ambition. He had affected penitence, and he had been treated with kindness. He had availed himself of the favor which had been shown to him to pretend to his countrymen that Caesar had promised him the chieftainship. He had petitioned earnestly to be excused from accompanying the expedition, and, Caesar having for this reason probably the more insisted upon it, he had persuaded the other chiefs that Caesar meant to destroy them, and that if they went to Britain they would never return. These whisperings were reported to Caesar. Dumnorix had come to Boulogne with the rest, and he ordered him to be watched. A long westerly wind had prevented Caesar from embarking as soon as he had wished. The weather changed at last, and the troops were ordered on board. Dumnorix slipped away in the confusion with a party of Aeduan horse, and it was now certain that he had sinister intentions. The embarkation was suspended. A detachment of cavalry was sent in pursuit, with directions to bring Dumnorix back dead or alive. Dumnorix resisted, and was killed.

No disturbance followed on his death. The remaining chiefs were loyal, or wished to appear loyal, and further delay was unnecessary. Labienus, whom Caesar thoroughly trusted, remained behind with three legions and two thousand horse to watch over Gaul; and on a fine summer evening, with a light air from the south, Caesar sailed at sunset on the 20th of July. He had five legions with him. He had as many cavalry as he had left with Labienus. His flotilla, swollen by volunteers, amounted to eight hundred vessels, small and great. At sunrise they were in midchannel, lying in a dead calm, with the cliffs of Britain plainly visible on their left hand. The tide was flowing. Oars were out; the legionaries worked with such enthusiasm that the transports kept abreast of the war-galleys. At noon they had reached the beach at Deal, where this time they found no enemy to oppose their landing; the Britons had been terrified at the multitude of ships and boats in which the power of Rome was descending on them, and had fled into the interior. The water was smooth, the disembarkation easy. A camp was drawn out and intrenched, and six thousand men, with a few hundred horse, were told off to guard it. The fleet was left riding quietly at anchor, the pilots ignorant of the meaning of the treacherous southern air which had been so welcome to them; and Caesar advanced inland as far as the Stour. The Britons, after an unsuccessful stand to prevent the Romans from crossing the river, retired into the woods, where they had made themselves a fortress with felled trees. The weak defence was easily stormed; the Britons were flying; the Romans were preparing to follow; when an express came from Deal to tell Caesar that a gale had risen again and the fleet was lying wrecked upon the shore. A second accident of the same kind might have seemed an omen of evil, but Caesar did not believe in omens. The even temperament of his mind was never discomposed, and at each moment he was able always to decide, and to do, what the moment required. The army was halted. He rode back himself to the camp, to find that forty of his vessels only were entirely ruined. The rest were injured, but not irreparably. They were hauled up within the lines of the camp. He selected the best mechanics out of the legions; he sent across to Labienus for more, and directed him to build fresh transports in the yards at Boulogne. The men worked night and day, and in little more than a week Caesar was able to rejoin his troops and renew his march.

The object of the invasion had been rather to secure the quiet of Gaul than the annexation of new subjects and further territory. But it could not be obtained till the Romans had measured themselves against the Britons, and had asserted their military superiority. The Britons had already shown themselves a fearless race, who could not be despised. They fought bravely from their cars and horses, retreated rapidly when overmatched, and were found dangerous when pursued. Encouraged by the report of the disaster to the fleet, Cassibelaunus, chief of the Cassi, whose head-quarters were at St. Albans, had collected a considerable army from both sides of the Thames, and was found in strength in Caesar's front when he again began to move. They attacked his foraging parties. They set on his flanking detachments. They left their cars, and fought on foot when they could catch an advantage; and remounted and were swiftly out of the reach of the heavily armed Roman infantry. The Gaulish horse pursued, but did not know the country, and suffered more harm than they inflicted. Thus the British gave Caesar considerable trouble, which he recorded to their credit. Not a word can be found in his Commentaries to the disparagement of brave and open adversaries. At length he forced them into a battle, where their best warriors were killed. The confederacy of tribes dissolved and never rallied again, and he pursued his march thenceforward with little molestation. He crossed the Medway, and reached the Thames seemingly at Sunbury. There was a ford there, but the river was still deep, the ground was staked, and Cassibelaunus with his own people was on the other side. The legions, however, paid small attention to Cassibelaunus; they plunged through with the water at their necks. The Britons dispersed, driving off their cattle, and watching his march from a distance. The tribes from the eastern counties made their submission, and at Caesar's orders supplied him with corn. Caesar marched on to St. Albans itself, then lying in the midst of forests and marshes, where the cattle, the Cassi's only wealth, had been collected for security. St. Albans and the cattle were taken; Cassibelaunus sued for peace; the days were drawing in; and Caesar, having no intention of wintering in Britain, considered he had done enough and need go no farther. He returned as he had come. The Kentish men had attacked the camp in his absence, but had been beaten off with heavy loss. The Romans had sallied out upon them, killed as many as they could catch, and taken one of their chiefs. Thenceforward they had been left in quiet. A nominal tribute, which was never paid, was assigned to the tribes who had submitted. The fleet was in order, and all was ready for departure. The only, but unhappily too valuable, booty which they had carried off consisted of some thousands of prisoners. These, when landed in

Gaul, were disposed of to contractors, to be carried to Italy and sold as slaves. Two trips were required to transport the increased numbers; but the passage was accomplished without accident, and the whole army was again at Boulogne.

Thus ended the expedition into Britain. It had been undertaken rather for effect than for material advantage; and everything which had been aimed at had been gained. The Gauls looked no more across the Channel for support of insurrections; the Romans talked with admiration for a century of the far land to which Caesar had borne the eagles; and no exploit gave him more fame with his contemporaries. Nor was it without use to have solved a geographical problem, and to have discovered with certainty what the country was, the white cliffs of which were visible from the shores which were now Roman territory. Caesar during his stay in Britain had acquired a fairly accurate notion of it. He knew that it was an island, and he knew its dimensions and shape. He knew that Ireland lay to the west of it, and Ireland, he had been told, was about half its size. He had heard of the Isle of Man, and how it was situated. To the extreme north above Britain he had ascertained that there were other islands, where in winter the sun scarcely rose above the horizon; and he had observed through accurate measurement by water-clocks that the midsummer nights in Britain were shorter than in the south of France and Italy. He had inquired into the natural products of the country. There were tin mines, he found, in parts of the island, and iron in small quantities; but copper was imported from the Continent. The vegetation resembled that of France, save that he saw no beech and no spruce pine. Of more consequence were the people and the distribution of them. The Britons of the interior he conceived to be indigenous. The coast was chiefly occupied by immigrants from Belgium, as could be traced in the nomenclature of places. The country seemed thickly inhabited. The flocks and herds were large; and farm buildings were frequent, resembling those in Gaul. In Kent especially, civilization was as far advanced as on the opposite continent. The Britons proper from the interior showed fewer signs of progress. They did not break the ground for corn; they had no manufactures; they lived on meat and milk, and were dressed in leather. They dyed their skins blue that they might look more terrible. They wore their hair long, and had long mustaches. In their habits they had not risen out of the lowest order of savagery. They had wives in common, and brothers and sisters, parents and children, lived together with promiscuous unrestraint. From such a country not much was to be gained in the way of spoil; nor had much been expected. Since Cicero's conversion, his brother Quintus had joined Caesar, and was now attending him as one of his lieutenant-generals. The brothers were in intimate correspondence. Cicero, though he watched the British expedition with interest, anticipated that Quintus would bring nothing of value back with him but slaves; and he warned his friend Atticus, who dealt extensively in such commodities, that the slaves from Britain would not be found of superior quality.[2]

[1] Nassau and Darmstadt.

[2] "Britannici belli exitus exspectatur. Constat enim, aditus insulae esse munitos mirificis molibus. Etiam illud jam cognitum est, neque argenti scrupulum esse ullum in ill?insul? neque ullam spem praedae, nisi ex mancipiis: ex quibus nullos puto te litteris aut musicis eruditos exspectare."-- Ad Atticum, iv. 16. It does not appear what Cicero meant by the "mirificae moles" which guarded the approaches to Britain, whether Dover Cliff or the masses of sand under water at the Goodwins.

CHAPTER XVII.

The summer had passed off gloriously for the Roman arms. The expedition to Britain had produced all the effects which Caesar expected from it, and Gaul was outwardly calm. Below the smooth appearance the elements of disquiet were silently working, and the winter was about to produce the most serious disaster and the sharpest trials which Caesar had yet experienced. On his return from Britain he held a council at Amiens. The harvest had been bad, and it was found expedient, for their better provision, to disperse the troops over a broader area than usual. There were in all eight legions, with part of another to be disposed of, and they were distributed in the following order. Lucius Roscius was placed in Normandy; Quintus Cicero at Charleroy, not far from the scene of the battle with the Nervii. Cicero had chosen this position for himself as peculiarly advantageous; and his brother speaks of Caesar's acquiescence in the arrangement as a special mark of favor to himself. Labienus was at Lavacherie, on the Ourthe, about seventy miles to the south-east of Cicero; and Sabinus and Cotta were at Tongres, among the Aduatuci, not far from Liege, an equal distance from him to the north-east. Caius Fabius had a legion at St. Pol, between Calais and Arras; Trebonius one at Amiens;

Marcus Crassus one at Montdidier; Munatius Plancus one across the Oise, near Compine. Roscius was far off, but in a comparatively quiet country. The other camps lay within a circle, two hundred miles in diameter, of which Bavay was the centre. Amiens was at one point on the circumference. Tongres, on the opposite side of it, to the north-east. Sabinus, being the most exposed, had, in addition to his legion, a few cohorts lately raised in Italy. Caesar, having no particular business to take him over the Alps, remained, with Trebonius attending to general business. His dispositions had been carefully watched by the Gauls. Caesar, they supposed, would go away as usual; they even believed that he had gone; and a conspiracy was formed in the north to destroy the legions in detail.

The instigator of the movement was Induciomarus, the leader of the patriot party among the Treveri, whose intrigues had taken Caesar to the Moselle before the first visit to Britain. At that time Induciomarus had been able to do nothing; but a fairer opportunity had arrived. The overthrow of the great German horde had affected powerfully the semi-Teutonic populations on the left bank of the Rhine. The Eburones, a large tribe of German race occupying the country between Liege and Cologne, had given in their submission; but their strength was still undiminished, and Induciomarus prevailed on their two chiefs, Ambiorix and Catavoleus, to attack Sabinus and Cotta. It was midwinter. The camp at Tongres was isolated. The nearest support was seventy miles distant. If one Roman camp was taken, Induciomarus calculated that the country would rise; the others could be separately surrounded, and Gaul would be free. The plot was well laid. An entrenched camp being difficult to storm, the confederates decided to begin by treachery. Ambiorix was personally known to many of the Roman officers. He sent to Sabiuus to say that he wished to communicate with him on a matter of the greatest consequence. An interview being granted, he stated that a general conspiracy had been formed through the whole of Gaul to surprise and destroy the legions. Each station was to be attacked on the same day, that they might be unable to support each other. He pretended himself to have remonstrated; but his tribe, he said, had been carried away by the general enthusiasm for liberty, and he could not keep them back. Vast bodies of Germans had crossed the Rhine to join in the war. In two days at the furthest they would arrive. He was under private obligations to Caesar, who had rescued his son and nephew in the fight with the Aduatuci, and out of gratitude he wished to save Sabinus from destruction, which was otherwise inevitable. He urged him to escape while there was still time, and to join either Labienus or Cicero, giving a solemn promise that he should not be molested on the road.

A council of officers was held on the receipt of this unwelcome information. It was thought unlikely that the Eburones would rise by themselves. It was probable enough, therefore, that the conspiracy was more extensive. Cotta, who was second in command, was of opinion that it would be rash and wrong to leave the camp without Caesar's orders. They had abundant provisions. They could hold their own lines against any force which the Germans could bring upon them, and help would not be long in reaching them. It would be preposterous to take so grave a step on the advice of an enemy. Sabinus unfortunately thought differently. He had been over-cautious in Brittany, though he had afterward redeemed his fault. Caesar, he persuaded himself, had left the country; each commander therefore must act on his own responsibility. The story told by Ambiorix was likely in itself. The Germans were known to be furious at the passage of the Rhine, the destruction of Ariovistus, and their other defeats. Gaul resented the loss of its independence. Ambiorix was acting like a true friend, and it would be madness to refuse his offer. Two days' march would bring them to their friends. If the alarm was false, they could return. If there was to be a general insurrection, the legions could not be too speedily brought together. If they waited, as Cotta advised, they would be surrounded, and in the end would be starved into surrender.

Cotta was not convinced, and the majority of officers supported him. The first duty of a Roman army, he said, was obedience to orders. Their business was to hold the post which had been committed to them, till they were otherwise directed. The officers were consulting in the midst of the camp, surrounded by the legionaries. "Have it as you wish," Sabinus exclaimed, in a tone which the men could hear; "I am not afraid of being killed. If things go amiss, the troops will understand where to lay the blame. If you allowed it, they might in forty-eight hours be at the next quarters, facing the chances of war with their comrades, instead of perishing here alone by sword or hunger."

Neither party would give way. The troops joined in the discussion. They were willing either to go or to stay, if their commanders would agree; but they said that it must be one thing or the other; disputes would be certain ruin. The discussion lasted till midnight. Sabinus was obstinate, Cotta at last withdrew his opposition, and the fatal resolution was formed to march at dawn. The remaining hours of the night were passed by the men in collecting such valuables as they wished to take with them. Everything seemed ingeniously done to increase the difficulty of remaining, and to add to the perils of the march by the exhaustion of the troops. The Meuse lay between them and Labienus, so they had selected to go to Cicero at Charleroy. Their course lay up the left bank of the little river Geer. Trusting to the promises of Ambiorix, they started in loose order, followed by a long train of carts and wagons. The Eburones lay, waiting for them, in a large valley, two miles from the camp. When most of the cohorts were entangled in the middle of the hollow, the enemy appeared suddenly, some in front, some on both sides of the valley, some behind threatening the baggage. Wise men, as Caesar says, anticipate possible difficulties, and decide beforehand what they will do if occasions arise. Sabinus had foreseen nothing and arranged nothing. Cotta, who had expected what might happen, was better prepared, and did the best that was possible. The men had scattered among the wagons, each to save or protect what he could. Cotta ordered them back, bade them leave the carts to their fate, and form together in a ring. He did right, Caesar thought; but the effect was unfortunate. The troops lost heart, and the enemy was encouraged, knowing that the baggage would only be abandoned when the position was desperate. The Eburones were under good command. They did not, as might have been expected, fly upon the plunder. They stood to their work, well aware that the carts would not escape them. They were not in great numbers. Caesar specially says that the Romans were as numerous as they. But everything else was against the Romans. Sabinus could give no directions. They were in a narrow meadow, with wooded hills on each side of them filled with enemies whom they could not reach. When they charged, the light-footed barbarians ran back; when they retired, they closed in upon them again, and not a dart, an arrow, or a stone missed its mark among the crowded cohorts. Bravely as the Romans fought, they were in a trap where their courage was useless to them. The battle lasted from dawn till the afternoon, and though they were falling fast, there was no flinching and no cowardice. Caesar, who inquired particularly into the minutest circumstances of the disaster, records by name the officers who distinguished themselves; he mentions one whose courage he had marked before, who was struck down with a lance through his thighs, and another who was killed in rescuing his son. The brave Cotta was hit in the mouth by a stone as he was cheering on his men. The end came at last. Sabinus, helpless and distracted, caught sight of Ambiorix in the confusion, and sent an interpreter to implore him to spare the remainder of the army. Ambiorix answered that Sabinus might come to him, if he pleased; he hoped he might persuade his tribe to be merciful; he promised that Sabinus himself should suffer no injury. Sabinus asked Cotta to accompany him. Cotta said he would never surrender to an armed enemy; and, wounded as he was, he stayed with the legion. Sabinus, followed by the rest of the surviving officers whom he ordered to attend him, proceeded to the spot where the chief was standing. They were commanded to lay down their arms. They obeyed, and were immediately killed; and with one wild yell the barbarians then rushed in a mass on the deserted cohorts. Cotta fell, and most of the others with him. The survivors, with the eagle of the legion, which they had still faithfully guarded, struggled back in the dusk to their deserted camp. The standard-bearer, surrounded by enemies, reached the fosse, flung the eagle over the rampart, and fell with the last effort. Those that were left fought on till night, and then, seeing that hope was gone, died like Romans on each other's swords--a signal illustration of the Roman greatness of mind, which had died out among the degenerate patricians, but was living in all its force in Caesar's legions. A few stragglers, who had been cut off during the battle from their comrades, escaped in the night through the woods, and carried the news to Labienus. Cicero, at Charleroy, was left in ignorance. The roads were beset, and no messenger could reach him.

Induciomarus understood his countrymen. The conspiracy with which he had frightened Sabinus had not as yet extended beyond a few northern chiefs, hut the success of Ambiorix produced the effect which he desired. As soon as it was known that two Roman generals had been cut off, the remnants of the Aduatuci and the Nervii were in arms for their own revenge. The smaller tribes along the Meuse and Sambre rose with them; and Cicero, taken by surprise, found himself surrounded before he had a thought of danger. The Gauls, knowing that their chances depended on the capture of the second camp before assistance could arrive, flung themselves so desperately on the entrenchments that the legionaries were barely able to repel the first assault. The assailants were driven back at last, and Cicero despatched messengers to Caesar to Amiens, to give him notice of the rising; but not a man was able to penetrate through the multitude of enemies which now swarmed in the woods. The troops worked gallantly, strengthening the weak points of their fortifications. In one night they raised a hundred and twenty towers on their walls. Again the Gauls tried a storm, and, though they failed a second time, they left the garrison no rest either by day or night. There was no leisure for sleep; not a hand could be spared from the lines to care for the sick or wounded. Cicero was in bad health, but he clung to his work till the men carried him by force to his tent and obliged him to lie down. The first surprise not having succeeded, the Nervian chiefs, who knew Cicero, desired a parley. They told the same story which Ambiorix had told, that the Germans had crossed the Rhine, and that all Gaul was in arms. They informed him of the destruction of Sabinus; they warned him that the same fate was hanging over himself, and that his only hope was in surrender. They did not wish, they said, to hurt either him or the Roman people; he and his troops would be free to go where they pleased, but they were determined to prevent the legions from quartering themselves permanently in their country.

There was but one Sabinus in the Roman army. Cicero answered, with a spirit worthy of his country, that Romans accepted no conditions from enemies in arms. The Gauls might, if they pleased, send a deputation to Caesar, and hear what he would say to them. For himself, he had no authority to listen to them. Force and treachery being alike unavailing, they resolved to starve Cicero out. They had watched the Roman strategy. They had seen and felt the value of the entrenchments. They made a bank and ditch all round the camp, and, though they had no tools but their swords with which to dig turf and cut trees, so many there were of them that the work was completed in three hours.[1] Having thus pinned the Romans in, they slung red-hot balls and flung darts carrying lighted straw over the ramparts of the camp on the thatched roofs of the soldiers' huts. The wind was high, the fire spread, and amidst the smoke and the blaze the Gauls again rushed on from all sides to the assault. Roman discipline was never more severely tried, and never showed its excellence more signally. The houses and stores of the soldiers were in flames behind them. The enemy were pressing on the walls in front, covered by a storm of javelins and stones and arrows, but not a man left his post to save his property or to extinguish the fire. They fought as they stood, striking down rank after rank of the Gauls, who still crowded on, trampling on the bodies of their companions, as the foremost lines fell dead into the ditch. Such as reached the wall never left it alive, for they were driven forward by the throng behind on the swords of the legionaries. Thousands of them had fallen, before, in desperation, they drew back at last.

But Cicero's situation was almost desperate too. The huts were destroyed. The majority of the men were wounded, and those able to bear arms were daily growing weaker in number. Caesar was 120 miles distant, and no word had reached him of the danger. Messengers were again sent off, but they were caught one after another, and were tortured to death in front of the ramparts, and the boldest men shrank from risking their lives on so hopeless an enterprise. At length a Nervian slave was found to make another adventure. He was a Gaul, and could easily disguise himself. A letter to Caesar was enclosed in the shaft of his javelin. He glided out of the camp in the dark, passed undetected among the enemies as one of themselves, and, escaping from their lines, made his way to Amiens.

Swiftness of movement was Caesar's distinguishing excellence. The legions were kept ready to march at an hour's notice. He sent an order to Crassus to join him instantly from Montdidier. He sent to Fabius at St. Pol to meet him at Arras. He wrote to Labienus, telling him the situation, and leaving him to his discretion to advance or to remain on his guard at Lavacherie, as might seem most prudent. Not caring to wait for the rest of his army, and leaving Crassus to take care of Amiens, he started himself, the morning after the information reached him, with Trebonius's legion to Cicero's relief. Fabius joined him, as he had been directed, at Arras. He had hoped for Labienus's presence also; but Labienus sent to say that he was surrounded by the Treveri, and dared not stir. Caesar approved his hesitation, and with but two legions, amounting in all to only 7,000 men, he hurried forward to the Nervian border. Learning that Cicero was still holding out, he wrote a letter to him in Greek, that it might be unintelligible if intercepted, to tell him that help was near. A Gaul carried the letter, and fastened it by a line to his javelin, which he flung over Cicero's rampart. The javelin stuck in the side of one of the towers and was unobserved for several days. The besiegers were better informed. They learnt that Caesar was at hand, that he had but a handful of men with him. By that time their own numbers had risen to 60,000, and, leaving Cicero to be dealt with at leisure, they moved off to envelop and destroy their great enemy. Caesar was well served by spies. He knew that Cicero was no longer in immediate danger, and there was thus no occasion for him to risk a battle at a disadvantage to relieve him. When he found the Gauls near him, he encamped, drawing his lines as narrowly as he could, that from the small show which he made they might imagine his troops to be even fewer than they were. He invited attack by an ostentation of timidity, and having tempted the Gauls to become the assailants, he flung open his gates, rushed out upon them with his whole force, and all but annihilated them. The patriot army was broken to pieces, and the unfortunate Nervii and Aduatuci never rallied from this second blow. Caesar could then go at his leisure to Cicero and his comrades, who had fought so nobly against such desperate odds. In every ten men he found that there was but one unwounded. He inquired with minute curiosity into every detail of the siege. In a general address he thanked Cicero and the whole legion. He thanked the officers man by man for their gallantry and fidelity. Now for the first time (and that he could have remained ignorant of it so long speaks for the passionate unanimity with which the Gauls had risen) he learnt from prisoners the fate of Sabinus. He did not underrate the greatness of the catastrophe. The soldiers in the army he treated always as friends and comrades in arms, and the loss of so many of them was as personally grievous to him as the effects of it might be politically mischievous. He made it the subject of a second speech to his own and to Cicero's troops, but he spoke to encourage and to console. A serious misfortune had happened, he said, through the fault of one of his generals, but it must be borne with equanimity, and had already been heroically expiated. The meeting with Cicero must have been an interesting one. He and the two Ciceros had been friends and companions in youth. It would have been well if Marcus Tullius could have remembered in the coming years the personal exertion with which Caesar had rescued a brother to whom he was so warmly attached.

Communications among the Gauls were feverishly rapid. While the Nervii were attacking Cicero, Induciomarus and the Treveri had surrounded Labienus at Lavacherie. Caesar had entered Cicero's camp at three o'clock in the afternoon. The news reached Induciomarus before midnight, and he had disappeared by the morning. Caesar returned to Amiens, but the whole country was now in a state of excitement. He had intended to go to Italy, but he abandoned all thoughts of departure. Rumors came of messengers hurrying to and fro, of meetings at night in lonely places, of confederacies among the patriots. Even Brittany was growing uneasy; a force had been collected to attack Roscius, though it had dispersed after the relief of Cicero. Caesar again summoned the chiefs to come to him, and between threats and encouragements succeeded in preventing a general rising. But the tribes on the upper Seine broke into disturbance. The Aedui and the Remi alone remained really loyal; and it was evident that only a leader was wanted to raise the whole of Gaul. Caesar himself admitted that nothing could be more natural. The more high-spirited of the Gauls were miserable to see that their countrymen had so lost conceit of themselves as to submit willingly to the Roman rule.

Induciomarus was busy all the winter soliciting help from the Germans, and promising money and lands. The Germans had had enough of fighting the Romans, and, as long as their own independence was not threatened, were disinclined to move; but Induciomarus, nothing daunted, gathered volunteers on all sides. His camp became a rallying point for disaffection. Envoys came privately to him from distant tribes. He, too, held his rival council, and a fresh attack on the camp of Labienus was to be the first step in a general war. Labienus, well informed of what was going on, watched him quietly from his entrenchments. When the Gauls approached, he affected fear, as Caesar had done, and he secretly formed a body of cavalry, of whose existence they had no suspicion. Induciomarus became careless. Day after day he rode round the entrenchments, insulting the Romans as cowards, and his men flinging their javelins over the walls. Labienus remained passive, till one evening, when, after one of these displays, the loose bands of the Gauls had scattered, he sent his horse out suddenly with orders to fight neither with small nor great, save with Induciomarus only, and promising a reward for his head. Fortune favored him. Induciomarus was overtaken and killed in a ford of the Ourthe, and for the moment the agitation was cooled down. But the impression which had been excited by the destruction of Sabinus was still telling through the country. Caesar expected fresh trouble in the coming summer, and spent the rest of the winter and spring in preparing for a new struggle. Future peace depended on convincing the Gauls of the inexhaustible resources of Italy; on showing them that any loss which might be inflicted could be immediately repaired, and that the army could and would be maintained in whatever strength might be necessary to coerce them. He raised two fresh legions in his own province. Pompey had formed a legion in the north of Italy, within Caesar's boundaries, for service in Spain. Caesar requested Pompey to lend him this legion for immediate purposes; and Pompey, who was still on good terms with Caesar, recognized the importance of the occasion, and consented without difficulty.

[Sidenote: B.C. 53.] Thus amply reinforced, Caesar, before the grass had begun to grow, took the field against the tribes which were openly disaffected. The first business was to punish the Belgians, who had attacked Cicero. He fell suddenly on the Nervii with four legions, seized their cattle, wasted their country, and carried off thousands of them to be sold into slavery. Returning to Amiens, he again called the chiefs about him, and, the Seine tribes refusing to put in an appearance, he transferred the council to Paris, and, advancing by rapid marches, he brought the Senones and Carnutes to pray for pardon.[2] He then turned on the Treveri and their allies, who, under Ambiorix, had destroyed Sabinus. Leaving Labienus with the additional legions to check the Treveri, he went himself into Flanders, where Ambiorix was hiding among the rivers and marshes. He threw bridges over the dikes, burnt the villages, and carried off an enormous spoil, of cattle and, alas! of men. To favor and enrich the tribes that submitted after a first defeat, to depopulate the determinately rebellious by seizing and selling as slaves those who had forfeited a right to his protection, was his uniform and, as the event proved, entirely successful policy. The persuasions of the Treveri had failed with the nearer German tribes; but some of the Suevi, who had never seen the Romans, were tempted to adventure over and try their fortunes; and the Treveri were waiting for them, to set on Labienus, in Caesar's absence. Labienus went in search of the Treveri, tempted them into an engagement by a feigned flight, killed many of them, and filled his camp with prisoners. Their German allies retreated again across the river, and the patriot chiefs, who had gone with Induciomarus, concealed themselves in the forests of Westphalia. Caesar thought it desirable to renew the admonition which he had given the Germans two years before, and again threw a bridge over the Rhine at the same place where he had made the first, but a little higher up the stream. Experience made the construction more easy. The bridge was begun and finished in a few days, but this time the labor was thrown away. The operation itself lost its impressiveness by repetition, and the barrenness of practical results was more evident than before. The Sueves, who had gone home, were far away in the interior. To lead the heavily armed legions in pursuit of wild light-footed marauders, who had not a town which could be burned, or a field of corn which could be cut for food, was to waste their strength to no purpose, and to prove still more plainly that in their own forests they were beyond the reach of vengeance. Caesar drew back again, after a brief visit to his allies the Ubii, cut two hundred feet of the bridge on the German side, and leaving the rest standing with a guard to defend it, he went in search of Ambiorix, who had as yet eluded him, in the Ardennes.

Ambiorix had added treachery to insurrection, and as long as he was free and unpunished the massacred legion had not been fully avenged. Caesar was particularly anxious to catch him, and once had found the nest warm which Ambiorix had left but a few moments before.

  In the pursuit he came again to Tongres, to the fatal camp which Sabinus had deserted and in which the last of the legionaries had killed each other, rather than degrade the Roman name by allowing themselves to be captured. The spot was fated, and narrowly escaped being the scene of a second catastrophe as frightful as the first. The entrenchments were standing as they were left, ready to be occupied. Caesar, finding himself encumbered by his heavy baggage in the pursuit of Ambiorix, decided to leave it there with Quintus Cicero and the 14th legion. He was going himself to scour Brabant and East Flanders as far as the Scheldt. In seven days he promised to return, and meanwhile he gave Cicero strict directions to keep the legion within the lines, and not to allow any of the men to stray. It happened that after Caesar recrossed the Rhine two thousand German horse had followed in bravado, and were then plundering between Tongres and the river. Hearing that there was a rich booty in the camp, that Caesar was away, and only a small party had been left to guard it, they decided to try to take the place by a sudden stroke. Cicero, seeing no sign of an enemy, had permitted his men to disperse in foraging parties. The Germans were on them before they could recover their entrenchments, and they had to form at a distance and defend themselves as they could. The gates of the camp were open, and the enemy were actually inside before the few maniples who were left there were able to collect and resist them. Fortunately Sextius Bacillus, the same officer who had so brilliantly distinguished himself in the battle with the Nervii, and had since been badly wounded, was lying sick in his tent, where he had been for five days, unable to touch food. Hearing the disturbance, Bacillus sprang out, snatched a sword, rallied such men as he could find, and checked the attack for a few minutes. Other officers rushed to his help, and the legionaries having their centurions with them recovered their steadiness. Sextius Bacillus was again severely hurt, and fainted, but he was carried off in safety. Some of the cohorts who were outside, and had been for a time cut off, made their way into the camp to join the defenders, and the Germans, who had come without any fixed purpose, merely for plunder, gave way and galloped off again. They left the Romans, however, still in the utmost consternation. The scene and the associations of it suggested the most gloomy anticipations.

They thought that German cavalry could never be so far from the Rhine, unless their countrymen were invading in force behind them. Caesar, it was supposed, must have been surprised and destroyed, and they and every Roman in Gaul would soon share the same fate. Brave as they were, the Roman soldiers seem to have been curiously liable to panics of this kind. The faith with which they relied upon their general avenged itself through the completeness with which they were accustomed to depend upon him. He returned on the day which he had fixed, and not unnaturally was displeased at the disregard of his orders. He did not, or does not in his Commentaries, professedly blame Cicero. But the Ciceros perhaps resented the loss of confidence which one of them had brought upon himself. Quintus Cicero cooled in his zeal, and afterward amused the leisure of his winter quarters with composing worthless dramas.

Ambiorix had again escaped, and was never taken. The punishment fell on his tribe. The Eburones were completely rooted out. The turn of the Carnutes and Senones came next. The people themselves were spared; but their leader, a chief named Acco, who was found to have instigated the revolt, was arrested and executed. Again the whole of Gaul settled into seeming quiet; and Caesar went to Italy, where the political frenzy was now boiling over.

[1] Caesar says their trenches were fifteen miles long. This is, perhaps, a mistake of the transcriber. A Roman camp did not usually cover more than a few acres.

[2] People about Sens, Melun, and Chartres.

CHAPTER XVIII.

[Sidenote: B.C. 55.] The conference at Lucca and the Senate's indifference had determined Cicero to throw in his lot with the trimmers. He had remonstrated with Pompey on the imprudence of prolonging Caesar's command. Pompey, he thought, would find out in time that he had made Caesar too strong for him; but Pompey had refused to listen, and Cicero had concluded that he must consider his own interests. His brother Quintus joined the army in Gaul to take part in the invasion of Britain, and to share the dangers and the honors of the winter which followed it. Cicero himself began a warm correspondence with Caesar, and through Quintus sent continued messages to him. Literature was a neutral ground on which he could approach his political enemy without too open discredit, and he courted eagerly the approval of a critic whose literary genius he esteemed as highly as his own. Men of genuine ability are rarely vain of what they can do really well. Cicero admired himself as a statesman with the most unbounded enthusiasm. He was proud of his verses, which were hopelessly commonplace. In the art in which he was without a rival he was modest and diffident. He sent his various writings for Caesar's judgment. "Like the traveller who has overslept himself," he said, "yet by extraordinary exertions reaches his goal sooner than if he had been earlier on the road, I will follow your advice and court this man. I have been asleep too long. I will correct my slowness with my speed; and as you say he approves my verses, I shall travel not with a common carriage, but with a four-in-hand of poetry." [1]

"What does Caesar say of my poems?" he wrote again. "He tells me in one of his letters that he has never read better Greek. At one place he writes [Greek: rathumotera] [somewhat careless]. This is his word. Tell me the truth, Was it the matter which did not please him, or the style?" "Do not be afraid," he added with candid simplicity; "I shall not think a hair the worse of myself." [2]

His affairs were still in disorder. Caesar had now large sums at his disposition. Cicero gave the highest proof of the sincerity of his conversion by accepting money from him. "You say," he observed in another letter, "that Caesar shows every day more marks of his affection for you. It gives me infinite pleasure. I can have no second thoughts in Caesar's affairs. I act on conviction, and am doing but my duty; but I am inflamed with love for him." [3]

With Pompey and Crassus Cicero seemed equally familiar. When their consulship was over, their provinces were assigned as had been determined. Pompey had Spain, with six legions. He remained himself at Rome, sending lieutenants in charge of them. Crassus aspired to equal the glory of his colleagues in the open field. He had gained some successes in the war with the slaves which persuaded him that he too could be a conqueror; and knowing as much of foreign campaigning as the clerks in his factories, he intended to use Syria as a base of operations against the Parthians, and to extend the frontier to the Indus. The Senate had murmured, but Cicero had passionately defended Crassus;[4] and as if to show publicly how entirely he had now devoted himself to the cause of the "Dynasts," he invited Crassus to dine with him the day before his departure for the East.

The position was not wholly pleasant to Cicero. "Self-respect in speech, liberty in choosing the course which we will pursue, is all gone," he wrote to Lentulus Spinther--"gone not more from me than from us all. We must assent, as a matter of course, to what a few men say, or we must differ from them to no purpose.--The relations of the Senate, of the courts of justice, nay, of the whole Commonwealth are changed.--The consular dignity of a firm and courageous statesman can no longer be thought of. It has been lost by the folly of those who estranged from the Senate the compact order of the equites and a very distinguished man [Caesar]." [5] And again: "We must go with the times. Those who have played a great part in public life have never been able to adhere to the same views on all occasions. The art of navigation lies in trimming to the storm. When you can reach your harbor by altering your course, it is a folly to persevere in struggling against the wind. Were I entirely free I should still act as I am doing; and when I am invited to my present attitude by the kindness of one set of men, and am driven to it by the injurious conduct of the other, I am content to do what I conceive will conduce at once to my own advantage and the welfare of the State.--Caesar's influence is enormous. His wealth is vast. I have the use of both, as if they were my own. Nor could I have crushed the conspiracy of a set of villains to ruin me, unless, in addition to the defences which I always possessed, I had secured the goodwill of the men in power." [6]

[Sidenote: B.C. 54.] Cicero's conscience could not have been easy when he was driven to such laborious apologies. He spoke often of intending to withdraw into his family, and devoting his time entirely to literature; but he could not bring himself to leave the political ferment; and he was possessed besides with a passionate desire to revenge himself on those who had injured him. An opportunity seemed to present itself. The persons whom he hated most, after Clodius, were the two consuls Gabinius and Piso, who had permitted his exile. They had both conducted themselves abominably in the provinces, which they had bought, he said, at the price of his blood. Piso had been sent to Macedonia, where he had allowed his army to perish by disease and neglect. The frontiers had been overrun with brigands, and the outcries of his subjects had been audible even in Rome against his tyranny and incapacity. Gabinius, in Syria, had been more ambitious, and had exposed himself to an indignation more violent because more interested. At a hint from Pompey, he had restored Ptolemy to Egypt on his own authority and without waiting for the Senate's sanction, and he had snatched for himself the prize for which the chiefs of the Senate had been contending. He had broken the law by leading his legions over the frontier. He had defeated the feeble Alexandrians, and the gratified Ptolemy had rewarded him with the prodigious sum of ten thousand talents--a million and a half of English money. While he thus enriched himself he had irritated the knights, who might otherwise have supported him, by quarrelling with the Syrian revenue farmers, and, according to popular scandal, he had plundered the province worse than it had been plundered even by the pirates.

When so fair a chance was thrown in his way, Cicero would have been more than human if he had not availed himself of it. He moved in the Senate for the recall of the two offenders, and in the finest of his speeches he laid bare their reputed iniquities. His position was a delicate one, because the senatorial party, could they have had their way, would have recalled Caesar also. Gabinius was Pompey's favorite, and Piso was Caesar's father- in-law. Cicero had no intention of quarrelling with Caesar; between his invectives, therefore, he was careful to interweave the most elaborate compliments to the conqueror of Gaul. He dwelt with extraordinary clearness on the value of Caesar's achievements. The conquest of Gaul, he said, was not the annexation of a province. It was the dispersion of a cloud which had threatened Italy from the days of Brennus. To recall Caesar would be madness. He wished to remain only to complete his work; the more honor to him that he was willing to let the laurels fade which were waiting for him at Rome, before he returned to wear them. There were persons who would bring him back, because they did not love him. They would bring him back only to enjoy a triumph. Gaul had been the single danger to the Empire. Nature had fortified Italy by the Alps. The mountain-barrier alone had allowed Rome to grow to its present greatness, but the Alps might now sink into the earth, Italy had no more to fear.[7]

The orator perhaps hoped that so splendid a vindication of Caesar in the midst of his worst enemies might have purchased pardon for his onslaught on the baser members of the "Dynastic" faction. He found himself mistaken. His eagerness to revenge his personal wrongs compelled him to drink the bitterest cup of humiliation which had yet been offered to him. He gained his immediate purpose. The two governors were recalled in disgrace, and Gabinius was impeached under the new Julian law for having restored Ptolemy without orders, and for the corrupt administration of his province. Cicero would naturally have conducted the prosecution; but pressure of some kind was laid on, which compelled him to stand aside. The result of the trial on the first of the two indictments was another of those mockeries of justice which made the Roman law-courts the jest of mankind. Pompey threw his shield over his instrument. He used his influence freely. The Egyptian spoils furnished a fund to corrupt the judges. The speech for the prosecution was so weak as to invite a failure, and Gabinius was acquitted by a majority of purchased votes. "You ask me how I endure such things," Cicero bitterly wrote, in telling the story to Atticus; "well enough, by Hercules, and I am entirely pleased with myself. We have lost, my friend, not only the juice and blood, but even the color and shape, of a commonwealth. No decent constitution exists in which I can take a part. How can you put up with such a state of things? you will say. Excellently well. I recollect how public affairs went awhile ago, when I was myself in office, and how grateful people were to me. I am not distressed now, that the power is with a single man. Those are miserable who could not bear to see me successful. I find much to console me." [8] "Gabinius is acquitted," he wrote to his brother.--"The verdict is so infamous that it is thought he will be convicted on the other charge; but, as you perceive, the constitution, the Senate, the courts, are all nought. There is no honor in any one of us.--Some persons, Sallust among them, say that I ought to have prosecuted him. I to risk my credit with such a jury! what if I had acted, and he had escaped then! but other motives influenced me. Pompey would have made a personal quarrel of it with me. He would have come into the city.[9]--He would have taken up with Clodius again. I know that I was wise, and I hope that you agree with me. I owe Pompey nothing, and he owes much to me; but in public matters (not to put it more strongly) he has not allowed me to oppose him; and when I was flourishing and he was less powerful than he is now, he let me see what he could do. Now when I am not even ambitious of power, and the constitution is broken down, and Pompey is omnipotent, why should I contend with him? Then, says Sallust, I ought to have pleased Pompey by defending Gabinius, as he was anxious that I should. A nice friend Sallust, who would have me push myself into dangerous quarrels, or cover myself with eternal infamy!" [10]

Unhappy Cicero, wishing to act honorably, but without manliness to face the consequences! He knew that it would be infamous for him to defend Gabinius, yet at the second trial Cicero, who had led the attack on him in the Senate, and had heaped invectives on him, the most bitter which he ever uttered against man, nevertheless actually did defend Gabinius. Perhaps he consoled himself with the certainty that his eloquence would be in vain, and that his extraordinary client this time could not escape conviction. Any way, he appeared at the bar as Gabinius's counsel. The Syrian revenue farmers were present, open-mouthed with their accusations. Gabinius was condemned, stripped of his spoils, and sent into banishment. Cicero was left with his shame. Nor was this the worst. There were still some dregs in the cup, which he was forced to drain. Publius Vatinius was a prominent leader of the military democratic party, and had often come in collision with Cicero. He had been tribune when Caesar was consul, and had stood by him against the Senate and Bibulus. He had served in Gaul in Caesar's first campaigns, and had returned to Rome, at Caesar's instance, to enter for higher office. He had carried the praetorship against Cato; and Cicero in one of his speeches had painted him as another Clodius or Catiline. When the praetorship was expired, he was prosecuted for corruption; and Cicero was once more compelled to appear on the other side, and defend him, as he had done Gabinius. Caesar and Pompey, wishing perhaps to break completely into harness the brilliant but still half unmanageable orator, had so ordered, and Cicero had complied. He was ashamed, but he had still his points of satisfaction. It was a matter of course that, as an advocate, he must praise the man whom, a year before, he had spattered with ignominy; but he had the pleasure of feeling that he was revenging himself on his conservative allies, who led the prosecution. "Why I praised Vatinius," he wrote to Lentulus, "I must beg you not to ask either in the case of this or of any other criminal. I put it to the judges that since certain noble lords, my good friends, were too fond of my adversary [Clodius], and in the Senate would go apart with him under my own eyes, and would treat him with warmest affection, they must allow me to have my Publius [Vatinius], since they had theirs [Clodius], and give them a gentle stab in return for their cuts at me." [11] Vatinius was acquitted. Cicero was very miserable. "Gods and men approved," he said; but his own conscience condemned him, and at this time his one consolation, real or pretended, was the friendship of Caesar. "Caesar's affectionate letters," he told his brother, "are my only pleasure; I attach little consequence to his promises; I do not thirst for honors, or regret my past glory. I value more the continuance of his good-will than the prospect of anything which he may do for me. I am withdrawing from public affairs, and giving myself to literature. But I am broken-hearted, my dear brother;--I am broken-hearted that the constitution is gone, that the courts of law are naught; and that now at my time of life, when I ought to be leading with authority in the Senate, I must be either busy in the Forum pleading, or occupying myself with my books at home. The ambition of my boyhood--

Aye to be first, and chief among my peers--is all departed. Of my enemies, I have left some unassailed, and some I even defend. Not only I may not think as I like, but I may not hate as I like,[12] and Caesar is the only person who loves me as I should wish to be loved, or, as some think, who desires to love me." [13]

[Sidenote: B.C. 53.] The position was the more piteous, because Cicero could not tell how events would fall out after all. Crassus was in the East, with uncertain prospects there. Caesar was in the midst of a dangerous war, and might be killed or might die. Pompey was but a weak vessel; a distinguished soldier, perhaps, but without the intellect or the resolution to control a proud, resentful, and supremely unscrupulous aristocracy. In spite of Caesar's victories, his most envenomed enemy, Domitius Ahenobarbus, had succeeded after all in carrying one of the consulships for the year 54. The popular party had secured the other, indeed; but they had returned Appius Claudius, Clodius's brother, and this was but a poor consolation. In the year that was to follow, the conservatives had bribed to an extent which astonished the most cynical observers. Each season the elections were growing more corrupt; but the proceedings on both sides in the fall of 54 were the most audacious that had ever been known, the two reigning consuls taking part, and encouraging and assisting in scandalous bargains. "All the candidates have bribed," wrote Cicero; "but they will be all acquitted, and no one will ever be found guilty again. The two consuls are branded with infamy." Memmius, the popular competitor, at Pompey's instance, exposed in the Senate an arrangement which the consuls had entered into to secure the returns. The names and signatures were produced. The scandal was monstrous, and could not be denied. The better kind of men began to speak of a dictatorship as the only remedy; and although the two conservative candidates were declared elected for 53, and were allowed to enter on their offices, there was a general feeling that a crisis had arrived, and that a great catastrophe could not be very far off. The form which it might assume was the problem of the hour.

Cicero, speaking two years before on the broad conditions of his time, had used these remarkable words: "No issue can be anticipated from discords among the leading men, except either universal ruin, or the rule of a conqueror, or a monarchy. There exists at present an unconcealed hatred implanted and fastened into the minds of our leading politicians. They are at issue among themselves. Opportunities are caught for mutual injury. Those who are in the second rank watch for the chances of the time. Those who might do better are afraid of the words and designs of their enemies." [14]

The discord had been suspended, and the intrigues temporarily checked, by the combination of Caesar and Pompey with Crassus, the chief of the moneyed commoners. Two men of equal military reputation, and one of them from his greater age and older services expecting and claiming precedency, do not easily work together. For Pompey to witness the rising glory of Caesar, and to feel in his own person the superior ascendency of Caesar's character, without an emotion of jealousy, would have demanded a degree of virtue which few men have ever possessed. They had been united so far by identity of conviction, by a military detestation of anarchy, by a common interest in wringing justice from the Senate for the army and people, by a pride in the greatness of their country, which they were determined to uphold. These motives, however, might not long have borne the strain but for other ties, which had cemented their union. Pompey had married Caesar's daughter, to whom he was passionately attached; and the personal competition between them was neutralized by the third element of the capitalist party represented by Crassus, which if they quarrelled would secure the supremacy of the faction to which Crassus attached himself. There was no jealousy on Caesar's part. There was no occasion for it. Caesar's fame was rising. Pompey had added nothing to his past distinctions, and the glory pales which does not grow in lustre. No man who had once been the single object of admiration, who had tasted the delight of being the first in the eyes of his countrymen, could find himself compelled to share their applause with a younger rival without experiencing a pang. So far Pompey had borne the trial well. He was on the whole, notwithstanding the Egyptian scandal, honorable and constitutionally disinterested. He was immeasurably superior to the fanatic Cato, to the shifty Cicero, or the proud and worthless leaders of the senatorial oligarchy. Had the circumstances remained unchanged, the severity of the situation might have been overcome. But two misfortunes coming near upon one another broke the ties of family connection, and by destroying the balance of parties laid Pompey open to the temptation of patrician intrigue. In the year 54 Caesar's great mother Aurelia, and his sister Julia, Pompey's wife, both died. A child which Julia had borne to Pompey died also, and the powerful if silent influence of two remarkable women, and the joint interest in an infant, who would have been Caesar's heir as well as Pompey's, were swept away together.

The political link was broken immediately after by a public disaster unequalled since the last consular army was overthrown by the Gauls on the Rhone; and the capitalists, left without a leader, drifted away to their natural allies in the Senate. Crassus had taken the field in the East, with a wild ambition of becoming in his turn a great conqueror. At first all had gone well with him. He had raised a vast treasure. He had plundered the wealthy temples in Phoenicia and Palestine to fill his military chest. He had able officers with him; not the least among them his son Publius Crassus, who had served with such distinction under Caesar. He crossed the Euphrates at the head of a magnificent army, expecting to carry all before him with the ease of an Alexander. Relying on his own idle judgment, he was tempted in the midst of a burning summer into the waterless plains of Mesopotamia; and on the 15th of June the great Roman millionaire met his miserable end, the whole force, with the exception of a few scattered cohorts, being totally annihilated.

The catastrophe in itself was terrible. The Parthians had not provoked the war. The East was left defenceless; and the natural expectation was that, in their just revenge, they might carry fire and sword through Asia Minor and Syria. It is not the least remarkable sign of the times that the danger failed to touch the patriotism of the wretched factions in Rome. The one thought of the leaders of the Senate was to turn the opportunity to advantage, wrest the constitution free from military dictation, shake off the detested laws of Caesar, and revenge themselves on the author of them. Their hope was in Pompey. If Pompey could be won over from Caesar, the army would be divided. Pompey, they well knew, unless he had a stronger head than his own to guide him, could be used till the victory was won, and then be thrust aside. It was but too easy to persuade him that he was the greatest man in the Empire; and that as the chief of a constitutional government, and with the Senate at his side, he would inscribe his name in the annals of his country as the restorer of Roman liberty.

The intrigue could not be matured immediately. The aristocracy had first to overcome their own animosities against Pompey, and Pompey himself was generous, and did not yield to the first efforts of seduction. The smaller passions were still at work among the baser senatorial chiefs, and the appetite for provinces and pillage. The Senate, even while Crassus was alive, had carried the consulships for 53 by the most infamous corruption. They meant now to attack Caesar in earnest, and their energies were addressed to controlling the elections for the next year. Milo was one of the candidates; and Cicero, who was watching the political current, reverted to his old friendship for him, and became active in the canvass. Milo was not a creditable ally. He already owed half a million of money, and Cicero, who was anxious for his reputation, endeavored to keep him within the bounds of decency. But Milo's mind was fastened on the province which was to redeem his fortunes, and he flung into bribery what was left of his wrecked credit with the desperation of a gambler. He had not been praetor, and thus was not legally eligible for the consulate. This, however, was forgiven. He had been aedile in 54, and as aedile he had already been magnificent in prodigality. But to secure the larger prize, he gave as a private citizen the most gorgeous entertainment which even in that monstrous age the city had yet wondered at. "Doubly, trebly foolish of him," thought Cicero, "for he was not called on to go to such expense, and he has not the means." "Milo makes me very anxious," he wrote to his brother. "I hope all will be made right by his consulship. I shall exert myself for him as much as I did for myself;[15] but he is quite mad," Cicero added; "he has spent ?0,000 on his games." Mad, but still, in Cicero's opinion, well fitted for the consulship, and likely to get it. All the "good," in common with himself, were most anxious for Milo's success. The people would vote for him as a reward for the spectacles, and the young and influential for his efforts to secure their favor.[16]

The reappearance of the "Boni," the "Good," in Cicero's letters marks the turn of the tide again in his own mind. The "Good," or the senatorial party, were once more the objects of his admiration. The affection for Caesar was passing off.

[Sidenote: B.C. 52.] A more objectionable candidate than Milo could hardly have been found. He was no better than a patrician gladiator, and the choice of such a man was a sufficient indication of the Senate's intentions. The popular party led by the tribunes made a sturdy resistance. There were storms in the Curia, tribunes imprisoning senators, and the Senate tribunes. Army officers suggested the election of military tribunes (lieutenant-generals), instead of consuls; and when they failed, they invited Pompey to declare himself Dictator. The Senate put on mourning, as a sign of approaching calamity. Pompey calmed their fears by declining so ambitious a position. But as it was obvious that Milo's chief object was a province which he might misgovern, Pompey forced the Senate to pass a resolution that consuls and praetors must wait five years from their term of office before a province was to be allotted to them. The temptation to corruption might thus in some degree be diminished. But senatorial resolutions did not pass for much, and what a vote had enacted a vote could repeal. The agitation continued. The tribunes, when the time came, forbade the elections. The year expired. The old magistrates went out of office, and Rome was left again without legitimate functionaries to carry on the government. All the offices fell vacant together.

Now once more Clodius was reappearing on the scene. He had been silent for two years, content or constrained to leave the control of the democracy to the three chiefs. One of them was now gone. The more advanced section of the party was beginning to distrust Pompey. Clodius, their favorite representative, had been put forward for the praetorship, while Milo was aspiring to be made consul, and Clodius had prepared a fresh batch of laws to be submitted to the sovereign people; one of which (if Cicero did not misrepresent it to inflame the aristocracy) was a measure of some kind for the enfranchisement of the slaves, or perhaps of the sons of slaves.[17] He was as popular as ever. He claimed to be acting for Caesar, and was held certain of success; if he was actually praetor, such was his extraordinary influence, and such was the condition of things in the city, that if Milo was out of the way he could secure consuls of his own way of thinking, and thus have the whole constitutional power in his hands.[18]

Thus both sides had reason for fearing and postponing the elections. Authority, which had been weak before, was now extinct. Rome was in a state of formal anarchy, and the factions of Milo and Clodius fought daily, as before, in the streets, with no one to interfere with them.

Violent humors come naturally to a violent end. Milo had long before threatened to kill Clodius. Cicero had openly boasted of his friend's intention to do it, and had spoken of Clodius in the Senate itself as Milo's predestined victim. On the evening of the 13th January, while the uncertainty about the elections was at its height, Clodius was returning from his country house, which was a few miles from Rome on "the Appian Way." Milo happened to be travelling accidentally down the same road, on his way to Lanuvium (Civita Indovina), and the two rivals and their escorts met. Milo's party was the largest. The leaders passed one another, evidently not intending a collision, but their followers, who were continually at sword's point, came naturally to blows. Clodius rode back to see what was going on; he was attacked and wounded, and took refuge in a house on the roadside. The temptation to make an end of his enemy was too strong for Milo to resist. To have hurt Clodius would, he thought, be as dangerous as to have made an end of him. His blood was up. The "predestined victim," who had thwarted him for so many years, was within his reach. The house was forced open. Clodius was dragged out bleeding, and was despatched, and the body was left lying where he fell, where a senator, named Sextus Tedius, who was passing an hour or two after, found it, and carried it the same night to Rome. The little which is known of Clodius comes only through Cicero's denunciations, which formed or colored later Roman traditions; and it is thus difficult to comprehend the affection which the people felt for him; but of the fact there can be no doubt at all; he was the representative of their political opinions, the embodiment, next to Caesar, of their practical hopes; and his murder was accepted as a declaration of an aristocratic war upon them, and the first blow in another massacre. On the following day, in the winter morning, the tribunes brought the body into the Forum. A vast crowd had collected to see it, and it was easy to lash them into fury. They dashed in the doors of the adjoining senate-house, they carried in the bier, made a pile of chairs and benches and tables, and burnt all that remained of Clodius in the ashes of the senate-house itself. The adjoining temples were consumed in the conflagration. The Senate collected elsewhere. They put on a bold front, they talked of naming an interrex--which they ought to have done before--and of holding the elections instantly, now that Clodius was gone. Milo still hoped, and the aristocracy still hoped for Milo. But the storm was too furious. Pompey came in with a body of troops, restored order, and took command of the city. The preparations for the election were quashed. Pompey still declined the dictatorship, but he was named, or he named himself, sole consul, and at once appointed a commission to inquire into the circumstances of Milo's canvass, and the corruption which had gone along with it. Milo himself was arrested and put on his trial for the murder. Judges were chosen who could be trusted, and to prevent intimidation the court was occupied by soldiers. Cicero undertook his friend's defence, but was unnerved by the stern, grim faces with which he was surrounded. The eloquent tongue forgot its office. He stammered, blundered, and sat down.[19] The consul expectant was found guilty and banished, to return a few years after like a hungry wolf in the civil war, and to perish as he deserved. Pompey's justice was even-handed. He punished Milo, but the senate-house and temples were not to be destroyed without retribution equally severe. The tribunes who had led on the mob were deposed, and suffered various penalties. Pompey acted with a soldier's abhorrence of disorder, and, so far, he did what Caesar approved and would himself have done in Pompey's place.

But there followed symptoms which showed that there were secret influences at work with Pompey, and that he was not the man which he had been. He had taken the consulate alone; but a single consul was an anomaly; as soon as order was restored it was understood that he meant to choose a colleague; and Senate and people were watching to see whom he would select as an indication of his future attitude. Half the world expected that he would name Caesar, but half the world was disappointed. He took Metellus Scipio, who had been the Senate's second candidate by the side of Milo, and had been as deeply concerned in bribery as Milo himself; shortly after, and with still more significance, he replaced Julia by Metellus Scipio's daughter, the widow of young Publius Crassus, who had fallen with his father.

Pompey, however, did not break with Caesar, and did not appear to intend to break with him. Communications passed between them on the matter of the consulship. The tribunes had pressed him as Pompey's colleague. Caesar himself, being then in the north of Italy, had desired, on being consulted, that the demand might not be insisted on. He had work still before him in Gaul which he could not leave unfinished; but he made a request himself that must be noticed, since the civil war formally grew out of it, and Pompey gave a definite pledge, which was afterwards broken.

One of the engagements at Lucca had been that, when Caesar's command should have expired, he was to be again consul. His term had still three years to run; but many things might happen in three years. A party in the Senate were bent on his recall. They might succeed in persuading the people to consent to it. And Caesar felt, as Pompey had felt before him, that, in the unscrupulous humor of his enemies at Rome he might be impeached or killed on his return, as Clodius had been, if he came back a private citizen unprotected by office to sue for his election. Therefore he had stipulated at Lucca that his name might be taken and that votes might be given for him while he was still with his army. On Pompey's taking the power into his hands, Caesar, while abandoning any present claim to share it, reminded him of this understanding, and required at the same time that it should be renewed in some authoritative form. The Senate, glad to escape on any terms from the present conjunction of the men whom they hoped to divide, appeared to consent. Cicero himself made a journey to Ravenna to see Caesar about it and make a positive arrangement with him. Pompey submitted the condition to the assembly of the people, by whom it was solemnly ratified. Every precaution was observed which would give the promise, that Caesar might be elected consul in his absence, the character of a binding engagement.[20]

It was observed with some surprise that Pompey, not long after, proposed and carried a law forbidding elections of this irregular kind, and insisting freshly on the presence of the candidates in person. Caesar's case was not reserved as an exception or in any way alluded to. And when a question was asked on the subject, the excuse given was that it had been overlooked by accident. Such accidents require to be interpreted by the use which is made of them.

[1] Ad Quintum Fratrem, ii. 15.

[2] "Ego enim ne pilo quidem minus me amabo."--Ibid., ii. 16. Other editions read "te."

[3] "Videor id judicio facere: jam enim debeo: sed amore sum incensus."--Ad Quintum Fratrem, iii. 1.

[4] Ad Crassum. Ad Familiares, v. 8.

[5] Ad Lentulum. Ad Fam., i. 8.

[6] Ibid., i. 9.

[7] De Provinciis Consularibus.

[8] To Atticus, iv. 16.

[9] Pompey, as proconsul with a province, was residing outside the walls.

[10] Ad Quintum fratrem, iii. 4.

[11] Ad Familiares, i. 9.

[12] "Meum non modo animum, sed ne odium quidem esse liberum."--Ad Quintum Fratrem, iii. 5.

[13] See the story in a letter to Atticus, lib. iv. 16-17.

[14] De Haruspicum Responsis.

[15] "Angit unus Milo. Sed velim finem afferat consulatus: in quo enitar non minus, quam sum enisus in nostro."--Ad Quintum Fratrem, iii. 9.

[16] Ad Familiares, ii. 6.

[17] "Incidebantur jam domi leges quae nos nostris servis addicerent.... Oppressisset omnia, possideret, teneret lege nov? quae est inventa apud eum cum reliquis legibus Clodianis. Servos nostros libertos suos fecisset."--Pro Milone, 32, 33. These strong expressions can hardly refer to a proposed enfranchisement of the libertini, or sons of freedmen, like Horace's father.

[18] "Caesaris potentiam suam esse dicebat.... An consules in praetore coercendo fortes fuissent? Primum, Milone occiso habuisset suos consules."--Pro Milone, 33.

[19] The Oratio pro Milone, published afterwards by Cicero, was the speech which he intended to deliver and did not.

[20] Suetonius, _De Vit?Julii Caesaris_. Cicero again and again acknowledges

in his letters to Atticus that the engagement had really been made. Writing to Atticus (vii. 1), Cicero says: "Non est locus ad tergiversandum. Contra Caesarem? Ubi illae sunt densae dexterae? Nam ut illi hoc liceret adjuvi rogatus ab ipso Ravennae de Caelio tribuno plebis. Ab ipso autem? Etiam a Cnaeo nostro in illo divino tertio consulatu. Aliter sensero?"

CHAPTER XIX.

The conquest of Gaul had been an exploit of extraordinary military difficulty. The intricacy of the problem had been enhanced by the venom of a domestic faction, to which the victories of a democratic general were more unwelcome than national disgrace. The discomfiture of Crassus had been more pleasant news to the Senate than the defeat of Ariovistus, and the passionate hope of the aristocracy had been for some opportunity which would enable them to check Caesar in his career of conquest and bring him home to dishonor and perhaps impeachment. They had failed. The efforts of the Gauls to maintain or recover their independence had been successively beaten down, and at the close of the summer of 53 Caesar had returned to the north of Italy, believing that the organization of the province which he had added to the Empire was all that remained to be accomplished. But Roman civilians had followed in the van of the armies. Roman traders had penetrated into the towns on the Seine and the Loire, and the curious Celts had learnt from them the distractions of their new rulers. Caesar's situation was as well understood among the Aedui and the Sequani as in the clubs and coteries of the capital of the Empire, and the turn of events was watched with equal anxiety. The victory over Sabinus, sharply avenged as it had been, kept alive the hope that their independence might yet be recovered. The disaffection of the preceding summer had been trampled out, but the ashes of it were still smouldering; and when it became known that Clodius, who was regarded as Caesar's tribune, had been killed, that the Senate was in power again, and that Italy was threatened with civil convulsions, their passionate patriotism kindled once more into flame. Sudden in their resolutions, they did not pause to watch how the balance would incline. Caesar was across the Alps. Either he would be deposed, or civil war would detain him in Italy. His legions were scattered between Auxerre and Sens, far from the Roman frontier. A simultaneous rising would cut them off from support, and they could be starved out or overwhelmed in detail, as Sabinus had been at Tongres and Cicero had almost been at Charleroy. Intelligence was swiftly exchanged. The chiefs of all the tribes established communications with each other. They had been deeply affected by the execution of Acco, the patriotic leader of the Carnutes. The death of Acco was an intimation that they were Roman subjects, and were to be punished as traitors if they disobeyed a Roman command. They buried their own dissensions. Except among the Aedui there was no longer a Roman faction and a patriot faction. The whole nation was inspired by a simultaneous impulse to snatch the opportunity, and unite in a single effort to assert their freedom. The understanding was complete. A day was fixed for a universal rising. The Carnutes began by a massacre which would cut off possibility of retreat, and, in revenge for Acco, slaughtered a party of Roman civilians who were engaged in business at Gien.[1] A system of signals had been quietly arranged. The massacre at Gien was known in a few hours in the south, and the Auvergne country, which had hitherto been entirely peaceful, rose in reply, under a young high-born chief named Vercingetorix. Gergovia, the principal town of the Arverni, was for the moment undecided.[2] The elder men there, who had known the Romans long, were against immediate action; but Vercingetorix carried the people away with him. His name had not appeared in the earlier campaigns, but his father had been a man of note beyond the boundaries of Auvergne; and he must himself have had a wide reputation among the Gauls, for everywhere, from the Seine to the Garonne, he was accepted as chief of the national confederacy. Vercingetorix had high ability and real organizing powers. He laid out a plan for the general campaign. He fixed a contingent of men and arms which each tribe was to supply, and failure brought instantaneous punishment. Mild offences were visited with the loss of eyes or ears; neglect of a more serious sort with death by fire in the wicker tower. Between enthusiasm and terror he had soon an army at his command, which he could increase indefinitely at his need. Part he left to watch the Roman province and prevent Caesar, if he should arrive, from passing through. With part he went himself to watch the Aedui, the great central race, where Roman authority had hitherto prevailed unshaken, but among whom, as he well knew, he had the mass of the people on his side. The Aedui were hesitating. They called their levies under arms, as if to oppose him, but they withdrew them again; and to waver at such a moment was to yield to the stream.

The Gauls had not calculated without reason on Caesar's embarrassments. The death of Clodius had been followed by the burning of the senate-house and by many weeks of anarchy. To leave Italy at such a moment might be to leave it a prey to faction or civil war. His anxiety was relieved at last by hearing that Pompey had acted, and that order was restored; and seeing no occasion for his own interference, and postponing the agitation for his second consulship, he hurried back to encounter the final and convulsive effort of the Celtic race to preserve their liberties. The legions were as yet in no danger. They were dispersed in the north of France, far from the scene of the present rising, and the northern tribes had suffered too desperately in the past years to be in a condition to stir without assistance. But how was Caesar to join them? The garrisons in the province could not be moved. If he sent for the army to come across to him, Vercingetorix would attack them on the march, and he could not feel confident of the result; while the line of the old frontier of the province was in the hands of the insurgents, or of tribes who could not be trusted to resist the temptation, if he passed through himself without more force than the province could supply. But Caesar had a resource which never failed him in the daring swiftness of his own movements. He sent for the troops which were left beyond the Alps. He had a few levies with him to fill the gaps in the old legions, and after a rapid survey of the stations on the provincial frontier he threw himself upon the passes of the Cevennes. It was still winter. The snow lay six feet thick on the mountains, and the roads at that season were considered impracticable even for single travellers. The Auvergne rebels dreamt of nothing so little as of Caesar's coming upon them at such a time and from such a quarter. He forced his way. He fell on them while they were lying in imagined security, Vercingetorix and his army being absent watching the Aedui, and, letting loose his cavalry, he laid their country waste. But Vercingetorix, he knew, would fly back at the news of his arrival; and he had already made his further plans. He formed a strong entrenched camp, where he left Decimus Brutus in charge, telling him that he would return as quickly as possible; and, unknown to any one, lest the troops should lose courage at parting with him, he flew across through an enemy's country with a handful of attendants to Vienne, on the Rhone, where some cavalry from the province had been sent to wait for him. Vercingetorix, supposing him still to be in the Auvergne, thought only of the camp of Brutus; and Caesar, riding day and night through the doubtful territories of the Aedui, reached the two legions which were quartered near Auxerre. Thence he sent for the rest to join him, and he was at the head of his army before Vercingetorix knew that only Brutus was in front of him. The Aedui, he trusted, would now remain faithful. But the problem before him was still most intricate. The grass had not begun to grow. Rapid movement was essential to prevent the rebel confederacy from consolidating itself; but rapid movements with a large force required supplies; and whence were the supplies to come? Some risks had to be run, but to delay was the most dangerous of all. On the defeat of the Helvetii, Caesar had planted a colony of them at Gorgobines, near Nevers, on the Loire. These colonists, called Boii, had refused to take part in the rising; and Vercingetorix, turning in contempt from Brutus, had gone off to punish them. Caesar ordered the Aedui to furnish his commissariat, sent word to the Boii that he was coming to their relief, swept through the Senones, that he might leave no enemy in his rear, and then advanced on Gien, where the Roman traders had been murdered, and which the Carnutes still occupied in force. There was a bridge there over the Loire, by which they tried to escape in the night. Caesar had beset the passage. He took the whole of them prisoners, plundered and burnt the town, gave the spoil to his troops, and then crossed the river and went up to help the Boii. He took Nevers. Vercingetorix, who was hastening to its relief, ventured his first battle with him; but the cavalry, on which the Gauls most depended, were scattered by Caesar's German horse. He was entirely beaten, and Caesar turned next to Avaricum (Bourges), a rich and strongly fortified town of the Bituriges. From past experience Caesar had gathered that the Gauls were easily excited and as easily discouraged. If he could reduce Bourges, he hoped that this part of the country would return to its allegiance. Perhaps he thought that Vercingetorix himself would give up the struggle. But he had to deal with a spirit and with a man different from any which he had hitherto encountered. Disappointed in his political expectations, baffled in strategy, and now defeated in open fight, the young chief of the Arverni had only learnt that he had taken a wrong mode of carrying on the war, and that he was wasting his real advantages. Battles in the field he saw that he would lose. But the Roman numbers were limited, and his were infinite. Tens of thousands of gallant young men, with their light, active horses, were eager for any work on which he might set them. They could scour the country far and wide. They could cut off Caesar's supplies. They could turn the fields into a blackened wilderness before him on whichever side he might turn. The hearts of the people were with him. They consented to a universal sacrifice. They burnt their farmsteads. They burnt their villages. Twenty towns (so called) of the Bituriges were consumed in a single day. The tribes adjoining caught the enthusiasm. The horizon at night was a ring of blazing fires. Vercingetorix was for burning Bourges also; but it was the sacred home of the Bituriges, the one spot which they implored to be allowed to save, the most beautiful city in all Gaul. Rivers defended it on three sides, and on the fourth there were swamps and marshes which could be passed only by a narrow ridge. Within the walls the people had placed the best of their property, and Vercingetorix, against his judgment, consented, in pity for their entreaties, that Avaricum should be defended. A strong garrison was left inside. Vercingetorix entrenched himself in the forests sixteen miles distant, keeping watch over Caesar's communications. The place could only be taken by regular approaches, during which the army had to be fed. The Aedui were growing negligent. The feeble Boii, grateful, it seemed, for Caesar's treatment of them, exerted themselves to the utmost, but their small resources were soon exhausted. For many days the legions were without bread. The cattle had been driven into the woods. It came at last to actual famine.[3] "But not one word was heard from them," says Caesar, "unworthy of the majesty of the Roman people or their own earlier victories." He told them that if the distress became unbearable he would raise the siege. With one voice they entreated him to persevere. They had served many years with him, they said, and had never abandoned any enterprise which they had undertaken. They were ready to endure any degree of hardship before they would leave unavenged their countrymen who had been murdered at Gien.

Vercingetorix, knowing that the Romans were in difficulties, ventured nearer. Caesar surveyed his position. It had been well chosen behind a deep morass. The legions clamored to be allowed to advance and attack him, but a victory, he saw, would be dearly purchased. No condemnation could be too severe for him, he said, if he did not hold the lives of his soldiers dearer than his own interest,[4] and he led them back without indulging their eagerness.

The siege work was unexpectedly difficult. The inhabitants of the Loire country were skilled artisans, trained in mines and iron works. The walls, built of alternate layers of stone and timber, were forty feet in thickness, and could neither be burnt nor driven in with the ram. The town could be taken only with the help of an agger--a bank of turf and fagots raised against the wall of sufficient height to overtop the fortifications. The weather was cold and wet, but the legions worked with such a will that in twenty-five days they had raised their bank at last, a hundred yards in width and eighty feet high. As the work drew near its end Caesar himself lay out all night among the men, encouraging them. One morning at daybreak he observed that the agger was smoking. The ingenious Gauls had undermined it and set it on fire. At the same moment they appeared along the walls with pitch-balls, torches, fagots, which they hurled in to feed the flames. There was an instant of confusion, but Caesar uniformly had two legions under arms while the rest were working. The Gauls fought with a courage which called out his warm admiration. He watched them at the points of greatest danger falling under the shots from the scorpions, and others stepping undaunted into their places to fall in the same way. Their valor was unavailing. They were driven in, and the flames were extinguished; the agger was level with the walls, and defence was no longer possible. The garrison intended to slip away at night through the ruins to join their friends outside. The wailing of the women was heard in the Roman camp, and escape was made impossible. The morning after, in a tempest of rain and wind, the place was stormed. The legionaries, excited by the remembrance of Gien and the long resistance, slew every human being that they found, men, women, and children all alike. Out of forty thousand who were within the walls, eight hundred only, that had fled at the first sound of the attack, made their way to the camp of Vercingetorix.

Undismayed by the calamity, Vercingetorix made use of it to sustain the determination of his followers. He pointed out to them that he had himself opposed the defence. The Romans had defeated them, not by superior courage, but by superior science. The heart of the whole nation was united to force the Romans out of Gaul, and they had only to persevere in a course of action where science would be useless, to be sure of success in the end. He fell back upon his own country, taking special care of the poor creatures who had escaped from the carnage; and the effect of the storming of Bourges was to make the national enthusiasm hotter and fiercer than before.

The Romans found in the town large magazines of corn and other provisions, which had been laid in for the siege, and Caesar remained there some days to refresh his troops. The winter was now over. The Aedui were giving him anxiety, and as soon as he could he moved to Decize, a frontier town belonging to them on the Loire, almost in the very centre of France. The anti-Roman faction were growing in influence. He called a council of the principal persons, and, to secure the fidelity of so important a tribe, he deposed the reigning chief and appointed another who had been nominated by the Druids.[5] He lectured the Aedui on their duty, bade them furnish him with ten thousand men, who were to take charge of the commissariat, and then divided his army. Labienus, with four legions, was sent to compose the country between Sens and Paris. He himself, with the remaining six legions, ascended the right bank of the Allier towards Gergovia in search of Vercingetorix. The bridges on the Allier were broken, but Caesar seized and repaired one of them and carried his army over.

The town of Gergovia stood on a high plateau, where the rivers rise which run into the Loire on one side and into the Dordogne on the other. The sides of the hill are steep, and only accessible at a very few places, and the surrounding neighborhood is broken with rocky valleys. Vercingetorix lay in force outside, but in a situation where he could not be attacked except at disadvantage, and with his communication with the fortress secured. He was departing again from his general plan for the campaign in allowing Gergovia to be defended; but it was the central home of his own tribe, and the result showed that he was right in believing it to be impregnable. Caesar saw that it was too strong to be stormed, and that it could only be taken after long operations. After a few skirmishes he seized a spur of the plateau which cut off the garrison from their readiest water-supply, and he formed an entrenched camp upon it. He was studying the rest of the problem when bad news came that the Aedui were unsteady again. The ten thousand men had been raised as he had ordered, but on their way to join him they had murdered the Roman officers in charge of them, and were preparing to go over to Vercingetorix. Leaving two legions to guard his works, he intercepted the Aeduan contingent, took them prisoners, and protected their lives. In his absence Vercingetorix had attacked the camp with determined fury. The fighting had been desperate, and Caesar only returned in time to save it. The reports from the Aedui were worse and worse. The patriotic faction had the upper hand, and with the same passionate determination to commit themselves irrevocably, which had been shown before at Gien, they had massacred every Roman in their territory. It was no time for delaying over a tedious siege: Caesar was on the point of raising it, when accident brought on a battle under the walls. An opportunity seemed to offer itself of capturing the place by escalade, which part of the army attempted contrary to orders. They fought with more than their usual gallantry. The whole scene was visible from the adjoining hills, the Celtic women, with long streaming hair, wildly gesticulating on the walls. The Romans were driven back with worse loss than they had yet met with in Gaul. Forty-six officers and seven hundred men had been killed.

Caesar was never more calm than under a reverse. He addressed the legions the next day. He complimented their courage, but he said it was for the general and not for them to judge when assaults should be tried. He saw the facts of the situation exactly as they were. His army was divided. Labienus was far away with a separate command. The whole of Gaul was in flames. To persevere at Gergovia would only be obstinacy, and he accepted the single military failure which he met with when present in person through the whole of his Gallic campaign.

Difficulties of all kinds were now thickening. Caesar had placed magazines in Nevers, and had trusted them to an Aeduan garrison. The Aeduans burnt the town and carried the stores over the Loire to their own strongest fortress, Bibracte (Mont Beauvray). The river had risen from the melting of the snows, and could not be crossed without danger; and to feed the army in its present position was no longer possible. To retreat upon the province would be a confession of defeat. The passes of the Cevennes would be swarming with enemies, and Labienus with his four legions in the west might be cut off. With swift decision he marched day and night to the Loire. He found a ford where the troops could cross with the water at their armpits. He sent his horse over and cleared the banks. The army passed safely. Food enough and in plenty was found in the Aeduans' country, and without waiting he pressed on toward Sens to reunite his forces. He understood the Gauls, and foresaw what must have happened.

Labienus, when sent on his separate command, had made Sens his headquarters. All down the Seine the country was in insurrection. Leaving the new Italian levies at the station, he went with his experienced troops down the left bank of the river till he came to the Essonne. He found the Gauls entrenched on the other side, and, without attempting to force the passage, he marched back to Melun, where he repaired a bridge which the Gauls had broken, crossed over, and descended without interruption to Paris. The town had been burnt, and the enemy were watching him from the further bank. At this moment he heard of the retreat from Gergovia, and of the rebellion of the Aedui. Such news, he understood at once, would be followed by a rising in Belgium. Report had said that Caesar was falling back on the province. He did not believe it. Caesar, he knew, would not desert him. His own duty, therefore, was to make his way back to Sens. But to leave the army of Gauls to accompany his retreat across the Seine, with the tribes rising on all sides, was to expose himself to the certainty of being intercepted. "In these sudden difficulties," says Caesar, "he took counsel from the valor of his mind." [6] He had brought a fleet of barges with him from Melun. These he sent down unperceived to a point at the bend of the river four miles below Paris, and directed them to wait for him there. When night fell he detached a few cohorts with orders to go up the river with boats as if they were retreating, splashing their oars, and making as much noise as possible. He himself with three legions stole silently in the darkness to his barges, and passed over without being observed. The Gauls, supposing the whole army to be in flight for Sens, were breaking up their camp to follow in boisterous confusion. Labienus fell upon them, telling the Romans to fight as if Caesar was present in person; and the courage with which the Gauls fought in their surprise only made the overthrow more complete. The insurrection in the north-west was for the moment paralysed, and Labienus, secured by his ingenious and brilliant victory, returned to his quarters without further accident. There Caesar came to him as he expected, and the army was once more together.

Meanwhile the failure at Gergovia had kindled the enthusiasm of the central districts into white-heat. The Aedui, the most powerful of all the tribes, were now at one with their countrymen, and Bibracte became the focus of the national army. The young Vercingetorix was elected sole commander, and his plan, as before, was to starve the Romans out. Flying bodies harassed the borders of the province, so that no reinforcements could reach them from the south. Caesar, however, amidst his conquests had the art of making staunch friends. What the province could not supply he obtained from his allies across the Rhine, and he furnished himself with bodies of German cavalry, which when mounted on Roman horses proved invaluable. In the new form which the insurrection had assumed the Aedui were the first to be attended to. Caesar advanced leisurely upon them, through the high country at the rise of the Seine and the Marne, toward Alesia, or Alice St. Reine. Vercingetorix watched him at ten miles' distance. He supposed him to be making for the province, and his intention was that Caesar should never reach it. The Celts at all times have been fond of emphatic protestations. The young heroes swore a solemn oath that they would not see wife or children or parents more till they had ridden twice through the Roman army. In this mood they encountered Caesar in the valley of the Vingeanne and they met the fate which necessarily befell them when their ungovernable multitudes engaged the legions in the open field. They were defeated with enormous loss: not they riding through the Roman army, but themselves ridden over and hewn down by the German horsemen and sent flying for fifty miles over the hills into Alice St. Reine. Caesar followed close behind, driving Vercingetorix under the lines of the fortress; and the siege of Alesia, one of the most remarkable exploits in all military history, was at once undertaken.

Alesia, like Gergovia, is on a hill sloping off all round, with steep and, in places, precipitous sides. It lies between two small rivers, the Ose and the Oserain, both of which fall into the Brenne, and thence into the Seine. Into this peninsula, with the rivers on each side of him, Vercingetorix had thrown himself with eighty thousand men. Alesia as a position was impregnable except to famine. The water-supply was secure. The position was of extraordinary strength. The rivers formed natural trenches. Below the town to the east they ran parallel for three miles through an open alluvial plain before they reached Brenne. In every other direction rose rocky hills of equal height with the central plateau, originally perhaps one wide table-land, through which the water had ploughed out the valleys. To attack Vercingetorix where he had placed himself was out of the question; but to blockade him there, to capture the leader of the insurrection and his whole army, and so in one blow make an end with it, on a survey of the situation seemed not impossible. The Gauls had thought of nothing less than of being besieged. The provisions laid in could not be considerable, and so enormous a multitude could not hold out many days.

At once the legions were set to work cutting trenches or building walls as the form of the ground allowed. Camps were formed at different spots, and twenty-three strong block-houses at the points which were least defensible. The lines where the circuit was completed were eleven miles long. The part most exposed was the broad level meadow which spread out to the west toward the Brenne river. Vercingetorix had looked on for a time, not understanding what was happening to him. When he did understand it, he made desperate efforts on his side to break the net before it closed about him. But he could do nothing. The Gauls could not be brought to face the Roman entrenchments. Their cavalry were cut to pieces by the German horse. The only hope was in help from without, and before the lines were entirely finished horsemen were sent out with orders to ride for their lives into every district in Gaul and raise the entire nation. The crisis had come. If the countrymen of Vercingetorix were worthy of their fathers, if the enthusiasm with which they had risen for freedom was not a mere emotion, but the expression of a real purpose, their young leader called on them to come now, every man of them, and seize Caesar in the trap into which he had betrayed himself. If, on the other hand, they were careless, if they allowed him and his eighty thousand men to perish without an effort to save them, the independence which they had ceased to deserve would be lost forever. He had food, he bade the messengers say, for thirty days; by thrifty management it might be made to last a few days longer. In thirty days he should look for relief.

The horsemen sped away like the bearers of the fiery cross. Caesar learnt from deserters that they had gone out, and understood the message which they carried. Already he was besieging an army far outnumbering his own. If he persevered, he knew that he might count with certainty on being attacked by a second army immeasurably larger. But the time allowed for the collection of so many men might serve also to prepare for their reception. Vercingetorix said rightly that the Romans won their victories, not by superior courage, but by superior science. The same power of measuring the exact facts of the situation which determined Caesar to raise the siege of Gergovia decided him to hold on at Alesia. He knew exactly, to begin with, how long Vercingetorix could hold out. It was easy for him to collect provisions within his lines which would feed his own army a few days longer. Fortifications the same in kind as those which prevented the besieged from breaking out would serve equally to keep the assailants off. His plan was to make a second line of works--an exterior line as well as an interior line; and as the extent to be defended would thus be doubled, he made them of a peculiar construction, to enable one man to do the work of two. There is no occasion to describe the rows of ditches, dry and wet; the staked pitfalls; the cervi, pronged instruments like the branching horns of a stag; the stimuli, barbed spikes treacherously concealed to impale the unwary and hold him fast when caught, with which the ground was sown in irregular rows; the vallus and the lorica, and all the varied contrivances of Roman engineering genius. Military students will read the particulars for themselves in Caesar's own language. Enough that the work was done within the time, with the legions in perfect good humor, and giving jesting names to the new instruments of torture as Caesar invented them. Vercingetorix now and then burst out on the working parties, but produced no effect. They knew what they were to expect when the thirty days were out; but they knew their commander, and had absolute confidence in his judgment.

Meanwhile, on all sides, the Gauls were responding to the call. From every quarter, even from far-off parts of Belgium, horse and foot were streaming along the roads. Commius of Arras, Caesar's old friend, who had gone with him to Britain, was caught with the same frenzy, and was hastening among the rest to help to end him. At last two hundred and fifty thousand of the best fighting men that Gaul could produce had collected at the appointed rendezvous, and advanced with the easy conviction that the mere impulse of so mighty a force would sweep Caesar off the earth. They were late in arriving. The thirty days had passed, and there were no signs of the coming deliverers. Eager eyes were straining from the heights of the plateau; but nothing was seen save the tents of the legions or the busy units of men at work on the walls and trenches. Anxious debates were held among the beleaguered chiefs. The faint-hearted wished to surrender before they were starved. Others were in favor of a desperate effort to cut their way through or die. One speech Caesar preserves for its remarkable and frightful ferocity. A prince of Auvergne said that the Romans conquered to enslave and beat down the laws and liberties of free nations under the lictors' axes, and he proposed that sooner than yield they should kill and eat those who were useless for fighting.

Vercingetorix was of noble nature. To prevent the adoption of so horrible an expedient, he ordered the peaceful inhabitants, with their wives and children, to leave the town. Caesar forbade them to pass his lines. Cruel--but war is cruel; and where a garrison is to be reduced by famine the laws of it are inexorable.

But the day of expected deliverance dawned at last. Five miles beyond the Brenne the dust-clouds of the approaching host were seen, and then the glitter of their lances and their waving pennons. They swam the river. They filled the plain below the town. From the heights of Alesia the whole scene lay spread under the feet of the besieged. Vercingetorix came down on the slope to the edge of the first trench, prepared to cross when the turn of battle should give him a chance to strike. Caesar sent out his German horse, and stood himself watching from the spur of an adjoining hill. The Gauls had brought innumerable archers with them. The horse flinched slightly under the showers of arrows, and shouts of triumph rose from the lines of the town;

but the Germans rallied again, sent the cavalry of the Gauls flying, and hewed down the unprotected archers. Vercingetorix fell back sadly to his camp on the hill, and then for a day there was a pause. The relieving army had little food with them, and, if they acted at all, must act quickly. They spread over the country collecting faggots to fill the trenches, and making ladders to storm the walls. At midnight they began their assault on the lines in the plain; and Vercingetorix, hearing by the cries that the work had begun, gave his own signal for a general sally. The Roman arrangements had been completed long before. Every man knew his post. The slings, the crossbows, the scorpions were all at hand and in order. Mark Antony and Caius Trebonius had each a flying division under them to carry help where the pressure was most severe. The Gauls were caught on the cervi, impaled on the stimuli, and fell in heaps under the bolts and balls which were poured from the walls. They could make no impression, and fell back at daybreak beaten and dispirited. Vercingetorix had been unable even to pass the moats and trenches, and did not come into action till his friends had abandoned the attack.

The Gauls had not yet taken advantage of their enormous numbers. Defeated on the level ground, they next tried the heights. The Romans were distributed in a ring now fourteen miles in extent. On the north side, beyond the Ose, the works were incomplete, owing to the nature of the ground, and their lines lay on the slope of the hills descending towards the river. Sixty thousand picked men left the Gauls' camp before dawn; they stole round by a distant route, and were allowed to rest concealed in a valley till the middle of the day. At noon they came over the ridge at the Romans' back; and they had the best of the position, being able to attack from above. Their appearance was the signal for a general assault on all sides, and for a determined sally by Vercingetorix from within. Thus before, behind, and everywhere, the legions were assailed at the same moment; and Caesar observes that the cries of battle in the rear are always more trying to men than the fiercest onset upon them in front; because what they cannot see they imagine more formidable than it is, and they depend for their own safety on the courage of others.

Caesar had taken his stand where he could command the whole action. There was no smoke in those engagements, and the scene was transparently visible. Both sides felt that the deciding trial had come. In the plain the Gauls made no more impression than on the preceding day. At the weak point on the north the Romans were forced back down the slope, and could not hold their positions. Caesar saw it, and sent Labienus with six cohorts to their help. Vercingetorix had seen it also, and attacked the interior lines at the same spot. Decimus Brutus was then despatched also, and then Caius Fabius. Finally, when the fighting grew desperate, he left his own station; he called up the reserves which had not yet been engaged, and he rode across the field, conspicuous in his scarlet dress and with his bare head, cheering on the men as he passed each point where they were engaged, and hastening to the scene where the chief danger lay. He sent round a few squadrons of horse to the back of the hills which the Gauls had crossed in the morning. He himself joined Labienus. Wherever he went he carried enthusiasm along with him. The legionaries flung away their darts and rushed upon the enemy sword in hand. The cavalry appeared above on the heights. The Gauls wavered, broke, and scattered. The German horse were among them, hewing down the brave but now helpless patriots who had come with such high hopes and had fought so gallantly. Out of the sixty thousand that had sallied forth in the morning, all but a draggled remnant lay dead on the hill-sides. Seventy-four standards were brought in to Caesar. The besieged retired into Alice again in despair. The vast hosts that were to have set them free melted away. In the morning they were streaming over the country, making back for their homes, with Caesar's cavalry behind them, cutting them down and capturing them in thousands.

The work was done. The most daring feat in the military annals of mankind had been successfully accomplished. A Roman army which could not at the utmost have amounted to fifty thousand men had held blockaded an army of eighty thousand--not weak Asiatics, but European soldiers, as strong and as brave individually as the Italians were; and they had defeated, beaten, and annihilated another army which had come expecting to overwhelm them, five times as large as their own.

Seeing that all was over, Vercingetorix called the chiefs about him. He had gone into the war, he said, for no object of his own, but for the liberty of his country. Fortune had gone against him; and he advised them to make their peace, either by killing him and sending his head to the conqueror or by delivering him up alive. A humble message of submission was despatched to Caesar. He demanded an unconditional surrender, and the Gauls, starving and hopeless, obeyed. The Roman general sat amidst the works in front of the camp while the chiefs one by one were produced before him. The brave

Vercingetorix, as noble in his calamity as Caesar himself in his success, was reserved to be shown in triumph to the populace of Rome. The whole of his army were prisoners of war. The Aedui and Arverni among them were set aside, and were dismissed after a short detention for political reasons. The remainder were sold to the contractors, and the proceeds were distributed as prize-money among the legions. Caesar passed the winter at Bibracte, receiving the submission of the chiefs of the Aedui and of the Auvergne. Wounds received in war soon heal if gentle measures follow a victory. If tried by the manners of his age, Caesar was the most merciful of conquerors. His high aim was, not to enslave the Gauls, but to incorporate them in the Empire; to extend the privileges of Roman citizens among them and among all the undegenerate races of the European provinces. He punished no one. He was gracious and considerate to all, and he so impressed the central tribes by his judgment and his moderation that they served him faithfully in all his coming troubles, and never more, even in the severest temptation, made an effort to recover their independence.

[Sidenote B.C. 51.] Much, however, remained to be done. The insurrection had shaken the whole of Gaul. The distant tribes had all joined in it, either actively or by sympathy; and the patriots who had seized the control, despairing of pardon, thought their only hope was in keeping rebellion alive. During winter they believed themselves secure. The Carnutes of the Eure and Loire, under a new chief named Gutruatus,[7] and the Bituriges, untaught by or savage at the fate of Bourges, were still defiant. When the winter was at its deepest, Caesar suddenly appeared across the Loire. He caught the country people unprepared, and captured them in their farms. The swiftness of his marches baffled alike flight and resistance; he crushed the whole district down, and he was again at his quarters in forty days. As a reward to the men who had followed him so cheerfully in the cold January campaign, he gave each private legionary 200 sesterces and each centurion 2,000. Eighteen days' rest was all that he allowed himself, and with fresh troops, and in storm and frost, he started for the Carnutes. The rebels were to have no rest till they submitted. The Bellovaci were now out also. The Remi alone of all the Gauls had continued faithful in the rising of Vercingetorix. The Bellovaci, led by Commius of Arras, were preparing to burn the territory of the Remi as a punishment. Commius was not as guilty, perhaps, as he seemed. Labienus had suspected him of intending mischief when he was on the Seine in the past summer, and had tried to entrap and kill him. Anyway Caesar's first object was to show the Gauls that no friends of Rome would be allowed to suffer. He invaded Normandy; he swept the country. He drove the Bellovaci and the Carnutes to collect in another great army to defend themselves; he set upon them with his usual skill; and destroyed them. Commius escaped over the Rhine to Germany. Gutruatus was taken. Caesar would have pardoned him; but the legions were growing savage at these repeated and useless commotions, and insisted on his execution. The poor wretch was flogged till he was insensible, and his head was cut off by the lictor's axe.

All Gaul was now submissive, its spirit broken, and, as the event proved, broken finally, except in the southwest. Eight years out of the ten of Caesar's government had expired. In one corner of the country only the dream still survived that, if the patriots could hold out till Caesar was gone, Celtic liberty might yet have a chance of recovering itself. A single tribe on the Dordogne, relying on the strength of a fortress in a situation resembling that of Gergovia, persisted in resistance to the Roman authority. The spirit of national independence is like a fire: so long as a spark remains a conflagration can again be kindled, and Caesar felt that he must trample out the last ember that was alive. Uxellodunum-- so the place was named--stood on an inaccessible rock, and was amply provisioned. It could be taken only as Edinburgh Castle was once taken, by cutting off its water; and the ingenious tunnel may still be seen by which the Roman engineers tapped the spring supplied the garrison. They, too, had then to yield, and the war in Gaul was over.

[Sidenote B.C. 50.] The following winter Caesar spent at Arras. He wished to hand over his conquests to his successor not only subdued, but reconciled, to subjection. He invited the chiefs of all the tribes to come to him. He spoke to them of the future which lay open to them as members of a splendid Imperial State. He gave them magnificent presents. He laid no impositions either on the leaders or their people, and they went to their homes personally devoted to their conqueror, contented with their condition, and resolved to maintain the peace which was now established--a unique experience in political history. The Norman Conquest of England alone in the least resembles it. In the spring of 50 Caesar went to Italy. Strange things had happened meanwhile in Rome. So long as there was a hope that Caesar would be destroyed by the insurrection, the ill-minded Senate had waited to let the Gauls do the work for him. The chance was gone. He had risen above his perils more brilliant than ever, and nothing now was left to them but to defy and trample on him. Servius Galba, who was favorable to Caesar, had stood for the consulship for 49, and had received a majority of votes. The election was set aside. Two patricians, Lentulus and Caius Marcellus, were declared chosen, and their avowed purpose was to strip the conqueror of Gaul of his honors and rewards.[8] The people of his own Cisalpine Province desired to show that they at least had no sympathy with such envenomed animosities. In the colonies in Lombardy and Venetia Caesar was received with the most passionate demonstrations of affection. The towns were dressed out with flags and flowers. The inhabitants crowded into the streets with their wives and children to look at him as he passed. The altars smoked with offerings; the temples were thronged with worshippers praying the immortal gods to bless the greatest of the Romans. He had yet one more year to govern. After a brief stay he rejoined his army. He spent the summer in organizing the administration of the different districts and assigning his officers their various commands. That he did not at this time contemplate any violent interference with the Constitution may be proved by the distribution of his legions, which remained stationed far away in Belgium and on the Loire.

[1] Above Orleans, on the Loire.

[2] Four miles from Clermont, on the Allier, in the Puy-de-D 彫 e.

[3] "Extrema fames."--_De Bell. Gall_., vii. 17.

[4] "Summ?se iniquitatis condemnari debere nisi eorum vitam su?salute habeat cariorem."

[5] _De Bell. Gall_., vii. 33.

[6] "Tantis subito difficultatibus objectis ab animi virtute consilium petebat."

[7] Gudrund? The word has a German sound.

[8] "Insolenter adversarii sui gloriabantur L. Lentulum et C. Marcellum consules creatos, qui omnem honorem et dignitatem Caesaris exspoliarent. Ereptum Servio Galbae consulatum cum is multo plus grati? suffragiisque valuisset, quod sibi conjunctus et familiaritate et necessitudine legationis

esset."--_Auli Hirtii De Bell. Gall_. viii. 50.

CHAPTER XX.

[Sidenote: B.C. 51.] Crassus had been destroyed by the Parthians. The nomination of his successor lay with the Senate, and the Senate gave a notable evidence of their incapacity for selecting competent governors for the provinces by appointing in his place Caesar's old colleague, Bibulus. In their whole number there was no such fool as Bibulus. When he arrived in Syria he shut himself into a fortified town, leaving the Parthians to plunder and burn at their pleasure. Cicero mocked at him. The Senate thanked him for his distinguished services. The few serious men in Rome thought that Caesar or Pompey should be sent out;[1] or, if they could not be spared, at least one of the consuls of the year--Sulpicius Rufus or Marcus Marcellus. But the consuls were busy with home politics and did not wish to go, nor did they wish that others should go and gather laurels instead of them. Therefore nothing was done at all,[2] and Syria was left to fate and Bibulus. The consuls and the aristocracy had, in fact, more serious matters to attend to. Caesar's time was running out, and when it was over he had been promised the consulship. That consulship the faction of the conservatives had sworn that he should never hold. Cato was threatening him with impeachment, blustering that he should be tried under a guard, as Milo had been.[3] Marcellus was saying openly that he would call him home in disgrace before his term was over. Como, one of the most thriving towns in the north of Italy, had been enfranchised by Caesar. An eminent citizen from Como happening to be at Rome, Marcellus publicly flogged him, and bade him go back and tell his fellow-townsmen the value of Caesar's gift to them, Cicero saw the folly of such actions;[4] but the aristocracy were mad--mad with pride and conscious guilt and fear. The ten years of Caesar's government would expire at the end of 49. The engagement had been entered into that he was to see his term out with his army and to return to Rome for 48--as consul. They remembered his first consulship and what he had done with it, and the laws which he had passed--laws which they could not repeal; yet how had they observed them? If he had been too strong for them all when he was but one of themselves, scarcely known beyond the Forum and senate-house, what would he do now, when he was recognized as the greatest soldier which Rome had produced, the army, the people, Italy, the provinces all adoring his name? Consul again he could not, must not be. Yet how could it be prevented? It was useless now to bribe the Comitia, to work with clubs and wire-pullers. The enfranchised citizens would come to vote for Caesar from every country town. The legionaries to a man would vote for him; and even in the venal city he was the idol of the hour. No fault could be found with his administration. His wars had paid their own expenses. He had doubled the pay of his troops, but his military chest was still full, and his own wealth seemed boundless. He was adorning the Forum with new and costly buildings. Senators, knights, young men of rank who had been extravagant, had been relieved by his generosity and were his pensioners. Gaul might have been impatient at its loss of liberty, but no word of complaint was heard against Caesar for oppressive government. The more genius he had shown the more formidable he was. Let him be consul, and he would be the master of them all.

Caesar had been credited with far-reaching designs. It has been assumed that in early life he had designed the overthrow of the Constitution; that he pursued his purpose steadily through every stage in his career, and that he sought the command of Gaul only to obtain an army devoted to him which would execute his will. It has not seemed incredible that a man of middle age undertook the conquest of a country of which nothing is known save that it was inhabited by warlike races, who more than once had threatened to overrun Italy and destroy Rome; that he went through ten years of desperate fighting exposed to a thousand dangers from the sword, from exposure and hardship; that for ten years he had banished himself from Rome, uncertain whether he would ever see it again; and that he had ventured upon all this with no other object than that of eventually controlling domestic politics. A lunatic might have entertained such a scheme, but not a Caesar. The Senate knew him. They knew what he had done. They knew what he would now do, and for this reason they feared and hated him. Caesar was a reformer. He had long seen that the Roman Constitution was too narrow for the functions which had fallen to it, and that it was degenerating into an instrument of tyranny and injustice. The courts of law were corrupt; the elections wore corrupt. The administration of the provinces was a scandal and a curse. The soil of Italy had become a monopoly of capitalists, and the inhabitants of it a population of slaves. He had exerted himself to stay the mischief at its fountain, to punish bribery, to punish the rapacity of proconsuls and propraetors, to purify the courts, to maintain respect for the law. He had endeavored to extend the franchise, to raise the position of the liberated slaves, to replace upon the land a free race of Roman citizens. The old Roman sentiment, the consciousness of the greatness of the country and of its mighty destinies, was chiefly now to be found in the armies. In the families of veteran legionaries, spread in farms over Italy and the provinces, the national spirit might revive; and, with a due share of political power conceded to them, an enlarged and purified constituency might control the votes of the venal populace of the city. These were Caesar's designs, so far as could have been gathered from his earlier actions; but the manipulation of elections, the miserable contests with disaffected colleagues and a hostile Senate, were dreary occupations for such a man as he was. He was conscious of powers which in so poor a sphere could find no expression. He had ambition doubtless--plenty of it--ambition not to pass away without leaving his mark on the history of his country. As a statesman he had done the most which could be done when he was consul the first time, and he had afterward sought a free field for his adventurous genius in a new country, and in rounding off into security the frontiers of the 'Empire on the side where danger was most threatening. The proudest self-confidence could not have allowed him at his time of life to calculate on returning to Rome to take up again the work of reformation.

But Cesar had conquered. He had made a name for himself as a soldier before which the Scipios and the Luculluses, the Syllas and Pompeys paled their glory. He was coming back to lay at his country's feet a province larger than Spain--not subdued only, but reconciled to subjugation; a nation of warriors, as much devoted to him as his own legions. The aristocracy had watched his progress with the bitterest malignity. When he was struggling with the last spasms of Gallic liberty, they had talked in delighted whispers of his reported ruin.[5] But his genius had risen above his difficulties and shone out more glorious than before. When the war was over the Senate had been forced to vote twenty days of thanksgiving. Twenty days were not enough for Roman, enthusiasm. The people made them into sixty.

If Caesar came to Rome as consul, the Senate knew too well what it might expect. What he had been before he would be again, but more severe as his power was greater. Their own guilty hearts perhaps made them fear another Marian proscription. Unless his command could be brought to an end in some far different form, their days of power were numbered, and the days of inquiry and punishment would begin.

[Sidenote: B.C. 50.] Cicero had for some time seen what was coming. He had preferred characteristically to be out of the way at the moment when he expected that the storm would break, and had accepted the government of Cilicia and Cyprus. He was thus absent while the active plot was in preparation. One great step had been gained--the Senate had secured Pompey. Caesar's greatness was too much for him. He could never again hope to be the first on the popular side, and he preferred being the saviour of the Constitution to playing second to a person whom he had patronized. Pompey ought long since to have been in Spain with his troops; but he had stayed at Rome to keep order, and he had lingered on with the same pretext. The first step was to weaken Caesar and to provide Pompey with a force in Italy. The Senate discovered suddenly that Asia Minor was in danger from, the Parthians. They voted that Caesar and Pompey must each spare a legion for the East. Pompey gave as his part the legion which he had lent to Caesar for the last campaign. Caesar was invited to restore it and to furnish another of his own. Caesar was then in Belgium. He saw the object of the demand perfectly clearly; but he sent the two legions without a word, contenting himself with making handsome presents to the officers and men on their leaving him. When they reached Italy the Senate found that they were wanted for home service, and they were placed under Pompey's command in Campania. The consuls chosen for the year 49 were Lucius Cornelius Lentulus and Caius Marcellus, both of them Caesar's open enemies. Caesar himself had been promised the consulship (there could be no doubt of his election, if his name was accepted in his absence) for the year 48. He was to remain with his troops till his term had run out, and to be allowed to stand while still in command. This was the distinct engagement which the assembly had ratified. After the consular election had been secured in the autumn of 50 to the conservative candidates, it was proposed that by a displacement of dates Caesar's government should expire, not at the close of the tenth year, but in the spring, on the 1st of March. Convenient constitutional excuses were found for the change. On the 1st of March he was to cease to be governor of Gaul. A successor was to be named to take over his army. He would then have to return to Rome, and would lie at the mercy of his enemies. Six months would intervene before the next elections, during which he might be impeached, incapacitated, or otherwise disposed of; while Pompey and his two legions could effectually prevent any popular disturbance in his favor. The Senate hesitated before decisively voting the recall. An intimation was conveyed to Caesar that he had been mistaken about his term, which would end sooner than he had supposed; and the world was waiting to see how he would take it. Atticus thought that he would give way. His having parted so easily with two legions did not look like resistance. Marcus Caelius, a correspondent of Cicero, who had been elected praetor for 49, and kept his friend informed how things were going on, wrote in the autumn:

"All is at a standstill about the Gallic government. The subject has been raised, and is again postponed. Pompey's view is plain that Caesar must leave his province after the 1st of March ... but he does not think that before that time the Senate can properly pass a resolution about it. After the 1st of March he will have no hesitation. When he was asked what he would do if a tribune interposed, he said it made no difference whether Caesar himself disobeyed the Senate or provided some one else to interfere with the Senate. Suppose, said one, Caesar wishes to be consul and to keep his army. Pompey answered, 'What if my son wishes to lay a stick on my back'.... It appears that Caesar will accept one or other of two conditions: either to remain in his province, and postpone his claim for the consulship; or, if he can be named for the consulship, then to retire. Curio is all against him. What he can accomplish, I know not; but I perceive this, that if Caesar means well, he will not be overthrown." [6]

The object of the Senate was either to ruin Caesar, if he complied with this order, or to put him in the wrong by provoking him to disobedience. The scheme was ingenious; but if the Senate could mine, Caesar could countermine. Caelius said that Curio was violent against him: and so Curio had been. Curio was a young man of high birth, dissolute, extravagant, and clever. His father, who had been consul five-and-twenty years before, was a strong aristocrat and a close friend of Cicero's. The son had taken the same line; but, among other loose companions, he had made the acquaintance, to his father's regret, of Mark Antony, and though they had hitherto been of opposite politics, the intimacy had continued. The Senate's influence had made Curio tribune for the year 49. Antony had been chosen tribune also. To the astonishment of everybody but Cicero, it appeared that these two, who were expected to neutralize each other, were about to work together, and to veto every resolution which seemed an unfair return for Caesar's services. Scandal said that young Curio was in money difficulties, and that Caesar had paid his debts for him. It was perhaps a lie invented by political malignity; but if Curio was purchasable, Caesar would not have hesitated to buy him. His habit was to take facts as they were, and, when satisfied that his object was just, to go the readiest way to it.

The desertion of their own tribune was a serious blow to the Senate. Caelius, who was to be praetor, was inclining to think that Caesar would win, and therefore might take his side also. The constitutional opposition would then be extremely strong; and even Pompey, fiercely as he had spoken, doubted what to do. The question was raised in the Senate, whether the tribunes' vetoes were to be regarded. Marcellus, who had flogged the citizen of Como, voted for defying them, but the rest were timid. Pompey did not know his own mind.[7] Caelius's account of his own feelings in the matter represented probably those of many besides himself.

"In civil quarrels," he wrote to Cicero, "we ought to go with the most honest party, as long as the contest lies within constitutional limits. When it is an affair of camps and battles, we must go with the strongest. Pompey will have the Senate and the men of consideration with him. All the discontented will go with Caesar. I must calculate the forces on both sides, before I decide on my own part." [8]

When the question next came on in the Senate, Curio, being of course instructed in Caesar's wishes, professed to share the anxiety lest there should be a military Dictatorship; but he said that the danger was as great from Pompey as from Caesar. He did not object to the recall of Caesar, but Pompey, he thought, should resign his province also, and the Constitution would then be out of peril. Pompey professed to be willing, if the Senate desired it; but he insisted that Caesar must take the first step. Curio's proposal was so fair, that it gained favor both in Forum and Senate. The populace, who hated Pompey, threw flowers upon the tribune as he passed. Marcellus, the consul, a few days later, put the question in the Senate: Was Caesar to be recalled? A majority answered Yes. Was Pompey to be deprived of his province? The same majority said No. Curio then proposed that both Pompey and Caesar should dismiss their armies. Out of three hundred and ninety-two senators present, three hundred and seventy agreed. Marcellus told them bitterly that they had voted themselves Caesar's slaves. But they were not all insane with envy and hatred, and in the midst of their terrors they retained some prudence, perhaps some conscience and sense of justice. By this time, however, the messengers who had been sent to communicate the Senate's views to Caesar had returned. They brought no positive answer from himself; but they reported that Caesar's troops were worn out and discontented, and certainly would refuse to support him in any violent action. How false their account of the army was, the Senate had soon reason to know; but it was true that one, and he the most trusted officer that Caesar had, Labienus, who had fought through so many battles with him in the Forum as well as in the field, whose high talents and character his Commentaries could never praise sufficiently--it was true that Labienus had listened to the offers made to him. Labienus had made a vast fortune in the war. He perhaps thought, as other distinguished officers have done, that he was the person that had won the victories; that without him Caesar, who was being so much praised and glorified, would have been nothing; and that he at least was entitled to an equal share of the honors and rewards that might be coming; while if Caesar was to be disgraced, he might have the whole recompense for himself. Caesar heard of these overtures; but he had refused to believe that Labienus could be untrue to him. He showed his confidence, and he showed at the same time the integrity of his own intentions, by appointing the officer who was suspected of betraying him Lieutenant-General of the Cisalpine Province. None the less it was true that Labienus had been won over. Labienus had undertaken for his comrades; and the belief that Caesar could not depend on his troops renewed Pompey's courage and gave heart to the faction which wished to precipitate extremities. The aspect of things was now altered. What before seemed rash and dangerous might be safely ventured. Caesar had himself followed the messengers to Ravenna. To raise the passions of men to the desired heat, a report was spread that he had brought his troops across and was marching on Rome. Curio hastened off to him, to bring back under his own hand a distinct declaration of his views.

It was at this crisis, in the middle of the winter 50-49, that Cicero returned to Rome. He had held his government but for two years, and instead of escaping the catastrophe, he found himself plunged into the heart of it. He had managed his province well. No one ever suspected Cicero of being corrupt or unjust. He had gained some respectable successes in putting down the Cilician banditti. He had been named imperator by his soldiers in the field after an action in which he had commanded; he had been flattering himself with the prospect of a triumph, and had laid up money to meet the cost of it. The quarrel between the two great men whom he had so long feared and flattered, and the necessity which might be thrown on him of declaring publicly on one side or the other, agitated him terribly. In October, as he was on his way home, he expressed his anxieties with his usual frankness to Atticus.

"Consider the problem for me," he said, "as it affects myself: you advised me to keep on terms both with Pompey and Caesar. You bade me adhere to one because he had been good to me, and to the other because he was strong. I have done so. I so ordered matters that no one could be dearer to either of them than I was. I reflected thus: while I stand by Pompey, I cannot hurt the Commonwealth; if I agree with Caesar, I need not quarrel with Pompey; so closely they appeared to be connected. But now they are at a sharp issue. Each regards me as his friend, unless Caesar dissembles; while Pompey is right in thinking that what he proposes I shall approve. I heard from both at the time at which I heard from you. Their letters were most polite. What am I to do? I don't mean in extremities. If it comes to fighting, it will be better to be defeated with one than to conquer with the other. But when I arrive at Rome, I shall be required to say if Caesar is to be proposed for the consulship in his absence, or if he is to dismiss his army. What must I answer? Wait till I have consulted Atticus? That will not do. Shall I go against Caesar? Where are Pompey's resources? I myself took Caesar's part about it. He spoke to me on the subject at Ravenna. I recommended his request to the tribunes as a reasonable one. Pompey talked with me also to the same purpose. Am I to change my mind? I am ashamed to oppose him now. Will you have a fool's opinion? I will apply for a triumph, and so I shall have an excuse for not entering the city. You will laugh. But oh, I wish I had remained in my province. Could I but have guessed what was impending! Think for me. How shall I avoid displeasing Caesar? He writes most kindly about a 'Thanksgiving' for my success." [9]

Caesar had touched the right point in congratulating Cicero on his military exploits. His friends in the Senate had been less delicate. Bibulus had. been thanked for hiding from the Parthians. When Cicero had hinted his expectations, the Senate had passed to the order of the day.

"Cato," he wrote, "treats me scurvily. He gives me praise for justice, clemency, and integrity, which I did not want. What I did want he will not let me have. Caesar promises me everything.--Cato has given a twenty days' thanksgiving to Bibulus. Pardon me, if this is more than I can bear.--But I am relieved from my worst fear. The Parthians have left Bibulus half alive." [10]

The shame wore off as Cicero drew near to Rome. He blamed the tribunes for insisting on what he had himself declared to be just. "Any way," he said, "I stick to Pompey. When they say to me, Marcus Tullius, what do you think? I shall answer, I go with Pompey; but privately I shall advise Pompey to come to terms.--We have to do with a man full of audacity and completely prepared. Every felon, every citizen who is in disgrace or ought to be in disgrace, almost all the young, the city mob, the tribunes, debtors, who are more numerous than I could have believed, all these are with Caesar. He wants nothing but a good cause, and war is always uncertain." [11]

Pompey had been unwell at the beginning of December, and had gone for a few days into the country. Cicero met him on the 10th. "We were two hours together," he said. "Pompey was delighted at my arrival. He spoke of my triumph, and promised to do his part. He advised me to keep away from the Senate, till it was arranged, lest I should offend the tribunes. He spoke of war as certain. Not a word did he utter pointing to a chance of compromise.--My comfort is that Caesar, to whom even his enemies had allowed a second consulship, and to whom fortune had given so much power, will not be so mad as to throw all this away." [12] Cicero had soon to learn that the second consulship was not so certain. On the 29th he had another long conversation with Pompey.

"Is there hope of peace?" he wrote, in reporting what had passed. "So far as I can gather from his very full expressions to me, he does not desire it. For he thinks thus: If Caesar be made consul, even after he has parted from his army, the constitution will be at an end. He thinks also that when Caesar hears of the preparations against him, he will drop the consulship for this year, to keep his province and his troops. Should he be so insane as to try extremities, Pompey holds him in utter contempt. I thought, when he was speaking, of the uncertainties of war; but I was relieved to hear a man of courage and experience talk like a statesman of the dangers of an insincere settlement.-- Not only he does not seek for peace, but he seems to fear it.--My own vexation is, that I must pay Caesar my debt, and spend thus what I had set apart for my triumph. It is indecent to owe money to a political antagonist." [13]

Events were hurrying on. Cicero entered Rome the first week in January, to find that the Senate had begun work in earnest. Curio had returned from Ravenna with a letter from Caesar. He had offered three alternatives. First, that the agreement already made might stand, and that he might be nominated, in his absence, for the consulship; or that when he left his army, Pompey should disband his Italian legions; or, lastly, that he should hand over Transalpine Gaul to his successor, with eight of his ten legions, himself keeping the north of Italy and Illyria with two, until his election. It was the first of January. The new consuls, Lentulus and Caius Marcellus, with the other magistrates, had entered on their offices, and were in their places in the Senate. Pompey was present, and the letter was introduced. The consuls objected to it being read, but they were overruled by the remonstrances of the tribunes. The reading over, the consuls forbade a debate upon it, and moved that the condition of the Commonwealth should be taken into consideration. Lentulus, the more impassioned of them, said that if the Senate would be firm, he would do his duty; if they hesitated and tried conciliation, he should take care of himself, and go over to Caesar's side. Metellus Scipio, Pompey's father- in-law, spoke to the same purpose. Pompey, he said, was ready to support the constitution, if the Senate were resolute. If they wavered, they would look in vain for future help from him. Marcus Marcellus, the consul of the preceding year, less wild than he had been when he flogged the Como citizen, advised delay, at least till Pompey was better prepared. Calidius, another senator, moved that Pompey should go to his province. Caesar's resentment at the detention of the two legions from the Parthian war he thought, was natural and justifiable. Marcus Rufus agreed with Calidius. But moderation was borne down by the violence of Lentulus; and the Senate, in spite of themselves,[14] voted, at Scipio's dictation, that Caesar must dismiss his army before a day which was to be fixed, or, in default, would be declared an enemy to the State. Two tribunes, Mark Antony and Cassius Longinus, interposed. The tribunes' veto was as old as their institution. It had been left standing even by Sylla. But the aristocracy were declaring war against the people. They knew that the veto was coming, and they had resolved to disregard it. The more passionate the speakers, the more they were cheered by Caesar's enemies. The sitting ended in the evening without a final conclusion; but at a meeting afterwards, at his house, Pompey quieted alarms by assuring the senators that there was nothing to fear. Caesar's army he knew to be disaffected. He introduced the officers of the two legions that had been taken from Caesar, who vouched for their fidelity to the constitution. Some of Pompey's veterans were present, called up from their farms; they were enthusiastic for their old commander. Piso, Caesar's father-in-law, and Roscius, a praetor, begged for a week's delay, that they might go to Caesar, and explain the Senate's pleasure. Others proposed to send a deputation to soften the harshness of his removal. But Lentulus, backed by Cato, would listen to nothing. Cato detested Caesar as the representative of everything which he most abhorred. Lentulus, bankrupt and loaded with debts, was looking for provinces to ruin, and allied sovereigns to lay presents at his feet. He boasted that he would be a second Sylla.[15] When the Senate met again in their places, the tribunes' veto was disallowed. They ordered a general levy through Italy. The consuls gave Pompey the command-in-chief, with the keys of the treasury. The Senate redistributed the provinces; giving Syria to Scipio, and in Caesar's place appointing Domitius Ahenobarbus, the most inveterate and envenomed of his enemies. Their authority over the provinces had been taken from them by law, but law was set aside. Finally, they voted the State in danger, suspended the constitution, and gave the consuls absolute power.

The final votes were taken on the 7th of January. A single week had sufficed for a discussion of the resolutions on which the fate of Rome depended. The Senate pretended to be defending the constitution. They had themselves destroyed the constitution, and established on the ruins of it a senatorial oligarchy. The tribunes fled at once to Caesar. Pompey left the city for Campania, to join his two legions and superintend the levies.

The unanimity which had appeared in the Senate's final determination was on the surface only. Cicero, though present in Rome, had taken no part, and looked on in despair. The "good" were shocked at Pompey's precipitation. They saw that a civil war could end only in a despotism. [16] "I have not met one man," Cicero said, "who does not think it would be better to make concessions to Caesar than to fight him.--Why fight now? Things are no worse than when we gave him his additional five years, or agreed to let him be chosen consul in his absence. You wish for my opinion. I think we ought to use every means to escape war. But I must say what Pompey says. I cannot differ from Pompey." [17]

A day later, before the final vote had been taken, he thought still that the Senate was willing to let Caesar keep his province, if he would dissolve his army. The moneyed interests, the peasant landholders, were all on Caesar's side; they cared not even if monarchy came so that they might have peace. "We could have resisted Caesar easily when he was weak," he wrote. "Now he has eleven legions and as many cavalry as he chooses with him, the Cisalpine provincials, the Roman populace, the tribunes, and the hosts of dissolute young men. Yet we are to fight with him, or take account of him unconstitutionally. Fight, you say, rather than be a slave. Fight for what? To be proscribed, if you are beaten; to be a slave still, if you win. What will you do then? you ask. As the sheep follows the flock and the ox the herd, so will I follow the 'good,' or those who are called good, but I see plainly what will come out of this sick state of ours. No one knows what the fate of war may be. But if the 'good' are beaten, this much is certain, that Caesar will be as bloody as Cinna, and as greedy of other men's properties as Sylla." [18]

Once more, and still in the midst of uncertainty:

"The position is this: We must either let Caesar stand for the consulship, he keeping his army with the Senate's consent, or supported by the tribunes; or we must persuade him to resign his province and his army, and so to be consul; or if he refuses, the elections can be held without him, he keeping his province; or if he forbids the election through the tribunes, we can hang on and come to an interrex; or, lastly, if he brings his army on us, we can fight. Should this be his choice, he will either begin at once, before we are ready, or he will wait till his election, when his friends will put in his name and it will not be received. His plea may then be the ill-treatment of himself, or it may be complicated further should a tribune interpose and be deprived of office, and so take refuge with him.... You will say persuade Caesar, then, to give up his army, and be consul. Surely, if he will agree, no objection can be raised; and if he is not allowed to stand while he keeps his army, I wonder that he does not let it go. But a certain person (Pompey) thinks that nothing is so much to be feared as that Caesar should be consul. Better thus, you will say, than with an army. No doubt. But a certain person holds that his consulship would be an irremediable misfortune. We must yield if Caesar will have it so. He will be consul again, the same man that he was before; then, weak as he was, he proved stronger than the whole of us. What, think you, will he be now? Pompey, for one thing, will surely be sent to Spain. Miserable every way; and the worst is, that Caesar cannot be refused, and by consenting will be taken into supreme favor by all the 'good.' They say, however, that he cannot be brought to this. Well, then, which is the worst of the remaining alternatives? Submit to what Pompey calls an impudent demand? Caesar has held his province for ten years. The Senate did not give it him. He took it himself by faction and violence. Suppose he had it lawfully, the time is up. His successor is named. He disobeys. He says that he ought to be considered. Let him consider us. Will he keep his army beyond the time for which the people gave it to him, in despite of the Senate? We must fight him then, and, as Pompey says, we shall conquer or die free men. If fight we must, time will show when or how. But if you have any advice to give, let me know it, for I am tormented day and night." [19]

These letters give a vivid picture of the uncertainties which distracted public opinion during the fatal first week of January. Caesar, it seems, might possibly have been consul had he been willing to retire at once into the condition of a private citizen, even though Pompey was still undisarmed. Whether in that position he would have lived to see the election-day is another question. Cicero himself, it will be seen, had been reflecting already that there were means less perilous than civil war by which dangerous persons might be got rid of. And there were weak points in his arguments which his impatience passed over. Caesar held a positive engagement about his consulship, which the people had ratified. Of the ten years which the people had allowed him, one was unexpired, and the Senate had no power to vote his recall without the tribunes' and the people's consent. He might well hesitate to put himself in the power of a faction so little scrupulous. It is evident, however, that Pompey and the two consuls were afraid that, if such overtures were made to him by a deputation from the Senate, he might perhaps agree to them; and by their rapid and violent vote they put an end to the possibility of an arrangement. Caesar, for no other crime than that as a brilliant democratic general he was supposed dangerous to the oligarchy, had been recalled from his command in the face of the prohibition of the tribunes, and was declared an enemy of his country unless he instantly submitted. After the experience of Marius and Sylla, the Senate could have paid no higher compliment to Caesar's character than in believing that he would hesitate over his answer.

[1] "Caelius ad Ciceronem," Ad Fam. viii. 10.

[2] Ibid.

[3] Suetonius, _De Vit?Julii Caesaris_.

[4] "Marcellus foede do Comensi. Etsi ille magistratum non gesserat, erat tamen Transpadanus. Ita mihi videtur non minus stomachi nostro ac Caesari fecisse."--To Atticus, v. 11.

[5] "Quod ad Caesarem crebri et non belli de eo rumores. Sed susurratores dumtaxat veniunt.... Neque adhuc certi quidquam est, neque haec incerta tamen vulgo jactantur. Sed inter paucos, quos tu nosti, palam secreto narrantur. At Domitius cum manus ad os apposuit!"--Caelius to Cicero, Ad Fam. viii. 1.

[6] Caelius to Cicero, Ad Fam. viii. 8.

[7] Ibid., viii. 13.

[8] Caelius to Cicero, Ad Fam. viii. 14.

[9] To Atticus, vii. 1, abridged.

[10] _Ibid._, vii. 2.

[11] _Ibid._, vii. 3.

[12] To Atticus, vii. 4.

[13] "Mihi autem illud molestissimum est, quod solvendi sunt nummi Caesari, et instrumentum triumphi eo conferendum. Est [Greek: amorphon hantipoliteuomenou chreopheiletaen] esse."--Ibid., vii. 8.

[14] "Inviti et coacti" is Caesar's expression. He wished, perhaps, to soften the Senate's action. (De Bello Civili, i. 2.)

[15] "Seque alterum fore Sullam inter suos gloriatur."--De Bello Civili, i. 4.

[16] "Tum certe tyrannus existet."--To Atticus, vii. 5.

[17] To Atticus, vii. 6.

[18] Ibid., vii. 7, abridged.

[19] To Atticus, vii. 9, abridged.

CHAPTER XXI.

Caesar, when the report of the Senate's action reached him, addressed his soldiers. He had but one legion with him, the 13th. But one legion would represent the rest. He told them what the Senate had done, and why they had done it. "For nine years he and his army had served their country loyally and with some success. They had driven the Germans over the Rhine; they had made Gaul a Roman province; and the Senate for answer had broken the constitution, and had set aside the tribunes because they spoke in his defence. They had voted the State in danger, and had called Italy to arms when no single act had been done by himself to justify them." The soldiers whom--Pompey supposed disaffected declared with enthusiasm that they would support their commander and the tribunes. They offered to serve without pay. Officers and men volunteered contributions for the expenses of the war. In all the army one officer alone proved false. Labienus kept his word to Pompey and stole away to Capua. He left his effects behind, and Caesar sent them after him untouched.

Finding that all the rest could be depended on, he sent back over the Alps for two more legions to follow him. He crossed the little river Rubicon, which bounded his province, and advanced to Rimini, where he met the tribunes, Antony, Cassius Longinus, and Curio, who were coming to him from Rome.[1] At Rimini the troops were again assembled. Curio told them what had passed. Caesar added a few more words. The legionaries, officers and privates, were perfectly satisfied; and Caesar, who, a resolution once taken, struck as swiftly as his own eagles, was preparing to go forward. He had but 5,000 men with him, but he understood the state of Italy, and knew that he had nothing to fear. At this moment Lucius Caesar, a distant kinsman, and the praetor Roscius arrived, as they said, with a private message from Pompey. The message was nothing. The object was no more than to gain time. But Caesar had no wish for war, and would not throw away a chance of avoiding it. He bade his kinsman tell Pompey that it was for him to compose the difficulties which had arisen without a collision. He had been himself misrepresented to his countrymen. He had been recalled from his command before his time; the promise given to him about his consulship had been broken. He had endured these injuries. He had proposed to the Senate that the forces on both sides should be disbanded. The Senate had refused. A levy had been ordered through Italy, and the legions designed for Parthia had been retained. Such an attitude could have but one meaning. Yet he was still ready to make peace. Let Pompey depart to Spain. His own troops should then be dismissed. The elections could be held freely, and Senate and people would be restored to their joint authority. If this was not enough, they two might meet and relieve each other's alarms and suspicions in a personal interview.

With this answer the envoys went, and Caesar paused at Rimini. Meanwhile the report reached Rome that Caesar had crossed the Rubicon. The aristocracy had nursed the pleasant belief that his heart would fail him, or that his army would desert him. His heart had not failed, his army had not deserted; and, in their terror, they saw him already in their midst like an avenging Marius. He was coming. His horse had been seen on the Apennines. Flight, instant flight, was the only safety. Up they rose, consuls, praetors, senators, leaving wives and children and property to their fate, not halting even to take the money out of the treasury, but contenting themselves with leaving it locked. On foot, on horseback, in litters, in carriages, they fled for their lives to find safety under Pompey's wing in Capua. In this forlorn company went Cicero, filled with contempt for what was round him.

"You ask what Pompey means to do," he wrote to Atticus. "I do not think he knows himself. Certainly none of us know.--It is all panic and blunder. We are uncertain whether he will make a stand, or leave Italy. If he stays, I fear his army is too unreliable. If not, where will he go, and how and what are his plans? Like you, I am afraid that Caesar will be a Phalaris, and that we may expect the very worst. The flight of the Senate, the departure of the magistrates, the closing of the treasury, will not stop him.--I am broken-hearted; so ill-advisedly, so against all my counsels, the whole business has been conducted. Shall I turn my coat, and join the victors? I am ashamed. Duty forbids me; but I am miserable at the thought of my children." [2]

A gleam of hope came with the arrival of Labienus, but it soon clouded. "Labienus is a hero," Cicero said. "Never was act more splendid. If nothing else comes of it, he has at least made Caesar smart.--We have a civil war on us, not because we have quarrelled among ourselves, but through one abandoned citizen. But this citizen has a strong army, and a large party attached to him.--What he will do I cannot say; he cannot even pretend to do anything constitutionally; but what is to become of us, with a general that cannot lead?--To say nothing of ten years of blundering, what could have been worse than this flight from Rome? His next purpose I know not. I ask, and can have no answer. All is cowardice and confusion. He was kept at home to protect us, and protection there is none. The one hope is in two legions invidiously detained and almost not belonging to us. As to the levies, the men enlist unwillingly, and hate the notion of a war." [3]

In this condition of things Lucius Caesar arrived with the answer from Rimini. A council of war was held at Teano to consider it; and the flames which had burnt so hotly at the beginning of the month were found to have somewhat cooled. Cato's friend Favonius was still defiant; but the rest, even Cato himself, had grown more modest. Pompey, it was plain, had no army, and could not raise an army. Caesar spoke fairly. It might be only treachery; but the Senate had left their families and their property in Rome. The public money was in Rome. They were willing to consent that Caesar should be consul, since so it must be. Unluckily for themselves, they left Pompey to draw up their reply. Pompey intrusted the duty to an incapable person named Sestius, and the answer was ill-written, awkward, and wanting on the only point which would have proved his sincerity. Pompey declined the proposed interview. Caesar must evacuate Rimini, and return to his province; afterwards, at some time unnamed, Pompey would go to Spain, and other matters should be arranged to Caesar's satisfaction. Caesar must give securities that he would abide by his promise to dismiss his troops; and meanwhile the consular levies would be continued.[4]

To Cicero these terms seemed to mean a capitulation clumsily disguised. Caesar interpreted them differently. To him it appeared that he was required to part with his own army, while Pompey was forming another. No time was fixed for the departure to Spain. He might be himself named consul, yet Pompey might be in Italy to the end of the year with an army independent of him. Evidently there was distrust on both sides, yet on Caesar's part a distrust not undeserved. Pompey would not see him. He had admitted to Cicero that he desired a war to prevent Caesar from being consul, and at this very moment was full of hopes and schemes for carrying it on successfully.

"Pompey writes," reported Cicero on the 28th of January, "that in a few days he will have a force on which he can rely. He will occupy Picenum,[5] and we are then to return to Rome. Labienus assures him that Caesar is utterly weak. Thus he is in better spirits." [6]

[Sidenote: February, B.C. 49.] A second legion had by this time arrived at Rimini. Caesar considered that if the Senate really desired peace, their disposition would be quickened by further pressure. He sent Antony across the mountains to Arezzo, on the straight road to Rome; and he pushed on himself toward Ancona, before Pompey had time to throw himself in the way. The towns on the way opened their gates to him. The municipal magistrates told the commandants that they could not refuse to entertain Caius Caesar, who had done such great things for the Republic. The officers fled. The garrisons joined Caesar's legions. Even a colony planted by Labienus sent a deputation with offers of service. Steadily and swiftly in gathering volume the army of the north came on. At Capua all was consternation. "The consuls are helpless," Cicero said. "There has been no levy. The commissioners do not even try to excuse their failure. With Caesar pressing forward and our general doing nothing, men will not give in their names. The will is not wanting, but they are without hope. Pompey, miserable and incredible though it be, is prostrate. He has no courage, no purpose, no force, no energy.... Caius Cassius came on the 7th to Capua, with an order from Pompey to the consuls to go to Rome and bring away the money from the treasury. How are they to go without an escort, or how return? The consuls say he must go himself first to Picenum. But Picenum is lost.--Caesar will soon be in Apulia, and Pompey on board ship. What shall I do? I should not doubt had there not been such shameful mis-management, and had I been myself consulted. Caesar invites me to peace, but his letter was written before his advance." [7]

Desperate at the lethargy of their commander, the aristocracy tried to force him into movement by acting on their own account. Domitius, who had been appointed Caesar's successor, was most interested in his defeat. He gathered a party of young lords and knights and a few thousand men, and flung himself into Corfinium, a strong position in the Apennines, directly in Caesar's path. Pompey had still his two legions, and Domitius sent an express to tell him that Caesar's force was still small, and that with a slight effort he might enclose him in the mountains. Meanwhile Domitius himself tried to break the bridge over the Pescara. He was too late. Caesar had by this time nearly 30,000 men.

The Cisalpine territories in mere enthusiasm had raised twenty-two cohorts for him. He reached the Pescara while the bridge was still standing. He surrounded Corfinium with the impregnable lines which had served him so well in Gaul, and the messenger sent to Capua came back with cold comfort. Pompey had simply ordered Domitius to retreat from a position which he ought not to have occupied, and to join him in Apulia. It was easy to say Retreat! No retreat was possible. Domitius and his companions proposed to steal away in the night. They were discovered. Their own troops arrested them, and carried them as prisoners to Caesar. Fortune had placed in his hands at the outset of the campaign the man who beyond others had been the occasion of it. Domitius would have killed Caesar like a bandit if he had caught him. He probably expected a similar fate for himself. Caesar received his captives calmly and coldly. He told them that they had made an ungrateful return to him for his services to his country; and then dismissed them all, restoring even Domitius's well-filled military chest, and too proud to require a promise from him that he would abstain personally from further hostility. His army, such as it was, followed the general example, and declared for Caesar.

The capture of Corfinium and the desertion of the garrison made an end of hesitation. Pompey and the consuls thought only of instant flight, and hurried to Brindisi, where ships were waiting for them; and Caesar, hoping that the evident feeling of Italy would have its effect with the reasonable part of the Senate, sent Cornelius Balbus, who was on intimate terms with many of them, to assure them of his eagerness for peace, and to tell Cicero especially that he would be well contented to live under Pompey's rule if he could have a guarantee for his personal safety.[8]

[Sidenote: March B.C. 49.] Cicero's trials had been great, and were not diminishing. The account given by Balbus was simply incredible to him. If Caesar was really as well disposed as Balbus represented, then the senatorial party, himself included, had acted like a set of madmen. It might be assumed, therefore, that Caesar was as meanly ambitious, as selfish, as revolutionary as their fears had represented him, and that his mildness was merely affectation. But what then? Cicero wished for himself to be on the right side, but also to be on the safe side. Pompey's was the right side, the side, that is, which, for his own sake, he would prefer to see victorious. But was Pompey's the safe side? or rather, would it be safe to go against him? The necessity for decision was drawing closer. If Pompey and the consuls went abroad, all loyal senators would be expected to follow them, and to stay behind would be held treason. Italy was with Caesar; but the East, with its treasures, its fleets, its millions of men, this was Pompey's, heart and soul. The sea was Pompey's. Caesar might win for the moment, but Pompey might win in the long run. The situation was most perplexing. Before the fall of Corfinium, Cicero had poured himself out upon it to his friend. "My connections, personal and political," he said, "attach me to Pompey. If I stay behind, I desert my noble and admirable companions, and I fall into the power of a man whom I know not how far I can trust. He shows in many ways that he wishes me well. I saw the tempest impending, and I long ago took care to secure his good-will. But suppose him to be my friend indeed, is it becoming in a good and valiant citizen, who has held the highest offices and done such distinguished things, to be in the power of any man? Ought I to expose myself to the danger, and perhaps disgrace, which would lie before me, should Pompey recover his position? This on one side; but now look at the other. Pompey has shown neither conduct nor courage, and he has acted throughout against my advice and judgment. I pass over his old errors: how he himself armed this man against the constitution; how he supported his laws by violence in the face of the auspices; how he gave him Further Gaul, married his daughter, supported Clodius, helped me back from exile indeed, but neglected me afterward; how he prolonged Caesar's command, and backed him up in everything; how in his third consulship, when he had begun to defend the constitution, he yet moved the tribunes to curry a resolution for taking Caesar's name in his absence, and himself sanctioned it by a law of his own; how he resisted Marcus Marcellus, who would have ended Caesar's government on the 1st of March. Let us forget all this: but what was ever more disgraceful than the flight from Rome? What conditions would not have been preferable? He will restore the constitution, you say, but when? by what means? Is not Picenum lost? Is not the road open to the city? Is not our money, public and private, all the enemy's? There is no cause, no rallying point for the friends of the constitution.... The rabble are all for Caesar, and many wish for revolution.... I saw from the first that Pompey only thought of flight: if I now follow him, whither are we to go? Caesar will seize my brother's property and mine, ours perhaps sooner than others', as an assault on us would be popular. If I stay, I shall do no more than many good men did in Cinna's time.--Caesar may be my friend, not certainly, but perhaps; and he may offer me a triumph which it would be dangerous to refuse, and invidious with the "good" to accept. Oh, most perplexing position!--while I write, word comes that Caesar is at

Corfinium. Domitius is inside, with a strong force and eager to fight. I cannot think Pompey will desert him." [9]

[Sidenote: February, B.C. 49.] Pompey did desert Domitius, as has been seen. The surrender of Corfinium, and the circumstances of it, gave Cicero the excuse which he evidently desired to find for keeping clear of a vessel that appeared to him to be going straight to shipwreck. He pleased himself with inventing evil purposes for Pompey, to justify his leaving him. He thought it possible that Domitius and his friends might have been purposely left to fall into Caesar's hands, in the hope that Caesar would kill them and make himself unpopular. Pompey, he was satisfied, meant as much to be a despot as Caesar. Pompey might have defended Rome, if he had pleased; but his purpose was to go away and raise a great fleet and a great Asiatic army, and come back and ruin Italy, and be a new "Sylla." [10] In his distress Cicero wrote both to Caesar and to Pompey, who was now at Brindisi. To Caesar he said that, if he wished for peace, he might command his services. He had always considered that Caesar had been wronged in the course which had been pursued toward him. Envy and ill-nature had tried to rob him of the honors which had been conferred on him by the Roman people. He protested that he had himself supported Caesar's claims, and had advised others to do the same. But he felt for Pompey also, he said, and would gladly be of service to him.[11]

To Pompey he wrote:

[Sidenote: March, B.C. 49.] "My advice was always for peace, even on hard terms. I wished you to remain in Rome. You never hinted that you thought of leaving Italy. I accepted your opinion, not for the constitution's sake, for I despaired of saving it. The constitution is gone, and cannot be restored without a destructive war; but I wished to be with you, and if I can join you now, I will. I know well that my conduct has not pleased those who desired to fight. I urged peace; not because I did not fear what they feared, but because I thought peace a less evil than war. When the war had begun and overtures were made to you, you responded so amply and so honorably that I hoped I had prevailed.... I was never more friendly with Caesar than they were; nor were they more true to the State than I. The difference between us is this, that while they and I are alike good citizens, I preferred an arrangement, and you, I thought, agreed with me. They chose to fight, and as their counsels have been taken, I can but do my duty as a member of the Commonwealth, and as a friend to you." [12]

* * * * *

In this last sentence Cicero gives his clear opinion that the aristocracy had determined upon war, and that for this reason and no other the attempted negotiations had failed. Caesar, hoping that a better feeling might arise after his dismissal of Domitius, had waited a few days at Corfinium. Finding that Pompey had gone to Brindisi, he then followed, trusting to overtake him before he could leave Italy, and again by messengers pressed him earnestly for an interview. By desertions, and by the accession of volunteers, Caesar had now six legions with him. If Pompey escaped, he knew that the war would be long and dangerous. If he could capture him, or persuade him to an agreement, peace could easily be preserved. When he arrived outside the town, the consuls with half the army had already gone. Pompey was still in Brindisi, with 12,000 men, waiting till the transports could return to carry him after them. Pompey again refused to see Caesar, and, in the absence of the consuls, declined further discussion. Caesar tried to blockade him, but for want of ships was unable to close the harbor. The transports came back, and Pompey sailed for Durazzo.[13]

A few extracts and abridgments of letters will complete the picture of this most interesting time.

Cicero to Atticus.[14]

"Observe the man into whose hands we have fallen. How keen he is, how alert, how well prepared! By Jove, if he does not kill any one, and spares the property of those who are so terrified, he will be in high favor. I talk with the tradesmen and farmers. They care for nothing but their lands, and houses, and money. They have gone right round. They fear the man they trusted, and love the man they feared; and all this through our own blunders. I am sick to think of it."

Balbus to Cicero.[15]

"Pompey and Caesar have been divided by perfidious villains. I beseech you,

Cicero, use your influence to bring them together again. Believe me, Caesar will not only do all you wish, but will hold you to have done him essential service. Would that I could say as much of Pompey, who I rather wish than hope may be brought to terms! You have pleased Caesar by begging Lentulus to stay in Italy, and you have more than pleased me. If he will listen to you, will trust to what I tell him of Caesar, and will go back to Rome, between you and him and the Senate, Caesar and Pompey may be reconciled. If I can see this, I shall have lived long enough. I know you will approve of Caesar's conduct at Corfinium."

Cicero to Atticus.[16]

"My preparations are complete. I wait till I can go by the upper sea; I cannot go by the lower at this season. I must start soon, lest I be detained. I do not go for Pompey's sake. I have long known him to be the worst of politicians, and I know him now for the worst of generals. I go because I am sneered at by the optimates. Precious optimates! What are they about now? Selling themselves to Caesar? The towns receive Caesar as a god. When this Pisistratus does them no harm, they are as grateful to him as if he had protected them from others. What receptions will they not give him? What honors will they not heap upon him? They are afraid, are they? By Hercules, it is Pompey that they are afraid of. Caesar's treacherous clemency enchants them. Who are these optimates, that insist that I must leave Italy, while they remain? Let them be who they may, I am ashamed to stay, though I know what to expect. I shall join a man who means not to conquer Italy, but to lay it waste."

Cicero to Atticus.[17]

"Ought a man to remain in his country after it has fallen under a tyranny? Ought a man to use any means to overthrow a tyranny, though he may ruin his country in doing it? Ought he not rather to try to mend matters by argument as opportunity offers? Is it right to make war on one's country for the sake of liberty? Should a man adhere at all risks to one party, though he considers them on the whole to have been a set of fools? Is a person who has been his country's greatest benefactor, and has been rewarded by envy and ill usage, to volunteer into danger for such a party? May he not retire, and live quietly with his family, and leave public affairs to their fate?

"I amused myself as times passes with these speculations."

Cicero to Atticus.[18]

"Pompey has sailed. I am pleased to find that you approve of my remaining. My efforts now are to persuade Caesar to allow me to be absent from the Senate, which is soon to meet. I fear he will refuse. I have been deceived in two points. I expected an arrangement; and now I perceive that Pompey has resolved upon a cruel and deadly war. By Heaven, he would have shown himself a better citizen, and a better man, had he borne anything sooner than have taken in hand such a purpose."

Cicero to Atticus.[19]

"Pompey is aiming at a monarchy after the type of Sylla. I know what I say. Never did he show his hand more plainly. Has he not a good cause? The very best. But mark me, it will be carried out most foully. He means to strangle Rome and Italy with famine, and then waste and burn the country, and seize the property of all who have any. Caesar may do as ill; but the prospect is frightful. The fleets from Alexandria, Colchis, Sidon, Cyprus, Pamphylia, Lycia, Rhodes, Chios, Byzantium, will be employed to cut off our supplies, and then Pompey himself will come in his wrath."

Cicero to Atticus.[20]

"I think I have been mad from the beginning of this business. Why did not I follow Pompey when things were at their worst? I found him (at Capua) full of fears. I knew then what he would do, and I did not like it. He made blunder on blunder. He never wrote to me, and only thought of flight. It was disgraceful. But now my love for him revives. Books and philosophy please me no more. Like the sad bird, I gaze night and day over the sea, and long to fly away.[21] Were flight the worst, it would be nothing, but I dread this terrible war, the like of which has never been seen. The word will be, 'Sylla could do thus and thus; and why should not I?' Sylla, Marius, Cinna, had each a constitutional cause, yet how cruel was their victory! I shrank from war because I saw that something still more cruel was now intended. I, whom some have called the saviour and parent of my country! I to bring Getes, and Armenians, and

Colchians upon Italy! I to famish my fellow-citizens and waste their lands! Caesar, I reflected, was in the first place but mortal; and then there were many ways in which he might be got rid of.[22] But, as you say, the sun has fallen out of the sky. The sick man thinks that while there is life there is hope. I continued to hope as long as Pompey was in Italy. Now your letters are my only consolation."

* * * * *

"Caesar was but mortal!" The rapture with which Cicero hailed Caesar's eventual murder explains too clearly the direction in which his thoughts were already running. If the life of Caesar alone stood between his country and the resurrection of the constitution, Cicero might well think, as others have done, that it was better that one man should die rather than the whole nation perish. We read the words with sorrow, and yet with pity. That Cicero, after his past flatteries of Caesar, after the praises which he was yet to heap on him, should yet have looked on his assassination as a thing to be desired, throws a saddening light upon his inner nature. But the age was sick with a moral plague, and neither strong nor weak, wise nor unwise, bore any antidote against infection.

[1] The vision on the Rubicon, with the celebrated saying that "the die is cast," is unauthenticated, and not at all consistent with Caesar's character.

[2] Ibid., vii. 12.

[3] "Delectus ... invitorum est et pugnando ab horrentium."--To Atticus, vii. 13.

[4] Compare Caesar's account of these conditions, De Bello Civili, i. 10, with Cicero to Atticus, vii. 17.

[5] Between the Apennines and the Adriatic, about Ancona; in the line of Caesar's march should he advance from Kimini.

[6] To Atticus, vii. 16.

[7] Ibid., vii. 21.

[8] "Balbus quidem major ad me scribit, nihil malle Caesarem, quam principe Pompeio sine metu vivere. Tu puto haec credis."--To Atticus, viii. 9.

[9] To Atticus, viii. 3.

[10] To Atticus, viii. 11.

[11] "Judicavique te bello violari, contra cujus honorem, populi Romani beneficio concessum, inimici atque invidi niterentur. Sed ut eo tempore non modo ipse fautor dignitatis tuae fui, verum etiam caeteris auctor ad te adjuvandum, sic me nunc Pompeii dignitas vehementer movet," etc.--_Cicero to Caesar, enclosed in a letter to Atticus_, ix. 11.

[12] Enclosed to Atticus, viii. 11.

[13] Pompey had for two years meditated on the course which he was now taking. Atticus had spoken of the intended flight from Italy as base. Cicero answers: "Hoc turpe Cnaeus noster biennio ante cogitavit: ita Sullaturit animus ejus, et diu proscripturit;" "so he apes Sylla and longs for a proscription."--To Atticus, ix. 10.

[14] To Atticus, viii. 13.

[15] Enclosed to Atticus, viii. 15.

[16] To Atticus, viii. 16.

[17] To Atticus, ix. 4.

[18] Ibid., ix. 6.

[19] To Atticus, ix. 7 and 9.

[20] Ibid.

[21] "Ita dies et noctes tanquam avis illa mare prospecto, evolare cupio."

[22] "Hunc primum mortalem esse, deinde etiam multis modis extingui posse cogitabam."--To Atticus, ix. 10.

CHAPTER XXII.

[Sidenote: April B.C. 49.] Pompey was gone, gone to cover the Mediterranean with fleets which were to starve Italy, and to raise an army which was to bring him back to play Sylla's game once more. The consuls had gone with him, more than half the Senate, and the young patricians, the descendants of the Metelli and the Scipios, with the noble nature melted out of them, and only the pride remaining. Caesar would have chased them at once, and have allowed them no time to organize, but ships were wanting, and he could not wait to form a fleet. Pompey's lieutenants, Afranius and Petreius and Varro, were in Spain, with six legions and the levies of the Province. These had to be promptly dealt with, and Sicily and Sardinia, on which Rome depended for its corn, had to be cleared of enemies, and placed in trustworthy hands. He sent Curio to Sicily and Valerius to Sardinia. Both islands surrendered without resistance, Cato, who was in command in Messina, complaining openly that he had been betrayed. Caesar went himself to Rome, which he had not seen for ten years. He met Cicero by appointment on the road, and pressed him to attend the Senate. Cicero's example, he said, would govern the rest. If his account of the interview be true, Cicero showed more courage than might have been expected from his letters to Atticus. He inquired whether, if he went, he might speak as he pleased; he could not consent to blame Pompey, and he should say that he disapproved of attacks upon him, either in Greece or Spain. Caesar said that he could not permit language of this kind. Cicero answered that he thought as much, and therefore preferred to stay away.[1]Caesar let him take his own course, and went on by himself. The consuls being absent, the Senate was convened by the tribunes, Mark Antony and Cassius Longinus, both officers in Caesar's army. The house was thin, but those present were cold and hostile. They knew by this time that they need fear no violence. They interpreted Caesar's gentleness into timidity, but they were satisfied that, let them do what they pleased, he would not injure them. He addressed the Senate with his usual clearness and simplicity. He had asked, he said, for no extraordinary honors. He had waited the legal period of ten years for a second consulship. A promise had been given that his name should be submitted, and that promise had been withdrawn. He dwelt on his forbearance, on the concessions which he had offered, and again on his unjust recall, and the violent suppression of the legal authority of the tribunes. He had proposed terms of peace, he said; he had asked for interviews, but all in vain. If the Senate feared to commit themselves by assisting him, he declared his willingness to carry on the government in his own name; but he invited them to send deputies to Pompey, to treat for an arrangement.

The Senate approved of sending a deputation; but Pompey had sworn, on leaving, that he would hold all who had not joined him as his enemies; no one, therefore, could be found willing to go. Three days were spent in unmeaning discussion, and Caesar's situation did not allow of trifling. With such people nothing could be done, and peace could be won only by the sword. By an edict of his own he restored the children of the victims of Sylla's proscription to their civil rights and their estates, the usurpers being mostly in Pompey's camp. The assembly of the people voted him the money in the treasury. Metellus, a tribune in Pompey's interest, forbade the opening of the doors, but he was pushed out of the way. Cesar took such money as he needed, and went with his best speed to join his troops in Gaul.

His singular gentleness had encouraged the opposition to him in Rome. In Gaul he encountered another result of his forbearance more practically trying. The Gauls themselves, though so lately conquered in so desperate a struggle, remained quiet. Then, if ever, they had an opportunity of reasserting their independence. They not only did not take advantage of it, but, as if they disdained the unworthy treatment of their great enemy, each tribe sent him, at his request, a body of horse, led by the bravest of their chiefs. His difficulty came from a more tainted source. Marseilles, the most important port in the western Mediterranean, the gate through which the trade of the Province passed in and out, had revolted to Pompey. Domitius Ahenobarbus, who had been dismissed at Corfinium, had been despatched to encourage and assist the townspeople with a squadron of Pompey's fleet. When Caesar arrived, Marseilles closed its gates, and refused to receive him. He could not afford to leave behind him an open door into the Province, and he could ill spare troops for a siege. Afranius and Petreius were already over the Ebro with 30,000 legionaries and with nearly twice as many Spanish auxiliaries. Yet Marseilles must be shut in, and quickly. Fabius was sent forward to hold the passes of the Pyrenees. Caesar's soldiers were set to work in the forest. Trees were cut down and sawn into planks. In thirty days twelve stout vessels, able to hold their own against Domitius, were built and launched and manned. The fleet thus extemporized was trusted to Decimus Brutus. Three legions were left to make approaches, and, if possible, to take the town on the land side; and, leaving Marseilles blockaded by sea and land, Caesar hurried on to the Spanish frontier. The problem before him was worthy of his genius. A protracted war in the peninsula would be fatal. Pompey would return to Italy, and there would be no one to oppose him there. The Spanish army had to be destroyed or captured, and that immediately; and it was stronger than Caesar's own, and was backed by all the resources of the province.

The details of a Roman campaign are no longer interesting. The results, with an outline of the means by which they were brought about, alone concern the modern reader. Pompey's lieutenant, having failed to secure the passes, was lying at Lerida, in Catalonia, at the junction of the Segre and the Naguera, with the Ebro behind them, and with a mountain range, the Sierra de Llena, on their right flank. Their position was impregnable to direct attack. From their rear they drew inexhaustible supplies. The country in front had been laid waste to the Pyrenees, and everything which Caesar required had to be brought to him from Gaul. In forty days from the time at which the armies came in sight of each other Afranius and Petreius, with all their legions, were prisoners. Varro, in the south, was begging for peace, and all Spain lay at Caesar's feet. At one moment he was almost lost. The melting of the snows in the mountains brought a flood down the Segre. The bridges were carried away, the fords were impassable, and his convoys were at the mercy of the enemy. News flew to Rome that all was over, that Caesar's army was starving, that he was cut off between the rivers, and in a few days must surrender. Marseilles still held out. Pompey's, it seemed, was to be the winning side, and Cicero and many others, who had hung back to watch how events would turn, made haste to join their friends in Greece before their going had lost show of credit.[2]

The situation was indeed most critical. Even Caesar's own soldiers became unsteady. He remarks that in civil wars generally men show less composure than in ordinary campaigns. But resource in difficulties is the distinction of great generals. He had observed in Britain that the coast fishermen used boats made out of frames of wicker covered with skins. The river banks were fringed with willows. There were hides in abundance on the carcasses of the animals in the camp. Swiftly in these vessels the swollen waters of the Segre were crossed; the convoys were rescued. The broken bridges were repaired. The communications of the Pompeians were threatened in turn, and they tried to fall back over the Ebro; but they left their position only to be intercepted, and after a few feeble struggles laid down their arms. Among the prisoners were found several of the young nobles who had been released at Corfinium. It appeared that they regarded Caesar as an outlaw with whom obligations were not binding. The Pompeian generals had ordered any of Caesar's soldiers who fell into their hands to be murdered. He was not provoked into retaliation. He again dismissed the whole of the captive force, officers and men, contenting himself with this time exacting a promise from them that they would not serve against him again. They gave their word and broke it. The generals and military tribunes made their way to Greece to Pompey. Of the rest, some enlisted in Caesar's legions; others scattered to combine again when opportunity allowed.

Varro, who commanded a legion in the south, behaved more honorably. He sent in his submission, entered into the same engagement, and kept it. He was an old friend of Caesar's, and better understood him. Caesar, after the victory at Lerida, went down to Cordova, and summoned the leading Spaniards and Romans to meet him there. All came and promised obedience. Varro gave in his accounts, with his ships, and stores, and money. Caesar then embarked at Cadiz, and went round to Tarragona, where his own legions were waiting for him. From Tarragona he marched back by the Pyrenees, and came in time to receive in person the surrender of Marseilles.

The siege had been a difficult one, with severe engagements both by land and sea. Domitius and his galleys had attacked the ungainly but useful vessels which Caesar had extemporized. He had been driven back with the loss of half his fleet. Pompey had sent a second squadron to help him, and this had fared no better. It had fled after a single battle and never reappeared. The land works had been assailed with ingenuity and courage. The agger had been burnt and the siege towers destroyed. But they had been repaired instantly by the industry of the legions, and Marseilles was at the last extremity when Caesar arrived. He had wished to spare the townspeople, and had sent orders that the place was not to be stormed. On his appearance the keys of the gates were brought to him without conditions. Again he pardoned every one; more, he said, for the reputation of the colony than for the merits of its inhabitants. Domitius had fled in a gale of wind, and once more escaped.

A third time he was not to be so fortunate.

[Sidenote: B.C. 48] Two legions were left in charge of Marseilles; others returned to their quarters in Gaul. Well as the tribes had behaved, it was unsafe to presume too much on their fidelity, and Caesar was not a partisan chief, but the guardian of the Roman Empire. With the rest of his army he returned to Rome at the beginning of the winter. All had been quiet since the news of the capitulation at Lerida. The aristocracy had gone to Pompey. The disaffection among the people of which Cicero spoke had existed only in his wishes, or had not extended beyond the classes who had expected from Caesar a general partition of property, and had been disappointed. His own successes had been brilliant. Spain, Gaul, and Italy, Sicily and Sardinia, were entirely his own. Elsewhere and away from his own eye things had gone less well for him. An attempt to make a naval force in the Adriatic had failed; and young Curio, who had done Caesar such good service as tribune, had met with a still graver disaster. After recovering Sicily, Curio had been directed to cross to Africa and expel Pompey's garrisons from the Province. His troops were inferior, consisting chiefly of the garrison which had surrendered at Corfinium. Through military inexperience he had fallen into a trap laid for him by Juba, King of Mauritania, and had been killed.

Caesar regretted Curio personally. The African misfortune was not considerable in itself, but it encouraged hopes and involved consequences which he probably foresaw. There was no present leisure, however, to attend to Juba. On arriving at the city he was named Dictator. As Dictator he held the consular elections, and, with Servilius Isauricus for a colleague, he was chosen consul for the year which had been promised to him, though under circumstances so strangely changed. With curious punctiliousness he observed that the legal interval had expired since he was last in office, and that therefore there was no formal objection to his appointment.

Civil affairs were in the wildest confusion. The Senate had fled; the administration had been left to Antony, whose knowledge of business was not of a high order; and over the whole of Italy hung the terror of Pompey's fleet and of an Asiatic invasion. Public credit was shaken. Debts had not been paid since the civil war began. Moneylenders had charged usurious interest for default, and debtors were crying for novae tabulae, and hoped to clear themselves by bankruptcy. Caesar had but small leisure for such matters.

Pompey had been allowed too long a respite, and unless he sought Pompey in Greece, Pompey would be seeking him at home, and the horrid scenes of Sylla's wars would be enacted over again. He did what he could, risking the loss of the favor of the mob by disappointing dishonest expectations. Estimates were drawn of all debts as they stood twelve months before. The principal was declared to be still due. The interest for the interval was cancelled. Many persons complained of injustice which they had met with in the courts of law during the time that Pompey was in power. Caesar refused to revise the sentences himself, lest he should seem to be encroaching on functions not belonging to him; but he directed that such causes should be heard again.

Eleven days were all he could afford to Rome. So swift was Caesar that his greatest exploits were measured by days. He had to settle accounts with Pompey while it was still winter, and while Pompey's preparations for the invasion of Italy were still incomplete; and he and his veterans, scarcely allowing themselves a breathing-time, went down to Brindisi.

It was now the beginning of January by the unreformed calendar (by the seasons the middle of October)--a year within a few days since Caesar had crossed the Rubicon. He had nominally twelve legions under him. But long marches had thinned the ranks of his old and best-tried troops. The change from the dry climate of Gaul and Spain to the south of Italy in a wet autumn had affected the health of the rest, and there were many invalids. The force available for field service was small for the work which was before it: in all not more than 30,000 men. Pompey's army lay immediately opposite Brindisi, at Durazzo. It was described afterward as inharmonious and ill-disciplined, but so far as report went at the time Caesar had never encountered so formidable an enemy. There were nine legions of Roman citizens with their complements full. Two more were coming up with Scipio from Syria. Besides these there were auxiliaries from the allied princes in the East; corps from Greece and Asia Minor, slingers and archers from Crete and the islands. Of money, of stores of all kinds, there was abundance, for the Eastern revenue had been all paid for the last year to Pompey, and he had levied impositions at his pleasure.

Such was the Senate's land army, and before Caesar could cross swords with it a worse danger lay in his path. It was not for nothing that Cicero said that

Pompey had been careful of his fleet. A hundred and thirty ships, the best which were to be had, were disposed in squadrons along the east shore of the Adriatic; the head-quarters were at Corfu; and the one purpose was to watch the passage and prevent Caesar from crossing over.

[Sidenote: January, B.C. 48.] Transports run down by vessels of war were inevitably sunk. Twelve fighting triremes, the remains of his attempted Adriatic fleet, were all that Caesar could collect for a convoy. The weather was wild. Even of transports he had but enough to carry half his army in a single trip. With such a prospect and with the knowledge that if he reached Greece at all he would have to land in the immediate neighborhood of Pompey's enormous host, surprise has been expressed that Caesar did not prefer to go round through Illyria, keeping his legions together. But Caesar had won many victories by appearing where he was least expected. He liked well to descend like a bolt out of the blue sky; and, for the very reason that no ordinary person would under such circumstances have thought of attempting the passage, he determined to try it. Long marches exhausted the troops. In bad weather the enemy's fleet preferred the harbors to the open sea; and perhaps he had a further and special ground of confidence in knowing that the officer in charge at Corfu was his old acquaintance, Bibulus-- Bibulus, the fool of the aristocracy, the butt of Cicero, who had failed in everything which he had undertaken, and had been thanked by Cato for his ill successes. Caesar knew the men with whom he had to deal. He knew Pompey's incapacity; he knew Bibulus's incapacity. He knew that public feeling among the people was as much on his side in Greece as in Italy. Above all, he knew his own troops, and felt that he could rely on them, however heavy the odds might be. He was resolved to save Italy at all hazards from becoming the theatre of war, and therefore the best road for him was that which would lead most swiftly to his end.

On the 4th January, then, by unreformed time, Caesar sailed with 15,000 men and 500 horses from Brindisi. The passage was rough but swift, and he landed without adventure at Acroceraunia, now Cape Linguetta, on the eastern shore of the Straits of Otranto. Bibulus saw him pass from the heights of Corfu, and put to sea, too late to intercept him--in time, however, unfortunately, to fall in with the returning transports. Caesar had started them immediately after disembarking, and had they made use of the darkness they might have gone over unperceived; they lingered and were overtaken; Bibulus captured thirty of them, and, in rage at his own blunder, killed every one that he found on board.

Ignorant of this misfortune, and expecting that Antony would follow him in a day or two with the remainder of the army, Caesar advanced at once toward Durazzo, occupied Apollonia, and entrenched himself on the left bank of the river Apsus. The country, as he anticipated, was well-disposed and furnished him amply with supplies. He still hoped to persuade Pompey to come to terms with him. He trusted, perhaps not unreasonably, that the generosity with which he had treated Marseilles and the Spanish legions might have produced an effect; and he appealed once more to Pompey's wiser judgment. Vibullius Rufus, who had been taken at Corfinium, and a second time on the Lerida, had since remained with Caesar. Rufus, being personally known as an ardent member of the Pompeian party, was sent forward to Durazzo with a message of peace.

"Enough had been done," Caesar said, "and Fortune ought not to be tempted further. Pompey had lost Italy, the two Spains, Sicily, and Sardinia, and a hundred and thirty cohorts of his soldiers had been captured. Caesar had lost Curio and the army of Africa. They were thus on an equality, and might spare their country the consequences of further rivalry. If either he or Pompey gained a decisive advantage, the victor would be compelled to insist on harder terms. If they could not agree, Caesar was willing to leave the question between them to the Senate and people of Rome, and for themselves, he proposed that they should each take an oath to disband their troops in three days."

Pompey, not expecting Caesar, was absent in Macedonia when he heard of his arrival, and was hurrying back to Durazzo. Caesar's landing had produced a panic in his camp. Men and officers were looking anxiously in each other's faces. So great was the alarm, so general the distrust, that Labienus had sworn in the presence of the army that he would stand faithfully by Pompey. Generals, tribunes, and centurions had sworn after him. They had then moved up to the Apsus and encamped on the opposite side of the river, waiting for Pompey to come up.

There was now a pause on both sides. Antony was unable to leave Brindisi, Bibulus being on the watch day and night. A single vessel attempted the passage. It was taken, and every one on board was massacred. The weather was still wild, and both sides suffered. If Caesar's transports could not put to sea, Bibulus's crews could not land either for fuel or water anywhere south of Apollonia. Bibulus held on obstinately till he died of exposure to wet and cold, so ending his useless life; but his death did not affect the situation favorably for Caesar; his command fell into abler hands.

[Sidenote: February, B.C. 48.] At length Pompey arrived. Vibullius Rufus delivered his message. Pompey would not hear him to the end. "What care I," he said, "for life or country if I am to hold both by the favor of Caesar? All men will think thus of me if I make peace now.... I left Italy. Men will say that Caesar has brought me back."

In the legions the opinion was different. The two armies were divided only by a narrow river. Friends met and talked. They asked each other for what purpose so desperate a war had been undertaken. The regular troops all idolized Caesar. Deputations from both sides were chosen to converse and consult, with Caesar's warmest approval. Some arrangement might have followed. But Labienus interposed. He appeared at the meeting as if to join in the conference; he was talking in apparent friendliness to Cicero's acquaintance, Publius Vatinius, who was serving with Caesar. Suddenly a shower of darts were hurled at Vatinius. His men flung themselves in front of him and covered his body; but most of them were wounded, and the assembly broke up in confusion, Labienus shouting, "Leave your talk of composition; there can be no peace till you bring us Caesar's head."

[Sidenote: April, B.C. 48.] Cool thinkers were beginning to believe that Caesar was in a scrape from which his good fortune would this time fail to save him. Italy was on the whole steady, but the slippery politicians in the capital were on the watch. They had been disappointed on finding that Caesar would give no sanction to confiscation of property, and a spark of fire burst out which showed that the elements of mischief were active as ever. Cicero's correspondent, Marcus Caelius, had thrown himself eagerly on Caesar's side at the beginning of the war. He had been left as praetor at Rome when Caesar went to Greece. He in his wisdom conceived that the wind was changing, and that it was time for him to earn his pardon from Pompey. He told the mob that Caesar would do nothing for them, that Caesar cared only for his capitalists. He wrote privately to Cicero that he was bringing them over to Pompey,[3] and he was doing it in the way in which pretended revolutionists so often play into the hands of reactionaries. He proposed a law in the Assembly in the spirit of Jack Cade, that no debts should be paid in Rome for six years, and that every tenant should occupy his house for two years free of rent. The administrators of the government treated him as a madman, and deposed him from office. He left the city pretending that he was going to Caesar. The once notorious Milo, who had been in exile since his trial for the murder of Clodius, privately joined him; and together they raised a band of gladiators in Campania, professing to have a commission from Pompey. Milo was killed. Caelius fled to Thurii, where he tried to seduce Caesar's garrison, and was put to death for his treachery. The familiar actors in the drama were beginning to drop. Bibulus was gone, and now Caelius and Milo. Fools and knaves are usually the first to fall in civil distractions, as they and their works are the active causes of them.

Meantime months passed away. The winter wore through in forced inaction, and Caesar watched in vain for the sails of his coming transports. The Pompeians had for some weeks blockaded Brindisi. Antony drove them off with armed boats; but still he did not start, and Caesar thought that opportunities had been missed.[4] He wrote to Antony sharply. The legions, true as steel, were ready for any risks sooner than leave their commander in danger. A south wind came at last, and they sailed. They were seen in mid-channel, and closely pursued. Night fell, and in the darkness they were swept past Durazzo, to which Pompey had again withdrawn, with the Pompeian squadron in full chase behind them. They ran into the harbor of Nymphaea, three miles north of Lissa, and were fortunate in entering it safely. Sixteen of the pursuers ran upon the rocks, and the crews owed their lives to Caesar's troops, who saved them. So Caesar mentions briefly, in silent contrast to the unvarying ferocity of the Pompeian leaders. Two only of the transports which had left Brindisi were missing in the morning. They had gone by mistake into Lissa, and were surrounded by the boats of the enemy, who promised that no one should be injured if they surrendered. "Here," says Caesar, in a characteristic sentence, "may be observed the value of firmness of mind." One of the vessels had two hundred and twenty young soldiers on board, the other two hundred veterans. The recruits were sea-sick and frightened. They trusted the enemy's fair words, and were immediately murdered. The others forced their pilot to run the ship ashore. They cut their way through a band of Pompey's cavalry, and joined their comrades without the loss of a man.

Antony's position was most dangerous, for Pompey's whole army lay between him and Caesar; but Caesar marched rapidly round Durazzo, and had joined his friend before Pompey knew that he had moved.

[Sidenote: May, B.C. 48.] Though still far outnumbered, Caesar was now in a condition to meet Pompey in the field, and desired nothing so much as a decisive action. Pompey would not give him the opportunity, and kept within his lines. To show the world, therefore, how matters stood between them, Caesar drew a line of strongly fortified posts round Pompey's camp and shut him in. Force him to surrender he could not, for the sea was open, and Pompey's fleet had entire command of it. But the moral effect on Italy of the news that Pompey was besieged might, it was hoped, force him out from his entrenchments. If Pompey could not venture to engage Caesar on his own chosen ground, and surrounded by his Eastern friends, his cause at home would be abandoned as lost. Nor was the active injury which Caesar was able to inflict inconsiderable. He turned the streams on which Pompey's camp depended for water. The horses and cattle died. Fever set in with other inconveniences. The labor of the siege was, of course, severe. The lines were many miles in length, and the difficulty of sending assistance to a point threatened by a sally was extremely great. The corn in the fields was still green, and supplies grew scanty. Meat Caesar's army had, but of wheat little or none; they were used to hardship, however, and bore it with admirable humor. They made cakes out of roots, ground into paste and mixed with milk; and thus, in spite of privation and severe work, they remained in good health, and deserters daily came into them.

So the siege of Durazzo wore on, diversified with occasional encounters, which Caesar details with the minuteness of a scientific general writing for his profession, and with those admiring mentions of each individual act of courage which so intensely endeared him to his troops. Once an accidental opportunity offered itself for a successful storm, but Caesar was not on the spot. The officer in command shrank from responsibility; and, notwithstanding the seriousness of the consequences, Caesar said that the officer was right.

[Sidenote: June, B.C. 48.] Pompey's army was not yet complete. Metellus Scipio had not arrived with the Syrian legions. Scipio had come leisurely through Asia Minor, plundering cities and temples and flaying the people with requisitions. He had now reached Macedonia, and Domitius Calvinus had been sent with a separate command to watch him. Caesar's own force, already too small for the business on hand, was thus further reduced, and at this moment there fell out one of those accidents which overtake at times the ablest commanders, and gave occasion for Caesar's observation, that Pompey knew not how to conquer.

There were two young Gauls with Caesar whom he had promoted to important positions. They were reported to have committed various peculations. Caesar spoke to them privately. They took offence and deserted. There was a weak spot in Caesar's lines at a point the furthest removed from the body of the army. The Gauls gave Pompey notice of it, and on this point Pompey flung himself with his whole strength. The attack was a surprise. The engagement which followed was desperate and unequal, for the reliefs were distant and came up one by one. For once Caesar's soldiers were seized with panic, lost their order, and forgot their discipline. On the news of danger he flew himself to the scene, threw himself into the thickest of the fight, and snatched the standards from the flying bearers. But on this single occasion he failed in restoring confidence. The defeat was complete; and, had Pompey understood his business, Caesar's whole army might have been overthrown. Nearly a thousand men were killed, with many field officers and many centurions. Thirty-two standards were lost, and some hundreds of legionaries were taken. Labienus begged the prisoners of Pompey. He called them mockingly old comrades. He asked them how veterans came to fly. They were led into the midst of the camp and were all killed.

Caesar's legions had believed themselves invincible. The effect of this misfortune was to mortify and infuriate them. They were eager to fling themselves again upon the enemy and win back their laurels; but Caesar saw that they were excited and unsteady, and that they required time to collect themselves. He spoke to them with his usual calm cheerfulness. He praised their courage. He reminded them of their many victories, and bade them not be cast down at a misadventure which they would soon repair; but he foresaw that the disaster would affect the temper of Greece and make his commissariat more difficult than it was already. He perceived that he must adopt some new plan of campaign, and with instant decision he fell back upon Apollonia.

[Sidenote: July, B.C 48.] The gleam of victory was the cause of Pompey's ruin. It was unlooked for, and the importance of it exaggerated. Caesar was supposed to be flying with the wreck of an army completely disorganized and disheartened. So sure were the Pompeians that it could never rally again that they regarded the war as over; they made no efforts to follow up a success which, if improved, might have been really decisive; and they gave Caesar the one thing which he needed, time to recover from its effects. After he had placed his sick and wounded in security at Apollonia, his first object was to rejoin Calvinus, who had been sent to watch Scipio, and might now be cut off. Fortune was here favorable. Calvinus, by mere accident, learnt his danger, divined where Caesar would be, and came to meet him. The next thing was to see what Pompey would do. He might embark for Italy. In this case Caesar would have to follow him by Illyria and the head of the Adriatic. Cisalpine Gaul was true to him, and could be relied on to refill his ranks. Or Pompey might pursue him in the hope to make an end of the war in Greece, and an opportunity might offer itself for an engagement under fairer terms. On the whole he considered the second alternative the more likely one, and with this expectation he led his troops into the rich plains of Thessaly for the better feeding which they so much needed. The news of his defeat preceded him. Gomphi, an important Thessalian town, shut its gates upon him; and, that the example might not be followed, Gomphi was instantly stormed and given up to plunder. One such lesson was enough. No more opposition was ventured by the Greek cities.

[Sidenote: August 9, B.C. 48.] Pompey meanwhile had broken up from Durazzo, and after being joined by Scipio was following leisurely. There were not wanting persons who warned him that Caesar's legions might still be dangerous. Both Cicero and Cato had advised him to avoid a battle, to allow Caesar to wander about Greece till his supplies failed and his army was worn out by marches. Pompey himself was inclined to the same opinion. But Pompey was no longer able to act on his own judgment. The senators who were with him in the camp considered that in Greece, as in Rome, they were the supreme rulers of the Roman Empire. All along they had held their sessions and their debates, and they had voted resolutions which they expected to see complied with. They had never liked Pompey. If Cicero was right in supposing that Pompey meant to be another Sylla, the senators had no intention of allowing it. They had gradually wrested his authority out of his hands, and reduced him to the condition of an officer of the Senatorial Directory. These gentlemen, more especially the two late consuls, Scipio and Lentulus, were persuaded that a single blow would now make an end of Caesar. His army was but half the size of theirs, without counting the Asiatic auxiliaries. The men, they were persuaded, were dispirited by defeat and worn out. So sure were they of victory that they were impatient of every day which delayed their return to Italy. They accused Pompey of protracting the war unnecessarily, that he might have the honor of commanding such distinguished persons as themselves. They had arranged everything that was to be done. Caesar and his band of cutthroats were in imagination already despatched. They had butchered hitherto every one of them who had fallen into their hands, and the same fate was designed for their political allies. They proposed to establish a senatorial court after their return to Italy, in which citizens of all kinds who had not actually fought on the Senate's side were to be brought up for trial. Those who should be proved to have been active for Caesar were to be at once killed, and their estates confiscated. Neutrals were to fare almost as badly, Not to have assisted the lawful rulers of the State was scarcely better than to have rebelled against them. They, too, were liable to death or forfeiture, or both. A third class of offenders was composed of those who had been within Pompey's lines, but had borne no part in the fighting. These cold-hearted friends were to be tried and punished according to the degree of their criminality. Cicero was the person pointed at in the last division. Cicero's clear judgment had shown him too clearly what was likely to be the result of a campaign conducted as he found it on his arrival, and he had spoken his thoughts with sarcastic freedom. The noble lords came next to a quarrel among themselves as to how the spoils of Caesar were to be divided. Domitius Ahenobarbus, Lentulus Spinther, and Scipio were unable to determine which of them was to succeed Caesar as Pontifex Maximus, and which was to have his palace and gardens in Rome. The Roman oligarchy were true to their character to the eve of their ruin. It was they, with their idle luxury, their hunger for lands and office and preferment, who had brought all this misery upon their country; and standing, as it were, at the very bar of judgment, with the sentence of destruction about to be pronounced upon them, their thoughts were still bent upon how to secure the largest share of plunder for themselves.

The battle of Pharsalia was not the most severe, still less was it the last, action of the war. But it acquired a special place in history, because it was a battle fought by the Roman aristocracy in their own persons in defence of their own supremacy. Senators and the sons of senators; the heirs of the names and fortunes of the ancient Roman families; the leaders of society in Roman saloons, and the chiefs of the political party of the optimates in the Curia and Forum, were here present on the field; representatives in person and in principle of the traditions of Sylla, brought face to face with the representative of Marius. Here were the men who had pursued Caesar through so many years with a hate so inveterate. Here were the haughty Patrician Guard, who had drawn their swords on him in the senate-house, young lords whose theory of life was to lounge through it in patrician insouciance. The other great actions were fought by the ignoble multitude whose deaths were of less significance. The plains of Pharsalia were watered by the precious blood of the elect of the earth. The battle there marked an epoch like no other in the history of the world.

For some days the two armies had watched each other's movements. Caesar, to give his men confidence, had again offered Pompey an opportunity of fighting. But Pompey had kept to positions where he could not be attacked. To draw him into more open ground, Caesar had shifted his camp continually. Pompey had followed cautiously, still remaining on his guard. His political advisers were impatient of these dilatory movements. They taunted him with cowardice. They insisted that he should set his foot on this insignificant adversary promptly and at once; and Pompey, gathering courage from their confidence, and trusting to his splendid cavalry, agreed at last to use the first occasion that presented itself.

One morning, on the Enipeus, near Larissa, the 9th of August, old style, or toward the end of May by real time, Caesar had broken up his camp and was preparing for his usual leisurely march, when he perceived a movement in Pompey's lines which told him that the moment which he had so long expected was come. Labienus, the evil genius of the Senate, who had tempted them into the war by telling them that his comrades were as disaffected as himself, and had fired Caesar's soldiers into intensified fierceness by his barbarities at Durazzo, had spoken the deciding word: "Believe not," Labienus had said, "that this is the army which defeated the Gauls and the Germans. I was in those battles, and what I say I know. That army has disappeared. Part fell in action; part perished of fever in the autumn in Italy. Many went home. Many were left behind unable to move. The men you see before you are levies newly drawn from the colonies beyond the Po. Of the veterans that were left, the best were killed at Durazzo."

A council of war had been held at dawn. There had been a solemn taking of oaths again. Labienus swore that he would not return to the camp except as a conqueror; so swore Pompey; so swore Lentulus, Scipio, Domitius; so swore all the rest. They had reason for their high spirits. Pompey had forty-seven thousand Roman infantry, not including his allies, and seven thousand cavalry. Caesar had but twenty-two thousand, and of horse only a thousand. Pompey's position was carefully chosen. His right wing was covered by the Enipeus, the opposite bank of which was steep and wooded. His left spread out into the open plain of Pharsalia. His plan of battle was to send forward his cavalry outside over the open ground, with clouds of archers and slingers, to scatter Caesar's horse, and then to wheel round and envelop his legions. Thus he had thought they would lose heart and scatter at the first shock. Caesar had foreseen what Pompey would attempt to do. His own scanty cavalry, mostly Gauls and Germans, would, he well knew, be unequal to the weight which would be thrown on them. He had trained an equal number of picked active men to fight in their ranks, and had thus doubled their strength. Fearing that this might be not enough, he had taken another precaution. The usual Roman formation in battle was in triple line. Caesar had formed a fourth line of cohorts specially selected to engage the cavalry; and on them, he said, in giving them their instructions, the result of the action would probably depend.

Pompey commanded on his own left with the two legions which he had taken from Caesar; outside him on the plain were his flying companies of Greeks and islanders, with the cavalry covering them. Caesar, with his favorite 10th, was opposite Pompey. His two faithful tribunes, Mark Antony and Cassius Longinus, led the left and centre. Servilia's son, Marcus Brutus, was in Pompey's army. Caesar had given special directions that Brutus, if recognized, should not be injured. Before the action began he spoke a few general words to such of his troops as could hear him. They all knew, he said, how earnestly he had sought for peace, how careful he had always been of his soldiers' lives, how unwilling to deprive the State of the services of any of her citizens, to whichever party they might belong. Crastinus, a centurion, of the 10th legion, already known to Caesar for his gallantry, called out, "Follow me, my comrades, and strike, and strike home, for your general. This one battle remains to be fought, and he will have his rights and we our liberty. General," he said, looking to Caesar, "I shall earn your thanks this day, dead or alive."

Pompey had ordered his first line to stand still to receive Caesar's charge.[5] They would thus be fresh, while the enemy would reach them exhausted--a mistake on Pompey's part, as Caesar thought; "for a fire and alacrity," he observes, "is kindled in all men when they meet in battle, and a wise general should rather encourage than repress their fervor."

The signal was given. Caesar's front rank advanced running. Seeing the Pompeians did not move, they halted, recovered breath, then rushed on, flung their darts, and closed sword in hand. At once Pompey's horse bore down, outflanking Caesar's right wing, with the archers behind and between them raining showers of arrows. Caesar's cavalry gave way before the shock, and the outer squadrons came wheeling round to the rear, expecting that there would be no one to encounter them. The fourth line, the pick and flower of the legions, rose suddenly in their way. Surprised and shaken by the fierceness of the attack on them, the Pompeians turned, they broke, they galloped wildly off. The best cavalry in those Roman battles were never a match for infantry when in close formation, and Pompey's brilliant squadrons were carpet-knights from the saloon and the circus. They never rallied, or tried to rally; they made off for the nearest hills. The archers were cut to pieces; and the chosen corps, having finished so easily the service for which they had been told off, threw themselves on the now exposed flank of Pompey's left wing. It was composed, as has been said, of the legions which had once been Caesar's, which had fought under him at the Vingeanne and at Alesia. They ill liked, perhaps, the change of masters, and were in no humor to stand the charge of their old comrades coming on with the familiar rush of victory. Caesar ordered up his third line, which had not yet been engaged; and at once on all sides Pompey's great army gave way, and fled. Pompey himself, the shadow of his old name, long harasssd out of self-respect by his senatorial directors, a commander only in appearance, had left the field in the beginning of the action. He had lost heart on the defeat of the cavalry, and had retired to his tent to wait the issue of the day.

The stream of fugitives pouring in told him too surely what the issue had been. He sprang upon his horse and rode off in despair. His legions were rushing back in confusion. Caesar, swift always at the right moment, gave the enemy no leisure to re-form, and fell at once upon the camp. It was noon, and the morning had been sultry; but heat and weariness were forgotten in the enthusiasm of a triumph which all then believed must conclude the war. A few companies of Thracians, who had been left on guard, made a brief resistance, but they were soon borne down. The beaten army, which a few hours before were sharing in imagination the lands and offices of their conquerors, fled out through the opposite gates, throwing away their arms, flinging down their standards, and racing, officers and men, for the rocky hills which at a mile's distance promised them shelter.

The camp itself was a singular picture. Houses of turf had been built for the luxurious patricians, with ivy trained over the entrances to shade their delicate faces from the summer sun; couches had been laid out for them to repose on after their expected victory; tables were spread with plate and wines, and the daintiest preparations of Roman cookery. Caesar commented on the scene with mournful irony. "And these men," he said, "accused my patient, suffering army, which had not even common necessaries, of dissoluteness and profligacy!"

Two hundred only of Caesar's men had fallen. The officers had suffered most. The gallant Crastinus, who had nobly fulfilled his promise, had been killed, among many others, in opening a way for his comrades. The Pompeians, after the first shock, had been cut down unresisting. Fifteen thousand of them lay scattered dead about the ground. There were few wounded in these battles. The short sword of the Romans seldom left its work unfinished.

"They would have it so," Caesar is reported to have said, as he looked sadly over the littered bodies in the familiar patrician dress.[6] "After all that I had done for my country, I, Caius Caesar, should have been condemned by them as a criminal if I had not appealed to my army."

[Sidenote: B.C. 48.] But Caesar did not wait to indulge in reflections. His object was to stamp the fire out on the spot, that it might never kindle again. More than half the Pompeians had reached the hills and were making for Larissa. Leaving part of his legions in the camp to rest, Caesar took the freshest the same evening, and by a rapid march cut off their line of retreat.

The hills were waterless, the weather suffocating. A few of the guiltiest of the Pompeian leaders, Labienus, Lentulus, Afranius, Petreius, and Metellus Scipio (Cicero and Cato had been left at Durazzo), contrived to escape in the night. The rest, twenty-four thousand of them, surrendered at daylight. They came down praying for mercy, which they had never shown, sobbing out their entreaties on their knees that the measure which they had dealt to others might not be meted out to them. Then and always Caesar hated unnecessary cruelty, and never, if he could help it, allowed executions in cold blood. He bade them rise, said a few gentle words to relieve their fears, and sent them back to the camp. Domitius Ahenobarbus, believing that for him at least there could be no forgiveness, tried to escape, and was killed. The rest were pardoned.

So ended the battle of Pharsalia. A hundred and eighty standards were taken and all the eagles of Pompey's legions. In Pompey's own tent was found his secret correspondence, implicating persons, perhaps, whom Caesar had never suspected, revealing the mysteries of the past three years. Curiosity and even prudence might have tempted him to look into it. His only wish was that the past should be forgotten: he burnt the whole mass of papers unread.

Would the war now end? That was the question. Caesar thought that it would not end as long as Pompey was at large. The feelings of others may be gathered out of abridgments from Cicero's letters:

Cicero to Plancius.[7]

"Victory on one side meant massacre, on the other slavery. It consoles me to remember that I foresaw these things, and as much feared the success of our cause as the defeat of it. I attached myself to Pompey's party more in hope of peace than from desire of war; but I saw, if we had the better, how cruel would be the triumph of an exasperated, avaricious, and insolent set of men; if we were defeated, how many of our wealthiest and noblest citizens must fall. Yet when I argued thus and offered my advice I was taunted for being a coward."

Cicero to Caius Cassius.[8]

"We were both opposed to a continuance of the war [after Pharsalia]. I, perhaps, more than you; but we agreed that one battle should be accepted as decisive, if not of the whole cause, yet of our own judgment upon it. Nor were there any who differed from us save those who thought it better that the Constitution should be destroyed altogether than be preserved with diminished prerogatives. For myself I could hope nothing from the overthrow of it, and much if a remnant could be saved.... And I thought it likely that, after that decisive battle, the victors would consider the welfare of the public, and that the vanquished would consider their own."

To Varro.[9]

"You were absent [at the critical moment]. I for myself perceived that our friends wanted war, and that Caesar did not want it, but was not afraid of it. Thus much of human purpose was in the matter. The rest came necessarily; for one side or the other would, of course, conquer. You and I both grieved to see how the State would suffer from the loss of either army and its generals; we knew that victory in a civil war was itself a most miserable disaster. I dreaded the success of those to whom I had attached myself. They threatened most cruelly those who had stayed quietly at home. Your sentiments and my speeches were alike hateful to them. If our side had won, they would have shown no forbearance."

To Marcus Marius.[10]

"When you met me on the 13th of May (49), you were anxious about the part which I was to take. If I stayed in Italy, you feared that I should be wanting in duty. To go to the war you thought dangerous for me. I was myself so disturbed that I could not tell what it was best for me to do. I consulted my reputation, however, more than my safety; and if I afterwards repented of my decision it was not for the peril to myself, but on account of the state of things which I found on my arrival at Pompey's camp. His forces were not very considerable, nor good of their kind. For the chiefs, if I except the general and a few others, they were rapacious in their conduct of the war, and so savage in their language that I dreaded to see them victorious. The most considerable among them were overwhelmed with debt. There was nothing good about them but their cause. I despaired of success and recommended peace. When Pompey would not hear of it, I advised him to protract the war. This for the time he approved, and he might have continued firm but for the confidence which he gathered from the battle at Durazzo. From that day the great man ceased to be a general. With a raw and inexperienced army he engaged legions in perfect discipline. On the defeat he basely deserted his camp and fled by himself. For me this was the end: I retired from a war in which the only alternatives before me were either to be killed in action or be taken prisoner, or fly to Juba in Africa, or hide in exile, or destroy myself."

To Caecina.[11]

"I would tell you my prophecies but that you would think I had made them after the event. But many persons can bear me witness that I first warned Pompey against attaching himself to Caesar, and then against quarrelling with him. Their union (I said) had broken the power of the Senate; their discord would cause a civil war. I was intimate with Caesar; I was most attached to Pompey; but my advice was for the good of them both.... I thought that Pompey ought to go to Spain. Had he done so, the war would not have been. I did not so much insist that Caesar could legally stand for the consulship as that his name should be accepted, because the people had so ordered at Pompey's own instance. I advised, I entreated. I preferred the most unfair peace to the most righteous war. I was overborne, not so much by Pompey (for on him I produced an effect) as by men who relied on Pompey's leadership to win them a victory, which would be convenient for their personal interests and private ambitions. No misfortune has happened in the war which I did not predict."

[1] To Atticus, ix. 18.

[2] "Tullia bids me wait till I see how things go in Spain, and she says you are of the same opinion. The advice would be good, if I could adapt my conduct to the issue of events there. But one of three alternatives must happen. Either Caesar will be driven back, which would please me best, or the war will be protracted, or he will be completely victorious. If he is defeated, Pompey will thank me little for joining him. Curio himself will then go over to him. If the war hangs on, how long am I to wait? If Caesar conquers, it is thought we may then have peace. But I consider, on the other hand, that it would be more decent to forsake Caesar in success than when beaten and in difficulties. The victory of Caesar means massacre, confiscation, recall of exiles, a clean

sweep of debts, every worst man raised to honor, and a rule which not only a Roman citizen but a Persian could not endure.... Pompey will not lay down his arms for the loss of Spain; he holds with Themistocles that those who are masters at sea will be the victors in the end. He has neglected Spain. He has given all his care to his ships. When the time comes he will return to Italy with an overwhelming fleet. And what will he say to me if he finds me still sitting here?--Let alone duty, I must think of the danger.... Every course has its perils; but I should surely avoid a course which is both ignominious and perilous also.

"I did not accompany Pompey when he went himself? I could not. I had not time. And yet, to confess the truth, I made a mistake which, perhaps, I should not have made. I thought there would be peace, and I would not have Caesar angry with me after he and Pompey had become friends again. Thus I hesitated; but I can overtake my fault if I lose no more time, and I am lost if I delay.--I see that Caesar cannot stand long. He will fall of himself if we do nothing. When his affairs were most flourishing, he became unpopular with the hungry rabble of the city in six or seven days. He could not keep up the mask. His harshness to Metellus destroyed his credit for clemency, and his taking money from the treasury destroyed his reputation for riches.

"As to his followers, how can men govern provinces who cannot manage their own affairs for two months together? Such a monarchy could not last half a year. The wisest men have miscalculated.... If that is my case, I must bear the reproach ... but I am sure it will be as I say. Caesar will fall, either by his enemies or by himself, who is his worst enemy.... I hope I may live to see it, though you and I should be thinking more of the other life than of this transitory one: but so it come, no matter whether I see it or foresee it."--To Atticus, x. 8.

[3] "Nam hic nunc praeter foeneratores paucos nec homo nec ordo quisquam est nisi Pompeianus. Equidem jam effeci ut maxime plebs et qui antea noster fuit populus vester esset."--Caelius to Cicero, Ad Fam., viii. 71.

[4] Caesar says nothing of his putting to sea in a boat, meaning to go over in person, and being driven back by the weather. The story is probably no more than one of the picturesque additions to reality made by men who find truth too tame for them.

[5] I follow Caesar's own account of the action. Appian is minutely circumstantial, and professes to describe from the narratives of eye-witnesses. But his story varies so far from Caesar's as to be irreconcilable with it, and Caesar's own authority is incomparably the best.

[6] Suetonius, quoting from Asinius Pollio, who was present at the battle.

[7] Ad Familiares, iv. 14.

[8] Ibid., xv. 15.

[9] Ad Fam., ix. 6.

[10] Ibid., vii. 3.

[11] Ad Fam., vi. 6.

CHAPTER XXIII.

The strength of the senatorial party lay in Pompey's popularity in the East. A halo was still supposed to hang about him as the creator of the Eastern Empire, and so long as he was alive and at liberty there was always a possibility that he might collect a new army. To overtake him, to reason with him, and, if reason failed, to prevent him by force from involving himself and the State in fresh difficulties, was Caesar's first object. Pompey, it was found, had ridden from the battlefield direct to the sea, attended by a handful of horse. He had gone on board a grain vessel, which carried him to Amphipolis. At Amphipolis he had stayed but a single night, and had sailed for Mitylene, where he had left his wife and his sons. The last accounts which the poor lady had heard of him had been such as reached Lesbos after the affair at Durazzo. Young patricians had brought her word that her husband had gained a glorious victory, that he had joined her father, Metellus Scipio, and that together they were pursuing Caesar with the certainty of overwhelming him. Rumor, cruel as usual,

Had brought smooth comforts false, worse than true wrongs.

Rumor had told Cornelia that Caesar had "stooped his head" before

Pompey's "rage." Pompey came in person to inform her of the miserable reality. At Mitylene Pompey's family were no longer welcome guests. They joined him on board his ship to share his fortunes, but what those fortunes were to be was all uncertain. Asia had seemed devoted to him. To what part of it should he go? To Cilicia? to Syria? to Armenia? To Parthia? For even Parthia was thought of. Unhappily the report of Pharsalia had flown before him, and the vane of sentiment had everywhere veered round. The Aegean islands begged him politely not to compromise them by his presence. He touched at Rhodes. Lentulus, flying from the battlefield, had tried Rhodes before him, and had been requested to pass on upon his way. Lentulus was said to be gone to Egypt. Polite to Pompey the Rhodians were, but perhaps he was generously unwilling to involve them in trouble in his behalf. He went on to Cilicia, the scene of his old glory in the pirate wars. There he had meant to land and take refuge either with the Parthians or with one of the allied princes. But in Cilicia he heard that Antioch had declared for Caesar. Allies and subjects, as far as he could learn, were all for Caesar. Egypt, whither Lentulus had gone, appeared the only place where he could surely calculate on being welcome. Ptolemy the Piper, the occasion of so much scandal, was no longer living, but he owed the recovery of his throne to Pompey. Gabinius had left a few thousand of Pompey's old soldiers at Alexandria to protect him against his subjects. These men had married Egyptian wives and had adopted Egyptian habits, but they could not have forgotten their old general. They were acting as guards at present to Ptolemy's four children, two girls, Cleopatra and Arsinoe, and two boys, each called Ptolemy. The father had bequeathed the crown to the two elder ones, Cleopatra, who was turned sixteen, and a brother two years younger. Here at least, among these young princes and their guardians, who had been their father's friends, their father's greatest benefactor might count with confidence on finding hospitality.

For Egypt, therefore, Pompey sailed, taking his family along with him. He had collected a few ships and 2,000 miscellaneous followers, and with them he arrived off Pelusium, the modern Damietta. His forlorn condition was a punishment sufficiently terrible for the vanity which had flung his country into war. But that it had been his own doing the letters of Cicero prove with painful clearness; and though he had partially seen his error at Capua, and would then have possibly drawn back, the passions and hopes which he had excited had become too strong for him to contend against. From the day of his flight from Italy he had been as a leaf whirled upon a winter torrent. Plain enough it had long been to him that he would not be able to govern the wild forces of a reaction which, if it had prevailed, would have brought back a more cruel tyranny than Sylla's. He was now flung as a waif on the shore of a foreign land; and if Providence on each occasion proportioned the penalties of misdoing to the magnitude of the fault, it might have been considered that adequate retribution had been inflicted on him. But the consequences of the actions of men live when the actions are themselves forgotten, and come to light without regard to the fitness of the moment. The senators of Rome were responsible for the exactions which Ptolemy Auletes had been compelled to wring out of his subjects. Pompey himself had entertained and supported him in Rome when he was driven from his throne, and had connived at the murder of the Alexandrians who had been sent to remonstrate against his restoration. It was by Pompey that he had been forced again upon his miserable subjects, and had been compelled to grind them with fresh extortions. It was not unnatural under these circumstances that the Egyptians were eager to free themselves from a subjection which bore more heavily on them than annexation to the Empire. A national party had been formed on Ptolemy's death to take advantage of the minority of his children. Cleopatra had been expelled. The Alexandrian citizens kept her brother in their hands, and were now ruling in his name; the demoralized Roman garrison had been seduced into supporting them, and they had an army lying at the time at Pelusium, to guard against Cleopatra and her friends.

Of all this Pompey knew nothing. When he arrived off the port he learnt that the young king with a body of troops was in the neighborhood, and he sent on shore to ask permission to land. The Egyptians had already heard of Pharsalia. Civil war among the Romans was an opportunity for them to assert their independence, or to secure their liberties by taking the side which seemed most likely to be successful. Lentulus had already arrived, and had been imprisoned--a not unnatural return for the murder of Dion and his fellow-citizens. Pompey, whose name more than that of any other Roman was identified with their sufferings, was now placing himself spontaneously in their hands. Why, by sparing him, should they neglect the opportunity of avenging their own wrongs, and of earning, as they might suppose that they would, the lasting gratitude of Caesar? The Roman garrison had no feeling for their once glorious commander. "In calamity," Caesar observes, "friends easily become foes." The guardians of the young king sent a smooth answer, bidding Pompey welcome. The water being shallow, they despatched Achillas, a prefect in the king's army, and Septimius, a Roman officer, whom Pompey personally knew, with a boat to conduct him on shore. His wife and friends distrusted the tone of the reception, and begged him to wait till he could land with his own guard. The presence of Septimius gave Pompey confidence. Weak men, when in difficulties, fall into a kind of despairing fatalism, as if tired of contending longer with adverse fortune. Pompey stepped into the boat, and when out of arrow-shot from the ship was murdered under his wife's eyes. His head was cut off and carried away. His body was left lying on the sands. A man who had been once his slave, and had been set free by him, gathered a few sticks and burnt it there; and thus the last rites were bestowed upon one whom, a few months before, Caesar himself would have been content to acknowledge as his superior.

So ended Pompey the Great. History has dealt tenderly with him on account of his misfortunes, and has not refused him deserved admiration for qualities as rare in his age as they were truly excellent. His capacities as a soldier were not extraordinary. He had risen to distinction by his honesty. The pirates who had swept the Mediterranean had bought their impunity by a tribute paid to senators and governors. They were suppressed instantly when a commander was sent against them whom they were unable to bribe. The conquest of Asia was no less easy to a man who could resist temptations to enrich himself. The worst enemy of Pompey never charged him with corruption or rapacity. So far as he was himself concerned, the restoration of Ptolemy was gratuitous, for he received nothing for it. His private fortune, when he had the world at his feet, was never more than moderate; nor as a politician did his faults extend beyond weakness and incompetence. Unfortunately he had acquired a position by his negative virtues which was above his natural level, and misled him into overrating his capabilities. So long as he stood by Caesar he had maintained his honor and his authority. He allowed men more cunning than himself to play upon his vanity, and Pompey fell--fell amidst the ruins of a Constitution which had been undermined by the villanies of its representatives. His end was piteous, but scarcely tragic, for the cause to which he was sacrificed was too slightly removed from being ignominious. He was no Phoebus Apollo sinking into the ocean, surrounded with glory. He was not even a brilliant meteor. He was a weak, good man, whom accident had thrust into a place to which he was unequal; and ignorant of himself, and unwilling to part with his imaginary greatness, he was flung down with careless cruelty by the forces which were dividing the world. His friend

Lentulus shared his fate, and was killed a few days later, while Pompey's ashes were still smoking. Two of Bibulus's sons, who had accompanied him, were murdered as well.

Caesar meanwhile had followed along Pompey's track, hoping to overtake him. In Cilicia he heard where he was gone; and learning something more accurately there of the state of Egypt, he took two legions with him, one of which had attended him from Pharsalia, and another which he had sent for from Achaia. With these he sailed for Alexandria. Together, so much had they been thinned by hard service, these legions mustered between them little over 3,000 men. The force was small, but Caesar considered that, after Pharsalia, there could be no danger for him anywhere in the Mediterranean. He landed without opposition, and was presented on his arrival, as a supposed welcome offering, with the head of his rival. Politically it would have been better far for him to have returned to Rome with Pompey as a friend. Nor, if it had been certain that Pompey would have refused to be reconciled, were services such as this a road to Caesar's favor. The Alexandrians speedily found that they were not to be rewarded with the desired independence. The consular fasces, the emblem of the hated Roman authority, were carried openly before Caesar when he appeared in the streets; and it was not long before mobs began to assemble with cries that Egypt was a free country, and that the people would not allow their king to be insulted. Evidently there was business to be done in Egypt before Caesar could leave it. Delay was specially inconvenient. A prolonged absence from Italy would allow faction time to rally again. But Caesar did not look on himself as the leader of a party, but as the guardian of Roman interests, and it was not his habit to leave any necessary work uncompleted. The etesian winds, too, had set in, which made it difficult for his heavy vessels to work out of the harbor. Seeing that troubles might rise, he sent a message to Mithridates of Pergamus,[1] to bring him reinforcements from Syria, while he himself at once took the government of Egypt into his hands. He forbade the Alexandrians to set aside Ptolemy's will, and insisted that the sovereignty must be vested jointly in Cleopatra and her brother as their father had ordered.[2]he cries of discontent grew bolder. Alexandria was a large, populous city, the common receptacle of vagabonds from all parts of the Mediterranean. Pirates, thieves, political exiles, and outlaws had taken refuge there, and had been received into the king's service. With the addition of the dissolute legionaries left by Gabinius, they made up 20,000 as dangerous ruffians as had ever been gathered into a single city. The more respectable citizens had no reason to love the Romans. The fate of Cyprus seemed a foreshadowing of their own. They too, unless they looked to themselves, would be absorbed in the devouring Empire. They had made an end of Pompey, and Caesar had shown no gratitude. Caesar himself was now in their hands. Till the wind changed they thought that he could not escape, and they were tempted, naturally enough, to use the chance which fate had given them.

Pothinus, a palace eunuch and one of young Ptolemy's guardians, sent secretly for the troops at Pelusium, and gave the command of them to Achillas, the officer who had murdered Pompey. The city rose when they came in, and Caesar found himself blockaded in the palace and the part of the city which joined the outer harbor. The situation was irritating from its absurdity, but more or less it was really dangerous. The Egyptian fleet which had been sent to Greece in aid of Pompey had come back, and was in the inner basin. It outnumbered Caesar's, and the Alexandrians were the best seamen in the Mediterranean. If they came out, they might cut his communications. Without hesitation he set fire to the docks; burnt or disabled the great part of the ships; seized the Pharos and the mole which connected it with the town; fortified the palace and the line of houses occupied by his troops; and in this position he remained for several weeks, defending himself against the whole power of Egypt. Of the time in which legend describes him as abandoned to his love for Cleopatra, there was hardly an hour of either day or night in which he was not fighting for his very life. The Alexandrians were ingenious and indefatigable. They pumped the sea into the conduits which supplied his quarters with water, for a moment it seemed with fatal effect. Fresh water was happily found by sinking wells. They made a new fleet; old vessels on the stocks were launched, others were brought down from the canals on the river. They made oars and spars out of the benches and tables of the professors' lecture rooms. With these they made desperate attempts to retake the mole. Once with a sudden rush they carried a ship, in which Caesar was present in person, and he was obliged to swim for his life.[3] Still, he held on, keeping up his men's spirits, and knowing that relief must arrive in time. He was never greater than in unlooked-for difficulties. He never rested. He was always inventing some new contrivance. He could have retired from the place with no serious loss. He could have taken to his ships and forced his way to sea in spite of the winds and the Alexandrians. But he felt that to fly from such an enemy would dishonor the

Roman name, and he would not entertain the thought of it.

[Sidenote: B.C. 47.] The Egyptians made desperate efforts to close the harbor. Finding that they could neither capture the Pharos nor make an impression on Caesar's lines, they affected to desire peace. Caesar had kept young Ptolemy with him as a security. They petitioned that he should be given up to them, promising on compliance to discontinue their assaults. Caesar did not believe them. But the boy was of no use to him; the army wished him gone, for they thought him treacherous; and his presence would not strengthen the enemy. Caesar, says Hirtius, considered that it would be more respectable to be fighting with a king than with a gang of ruffians. Young Ptolemy was released, and joined his countrymen, and the war went on more fiercely than before. Pompey's murderers were brought to justice in the course of it. Pothinus fell into Caesar's hands, and was executed. Ganymede, another eunuch, assassinated Achillas, and took his place as commander-in-chief. Reinforcements began to come in. Mithridates had not yet been heard of; but Domitius Calvinus, who had been left in charge of Asia Minor, and to whom Caesar had also sent, had despatched two legions to him. One arrived by sea at Alexandria, and was brought in with some difficulty. The other was sent by land, and did not arrive in time to be of service. There was a singular irony in Caesar being left to struggle for months with a set of miscreants, but the trial came to an end at last. Mithridates, skilful, active, and faithful, had raised a force with extraordinary rapidity in Cilicia and on the Euphrates. He had marched swiftly through Syria; and in the beginning of the new year Caesar heard the welcome news that he had reached Pelusium, and had taken it by storm. Not delaying for a day, Mithridates had gone up the bank of the Nile to Cairo. A division of the Egyptian army lay opposite to him, in the face of whom he did not think it prudent to attempt to cross, and from thence he sent word of his position to Caesar. The news reached Caesar and the Alexandrians at the same moment. The Alexandrians had the easiest access to the scene. They had merely to ascend the river in their boats. Caesar was obliged to go round by sea to Pelusium, and to follow the course which Mithridates had taken himself. Rapidity of movement made up the difference. Taking with him such cohorts as could be spared from his lines, Caesar had joined Mithridates before the Alexandrians had arrived. Together they forced the passage; and Ptolemy came only for his camp to be stormed, his army to be cut to pieces, and himself to be drowned in the Nile, and so end his brief and miserable life.

Alexandria immediately capitulated. Arsinoe, the youngest sister, was sent to Rome. Cleopatra and her surviving brother were made joint sovereigns; and Roman rumor, glad to represent Caesar's actions in monstrous characters, insisted in after years that they were married. The absence of contemporary authority for the story precludes also the possibility of denying it. Two legions were left in Egypt to protect them if they were faithful, or to coerce them if they misconducted themselves. The Alexandrian episode was over, and Caesar sailed for Syria. His long detention over a complication so insignificant had been unfortunate in many ways. Scipio and Cato, with the other fugitives from Pharsalia, had rallied in Africa, under the protection of Juba. Italy was in confusion. The popular party, now absolutely in the ascendant, were disposed to treat the aristocracy as the aristocracy would have treated them had they been victorious. The controlling hand was absent; the rich, long hated and envied, were in the power of the multitude, and wild measures were advocated, communistic, socialistic, such as are always heard of in revolutions, meaning in one form or another the equalization of wealth, the division of property, the poor taking their turn on the upper crest of fortune and the rich at the bottom. The tribunes were outbidding one another in extravagant proposals, while Caesar's legions, sent home from Greece to rest after their long service, were enjoying their victory in the license which is miscalled liberty. They demanded the lands, or rewards in money, which had been promised them at the end of the war. Discipline was relaxed or abandoned. Their officers wore unable, perhaps unwilling, to control them. They, too, regarded the Commonwealth as a spoil which their swords had won, and which they were entitled to distribute among themselves.

In Spain, too, a bad feeling had revived. After Caesar's departure his generals had oppressed the people, and had quarrelled with one another. The country was disorganized and disaffected. In Spain, as in Egypt, there was a national party still dreaming of independence. The smouldering traditions of Sertorius were blown into flame by the continuance of the civil war. The proud motley race of Spaniards, Italians, Gauls, indigenous mountaineers, Moors from Africa, the remnants of the Carthaginian colonies, however they might hate one another, yet united in resenting an uncertain servitude under the alternate ascendency of Roman factions. Spain was ripe for revolt. Gaul alone, Caesar's own province, rewarded him for the use which he had made of his victory, by unswerving loyalty and obedience.

On his landing in Syria, Caesar found letters pressing for his instant return to Rome. Important persons were waiting to give him fuller information than could be safely committed to writing. He would have hastened home at once, but restless spirits had been let loose everywhere by the conflict of the Roman leaders. Disorder had broken out near at hand. The still recent defeat of Crassus had stirred the ambition of the Asiatic princes; and to leave the Eastern frontier disturbed was to risk a greater danger to the Empire than was to be feared from the impatient politics of the Roman mob, or the dying convulsions of the aristocracy.

Pharnaces, a legitimate son of Mithridates the Great, had been left sovereign of Upper Armenia. He had watched the collision between Pompey and Caesar with a neutrality which was to plead for him with the conqueror, and he had intended to make his own advantage out of the quarrels between his father's enemies. Deiotarus, tributary king of Lower Armenia and Colchis, had given some help to Pompey, and had sent him men and money; and on Pompey's defeat, Pharnaces had supposed that he might seize on Deiotarus's territories without fear of Caesar's resentment. Deiotarus had applied to Domitius Calvinus for assistance; which Calvinus, weakened as he was by the despatch of two of his legions to Egypt, had been imperfectly able to give. Pharnaces had advanced into Cappadocia. When Calvinus ordered him to retire, he had replied by sending presents, which had hitherto proved so effective with Roman proconsuls, and by an equivocating profession of readiness to abide by Caesar's decision. Pharnaces came of a dangerous race. Caesar's lieutenant was afraid that, if he hesitated, the son of Mithridates might become as troublesome as his father had been. He refused the presents. Disregarding his weakness, he sent a peremptory command to Pharnaces to fall back within his own frontiers, and advanced to compel him if he refused. In times of excitement the minds of men are electric, and news travels with telegraphic rapidity if not with telegraphic accuracy. Pharnaces heard that Caesar was shut up in Alexandria and was in a position of extreme danger, that he had sent for all his Asiatic legions, and that Calvinus had himself been summoned to his assistance. Thus he thought that he might safely postpone compliance till the Roman army was gone, and he had the country to himself. The reports from Egypt were so unfavorable that, although as yet he had received no positive orders, Calvinus was in daily expectation that he would be obliged to go. It would be unsafe, he thought, to leave an insolent barbarian unchastised. He had learnt in Caesar's school to strike quickly. He had not learnt the comparison between means and ends, without which celerity is imprudence. He had but one legion left; but he had a respectable number of Asiatic auxiliaries, and with them he ventured to attack Pharnaces in an intricate position. His Asiatics deserted. The legion behaved admirably; but in the face of overwhelming numbers, it could do no more than cut its way to security. Pharnaces at once reclaimed his father's kingdom, and overran Pontus, killing, mutilating, or imprisoning every Roman that he encountered; and in this condition Caesar found Asia Minor on his coming to Syria.

It was not in Caesar's character to leave a Roman Province behind him in the hands of an invader, for his own political interests. He saw that he must punish Pharnaces before he returned to Rome, and he immediately addressed himself to the work. He made a hasty progress through the Syrian towns, hearing complaints and distributing rewards and promotions. The allied chiefs came to him from the borders of the Province to pay their respects. He received them graciously, and dismissed them pleased and satisfied. After a few days spent thus, he sailed for Cilicia, held a council at Tarsus, and then crossed the Taurus, and went by forced marches through Cappadocia to Pontus. He received a legion from Deiotarus which had been organized in Roman fashion. He sent to Calvinus to meet him with the survivors of his lost battle; and when they arrived, he reviewed the force which was at his disposition. It was not satisfactory. He had brought a veteran legion with him from Egypt, but it was reduced to a thousand strong. He had another which he had taken up in Syria; but even this did not raise his army to a point which could assure him of success. But time pressed, and skill might compensate for defective numbers.

Pharnaces, hearing that Caesar was at hand, promised submission. He sent Caesar a golden crown, in anticipation perhaps that he was about to make himself king. He pleaded his desertion of Pompey as a set-off against his faults. Caesar answered that he would accept the submission, if it were sincere; but Pharnaces must not suppose that good offices to himself could atone for injuries to the Empire.[4] The provinces which he had invaded must be instantly evacuated; his Roman prisoners must be released, and their property must be restored to them.

Pharnaces was a politician, and knew enough of Caesar's circumstances to mislead him. The state of Rome required Caesar's presence. A campaign in Asia would occupy more time than he could afford, and Pharnaces calculated that he must be gone in a few days or weeks. The victory over Calvinus had strengthened his ambition of emulating his father. He delayed his answer, shifted from place to place, and tried to protract the correspondence till Caesar's impatience to be gone should bring him to agree to a compromise.

Caesar cut short negotiations. Pharnaces was at Zela, a town in the midst of mountains behind Trebizond, and the scene of a great victory which had been won by Mithridates over the Romans. Caesar defied auguries. He seized a position at night on the brow of a hill directly opposite to the Armenian camp, and divided from it by a narrow valley. As soon as day broke the legions were busy intrenching with their spades and pickaxes. Pharnaces, with the rashness which if it fails is madness, and if it succeeds is the intuition of genius, decided to fall on them at a moment when no sane person could rationally expect an attack; and Caesar could not restrain his astonishment when he saw the enemy pouring down the steep side of the ravine, and breasting the ascent on which he stood. It was like the battle of Maubeuge over again, with the difference that he had here to deal with Asiatics, and not with the Nervii. There was some confusion while the legions were exchanging their digging tools for their arms. When the exchange had been made, there was no longer a battle, but a rout. The Armenians were hurled back down the hill, and slaughtered in masses at the bottom of it. The camp was taken. Pharnaces escaped for the moment, and made his way into his own country; but he was killed immediately after, and Asia Minor was again at peace.

Caesar, calm as usual, but well satisfied to have ended a second awkward business so easily, passed quickly down to the Hellespont, and had landed in Italy before it was known that he had left Pontus.

[1] Supposed to have been a natural son of Mithridates the Great. The reason for the special confidence which Caesar placed in him does not appear. The danger at Alexandria, perhaps, did not appear at the moment particularly serious.

[2] Roman scandal discovered afterward that Caesar had been fascinated by the charms of Cleopatra, and allowed his politics to be influenced by a love

affair. Roman fashionable society hated Caesar, and any carrion was welcome to them which would taint his reputation. Cleopatra herself favored the story, and afterward produced a child, whom she named Caesarion. Oppius, Caesar's most intimate friend, proved that the child could not have been his--of course, therefore, that the intrigue was a fable; and the boy was afterward put to death by Augustus as an impostor. No one claims immaculate virtue for Caesar. An amour with Cleopatra may have been an accident of his presence in Alexandria. But to suppose that such a person as Caesar, with the concerns of the world upon his hands, would have allowed his public action to be governed by a connection with a loose girl of sixteen is to make too large a demand upon human credulity; nor is it likely that, in a situation of so much danger and difficulty as that in which he found himself, he would have added to his embarrassments by indulging in an intrigue. The report proves nothing, for whether true or false it was alike certain to arise. The salons of Rome, like the salons of London and Paris, took their revenge on greatness by soiling it with filth; and happily Suetonius, the chief authority for the scandal, couples it with a story which is demonstrably false. He says that Caesar made a long expedition with Cleopatra in a barge upon the Nile; that he was so fascinated with her that he wished to extend his voyage to Aethiopia, and was prevented only by the refusal of his army to follow him. The details of Caesar's stay at Alexandria, so minutely given by Hirtius, show that there was not a moment when such an expedition could have been contemplated. During the greater part of the time he was blockaded in the palace. Immediately after the insurrection was put down, he was obliged to hurry off on matters of instant and urgent moment. Of the story of Cleopatra's presence in Rome at the time of his murder, more will be said hereafter.

[3] Legend is more absurd than usual over this incident. It pretends that he swam with one hand, and carried his Commentaries, holding them above water, with the other. As if a general would take his MSS. with him into a hot action!

[4] "Neque provinciarum injurias condonari iis posse qui fuissent in se officiosi."--De Bello Alexandrino, 70.

CHAPTER XXIV.

Cicero considered that the Civil War ought to have ended with Pharsalia;

and in this opinion most reasonable men among the conservatives were agreed. They had fought one battle; and it had gone against them. To continue the struggle might tear the Empire to pieces, but could not retrieve a lost cause; and prudence and patriotism alike recommended submission to the verdict of fortune. It is probable that this would have been the result, could Caesar have returned to Italy immediately after his victory. Cicero himself refused to participate in further resistance. Cato offered him a command at Corcyra, but he declined it with a shudder, and went back to Brindisi; and all but those whose consciences forbade them to hope for pardon, or who were too proud to ask for it, at first followed his example. Scipio, Cato, Labienus, Afranius, Petreius, were resolute to fight on to the last; but even they had no clear outlook, and they wandered about the Mediterranean, uncertain what to do, or whither to turn. Time went on, however, and Caesar did not appear. Rumor said at one time that he was destroyed at Alexandria. The defeat of Calvinus by Pharnaces was an ascertained fact. Spain was in confusion. The legions in Italy were disorganized, and society, or the wealthy part of society, threatened by the enemies of property, began to call for some one to save it. All was not lost. Pompey's best generals were still living. His sons, Sextus and Cnaeus, were brave and able. The fleet was devoted to them and to their father's cause, and Caesar's officers had failed, in his absence, to raise a naval force which could show upon the sea. Africa was a convenient rallying point. Since Curio's defeat, King Juba had found no one to dispute his supremacy, and between Juba and the aristocracy who were bent on persisting in the war, an alliance was easily formed. While Caesar was perilling his own interest to remain in Asia to crush Pharnaces, Metellus Scipio was offering a barbarian chief the whole of Roman Africa, as the price of his assistance, in a last effort to reverse the fortune of Pharsalia. Under these scandalous conditions, Scipio, Labienus, Cato, Afranius, Petreius, Faustus Sylla, the son of the Dictator, Lucius Caesar, and the rest of the irreconcilables, made Africa their new centre of operations. Here they gathered to themselves the inheritors of the Syllan traditions, and made raids on the Italian coasts and into Sicily and Sardinia. Seizing Caesar's officers when they could find them, they put them invariably to death without remorse. Cicero protested honorably against the employment of treacherous savages, even for so sacred a cause as the defence of the constitution;[1] but Cicero was denounced as a traitor seeking favor with the conqueror, and the desperate work went on. Caesar's long detention in the East gave the confederates time. The young Pompeys were strong at sea. From Italy there was an easy passage for adventurous disaffection. The shadow of a Pompeian Senate sat once more, passing resolutions, at Utica; while Cato was busy organizing an army, and had collected as many as thirteen legions out of the miscellaneous elements which drifted in to him. Caesar had sent orders to Cassius Longinus to pass into Africa from Spain, and break up these combinations; but Longinus had been at war with his own provincials. He had been driven out of the Peninsula, and had lost his own life in leaving it. Caesar, like Cicero, had believed that the war had ended at Pharsalia. He found that the heads of the Hydra had sprouted again, and were vomiting the old fire and fury. Little interest could it give Caesar to match his waning years against the blinded hatred of his countrymen. Ended the strife must be, however, before order could be restored in Italy, and wretched men take up again the quiet round of industry. Heavy work had to be done in Rome. Caesar was consul now--annual consul, with no ten years' interval any longer possible. Consul, dictator, whatever name the people gave him, he alone held the reins; he alone was able to hold them. Credit had to be restored; debtors had to be brought to recognize their liabilities. Property had fallen in value since the Civil Wars, and securities had to be freshly estimated. The Senate required reformation; men of fidelity and ability were wanted for the public offices. Pompey and Pompey's friends would have drowned Italy in blood. Caesar disappointed expectation by refusing to punish any one of his political opponents. He killed no one. He deprived no one of his property. He even protected the money-lenders, and made the Jews his constant friends. Debts he insisted must be paid, bonds fulfilled, the rights of property respected, no matter what wild hopes imagination might have indulged in. Something only he remitted of the severity of interest, and the poor in the city were allowed their lodgings rent free for a year.

He restored quiet, and gave as much satisfaction as circumstances permitted. His real difficulty was with the legions, who had come back from Greece. They had deserved admirably well, but they were unfortunately over-conscious of their merits. Ill-intentioned officers had taught them to look for extravagant rewards. Their expectations had not been fulfilled; and when they supposed that their labors were over, they received orders to prepare for a campaign in Africa. Sallust, the historian, was in command of their quarters in Campania. They mutinied, and almost killed him. He fled to Rome. The soldiers of the favored 10th legion pursued him to the gates, and demanded speech with Caesar. He bade them come to him, and with his usual fearlessness told them to bring their swords.

The army was Caesar's life. In the army lay the future of Rome, if Rome was to have a future. There, if anywhere, the national spirit survived. It was a trying moment; but there was a calmness in Caesar, a rising from a profound indifference to what man or fortune could give or take from him, which no extremity could shake.

The legionaries entered the city, and Caesar directed them to state their complaints. They spoke of their services and their sufferings. They said that they had been promised rewards, but their rewards so far had been words, and they asked for their discharge. They did not really wish for it. They did not expect it. But they supposed that Caesar could not dispense with them, and that they might dictate their own terms.

During the wars in Gaul, Caesar had been most munificent to his soldiers. He had doubled their ordinary pay. He had shared the spoils of his conquests with them. Time and leisure had alone been wanting to him to recompense their splendid fidelity in the campaigns in Spain and Greece. He had treated them as his children; no commander had ever been more careful of his soldiers' lives; when addressing the army he had called them always "commilitones," "comrades," "brothers-in-arms."

The familiar word was now no longer heard from him. "You say well, quirites," [2] he answered; "you have labored hard, and you have suffered much; you desire your discharge--you have it. I discharge you who are present. I discharge all who have served their time. You shall have your recompense. It shall never be said of me that I made use of you when I was in danger, and was ungrateful to you when the peril was past."

"Quirites" he had called them; no longer Roman legionaries, proud of their achievements, and glorying in their great commander, but "quirites"--plain citizens. The sight of Caesar, the familiar form and voice, the words, every sentence of which they knew that he meant, cut them to the heart. They were humbled, they begged to be forgiven. They said they would go with him to Africa, or to the world's end. He did not at once accept their penitence. He told them that lands had been allotted to every soldier out of the ager publicus, or out of his own personal estates. Suetonius says that the sections had been carefully taken so as not to disturb existing occupants; and thus it appeared that he had been thinking of them and providing for them when they supposed themselves forgotten. Money, too, he had ready for each, part in hand, part in bonds bearing interest, to be redeemed when the war should be over. Again, passionately, they implored to be allowed to continue with him. He relented, but not entirely.

"Let all go who wish to go," he said; "I will have none serve with me who serve unwillingly."

"All, all!" they cried; "not one of us will leave you"--and not one went. The mutiny was the greatest peril, perhaps, to which Caesar had ever been exposed. No more was said; but Caesar took silent notice of the officers who had encouraged the discontented spirit. In common things, Dion Cassius says, he was the kindest and most considerate of commanders. He passed lightly over small offences; but military rebellion in those who were really responsible he never forgave.

[Sidenote: B.C. 46.] The African business could now be attended to. It was again midwinter. Winter campaigns were trying, but Caesar had hitherto found them answer to him; the enemy had suffered more than himself; while, as long as an opposition Senate was sitting across the Mediterranean, intrigue and conspiracy made security impossible at home. Many a false spirit now fawning at home on Caesar was longing for his destruction. The army with which he would have to deal was less respectable than that which Pompey had commanded at Durazzo, but it was numerically as strong or stronger. Cato, assisted by Labienus, had formed into legions sixty thousand Italians. They had a hundred and twenty elephants, and African cavalry in uncounted multitudes. Caesar perhaps despised an enemy too much whom he had so often beaten. He sailed from Lilybaeum on the 19th of December, with a mere handful of men, leaving the rest of his troops to follow as they could. No rendezvous had been positively fixed, for between the weather and the enemy it was uncertain where the troops would be able to land, and the generals of the different divisions were left to their discretion. Caesar on arriving seized and fortified a defensible spot at Ruspinum.[3] The other legions dropped in slowly, and before a third of them had arrived the enemy were swarming about the camp, while the Pompeys were alert on the water to seize stray transports or provision ships. There was skirmishing every day in front of Caesar's lines. The Numidian horse surrounded his thin cohorts like swarms of hornets. Labienus himself rode up on one occasion to a battalion which was standing still under a shower of arrows, and asked in mockery who they were. A soldier of the 10th legion lifted his cap that his face might be recognized, hurled his javelin for answer, and brought Labienus's horse to the ground. But courage was of no avail in the face of overwhelming numbers. Scipio's army collected faster than Caesar's, and Caesar's young soldiers showed some uneasiness in a position so unexpected. Caesar, however, was confident and in high spirits.[4] Roman residents in the African province came gradually in to him, and some African tribes, out of respect, it was said, for the memory of Marius. A few towns declared against the Senate in indignation at Scipio's promise that the province was to be abandoned to Juba. Scipio replied with burning the Roman country houses and wasting the lands, and still killing steadily every friend of Caesar that he could lay hands on. Caesar's steady clemency had made no difference. The senatorial faction went on as they had begun till at length their ferocity was repaid upon them.

The reports from the interior became unbearable. Caesar sent an impatient message to Sicily that, storm or calm, the remaining legions must come to him, or not a house would be left standing in the province. The officers were no longer what they had been. The men came, but bringing only their arms and tools, without change of clothes and without tents, though it was the rainy season. Good will and good hearts, however, made up for other shortcomings. Deserters dropped in thick from the Senate's army. King Juba, it appeared, had joined them, and Roman pride had been outraged, when Juba had been seen taking precedence in the council of war, and Metellus Scipio exchanging his imperial purple in the royal presence for a plain dress of white.

[Sidenote: April 6, B.C. 46.] The time of clemency was past. Publius Ligarius was taken in a skirmish. He had been one of the captives at Lerida who had given his word to serve no further in the war. He was tried for breaking his engagement, and was put to death. Still, Scipio's army kept the field in full strength, the loss by desertions being made up by fresh recruits sent from Utica by Cato. Caesar's men flinched from facing the elephants, and time was lost while other elephants were fetched from Italy, that they might handle them and grow familiar with them. Scipio had been taught caution by the fate of Pompey, and avoided a battle, and thus three months wore away before a decisive impression had been made. But the clear dark eyes of the conqueror of Pharsalia had taken the measure of the situation and comprehended the features of it. By this time he had an effective squadron of ships, which had swept off Pompey's cruisers; and if Scipio shrank from an engagement it was possible to force him into it. A division of Scipio's troops were in the peninsula of Thapsus.[5] If Thapsus was blockaded at sea and besieged by land, Scipio would be driven to come to its relief, and would have to fight in the open country. Caesar occupied the neck of the peninsula, and the result was what he knew it must be. Scipio and Juba came down out of the hills with their united armies. Their legions were beginning to form intrenchments, and Caesar was leisurely watching their operations, when at the sight of the enemy an irresistible enthusiasm ran through his lines. The cry rose for instant attack; and Caesar, yielding willingly to the universal impulse, sprang on his horse and led the charge in person. There was no real fighting. The elephants which Scipio had placed in front wheeled about and plunged back into the camp, trumpeting and roaring. The vallum was carried at a rush, and afterward there was less a battle than a massacre. Officers and men fled for their lives like frightened antelopes, or flung themselves on their knees for mercy. This time no mercy was shown. The deliberate cruelty with which the war had been carried on had done its work at last. The troops were savage, and killed every man that they overtook. Caesar tried to check the carnage, but his efforts were unavailing. The leaders escaped for the time by the speed of their horses. They scattered with a general purpose of making for Spain. Labienus reached it, but few besides him. Afranius and Faustus Sylla with a party of cavalry galloped to Utica, which they expected to hold till one of the Pompeys could bring vessels to take them off. The Utican towns-people had from the first shown an inclination for Caesar. Neither they nor any other Romans in Africa liked the prospect of being passed over to the barbarians.

[Sidenote: B.C. 46.] Cowards smarting under defeat are always cruel. The fugitives from Thapsus found that Utica would not be available for their purpose, and in revenge they began to massacre the citizens. Cato was still in the town. Cato was one of those better natured men whom revolution yokes so often with base companionship. He was shocked at the needless cruelty, and bribed the murderous gang to depart. They were taken soon afterward by Caesar's cavalry. Afranius and Sylla were brought into the camp as prisoners. There was a discussion in the camp as to what was to be done with them. Caesar wished to be lenient, but the feeling in the legions was too strong. The system of pardons could not be continued in the face of hatred so envenomed. The two commanders were executed; Caesar contenting himself with securing Sylla's property for his wife, Pompeia, the great Pompey's daughter. Cato Caesar was most anxious to save; but Cato's enmity was so ungovernable that he grudged Caesar the honor of forgiving him. His animosity had been originally the natural antipathy which a man of narrow understanding instinctively feels for a man of genius. It had been converted by perpetual disappointment into a monomania, and Caesar had become to him the incarnation of every quality and every principle which he most abhorred. Cato was upright, unselfish, incorruptibly pure in deed and word; but he was a fanatic whom no experience could teach, and he adhered to his convictions with the more tenacity, because fortune or the disposition of events so steadily declared them to be mistaken. He would have surrendered Caesar to the Germans as a reward for having driven them back over the Rhine. He was one of those who were most eager to impeach him for the acts of his consulship, though the acts themselves were such as, if they had been done by another, he would himself have most warmly approved; and he was tempted by personal dislike to attach himself to men whose object was to reimpose upon his country a new tyranny of Sylla. His character had given respectability to a cause which, if left to its proper defenders, would have appeared in its natural baseness, and thus on him rested the responsibility for the color of justice in which it was disguised. That after all which had passed he should be compelled to accept his pardon at Caesar's hands was an indignity to which he could not submit, and before the conqueror could reach Utica he fell upon his sword and died. Ultimus Romanorum has been the epitaph which posterity has written on the tomb of Cato. Nobler Romans than he lived after him; and a genuine son of the old Republic would never have consented to surrender an imperial province to a barbarian prince. But at least he was an open enemy. He would not, like his nephew Brutus, have pretended to be Caesar's friend, that he might the more conveniently drive a dagger into his side.

The rest of the party was broken up. Scipio sailed for Spain, but was driven back by foul weather into Hippo, where he was taken and killed. His correspondence was found and taken to Caesar, who burnt it unread, as he had burnt Pompey's. The end of Juba and Petreius had a wild splendor about it. They had fled together from Thapsus to Zama, Juba's own principal city, and they were refused admission. Disdaining to be taken prisoners, as they knew they inevitably would be, they went to a country house in the neighborhood belonging to the king. There, after a last sumptuous banquet, they agreed to die like warriors by each other's hand. Juba killed Petreius, and then ran upon his own sword.

So the actors in the drama were passing away. Domitius, Pompey, Lentulus, Ligarius, Metellus Scipio, Afranius, Cato, Petreius, had sunk into bloody graves. Labienus had escaped clear from the battle; and knowing that if Caesar himself would pardon him Caesar's army never would, he made his way to Spain, where one last desperate hope remained. The mutinous legions of Cassius Longinus had declared for the Senate. Some remnants of Pompey's troops who had been dismissed after Lerida had been collected again and joined them; and these, knowing, as Labienus knew, that they had sinned beyond forgiveness, were prepared to fight to the last and die at bay.

One memorable scene in the African campaign must not be forgotten. While Caesar was in difficulty at Ruspinum, and was impatiently waiting for his legions from Sicily, there arrived a general officer of the 10th, named Caius Avienus, who had occupied the whole of one of the transports with his personal servants, horses, and other conveniences, and had not brought with him a single soldier. Avienus had been already privately noted by Caesar as having been connected with the mutiny in Campania. His own habits in the field were simple in the extreme, and he hated to see his officers self-indulgent. He used the opportunity to make an example of him and of one or two others at the same time.

He called his tribunes and centurions together. "I could wish," he said, "that certain persons would have remembered for themselves parts of their past conduct which, though I overlooked them, were known to me; I could wish they would have atoned for these faults by special attention to their duties. As they have not chosen to do this, I must make an example of them as a warning to others.

"You, Caius Avienus, instigated soldiers in the service of the State to mutiny against their commanders. You oppressed towns which were under your charge. Forgetting your duty to the army and to me, you filled a vessel with your own establishment which was intended for the transport of troops; and at a difficult moment we were thus left, through your means, without the men whom we needed. For these causes, and as a mark of disgrace, I dismiss you from the service, and I order you to leave Africa by the first ship which sails.

"You, Aulus Fonteius [another tribune], have been a seditious and a bad officer. I dismiss you also.

"You, Titus Salienus, Marcus Tiro, Caius Clusinas, centurions, obtained your commissions by favor, not by merit. You have shown want of courage in the field; your conduct otherwise has been uniformly bad; you have encouraged a mutinous spirit in your companies. You are unworthy to serve under my command. You are dismissed, and will return to Italy."

The five offenders were sent under guard on board ship, each noticeably being allowed a single slave to wait upon him, and so were expelled from the country.

This remarkable picture of Caesar's method of enforcing discipline is described by a person who was evidently present;[6] and it may be taken as a correction to the vague stories of his severity to these officers which are told by Dion Cassius.

[1] To Atticus, xi. 7.

[2] Citizens.

[3] Where the African coast turns south from Cape Bon.

[4] "Animum enim altum et erectum prae se gerebat."--De Bello Africano.

[5] Between Carthage and Utica.

[6] De Bella Africano, c. 54. This remarkably interesting narrative is attached to Caesar's Commentaries. The author is unknown.

CHAPTER XXV.

[Sidenote: B.C. 45.] The drift of disaffection into Spain was held at first to be of little moment. The battle of Thapsus, the final breaking up of the senatorial party, and the deaths of its leaders, were supposed to have brought an end at last to the divisions which had so long convulsed the Empire. Rome put on its best dress. The people had been on Caesar's side from the first. Those who still nursed in their hearts the old animosity were afraid to show it, and the nation appeared once more united in enthusiasm for the conqueror. There were triumphal processions which lasted for four days. There were sham fights on artificial lakes, bloody gladiator shows, which the Roman populace looked for as their special delight. The rejoicings being over, business began. Caesar was, of course, supreme. He was made inspector of public morals, the censorship being deemed inadequate to curb the inordinate extravagance. He was named Dictator for ten years, with a right of nominating the person whom the people were to choose for their consuls and praetors. The clubs and caucuses, the bribery of the tribes, the intimidation, the organized bands of voters formed out of the clients of the aristocracy, were all at an end. The courts of law were purified. No more judges were to be bought with money or by fouler temptations. The Leges Julias became a practical reality. One remarkable and darable reform was undertaken and carried through amidst the jests of Cicero and the other wits of the time--the revision of the Roman calendar. The distribution of the year had been governed hitherto by the motions of the moon. The twelve annual moons had fixed at twelve the number of the months, and the number of days required to bring the lunar year into correspondence with the solar had been supplied by irregular intercalations, at the direction of the Sacred College. But the Sacred College during the last distracted century had neglected their office. The lunar year was now sixty-five days in advance of the sun. The so-called winter was really the autumn, the spring the winter. The summer solstice fell at the beginning of the legal September. On Caesar as Pontifex Maximus devolved the duty of bringing confusion into order, and the completeness with which the work was accomplished at the first moment of his leisure shows that he had found time in the midst of his campaigns to think of other things than war or politics. Sosigenes, an Alexandrian astronomer, was called in to superintend the reform. It is not unlikely that he had made acquaintance with Sosigenes in Egypt, and had discussed the problem with him in the hours during which he is supposed to have amused himself "in the arms of Cleopatra." Sosigenes, leaving the moon altogether, took the sun for the basis of the new system. The Alexandrian observers had discovered that the annual course of the sun was completed in 365 days and six hours. The lunar twelve was allowed to remain to fix the number of the months. The numbers of days in each month were adjusted to absorb 365 days. The superfluous hours were allowed to accumulate, and every fourth year an additional day was to be intercalated. An arbitrary step was required to repair the negligence of the past. Sixty-five days had still to be made good. The new system, depending wholly on the sun, would naturally have commenced with the winter solstice. But Caesar so far deferred to usage as to choose to begin, not with the solstice itself, but with the first new moon which followed. It so happened in that year that the new moon was eighty days after the solstice; and thus the next year started, as it continues to start, from the 1st of January. The eight days were added to the sixty-five, and the current year was lengthened by nearly three months. It pleased Cicero to mock, as if Caesar, not contented with the earth, was making himself the master of the heavens. "Lyra," he said, "was to set according to the edict;" but the unwise man was not Caesar in this instance.[1]

While Sosigenes was at work with the calendar, Caesar personally again revised the Senate. He expelled every member who had been guilty of extortion or corruption; he supplied the vacancies with officers of merit, with distinguished colonists, with foreigners, with meritorious citizens, even including Gauls, from all parts of the Empire. Time, unfortunately, had to pass before these new men could take their places, but meanwhile he treated the existing body with all forms of respect, and took no step on any question of public moment till the Senate had deliberated on it. As a fitting close to the war he proclaimed an amnesty to all who had borne arms against him. The past was to be forgotten, and all his efforts were directed to the regeneration of Roman society. Cicero paints the habits of fashionable life in colors which were possibly exaggerated; but enough remains of authentic fact to justify the general truth of the picture. Women had forgotten their honor, children their respect for parents. Husbands had murdered wives, and wives husbands. Parricide and incest formed common incidents of domestic Italian history; and, as justice had been ordered in the last years of the Republic, the most abandoned villain who came into court with a handful of gold was assured of impunity. Rich men, says Suetonius, were never deterred from crime by a fear of forfeiting their estates; they had but to leave Italy, and their property was secured to them. It was held an extraordinary step toward improvement when Caesar abolished the monstrous privilege, and ordered that parricides should not only be exiled, but should forfeit everything that belonged to them, and that minor felons should forfeit half their estates.

Cicero had prophesied so positively that Caesar would throw off the mask of clemency when the need for it was gone, that he was disappointed to find him persevere in the same gentleness, and was impatient for revenge to begin. So bitter Cicero was that he once told Atticus he could almost wish himself to be the object of some cruel prosecution, that the tyrant might have the disgrace of it.[2]

He could not deny that "the tyrant" was doing what, if Rome was to continue an ordered commonwealth, it was essential must be done. Caesar's acts were unconstitutional! Yes; but constitutions are made for men, not men for constitutions, and Cicero had long seen that the Constitution was at an end. It had died of its own iniquities. He had perceived in his better moments that Caesar and Caesar only could preserve such degrees of freedom as could be retained without universal destruction. But he refused to be comforted. He considered it a disgrace to them all that Caesar was alive.[3] Why did not somebody kill him? Kill him? And what then? On that side too the outlook was not promising. News had come that Labienus and young Cnaeus Pompey had united their forces in Spain. The whole Peninsula was in revolt, and the counter-revolution was not impossible after all. He reflected with terror on the sarcasms which he had flung on young Pompey. He knew him to be a fool and a savage. "Hang me," he said, "if I do not prefer an old and kind master to trying experiments with a new and cruel one. The laugh will be on the other side then." [4]

Far had Cicero fallen from his dream of being the greatest man in Rome! Condemned to immortality by his genius, yet condemned also to survive in the portrait of himself which he has so unconsciously and so innocently drawn.

The accounts from Spain were indeed most serious. It is the misfortune of men of superior military ability that their subordinates are generally failures when trusted with independent commands. Accustomed to obey implicitly the instructions of their chief, they have done what they have been told to do, and their virtue has been in never thinking for themselves. They succeed, and they forget why they succeed, and in part attribute their fortune to their own skill. With Alexander's generals, with Caesar's, with Cromwell's, even with some of Napoleon's, the story has been the same. They have been self-confident, yet when thrown upon their own resources they have driven back upon a judgment which has been inadequately trained. The mind which guided them is absent. The instrument is called on to become self-acting, and necessarily acts unwisely. Caesar's lieutenants while under his own eye had executed his orders with the precision of a machine. When left to their own responsibility they were invariably found wanting. Among all his officers there was not a man of real eminence. Labienus, the ablest of them, had but to desert Caesar, to commit blunder upon blunder, and to ruin the cause to which he attached himself. Antony, Lepidus, Trebonius, Calvinus, Cassius Longinus, Quintus Cicero, Sabinus, Decimus Brutus, Vatinius, were trusted with independent authority, only to show themselves unfit to use it. Cicero had guessed shrewdly that Caesar's greatest difficulties would begin with his victory. He had not a man who was able to govern under him away from his immediate eye.

Cassius Longinus, Trebonius, and Marcus Lepidus had been sent to Spain after the battle of Pharsalia. They had quarrelled among themselves. They had driven the legions into mutiny. The authority of Rome had broken down as entirely as when Sertorius was defying the Senate; and Spain had become the receptacle of all the active disaffection which remained in the Empire. Thither had drifted the wreck of Scipio's African army. Thither had gathered the outlaws, pirates, and banditti of Italy and the Islands. Thither too had come flights of Numidians and Moors in hopes of plunder; and Pompey's sons and Labienus had collected an army as numerous as that which had been defeated at Thapsus, and composed of materials far more dangerous and desperate. There were thirteen legions of them in all, regularly formed, with eagles and standards; two which had deserted from Trebonius; one made out of Roman Spanish settlers, or old soldiers of Pompey's who had been dismissed at Lerida; four out of the remnants of the campaign in Africa; the rest a miscellaneous combination of the mutinous legions of Longinus and outlawed adventurers who knew that there was no forgiveness for them, and were ready to fight while they could stand. It was the last cast of the dice for the old party of the aristocracy. Appearances were thrown off. There were no more Catos, no more phantom Senates to lend to rebellion the pretended dignity of a national cause. The true barbarian was there in his natural colors.

Very reluctantly Caesar found that he must himself grapple with this last convulsion. The sanguinary obstinacy which no longer proposed any object to itself save defiance and revenge, was converting a war which at first wore an aspect of a legitimate constitutional struggle, into a conflict with brigands. Clemency had ceased to be possible, and Caesar would have gladly left to others the execution in person of the sharp surgery which was now necessary. He was growing old: fifty-five this summer. His health was giving way. For fourteen years he had known no rest. That he could have endured so long such a strain on mind and body was due only to his extraordinary abstinence, to the simplicity of his habits, and the calmness of temperament which in the most anxious moments refused to be agitated. But the work was telling at last on his constitution, and he departed on his last campaign with confessed unwillingness. The future was clouded with uncertainty. A few more years of life might enable him to introduce into the shattered frame of the Commonwealth some durable elements. His death in the existing confusion might be as fatal as Alexander's. That some one person not liable to removal under the annual wave of electoral agitation must preside over the army and the administration, had been evident in lucid moments even to Cicero. To leave the prize to be contended for among the military chiefs was to bequeath a legacy of civil wars and probable disruption; to compound with the embittered remnants of the aristocracy who were still in the field would intensify the danger; yet time and peace alone could give opportunity for the conditions of a permanent settlement to shape themselves. The name of Caesar had become identified with the stability of the Empire. He no doubt foresaw that the only possible chief would be found in his own family. Being himself childless, he had adopted his sister's grandson, Octavius, afterward Augustus, a fatherless boy of seventeen; and had trained him under his own eye. He had discerned qualities doubtless in his nephew which, if his own life was extended for a few years longer, might enable the boy to become the representative of his house and perhaps the heir of his power. In the unrecorded intercourse between the uncle and his niece's child lies the explanation of the rapidity with which the untried Octavius seized the reins when all was again chaos, and directed the Commonwealth upon the lines which it was to follow during the remaining centuries of Roman power.

Octavius accompanied Caesar into Spain. They travelled in a carriage, having as a third with them the general whom Caesar most trusted and liked, and whom he had named in his will as one of Octavius's guardians, Decimus Brutus--the same officer who had commanded his fleet for him at Quiberon and at Marseilles, and had now been selected as the future governor of Cisalpine Gaul. Once more it was midwinter when they left Rome. They travelled swiftly; and Caesar, as usual, himself brought the news that he was coming. But the winter season did not bring to him its usual advantages, for the whole Peninsula had revolted, and Pompey and Labienus were able to shelter their troops in the towns, while Caesar was obliged to keep the field. Attempts here and there to capture detached positions led to no results. On both sides now the war was carried on upon the principles which the Senate had adopted from the first. Prisoners from the revolted legions were instantly executed, and Cnaeus Pompey murdered the provincials whom he suspected of an inclination for Caesar. Attagona was at last taken. Caesar moved on Cordova; and Pompey, fearing that the important cities might seek their own security by coming separately to terms, found it necessary to risk a battle.

[Sidenote: March 17, B.C. 45.] [Sidenote: B.C. 45.] The scene of the conflict which ended the civil war was the plain of Munda. The day was the 17th of March, B.C. 45. Spanish tradition places Munda on the Mediterranean, near Gibraltar. The real Munda was on the Guadalquiver, so near to Cordova that the remains of the beaten army found shelter within its walls after the battle. Caesar had been so invariably victorious in his engagements in the open field that the result might have been thought a foregone conclusion. Legendary history reported in the next generation that the elements had been pregnant with auguries. Images had sweated; the sky had blazed with meteors; celestial armies, the spirits of the past and future, had battled among the constellations. The signs had been unfavorable to the Pompeians; the eagles of their legions had dropped the golden thunderbolts from their talons, spread their wings, and had flown away to Caesar. In reality, the eagles had remained in their places till the standards fell from the hands of their dead defenders; and the battle was one of the most desperate in which Caesar had ever been engaged. The numbers were nearly equal--the material on both sides equally good. Pompey's army was composed of revolted Roman soldiers. In arms, in discipline, in stubborn fierceness, there was no difference. The Pompeians had the advantage of situation, the village of Munda, with the hill on which it stood, being in the centre of their lines. The Moorish and Spanish auxiliaries, of whom there were large bodies on either side, stood apart when the legions closed; they having no further interest in the matter than in siding with the conqueror, when fortune had decided who the conqueror was to be. There were no manoeuvres; no scientific evolutions. The Pompeians knew that there was no hope for them if they were defeated. Caesar's men, weary and savage at the protraction of the war, were determined to make a last end of it; and the two armies fought hand to hand with their short swords, with set teeth and pressed lips, opened only with a sharp cry as an enemy fell dead. So equal was the struggle, so doubtful at one moment the issue of it, that Caesar himself sprang from his horse, seized a standard, and rallied a wavering legion. It seemed as if the men meant all to stand and kill or be killed as long as daylight lasted. The ill fate of Labienus decided the victory. He had seen, as he supposed, some movement which alarmed him among Caesar's Moorish auxiliaries, and had galloped conspicuously across the field to lead a division to check them. A shout rose, "He flies--he flies!" A panic ran along the Pompeian lines. They gave way, and Caesar's legions forced a road between their ranks. One wing broke off and made for Cordova; the rest plunged wildly within the ditch and walls of Munda, the avenging sword smiting behind into the huddled mass of fugitives. Scarcely a prisoner was taken. Thirty thousand fell on the field, among them three thousand Roman knights, the last remains of the haughty youths who had threatened Caesar with their swords in the senate-house, and had hacked Clodius's mob in the Forum. Among them was slain Labienus--his desertion of his general, his insults and his cruelties to his comrades, expiated at last in his own blood. Attius Varus was killed also, who had been with Juba when he destroyed Curio. The tragedy was being knitted up in the deaths of the last actors in it. The eagles of the thirteen legions were all taken. The two Pompeys escaped on their horses, Sextus disappearing in the mountains of Grenada or the Sierra Morena; Cnaeus flying for Gibraltar, where he hoped to find a friendly squadron.

Munda was at once blockaded, the enclosing wall--savage evidence of the temper of the conquerors--being built of dead bodies pinned together with lances, and on the top of it a fringe of heads on swords' points with the faces turned toward the town. A sally was attempted at midnight, and failed. The desperate wretches then fought among themselves, till at length the place was surrendered, and fourteen thousand of those who still survived were taken, and spared. Their comrades, who had made their way into Cordova, were less fortunate. When the result of the battle was known, the leading citizen, who had headed the revolt against Caesar, gathered all that belonged to him into a heap, poured turpentine over it, and, after a last feast with his family, burnt himself, his house, his children, and servants. In the midst of the tumult the walls were stormed. Cordova was given up to plunder and massacre, and twenty-two thousand miserable people--most of them, it may be hoped, the fugitives from Munda--were killed. The example sufficed. Every town opened its gates, and Spain was once more submissive. Sextus Pompey successfully concealed himself. Cnaeus reached Gibraltar, but to find that most of the ships which he looked for had been taken by Caesar's fleet. He tried to cross to the African coast, but was driven back by bad weather, and search parties were instantly on his track. He had been wounded; he had sprained his ankle in his flight. Strength and hope were gone. He was carried on a litter to a cave on a mountain side, where his pursuers found him, cut off his head, and spared Cicero from further anxiety.

Thus bloodily ended the Civil War, which the Senate of Rome had undertaken against Caesar, to escape the reforms which were threatened by his second consulship. They had involuntarily rendered their country the best service which they were capable of conferring upon it, for the attempts which Caesar would have made to amend a system too decayed to benefit by the process had been rendered forever impossible by their persistence. The free constitution of the Republic had issued at last in elections which were a mockery of representation, in courts of law which were an insult to justice, and in the conversion of the Provinces of the Empire into the feeding-grounds of a gluttonous aristocracy. In the army alone the Roman character and the Roman honor survived. In the Imperator, therefore, as chief of the army, the care of the Provinces, the direction of public policy, the sovereign authority in the last appeal, could alone thenceforward reside. The Senate might remain as a Council of State; the magistrates might bear their old names, and administer their old functions. But the authority of the executive government lay in the loyalty, the morality, and the patriotism of the legions to whom the power had been transferred. Fortunately for Rome, the change came before decay had eaten into the bone, and the genius of the Empire had still a refuge from platform oratory and senatorial wrangling in the hearts of her soldiers.

Caesar did not immediately return to Italy. Affairs in Rome were no longer pressing, and, after the carelessness and blunders of his lieutenants, the administration of the Peninsula required his personal inspection. From open revolts in any part of the Roman dominions he had nothing more to fear. The last card had been played, and the game of open resistance was lost beyond recovery. There might be dangers of another kind: dangers from ambitious generals, who might hope to take Caesar's place on his death; or dangers from constitutional philosophers, like Cicero, who had thought from the first that the Civil War had been a mistake, "that Caesar was but mortal, and that there were many ways in which a man might die." A reflection so frankly expressed, by so respectable a person, must have occurred to many others as well as to Cicero; Caesar could not but have foreseen in what resources disappointed fanaticism or baffled selfishness might seek refuge. But of such possibilities he was prepared to take his chance; he did not fly from them, he did not seek them; he took his work as he found it, and remained in Spain through the summer, imposing fines and allotting rewards, readjusting the taxation, and extending the political privileges of the Roman colonies. It was not till late in the autumn that he again turned his face toward Rome.

[1] In connection with this subject it is worth while to mention another change in the division of time, not introduced by Caesar, but which came into general use about a century after. The week of seven days was unknown to the Greeks and to the Romans of the Commonwealth, the days of the month being counted by the phases of the moon. The seven-days division was supposed by the Romans to be Egyptian. We know it to have been Jewish, and it was probably introduced to the general world on the first spread of Christianity. It was universally adopted at any rate after Christianity had been planted in different parts of the Empire, but while the Government and the mass of the people were still unconverted to the new religion. The week was accepted for its convenience; but while accepted it was paganized; and the seven days were allotted to the five planets and the sun and moon in the order which still survives among the Latin nations, and here in England with a further introduction of Scandinavian mythology. The principle of the distribution was what is popularly called "the music of the spheres," and turns on a law of Greek music, which is called by Don Cassius the [Greek: armonia dia teddaron]. Assuming the earth to be the centre of the universe, the celestial bodies which have a proper movement of their own among the stars were arranged in the order of their apparent periods of revolution-- Saturn, Jupiter, Mars, the Sun, Venus, Mercury, the Moon. The Jewish Jehovah was identified by the Graeco-Romans with Saturn, the oldest of the heathen personal gods. The Sabbath was the day supposed to be specially devoted to him. The first day of the week was, therefore, given to Saturn. Passing over Jupiter and Mars, according to the laws of the [Greek: armonia], the next day was given to the Sun; again passing over two, the next to the

Moon, and so on, going round again to the rest, till the still existing order came out. Dies Saturni, dies Solis, dies Lunae, dies Martis, dies Mercurri, dies Jovis, and dies Veneris. See Dion Cassius, Historia Romana, lib. xxxvii. c. 18. Dion Cassius gives a second account of the distribution, depending on the twenty-four hours of the day. But the twenty-four hours being a division purely artificial, this explanation is of less interest.

[2] To Atticus, x. 12.

[3] "Cum vivere ipsum turpe sit nobis."--To Atticus, xiii. 28.

[4] "Peream nisi sollicitus sum, ac malo veterem et clementem dominum habere, quam novum et crudelem experiri. Scis, Cnaeus quam sit fatuus. Scis, quomodo crudelitatem virtutem putet. Scis, quam se semper a nobis derisum putet. Vereor, ne nos rustice gladio velit [Greek: antimuktaerisai]"--_To Caius Cassius, Ad Fam_. xv. 19.

CHAPTER XXVI.

Caesar came back to Rome to resume the suspended work of practical reform. His first care was to remove the fears which the final spasm of rebellion had again provoked. He had already granted an amnesty. But the optimates were conscious that they had desired and hoped that the Pompeys might be victorious in Spain. Caesar invited the surviving leaders of the party to sue for pardon on not unbecoming conditions. Hitherto they had kept no faith with him, and on the first show of opportunity had relapsed into defiance. His forbearance had been attributed to want of power rather than of will to punish; when they saw him again triumphant, they assumed that the representative of the Marian principles would show at last the colors of his uncle, and that Rome would again run with blood. He knew them all. He knew that they hated him, and would continue to hate him; but he supposed that they had recognized the hopelessness and uselessness of farther conspiracy. By destroying him they would fall only under the rod of less scrupulous conquerors; and therefore he was content that they should ask to be forgiven. To show further that the past was really to be forgotten, he drew no distinction between his enemies and his friends, and he recommended impartially for office those whose rank or services to the State entitled them to look for promotion. Thus he pardoned and advanced Caius Cassius, who would have killed him in Cilicia.[1] But Cassius had saved Syria from being overrun by the Parthians after the death of Crassus; and the service to the State outweighed the injury to himself. So he pardoned and advanced Marcus Brutus, his friend Servilia's son, who had fought against him at Pharsalia, and had been saved from death there by his special orders. So he pardoned and protected Cicero; so Marcus Marcellus, who, as consul, had moved that he should be recalled from his government, and had flogged the citizen of Como, in scorn of the privileges which Caesar had granted to the colony. So he pardoned also Quintus Ligarius,[2] who had betrayed his confidence in Africa; so a hundred others, who now submitted, accepted his favors, and bound themselves to plot against him no more. To the widows and children of those who had fallen in the war he restored the estates and honors of their families. Finally, as some were still sullen, and refused to sue for a forgiveness which might imply an acknowledgment of guilt, he renewed the general amnesty of the previous year; and, as a last evidence that his victory was not the triumph of democracy, but the consolidation of a united Empire, he restored the statues of Sylla and Pompey, which had been thrown down in the revolution, and again dedicated them with a public ceremonial.

Having thus proved that, so far as he was concerned, he nourished no resentment against the persons of the optimates, or against their principles, so far as they were consistent with the future welfare of the Roman State, Caesar set himself again to the reorganization of the administration. Unfortunately, each step that he took was a fresh crime in the eyes of men whose pleasant monopoly of power he had overthrown. But this was a necessity of the revolution. They had fought for their supremacy, and had lost the day.

He increased the number of the Senate to nine hundred, filling its ranks from eminent provincials; introducing even barbarian Gauls, and, still worse, libertini, the sons of liberated slaves, who had risen to distinction by their own merit. The new members came in slowly, and it is needless to say were unwillingly received; a private handbill was sent round, recommending the coldest of greetings to them.[3]

The inferior magistrates were now responsible to himself as Dictator. He added to their numbers also, and to check the mischiefs of the annual elections, he ordered that they should be chosen for three years. He cut short the corn grants, which nursed the city mob in idleness; and from among the impoverished citizens he furnished out masses of colonists to repair the decay of ancient cities. Corinth rose from its ashes under Caesar's care. Eighty thousand Italians were settled down on the site of Carthage. As inspector of morals, Caesar inherited in an invigorated form the power of the censors. Senators and officials who had discredited themselves by dishonesty were ruthlessly degraded. His own private habits and the habits of his household were models of frugality. He made an effort, in which Augustus afterward imitated him, to check the luxury which was eating into the Roman character. He forbade the idle young patricians to be carried about by slaves in litters. The markets of the world had been ransacked to provide dainties for these gentlemen. He appointed inspectors to survey the dealers' stalls, and occasionally prohibited dishes were carried off from the dinner table under the eyes of the disappointed guests,[4] Enemies enough Caesar made by these measures; but it could not be said of him that he allowed indulgences to himself which he interdicted to others. His domestic economy was strict and simple, the accounts being kept to a sesterce. His frugality was hospitable. He had two tables always, one for his civilian friends, another for his officers, who dined in uniform. The food was plain, but the best of its kind; and he was not to be played with in such matters. An unlucky baker who supplied his guests with bread of worse quality than he furnished for himself was put in chains. Against moral offences he was still more severe. He, the supposed example of licentiousness with women, executed his favorite freedman for adultery with a Roman lady. A senator had married a woman two days after her divorce from her first husband; Caesar pronounced the marriage void.

[Sidenote: B.C. 45-44.] Law reforms went on. Caesar appointed a commission to examine the huge mass of precedents, reduce them to principles, and form a Digest. He called in Marcus Varro's help to form libraries in the great towns. He encouraged physicians and men of science to settle in Rome, by offering them the freedom of the city. To maintain the free population of Italy, he required the planters and farmers to employ a fixed proportion of free laborers on their estates. He put an end to the pleasant tours of senators at the expense of the provinces; their proper place was Italy, and he allowed them to go abroad only when they were in office or in the service of the governors. He formed large engineering plans, a plan to drain the Pontine marches and the Fucine lake, a plan to form a new channel for the Tiber, another to improve the roads, another to cut the Isthmus of

Corinth. These were his employments during the few months of life which were left to him after the close of the war. His health was growing visibly weaker, but his superhuman energy remained unimpaired. He was even meditating and was making preparation for a last campaign. The authority of Rome on the eastern frontier had not recovered from the effects of the destruction of the army of Crassus. The Parthians were insolent and aggressive. Caesar had determined to go in person to bring them to their senses as soon as he could leave Rome. Partly, it was said that he felt his life would be safer with the troops; partly, he desired to leave the administration free from his overpowering presence, that it might learn to go alone; partly and chiefly, he wished to spend such time as might remain to him where he could do most service to his country. But he was growing weary of the thankless burden. He was heard often to say that he had lived long enough. Men of high nature do not find the task of governing their fellow-creatures particularly delightful.

The Senate meanwhile was occupied in showing the sincerity of their conversion by inventing honors for their new master, and smothering him with distinctions since they had failed to defeat him in the field. Few recruits had yet joined them, and they were still substantially the old body. They voted Caesar the name of Liberator. They struck medals for him, in which he was described as Pater Patriae, an epithet which Cicero had once with quickened pulse heard given to himself by Pompey. "Imperator" had been a title conferred hitherto by soldiers in the field on a successful general. It was now granted to Caesar in a special sense, and was made hereditary in his family, with the command-in-chief of the army for his life. The Senate gave him also the charge of the treasury. They made him consul for ten years. Statues were to be erected to him in the temples, on the Rostra, and in the Capitol, where he was to stand as an eighth among the seven Kings of Rome. In the excess of their adoration, they desired even to place his image in the Temple of Quirinus himself, with an inscription to him as [Greek: Theos animaetos], the invincible god. Golden chairs, gilt chariots, triumphal robes were piled one upon another with laurelled fasces and laurelled wreaths. His birthday was made a perpetual holiday, and the month Quinctilis[5] was renamed, in honor of him, July. A temple to Concord was to be erected in commemoration of his clemency. His person was declared sacred, and to injure him by word or deed was to be counted sacrilege. The Fortune of Caesar was introduced into the constitutional oath, and the Senate took a solemn pledge to maintain his acts inviolate. Finally, they arrived at a conclusion that he was not a man at all; no longer Caius Julius, but Divus Julius, a god or the son of god. A temple was to be built to Caesar as another Quirinus, and Antony was to be his priest.

Caesar knew the meaning of all this. He must accept their flattery and become ridiculous, or he must appear to treat with contumely the Senate which offered it. The sinister purpose started occasionally into sight. One obsequious senator proposed that every woman in Rome should be at his disposition, and filthy libels against him were set floating under the surface. The object, he perfectly understood, "was to draw him into a position more and more invidious, that he might the sooner perish." [6] The praise and the slander of such men were alike indifferent to him. So far as he was concerned, they might call him what they pleased; god in public, and devil in their epigrams, if it so seemed good to them. It was difficult for him to know precisely how to act, but he declined his divine honors; and he declined the ten years' consulship. Though he was sole consul for the year, he took a colleague, and when his colleague died on the last day of office, he named another, that the customary forms might be observed. Let him do what he would, malice still misconstrued him. Cicero, the most prominent now of his senatorial flatterers, was the sharpest with his satire behind the scenes. "Caesar," he said, "had given so active a consul that there was no sleeping under him." [7]

Caesar was more and more weary of it. He knew that the Senate hated him; he knew that they would kill him, if they could. All these men whose lips were running over with adulation, were longing to drive their daggers into him. He was willing to live, if they would let him live; but, for himself, he had ceased to care about it. He disdained to take precautions against assassination. On his first return from Spain, he had been attended by a guard; but he dismissed it in spite of the remonstrances of his friends, and went daily into the senate-house alone and unarmed. He spoke often of his danger with entire openness; but he seemed to think that he had some security in the certainty that, if he was murdered, the Civil War would break out again, as if personal hatred was ever checked by fear of consequences. It was something to feel that he had not lived in vain. The Gauls were settling into peaceful habits. The soil of Gaul was now as well cultivated as Italy. Barges loaded with merchandise were passing freely along the Rhone and the Loire, the Moselle, and the Rhine. [8] The best of the chiefs were made senators of Rome, and the people were happy and contented. What he had done for Gaul he might, if he lived, do for Spain, and Africa, and the East. But it was the concern of others more than of himself. "Better," he said, "to die at once than live in perpetual dread of treason."

[Sidenote: B.C. 44.] But Caesar was aware that conspiracies were being formed against him; and that he spoke freely of his danger, appears from a speech delivered in the middle of the winter by Cicero in Caesar's presence. It has been seen that Cicero had lately spoken of Caesar's continuance in life as a disgrace to the State. It has been seen also that he had long thought of assassination as the readiest means of ending it. He asserted afterward that he had not been consulted when the murder was actually accomplished; but the perpetrators were assured of his approbation, and when Caesar was killed he deliberately claimed for himself a share of the guilt, if guilt there could be in what he regarded as the most glorious achievement in human history,[9] It maybe assumed, therefore, that Cicero's views upon the subject had remained unchanged since the beginning of the Civil War, and that his sentiments were no secret among his intimate friends.

Cicero is the second great figure in the history of the time. He has obtained the immortality which he so much desired, and we are, therefore, entitled and obliged to scrutinize his conduct with a niceness which would be ungracious and unnecessary in the case of a less distinguished man. After Pharsalia he had concluded that the continuance of the war would be unjustifiable. He had put himself in communication with Antony and Caesar's friend and secretary Oppius, and at their advice he went from Greece to Brindisi, to remain there till Caesar's pleasure should be known. He was very miserable. He had joined Pompey with confessed reluctance, and family quarrels had followed on Pompey's defeat. His brother Quintus, whom he had drawn away from Caesar, regretted having taken his advice. His sons and nephews were equally querulous and dissatisfied; and for himself, he dared not appear in the streets of Brindisi, lest Caesar's soldiers should insult or injure him. Antony, however, encouraged him to hope. He assured him that Caesar was well disposed to him, and would not only pardon him, but would show him every possible favor,[10] and with these expectations he contrived for a while to comfort himself. He had regarded the struggle as over, and Caesar's side as completely victorious. But gradually the scene seemed to change. Caesar was long in returning. The optimates rallied in Africa, and there was again a chance that they might win after all. His first thought was always for himself. If the constitution survived under Caesar, as he was inclined to think that in some shape it would, he had expected that a place would be found in it for him.[11] But how if Caesar himself should not survive? How if he should be killed in Alexandria? How if he should be defeated by Metellus Scipio? He described himself as excruciated with anxiety.[12] Through the year which followed he wavered from day to day as the prospect varied, now cursing his folly for having followed the Senate to Greece, now for having deserted them, blaming himself at one time for his indecision, at another for having committed himself to either side.[13]

Gradually his alarms subsided. The Senate's party was finally overthrown. Caesar wrote to him affectionately, and allowed him to retain his title as Imperator. When it appeared that he had nothing personally to fear, he recovered his spirits, and he recovered along with them a hope that the constitution might be restored, after all, by other means than war. "Caesar could not live forever, and there were many ways in which a man might die."

Caesar had dined with him in the country, on his way home from Spain. He had been as kind as Cicero could wish, but had avoided politics. When Caesar went on to Rome, Cicero followed him, resumed his place in the Senate, which was then in the full fervor of its affected adulation, and took an early opportunity of speaking. Marcus Marcellus had been in exile since Pharsalia. The Senate had interceded for his pardon, and Caesar had granted it, and granted it with a completeness which exceeded expectation. Cicero rose to thank him in his presence, in terms which most certainly did not express his real feelings, whatever may have been the purpose which they concealed.

* * * * *

"He had long been silent," he said, "not from fear, but from grief and diffidence. The time for silence was past. Thenceforward he intended to speak his thoughts freely in his ancient manner. Such kindness, such unheard-of generosity, such moderation in power, such incredible and almost godlike wisdom, he felt himself unable to pass over without giving expression to his emotions." [14] No flow of genius, no faculty of speech or writing, could adequately describe Caesar's actions, yet on that day he had achieved a yet greater glory. Often had Cicero thought, and often had said to others, that no king or general had ever performed such exploits as Caesar. In war, however, officers, soldiers, allies, circumstances, fortune, claimed a share in the result; and there were victories greater than could be won on the battlefield, where the honor was undivided.

"To have conquered yourself," he said, addressing Caesar directly, "to have restrained your resentment, not only to have restored a distinguished opponent to his civil rights, but to have given him more than he had lost, is a deed which raises you above humanity, and makes you most like to God. Your wars will be spoken of to the end of time in all lands and tongues; but in tales of battles we are deafened by the shoutings and the blare of trumpets. Justice, mercy, moderation, wisdom, we admire even in fiction, or in persons whom we have never seen; how much more must we admire them in you, who are present here before us, and in whose face we read a purpose to restore us to such remnants of our liberty as have survived the war! How can we praise, how can we love you sufficiently? By the gods, the very walls of this house are eloquent with gratitude.... No conqueror in a civil war was ever so mild as you have been. To-day you have surpassed yourself. You have overcome victory in giving back the spoils to the conquered. By the laws of war we were under your feet, to be destroyed, if you so willed. We live by your goodness.... Observe, conscript fathers, how comprehensive is Caesar's sentence. We were in arms against him, how impelled I know not. He cannot acquit us of mistake, but he holds us innocent of crime, for he has given us back Marcellus at your entreaty. Me, of his own free will, he has restored to myself and to my country. He has brought back the most illustrious survivors of the war. You see them gathered here in this full assembly. He has not regarded them as enemies. He has concluded that you entered into the conflict with him rather in ignorance and unfounded fear than from any motives of ambition or hostility.

"For me, I was always for peace. Caesar was for peace, so was Marcellus. There were violent men among you, whose success Marcellus dreaded. Each party had a cause. I will not compare them. I will compare rather the victory of the one with the possible victory of the other. Caesar's wars ended with the last battle. The sword is now sheathed. Those whom we have lost fell in the fury of the fight, not one by the resentment of the conqueror. Caesar, if he could, would bring back to life many who lie dead. For the others, we all feared what they might do if the day had been theirs. They not only threatened those who were in arms against them, but those who sate quietly at home."

* * * * *

Cicero then said that he had heard a fear of assassination expressed by Caesar. By whom, he asked, could such an attempt be made? Not by those whom he had forgiven, for none were more attached to him. Not by his comrades, for they could not be so mad as to conspire against the general to whom they owed all that they possessed. Not by his enemies, for he had no enemies. Those who had been his enemies were either dead through their own obstinacy, or were alive through his generosity. It was possible, however, he admitted, that there might be some such danger.

* * * * *

"Be you, therefore," he said, again speaking to Caesar,--"be you watchful, and let us be diligent. Who is so careless of his own and the common welfare as to be ignorant that on your preservation his own depends, and that all our lives are bound up in yours? I, as in duty bound, think of you by night and day; I ponder over the accidents of humanity, the uncertainty of health, the frailty of our common nature, and I grieve to think that the Commonwealth which ought to be immortal should hang on the breath of a single man. If to these perils be added a nefarious conspiracy, to what god can we turn for help? War has laid prostrate our institutions; you alone can restore them. The courts of justice need to be reconstituted, credit to be recovered, license to be repressed, the thinned ranks of the citizens to be repaired. The bonds of society are relaxed. In such a war, and with such a temper in men's hearts, the State must have lost many of its greatest ornaments, be the event what it would. These wounds need healing, and you alone can heal them. With sorrow I have heard you say that you have lived long enough. For nature it may be that you have, and perhaps for glory. But for your country you have not. Put away, I beseech you, this contempt of death. Be not wise at our expense. You repeat often, I am told, that you do not wish for longer life. I believe you mean it; nor should I blame you, if you had to think only of yourself. But by your actions you have involved the welfare of each citizen and of the whole Commonwealth in your own. Your work is unfinished: the foundations are hardly laid, and is it for you to be measuring calmly your term of days by your own desires?... If, Caesar, the result of your immortal deeds is to be no more than this, that, after defeating your enemies, you are to leave the State in the condition in which it now stands, your splendid qualities will be more admired than honored. It remains for you to rebuild the constitution. Live till this is done. Live till you see your country tranquil, and at peace. Then, when your last debt is paid, when you have filled the measure of your existence to overflowing, then say, if you will, that you have had enough of life. Your life is not the life which is bounded by the union of your soul and body, your life is that which shall continue fresh in the memory of ages to come, which posterity will cherish, and eternity itself keep guard over. Much has been done which men will admire: much remains to be done, which they can praise. They will read with wonder of empires and provinces, of the Rhine, the ocean, and the Nile, of battles without number, of amazing victories, of countless monuments and triumphs; but unless this Commonwealth be wisely re-established in institutions by you bestowed upon us, your name will travel widely over the world, but will have no stable habitation; and those who come after us will dispute about you as we have disputed. Some will extol you to the skies, others will find something wanting and the most important element of all. Remember the tribunal before which you will hereafter stand. The ages that are to be will try you, with minds, it may be, less prejudiced than ours, uninfluenced either by desire to please you or by envy of your greatness.

"Our dissensions have been crushed by the arms, and extinguished by the lenity of the conqueror. Let all of us, not the wise only, but every citizen who has ordinary sense, be guided by a single desire. Salvation there can be none for us, Caesar, unless you are preserved. Therefore, we exhort you, we beseech you, to watch over your own safety. You believe that you are threatened by a secret peril. From my own heart I say, and I speak for others as well as myself, we will stand as sentries over your safety, and we will interpose our own bodies between you and any danger which may menace you." [15]

* * * * *

Such, in compressed form, for necessary brevity, but deserving to be studied in its own brilliant language, was the speech delivered by Cicero, in the

Senate in Caesar's presence, within a few weeks of his murder. The authenticity of it has been questioned, but without result beyond creating a doubt whether it was edited and corrected, according to his usual habit, by Cicero himself. The external evidence of genuineness is as good as for any of his other orations, and the Senate possessed no other speaker known to us, to whom, with any probability, so splendid an illustration of Roman eloquence could be assigned.

Now, therefore, let us turn to the second Philippic delivered in the following summer when the deed had been accomplished which Cicero professed to hold in so much abhorrence. Then, fiercely challenging for himself a share in the glory of tyrannicide, he exclaimed:

* * * * *

"What difference is there between advice beforehand and approbation afterward? What does it matter whether I wished it to be done, or rejoiced that it was done? Is there a man, save Antony and those who were glad to have Caesar reign over us, that did not wish him to be killed, or that disapproved when he was killed? All were in fault, for all the Boni joined in killing him, so far as lay in them. Some were not consulted, some wanted courage, some opportunity. All were willing," [16]

Expressions so vehemently opposite compel us to compare them. Was it that Cicero was so carried away by the stream of his oratory, that he spoke like an actor, under artificial emotion which the occasion called for? Was it that he was deliberately trying to persuade Caesar that from the Senate he had nothing to fear, and so to put him off his guard? If, as he declared, he himself and the Boni, who were listening to him, desired so unanimously to see Caesar killed, how else can his language be interpreted? Cicero stands before the tribunal of posterity, to which he was so fond of appealing. In him, too, while "there is much to admire," "something may be found wanting."

Meanwhile the Senate went its way, still inventing fresh titles and conferring fresh powers. Caesar said that these vain distinctions needed limitation, rather than increase; but the flattery had a purpose in it, and would not be checked.

One day a deputation waited on him with the proffer of some "new marvel." [17] He was sitting in front of the Temple of Venus Genetrix, and when the senators approached he neglected to rise to receive them. Some said that he was moving, but that Cornelius Balbus pulled him down. Others said that he was unwell. Pontius Aquila, a tribune, had shortly before refused to rise to Caesar. The senators thought he meant to read them a lesson in return. He intended to be king, it seemed; the constitution was gone, another Tarquin was about to seize the throne of Republican Rome.

Caesar was king in fact, and to recognize facts is more salutary than to ignore them. An acknowledgment of Caesar as king might have made the problem of reorganization easier than it proved. The army had thought of it. He was on the point of starting for Parthia, and a prophecy had said that the Parthians could only be conquered by a king.--But the Roman people were sensitive about names. Though their liberties were restricted for the present, they liked to hope that one day the Forum might recover its greatness. The Senate, meditating on the insult which they had received, concluded that Caesar might be tempted, and that if they could bring him to consent he would lose the people's hearts. They had already made him Dictator for life; they voted next that he really should be King, and, not formally perhaps, but tentatively, they offered him the crown. He was sounded as to whether he would accept it. He understood the snare, and refused. What was to be done next? He would soon be gone to the East. Rome and its hollow adulations would lie behind him, and their one opportunity would be gone also. They employed some one to place a diadem on the head of his statue which stood upon the Rostra.[18] It was done publicly, in the midst of a vast crowd, in Caesar's presence. Two eager tribunes tore the diadem down, and ordered the offender into custody. The treachery of the Senate was not the only danger. His friends in the army had the same ambition for him. A few days later, as he was riding through the streets, he was saluted as King by the mob. Caesar answered calmly that he was not King but Caesar, and there the matter might have ended; but the tribunes rushed into the crowd to arrest the leaders; a riot followed, for which Caesar blamed them; they complained noisily; he brought their conduct before the Senate, and they were censured and suspended. But suspicion was doing its work, and honest republican hearts began to heat and kindle.

The kingship assumed a more serious form on the 15th of February at the

Lupercalia--the ancient carnival. Caesar was in his chair, in his consular purple, wearing a wreath of bay, wrought in gold. The honor of the wreath was the only distinction which he had accepted from the Senate with pleasure. He retained a remnant of youthful vanity, and the twisted leaves concealed his baldness. Antony, his colleague in the consulship, approached with a tiara, and placed it on Caesar's head, saying, "The people give you this by my hand." That Antony had no sinister purpose is obvious. He perhaps spoke for the army;[19] or it may be that Caesar himself suggested Antony's action, that he might end the agitation of so dangerous a subject. He answered in a loud voice "that the Romans had no king but God," and ordered that the tiara should be taken to the Capitol, and placed on the statue of Jupiter Olympius. The crowd burst into an enthusiastic cheer; and an inscription on a brass tablet recorded that the Roman people had offered Caesar the crown by the hands of the consul, and that Caesar had refused it.

The question of the kingship was over; but a vague alarm had been created, which answered the purpose of the optimates. Caesar was at their mercy any day. They had sworn to maintain all his acts. They had sworn, after Cicero's speech, individually and collectively to defend his life. Caesar, whether he believed them sincere or not, had taken them at their word, and came daily to the Senate unarmed and without a guard. He had a protection in the people. If the optimates killed him without preparation, they knew that they would be immediately massacred. But an atmosphere of suspicion and uncertainty had been successfully generated, of which they determined to take immediate advantage. There were no troops in the city. Lepidus, Caesar's master of the horse, who had been appointed governor of Gaul, was outside the gates, with a few cohorts; but Lepidus was a person of feeble character, and they trusted to be able to deal with him.

Sixty senators, in all, were parties to the immediate conspiracy. Of these nine-tenths were members of the old faction whom Caesar had pardoned, and who, of all his acts, resented most that he had been able to pardon them. They were the men who had stayed at home, like Cicero, from the fields of Thapsus and Munda, and had pretended penitence and submission that they might take an easier road to rid themselves of their enemy. Their motives were the ambition of their order and personal hatred of Caesar; but they persuaded themselves that they were animated by patriotism, and as, in their hands, the Republic had been a mockery of liberty, so they aimed at restoring it by a mock tyrannicide. Their oaths and their professions were nothing to them. If they were entitled to kill Caesar, they were entitled equally to deceive him. No stronger evidence is needed of the demoralization of the Roman Senate than the completeness with which they were able to disguise from themselves the baseness of their treachery. One man only they were able to attract into co-operation who had a reputation for honesty, and could be conceived, without absurdity, to be animated by a disinterested purpose.

Marcus Brutus was the son of Cato's sister Servilia, the friend, and a scandal said the mistress, of Caesar. That he was Caesar's son was not too absurd for the credulity of Roman drawing-rooms. Brutus himself could not have believed in the existence of such a relation, for he was deeply attached to his mother; and although, under the influence of his uncle Cato, he had taken the Senate's side in the war, he had accepted afterward not pardon only from Caesar, but favors of many kinds, for which he had professed, and probably felt, some real gratitude. He had married Cato's daughter Portia, and on Cato's death had published a eulogy upon him. Caesar left him free to think and write what he pleased. He had made him praetor; he had nominated him to the governorship of Macedonia. Brutus was perhaps the only member of the senatorial party in whom Caesar felt genuine confidence. His known integrity, and Caesar's acknowledged regard for him, made his accession to the conspiracy an object of particular importance. The name of Brutus would be a guarantee to the people of rectitude of intention. Brutus, as the world went, was of more than average honesty. He had sworn to be faithful to Caesar as the rest had sworn, and an oath with him was not a thing to be emotionalized away; but he was a fanatical republican, a man of gloomy habits, given to dreams and omens, and easily liable to be influenced by appeals to visionary feelings. Caius Cassius, his brother-in-law, was employed to work upon him. Cassius, too, was praetor that year, having been also nominated to office by Caesar. He knew Brutus, he knew where and how to move him. He reminded him of the great traditions of his name. A Brutus had delivered Rome from the Tarquins. The blood of a Brutus was consecrated to liberty. This, too, was mockery; Brutus, who expelled the Tarquins, put his sons to death, and died childless; Marcus Brutus came of good plebeian family, with no glories of tyrannicide about them; but an imaginary genealogy suited well with the spurious heroics which veiled the motives of Caesar's murderers.

Brutus, once wrought upon, became with Cassius the most ardent in the cause which assumed the aspect to him of a sacred duty. Behind them were the crowd of senators of the familiar faction, and others worse than they, who had not even the excuse of having been partisans of the beaten cause; men who had fought at Caesar's side till the war was over, and believed, like Labienus, that to them Caesar owed his fortune, and that he alone ought not to reap the harvest. One of these was Trebonius, who had misconducted himself in Spain, and was smarting under the recollection of his own failures. Trebonius had long before sounded Antony on the desirableness of removing their chief. Antony, though he remained himself true, had unfortunately kept his friend's counsel. Trebonius had been named by Caesar for a future consulship, but a distant reward was too little for him. Another and a yet baser traitor was Decimus Brutus, whom Caesar valued and trusted beyond all his officers, whom he had selected as guardian for Augustus, and had noticed, as was seen afterward, with special affection in his will. The services of these men were invaluable to the conspirators on account of their influence with the army. Decimus Brutus, like Labienus, had enriched himself in Caesar's campaigns, and had amassed near half a million of English money.[20] It may have been easy to persuade him and Trebonius that a grateful Republic would consider no recompense too large to men who would sacrifice their commander to their country. To Caesar they could be no more than satellites; the first prizes of the Empire would be offered to the choice of the saviours of the constitution.

So composed was this memorable band, to whom was to fall the bad distinction of completing the ruin of the senatorial rule. Caesar would have spared something of it; enough, perhaps, to have thrown up shoots again as soon as he had himself passed away in the common course of nature. By combining in a focus the most hateful characteristics of the order, by revolting the moral instincts of mankind by ingratitude and treachery, they stripped their cause by their own hands of the false glamour which they hoped to throw over it. The profligacy and avarice, the cynical disregard of obligation, which had marked the Senate's supremacy for a century, had exhibited abundantly their unfitness for the high functions which had descended to them; but custom and natural tenderness for a form of government, the past history of which had been so glorious, might have continued still to shield them from the penalty of their iniquities. The murder of Caesar filled the measure of their crimes, and gave the last and necessary impulse to the closing act of the revolution.

Thus the ides of March drew near. Caesar was to set out in a few days for Parthia. Decimus Brutus was going, as governor, to the north of Italy, Lepidus to Gaul, Marcus Brutus to Macedonia, and Trebonius to Asia Minor. Antony, Caesar's colleague in the consulship, was to remain in Italy. Dolabella, Cicero's son-in-law, was to be consul with him as soon as Caesar should have left for the East. The foreign appointments were all made for five years, and in another week the party would be scattered. The time for action had come, if action there was to be. Papers were dropped in Brutus's room, bidding him awake from his sleep. On the statue of Junius Brutus some hot republican wrote "Would that thou wast alive!" The assassination in itself was easy, for Caesar would take no precautions. So portentous an intention could not be kept entirely secret; many friends warned him to beware; but he disdained too heartily the worst that his enemies could do to him to vex himself with thinking of them, and he forbade the subject to be mentioned any more in his presence. Portents, prophecies, soothsayings, frightful aspects in the sacrifices, natural growths of alarm and excitement, were equally vain. "Am I to be frightened," he said, in answer to some report of the haruspices, "because a sheep is without a heart?"

[Sidenote: March 14, B.C. 44.] An important meeting of the Senate had been called for the ides (the 15th) of the month. The Pontifices, it was whispered, intended to bring on again the question of the kingship before Caesar's departure. The occasion would be appropriate. The senate-house itself was a convenient scene of operations. The conspirators met at supper the evening before at Cassius's house. Cicero, to his regret, was not invited. The plan was simple, and was rapidly arranged. Caesar would attend unarmed. The senators not in the secret would be unarmed also. The party who intended to act were to provide themselves with poniards, which could be easily concealed in their paper boxes. So far all was simple; but a question rose whether Caesar only was to be killed, or whether Antony and Lepidus were to be despatched along with him. They decided that Caesar's death would be sufficient. To spill blood without necessity would mar, it was thought, the sublimity of their exploit. Some of them liked Antony. None supposed that either he or Lepidus would be dangerous when Caesar was gone. In this resolution Cicero thought that they made a fatal mistake;[21] fine emotions were good in their place, in the perorations of speeches and such like; Antony, as Cicero admitted, had been signally kind to him; but the killing Caesar was a serious business, and his friends should have died along with him. It was determined otherwise. Antony and Lepidus were not to be touched. For the rest, the assassins had merely to be in their places in the Senate in good time. When Caesar entered, Trebonius was to detain Antony in conversation at the door. The others were to gather about Caesar's chair on pretence of presenting a petition, and so could make an end. A gang of gladiators were to be secreted in the adjoining theatre to be ready should any unforeseen difficulty present itself.

The same evening, the 14th of March, Caesar was at a "Last Supper" at the house of Lepidus. The conversation turned on death, and on the kind of death which was most to be desired. Caesar, who was signing papers while the rest wore talking, looked up and said, "A sudden one." When great men die, imagination insists that all nature shall have felt the shock. Strange stories were told in after years of the uneasy labors of the elements that night.

A little ere the mightiest Julius fell, The graves did open, and the sheeted dead Did squeak and jibber in the Roman streets.

The armor of Mars, which stood in the hall of the Pontifical Palace, crashed down upon the pavement. The door of Caesar's room flew open. Calpurnia dreamt her husband was murdered, and that she saw him ascending into heaven, and received by the hand of God.[22] In the morning the sacrifices were again unfavorable. Caesar was restless. Some natural disorder affected his spirits, and his spirits were reacting on his body. Contrary to his usual habit, he gave way to depression. He decided, at his wife's entreaty, that he would not attend the Senate that day.

[Sidenote: March 15, B.C. 44.] The house was full. The conspirators were in their places with their daggers ready. Attendants came in to remove Caesar's chair. It was announced that he was not coming. Delay might be fatal. They conjectured that he already suspected something. A day's respite, and all might be discovered. His familiar friend whom he trusted--the coincidence is striking!--was employed to betray him. Decimus Brutus, whom it was impossible for him to distrust, went to entreat his attendance, giving reasons to which he knew that Caesar would listen, unless the plot had been actually betrayed. It was now eleven in the forenoon. Caesar shook off his uneasiness, and rose to go. As he crossed the hall, his statue fell, and shivered on the stones. Some servant, perhaps, had heard whispers, and wished to warn him. As he still passed on, a stranger thrust a scroll into his hand, and begged him to read it on the spot. It contained a list of the conspirators, with a clear account of the plot. He supposed it to be a petition, and placed it carelessly among his other papers. The fate of the Empire hung upon a thread, but the thread was not broken, As Caesar had lived to reconstruct the Roman world, so his death was necessary to finish the work. He went on to the Curia, and the senators said to themselves that the augurs had foretold his fate, but he would not listen; he was doomed for his "contempt of religion." [23]

Antony, who was in attendance, was detained, as had been arranged, by Trebonius. Caesar entered, and took his seat. His presence awed men, in spite of themselves, and the conspirators had determined to act at once, lest they should lose courage to act at all. He was familiar and easy of access. They gathered round him. He knew them all. There was not one from whom he had not a right to expect some sort of gratitude, and the movement suggested no suspicion. One had a story to tell him; another some favor to ask. Tullius Cimber, whom he had just made governor of Bithynia, then came close to him, with some request which he was unwilling to grant. Cimber caught his gown, as if in entreaty, and dragged it from his shoulders. Cassius,[24] who was standing behind, stabbed him in the throat. He started up with a cry, and caught Cassius's arm. Another poniard entered his breast, giving a mortal wound. He looked round, and seeing not one friendly face, but only a ring of daggers pointing at him, he drew his gown over his head, gathered the folds about him that he might fall decently, and sank down without uttering another word,[25] Cicero was present. The feelings with which he watched the scene are unrecorded, but may easily be imagined. Waving his dagger, dripping with Caesar's blood, Brutus shouted to Cicero by name, congratulating him that liberty was restored.[26] The Senate rose with shrieks and confusion, and rushed into the Forum. The crowd outside caught the words that Caesar was dead, and scattered to their houses. Antony, guessing that those who had killed Caesar would not spare himself, hurried off into concealment. The murderers, bleeding some of them from wounds which they had given one another in their eagerness, followed, crying that the tyrant was dead, and that Rome was free; and the body of the great Caesar was left alone in the house where a few weeks before Cicero told him that he was so necessary to his country that every senator would die before harm should reach him!

[1] Apparently when Caesar touched there on his way to Egypt, after Pharsalia. Cicero says (Philippic ii. 11): "Quid? C. Cassius ... qui etiam sine his clarissimis viris, hanc rem in Cilicia ad ostium fluminis Cydni confecisset, si ille ad eam ripam quam constituerat, non ad contrariam, navi appulisset."

[2] To be distinguished from Publius Ligarius, who had been put to death before Thapsus.

[3] The Gauls were especially obnoxious, and epigrams were circulated to insult them:--

"Gallos Caesar in triumphum ducit, idem in Curiam. Galli braccas deposuerunt, latum clavum sumpserunt"

SUETONIUS, Vita Jullii Caesaris, 80.

[4] Suetonius.

[5] The fifth, dating the beginning of the year, in the old style, from March.

[6] Dion Cassius.

[7] The second consul who had been put in held office but for a few hours.

[8] Dion Cassius.

[9] See the 2nd Philippic, passim. In a letter to Decimus Brutus, he says: "Quare hortatione tu quidem non egos, si ne ill?quidem in re, quae a te gesta est post hominum memoriam maxim? hortatorem desider 鈘 ti." Ad Fam. xi. 5.

[10] To Atticus, xi. 5, 6.

[11] _Ad Caelium, Ad Fam_. ii. 16.

[12] To Atticus, xi. 7.

[13] See To Atticus, xi. 7-9; _To Terentia, Ad Fam_. xiv. 12.

[14] "Tantam enim mansuetudinem, tam inusitatam inauditamque clementiam, tantum in summ?potestate rerum omnium modum, tam denique incredibilem sapientiam ac paene divinam tacitus nullo modo praeterire possum."--Pro Marco Marcello, 1.

[15] Pro Marco Marcello, abridged.

[16] "Non intelligis, si id quod me arguis voluisse interfici Caesarem crimen sit, etiam laetatum esse morte Caesaris crimen esse? Quid enim interest inter suasorem facti et approbatorem? Aut quid refert utrum voluerim fieri an gaudeam factum? Ecquis est igitur te excepto et iis qui illum regnare gaudebant, qui illud aut fieri noluerit, aut factum improbarit? Omnes enim in culp? Etenim omnes boni quantum in ipsis fuit Caesarem occiderunt. Aliis consilium, aliis animus, aliis occasio defuit. Voluntas nemini."--_2nd Philippic_, 12.

[17] Dion Cassius.

[18] So Dion Cassius states, on what authority we know not. Suetonius says that as Caesar was returning from the Latin festival some one placed a laurel crown on the statue, tied with a white riband.

[19] The fact is certain. Cicero taunted Antony with it in the Senate, in the Second Philippic.

[20] "Cum ad rem publicam liberandam accessi, HS. mihi fuit quadringenties amplius."--_Decimus Brutus to Cicero, Ad Fam_. xi. 10.

[21] "Vellem Idibus Martiis me ad coenam invitses. Reliquiarum nihil fuisset."--_Ad Cassium, Ad Fam_. xii. 4. And again: "Quam vellem ad illas pulcherrimas epulas me Idibus Martiis invit鈠ses! Reliquiarum nihil haberemus."--_Ad Trebonium, Ad Fam_. x. 28.

[22] Dion Cassius, _C. Julius Caesar_, xliv. 17.

[23] "Spret?religione."--Suetonius.

[24] Not perhaps Caius Cassius, but another. Suetonius says "alter e Cassiis."

[25] So says Suetonius, the best extant authority, who refers to the famous words addressed to Brutus only as a legend: "Atque ita tribus et viginti plagis confossus est, uno modo ad primum ictum gemitu sine voce edito. Etsi tradiderunt quidam Marco Bruto irruenti dixisse [Greek: kai su ei ekeinon kai su teknon]"--Julius Caesar, 82.

[26] "Cruentum alte extollens Marcus Brutus pugionem, Ciceronem nominatim exclamavit atque ei recuperatam libertatem est gratulatus."--Philippic ii. 12.

CHAPTER XXVII.

[Sidenote: March 16, B.C. 44.] The tyrannicides, as the murderers of Caesar called themselves, had expected that the Roman mob would be caught by the cry of liberty, and would hail them as the deliverers of their country. They found that the people did not respond as they had anticipated. The city was stunned. The Forum was empty. The gladiators, whom they had secreted in the Temple, broke out and plundered the unprotected booths. A dead and ominous silence prevailed everywhere. At length a few citizens collected in knots. Brutus spoke, and Cassius spoke. They extolled their old constitution. They said that Caesar had overthrown it; that they had slain him, not from private hatred or private interest, but to restore the liberties of Rome. The audience was dead and cold. No answering shouts came back to reassure them. The citizens could not forget that these men who spoke so fairly had a few days before fawned on Caesar as the saviour of the Empire, and, as if human honors were too little, had voted a temple to him as a god. The fire would not kindle. Lepidus came in with troops, and occupied the Forum. The conspirators withdrew into the Capitol, where Cicero and others joined them, and the night was passed in earnest discussion what next was to be done. They had intended to declare that Caesar had been a tyrant, to throw his body into the Tiber, and to confiscate his property to the State. They discovered to their consternation that, if Caesar was a tyrant, all his acts would be invalidated. The praetors and tribunes held their offices, the governors their provinces, under Caesar's nomination. If Caesar's acts were set aside, Decimus Brutus was not governor of North Italy, nor Marcus Brutus of Macedonia; nor was Dolabella consul, as he had instantly claimed to be on Caesar's death. Their names, and the names of many more whom Caesar had promoted, would have to be laid before the Comitia, and in the doubtful humor of the people they little liked the risk. That the dilemma should have been totally unforeseen was characteristic of the men and their capacity.

Nor was this the worst. Lands had been allotted to Caesar's troops. Many thousands of colonists were waiting to depart for Carthage and Corinth and other places where settlements had been provided for them. These arrangements would equally fall through, and it was easy to know what would follow. Antony and Lepidus, too, had to be reckoned with. Antony, as the surviving consul, was the supreme lawful authority in the city; and Lepidus and his soldiers might have a word to say if the body of their great commander was flung into the river as the corpse of a malefactor. Interest and fear suggested more moderate counsels. The conspirators determined that Caesar's appointments must stand; his acts, it seemed, must stand also; and his remains, therefore, must be treated with respect. Imagination took another flight. Caesar's death might be regarded as a sacrifice, an expiatory offering for the sins of the nation; and the divided parties might embrace in virtue of the atonement. They agreed to send for Antony, and invite him to assist in saving society; and they asked Cicero to be their messenger. Cicero, great and many as his faults might be, was not a fool. He declined to go on so absurd a mission. He knew Antony too well to dream that he could be imposed on by fantastic illusions. Antony, he said, would promise anything, but if they trusted him, they would have reason to repent.[1] Others, however, undertook the office. Antony agreed to meet them, and the next morning the Senate was assembled in the Temple of Terra.

Antony presided as consul, and after a few words from him Cicero rose. He disapproved of the course which his friends were taking; he foresaw what must come of it; but he had been overruled, and he made the best of what he could not help. He gave a sketch of Roman political history. He went back to the secession to Mount Aventine. He spoke of the Gracchi, of Saturninus and Glaucia, of Marius and Sylla, of Sertorius and Pompey, of Caesar and the still unforgotten Clodius. He described the fate of Athens and of other Grecian states into which faction had penetrated. If Rome continued divided, the conquerors would rule over its ruins; therefore he appealed to the two factions to forget their rivalries and to return to peace and concord. But they must decide at once, for the signs were already visible of a fresh conflict.

"Caesar is slain," he said. "The Capitol is occupied by the optimates, the Forum by soldiers, and the people are full of terror. Is violence to be again answered by more violence? These many years we have lived less like men than like wild beasts in cycles of recurring revenge. Let us forget the past. Let us draw a veil over all that has been done, not looking too curiously into the acts of any man. Much may be said to show that Caesar deserved his death, and much against those who have killed him. But to raise the question will breed fresh quarrels; and if we are wise we shall regard the scene which we have witnessed as a convulsion of nature which is now at an end. Let Caesar's ordinances, let Caesar's appointments be maintained. None such must be heard of again. But what is done cannot be undone." [2]

Admirable advice, were it as easy to act on good counsel as to give it. The murder of such a man as Caesar was not to be so easily smoothed over. But the delusive vision seemed for a moment to please. The Senate passed an act of oblivion. The agitation in the army was quieted when the men heard that their lands were secure. But there were two other questions which required an answer, and an immediate one. Caesar's body, after remaining till evening on the floor of the senate-house, had been carried home in the dusk in a litter by three of his servants, and was now lying in his palace. If it was not to be thrown into the Tiber, what was to be done with it? Caesar had left a will, which was safe with his other papers in the hands of Antony. Was the will to be read and recognized? Though Cicero had advised in the Senate that the discussion whether Caesar had deserved death should not be raised, yet it was plain to him and to every one that, unless Caesar was held guilty of conspiring against the Constitution, the murder was and would be regarded as a most execrable crime. He dreaded the effect of a public funeral. He feared that the will might contain provisions which would rouse the passions of the people. Though Caesar was not for various reasons to be pronounced a tyrant, Cicero advised that he should be buried privately, as if his name was under a cloud, and that his property should be escheated to the nation. But the humor of conciliation and the theory of "the atoning sacrifice" had caught the Senate. Caesar had done great things for his country. It would please the army that he should have an honorable sepulture.

[Sidenote: March, B.C. 44.] If they had refused, the result would not have been greatly different. Sooner or later, when the stunning effects of the shock had passed off, the murder must have appeared to Rome and Italy in its true colors. The optimates talked of the Constitution. The Constitution in their hands had been a parody of liberty. Caesar's political life had been spent in wresting from them the powers which they had abused. Caesar had punished the oppressors of the provinces. Caesar had forced the nobles to give the people a share of the public lands. Caesar had opened the doors of citizenship to the libertini, the distant colonists, and the provincials. It was for this that the Senate hated him. For this they had fought against him; for this they murdered him. No Roman had ever served his country better in peace or war, and thus he had been rewarded.

Such thoughts were already working in tens of thousands of breasts. A feeling of resentment was fast rising, with as yet no certain purpose before it. In this mood the funeral could not fail to lead to some fierce explosion. For this reason Antony had pressed for it, and the Senate had given their consent.

The body was brought down to the Forum and placed upon the Rostra. The dress had not been changed; the gown, gashed with daggers and soaked in blood, was still wrapped about it. The will was read first. It reminded the Romans that they had been always in Caesar's thoughts, for he had left each citizen seventy-five drachmas (nearly ? of English money), and he had left them his gardens on the Tiber as a perpetual recreation ground, a possession which Domitius Ahenobarbus had designed for himself before Pharsalia. He had made Octavius his general heir; among the second heirs, should Octavius fail, he had named Decimus Brutus, who had betrayed him. A deep movement of emotion passed through the crowd when, besides the consideration for themselves, they heard from this record, which could not lie, a proof of the confidence which had been so abused. Antony, after waiting for the passion to work, then came forward.

Cicero had good reason for his fear of Antony. He was a loose soldier, careless in his life, ambitious, extravagant, little more scrupulous perhaps than any average Roman gentleman. But for Caesar his affection was genuine. The people were in intense expectation. He produced the body, all bloody as it had fallen, and he bade a herald first read the votes which the Senate had freshly passed, heaping those extravagant honors upon Caesar which he had not desired, and the oath which the senators had each personally taken to defend him from violence. He then spoke--spoke with the natural vehemence of a friend, yet saying nothing which was not literally true. The services of Caesar neither needed nor permitted the exaggeration of eloquence.

He began with the usual encomiums. He spoke of Caesar's family, his birth, his early history, his personal characteristics, his thrifty private habits, his public liberality; he described him as generous to his friends, forbearing with his enemies, without evil in himself, and reluctant to believe evil of others.

"Power in most men," he said, "has brought their faults to light. Power in Caesar brought into prominence his excellences. Prosperity did not make him insolent for it gave him a sphere which corresponded to his nature. His first services in Spain a deserved triumph; of his laws I could speak forever. His campaigns in Gaul are known to you all. That land from which the Teutons and Cimbri poured over the Alps is now as well ordered as Italy. Caesar would have added Germany and Britain to your Empire, but his enemies would not have it so. They regarded the Commonwealth as the patrimony of themselves. They brought him home. They went on with their usurpations till you yourselves required his help. He set you free. He set Spain free. He labored for peace with Pompey, but Pompey preferred to go into Greece, to bring the powers of the East upon you, and he perished in his obstinacy.

"Caesar took no honor to himself for this victory. He abhorred the necessity of it. He took no revenge. He praised those who had been faithful to Pompey, and he blamed Pharnaces for deserting him. He was sorry for Pompey's death, and he treated his murderers as they deserved. He settled Egypt and Armenia. He would have disposed of the Parthians had not fresh seditions recalled him to Italy. He quelled those seditions. He restored peace in Africa and Spain, and again his one desire was to spare his fellow-citizens. There was in him an 'inbred goodness.'[3] He was always the same--never carried away by anger, and never spoilt by success. He did not retaliate for the past; he never tried by severity to secure himself for the future. His effort throughout was to save all who would allow themselves to be saved. He repaired old acts of injustice. He restored the families of those who had been proscribed by Sylla, but he burnt unread the correspondence of Pompey and Scipio, that those whom it compromised might neither suffer injury nor fear injury. You honored him as your father; you loved him as your benefactor; you made him chief of the

State, not being curious of titles, but regarding the most which you could give as less than he had deserved at your hands. Toward the gods he was High Priest. To you he was Consul; to the army he was Imperator; to the enemies of his country, Dictator. In sum he was Pater Patriae. And this your father, your Pontifex, this hero, whose person was declared inviolable, lies dead-- dead, not by disease or age, not by war or visitation of God, but here at home, by conspiracy within your own walls, slain in the Senate-house, the warrior unarmed, the peacemaker naked to his foes, the righteous judge in the seat of judgment. He whom no foreign enemy could hurt has been killed by his fellow-countrymen--he, who had so often shown mercy, by those whom he had spared. Where, Caesar, is your love for mankind? Where is the sacredness of your life? Where are your laws? Here you lie murdered--here in the Forum, through which so often you marched in triumph wreathed with garlands; here upon the Rostra from which you were wont to address your people. Alas for your gray hairs dabbled in blood! alas for this lacerated robe in which you were dressed for the sacrifice!"[4]

Antony's words, as he well knew, were a declaration of irreconcilable war against the murderers and their friends. As his impassioned language did its work the multitude rose into fury. They cursed the conspirators. They cursed the Senate who had sate by while the deed was being done. They had been moved to fury by the murder of Clodius. Ten thousand Clodiuses, had he been all which their imagination painted him, could not equal one Caesar. They took on themselves the order of the funeral. They surrounded the body, which was reverently raised by the officers of the Forum. Part proposed to carry it to the Temple of Jupiter, in the Capitol, and to burn it under the eyes of the assassins; part to take it into the Senate-house and use the meeting-place of the Optimates a second time as the pyre of the people's friend. A few legionaries, perhaps to spare the city a general conflagration, advised that it should be consumed where it lay. The platform was torn up and the broken timbers piled into a heap. Chairs and benches were thrown on to it, the whole crowd rushing wildly to add a chip or splinter. Actors flung in their dresses, musicians their instruments, soldiers their swords. Women added their necklaces and scarves. Mothers brought up their children to contribute toys and playthings. On the pile so composed the body of Caesar was reduced to ashes. The remains were collected with affectionate care and deposited in the tomb of the Caesars, in the Campus Martius. The crowd, it was observed, was composed largely of libertini and of provincials whom Caesar had enfranchised. The demonstrations of sorrow were most remarkable among the Jews, crowds of whom continued for many nights to collect and wail in the Forum at the scene of the singular ceremony.

When the people were in such a mood, Rome was no place for the conspirators. They scattered over the Empire; Decimus Brutus, Marcus Brutus, Cassius, Cimber, Trebonius retreated to the provinces which Caesar had assigned them, the rest clinging to the shelter of their friends. The legions--a striking tribute to Roman discipline--remained by their eagles, faithful to their immediate duties, and obedient to their officers, till it could be seen how events would turn. Lepidus joined the army in Gaul; Antony continued in Rome, holding the administration in his hands and watching the action of the Senate. Caesar was dead. But Caesar still lived. "It was not possible that the grave should hold him." The people said that he was a god, and had gone back to heaven, where his star had been seen ascending;[5] his spirit remained on earth, and the vain blows of the assassins had been but "malicious mockery." "We have killed the king," exclaimed Cicero in the bitterness of his disenchantment, "but the kingdom is with us still;" "we have taken away the tyrant: the tyranny survives." Caesar had not overthrown the oligarchy; their own incapacity, their own selfishness, their own baseness had overthrown them. Caesar had been but the reluctant instrument of the power which metes out to men the inevitable penalties of their own misdeeds. They had dreamt that the Constitution was a living force which would revive of itself as soon as its enemy was gone. They did not know that it was dead already, and that they had themselves destroyed it. The Constitution was but an agreement by which the Roman people had consented to abide for their common good. It had ceased to be for the common good. The experience of fifty miserable years had proved that it meant the supremacy of the rich, maintained by the bought votes of demoralized electors. The soil of Italy, the industry and happiness of tens of millions of mankind, from the Rhine to the Euphrates, had been the spoil of five hundred families and their relatives and dependents, of men whose occupation was luxury, and whose appetites were for monstrous pleasures. The self-respect of reasonable men could no longer tolerate such a rule in Italy or out of it. In killing Caesar the optimates had been as foolish as they were treacherous; for Caesar's efforts had been to reform the Constitution, not to abolish it. The civil war had risen from their dread of his second consulship, which they had feared would make an end of their corruptions;

and that the Constitution should be purged of the poison in its veins was the sole condition on which its continuance was possible. The obstinacy, the ferocity, the treachery of the aristocracy had compelled Caesar to crush them; and the more desperate their struggles the more absolute the necessity became. But he alone could have restored as much of popular liberty as was consistent with the responsibilities of such a government as the Empire required. In Caesar alone were combined the intellect and the power necessary for such a work; and they had killed him, and in doing so had passed final sentence on themselves. Not as realities any more, but as harmless phantoms, the forms of the old Republic were henceforth to persist. In the army only remained the imperial consciousness of the honor and duty of Roman citizens, To the army, therefore, the rule was transferred. The Roman nation had grown as the oak grows, self-developed in severe morality, each citizen a law to himself, and therefore capable of political freedom in an unexampled degree. All organizations destined to endure spring from forces inherent in themselves, and must grow freely, or they will not grow at all. When the tree reaches maturity, decay sets in; if it be left standing, the disintegration of the fibre goes swiftly forward; if the stem is severed from the root, the destroying power is arrested, and the timber will endure a thousand years. So it was with Rome. The Constitution under which the Empire had sprung up was poisoned, and was brought to a violent end before it had affected materially for evil the masses of the people. The solid structure was preserved--not to grow any longer, not to produce a new Camillus or a new Regulus, a new Scipio Africanus or a new Tiberius Gracchus, but to form an endurable shelter for civilized mankind, until a fresh spiritual life was developed out of Palestine to remodel the conscience of humanity.

A gleam of hope opened to Cicero in the summer. Octavius, who was in Greece at the time of the murder, came to Rome to claim his inheritance. He was but eighteen, too young for the burden which was thrown upon him; and being unknown, he had the confidence of the legions to win. The army, dispersed over the provinces, had as yet no collective purpose. Antony, it is possible, was jealous of him, and looked on himself as Caesar's true representative and avenger. Octavius, finding Antony hostile, or at least indifferent to his claims, played with the Senate with cool foresight till he felt the ground firm under his feet. Cicero boasted that he would use Octavius to ruin Antony, and would throw him over when he had served his purpose. "Cicero will learn," Octavius said, when the words were reported to him, "that I shall not be played with so easily."

[Sidenote: B.C. 44-43.] [Sidenote: B.C. 43.] For a year the confusion lasted; two of Caesar's officers, Hirtius and Pausa, were chosen consuls by the senatorial party, to please the legions; and Antony contended dubiously with them and Decimus Brutus for some months in the North of Italy. But Antony joined Lepidus, and the Gallic legions with judicial fitness brought Cicero's dreams to the ground. Cicero's friend, Plancus, who commanded in Normandy and Belgium, attempted a faint resistance, but was made to yield to the resolution of his troops. Octavius and Antony came to an understanding; and Caesar's two generals, who were true to his memory, and Octavius, who was the heir of his name, crossed the Alps, at the head of the united army of Gaul, to punish the murder and restore peace to the world. No resistance was possible. Many of the senators, like Cicero, though they had borne no part in the assassination, had taken the guilt of it upon themselves by the enthusiasm of their approval. They were all men who had sworn fidelity to Caesar, and had been ostentatious in their profession of devotion to him. It had become too plain that from such persons no repentance was to be looked for. They were impelled by a malice or a fanaticism which clemency could not touch or reason influence. So long as they lived they would still conspire; and any weapons, either of open war or secret treachery, would seem justifiable to them in the cause which they regarded as sacred. Caesar himself would, no doubt, have again pardoned them. Octavius, Antony, and Lepidus were men of more common mould. The murderers of Caesar, and those who had either instigated them secretly or applauded them afterward, were included in a proscription list, drawn by retributive justice on the model of Sylla's. Such of them as were in Italy were immediately killed. Those in the provinces, as if with the curse of Cain upon their heads, came one by one to miserable ends. Brutus and Cassius fought hard and fell at Philippi. In three years the tyrannicides of the ides of March, with their aiders and abettors, were all dead, some killed in battle, some in prison, some dying by their own hand--slain with the daggers with which they had stabbed their master.

Out of the whole party the fate of one only deserves special notice, a man whose splendid talents have bought forgiveness for his faults, and have given him a place in the small circle of the really great whose memory is not allowed to die.

[Sidenote: Dec. 7, B.C. 43.] After the dispersion of the conspirators which followed Caesar's funeral, Cicero had remained in Rome. His timidity seemed to have forsaken him, and he had striven, with an energy which recalled his brightest days, to set the Constitution again upon its feet. Antony charged him in the Senate with having been the contriver of Caesar's death. He replied with invectives fierce and scurrilous as those which he had heaped upon Catiline and Clodius. A time had been when he had affected to look on Antony as his preserver. Now there was no imaginable infamy in which he did not steep his name. He spoke of the murder as the most splendid achievement recorded in history, and he regretted only that he had not been taken into counsel by the deliverers of their country. Antony would not then have been alive to rekindle civil discord. When Antony left Rome, Cicero was for a few months again the head of the State. He ruled the Senate, controlled the Treasury, corresponded with the conspirators in the provinces, and advised their movements. He continued sanguine himself, and he poured spirit into others. No one can refuse admiration to the last blaze of his expiring powers. But when he heard that Antony and Lepidus and Octavius had united, and were coming into Italy with the whole Western army, he saw that all was over. He was now sixty-three--too old for hope. He could hardly have wished to live, and this time he was well assured that there would be no mercy for him. Caesar would have spared a man whom he esteemed in spite of his infirmities. But there was no Caesar now, and fair speeches would serve his turn no longer. He retired from the city with his brother Quintus, and had some half-formed purpose of flying to Brutus, who was still in arms in Macedonia. He even embarked, but without a settled resolution, and he allowed himself to be driven back by a storm. Theatrical even in extremities, he thought of returning to Rome and of killing himself in Caesar's house, that he might bring the curse of his blood upon Octavius. In these uncertainties he drifted into his own villa at Formiae,[6] saying in weariness, and with a sad note of his old self-importance, that he would die in the country which he had so often saved. Here, on the 4th of December, B.C. 43, Popilius Loenas, an officer of Antony's, came to find him. Peasants from the neighborhood brought news to the villa that the soldiers were approaching. His servants thrust him into a litter and carried him down through the woods toward the sea. Loenas followed and overtook him. To his slaves he had been always the gentlest of masters. They would have given their lives in his defence if he would have allowed them; but he bade them set the litter down and save themselves. He thrust out his head between the curtains, and it was instantly struck off.

So ended Cicero, a tragic combination of magnificent talents, high aspirations, and true desire to do right, with an infirmity of purpose and a latent insincerity of character which neutralized and could almost make us forget his nobler qualities. It cannot be said of Cicero that he was blind to the faults of the party to which he attached himself. To him we owe our knowledge of what the Roman aristocrats really were, and of the hopelessness of expecting that they could have been trusted any longer with the administration of the Empire, if the Empire itself was to endure. Cicero's natural place was at Caesar's side; but to Caesar alone of his contemporaries he was conscious of an inferiority which was intolerable to him. In his own eyes he was always the first person. He had been made unhappy by the thought that posterity might rate Pompey above himself. Closer acquaintance had reassured him about Pompey, but in Caesar he was conscious of a higher presence, and he rebelled against the humiliating acknowledgment. Supreme as an orator he could always be, and an order of things was, therefore, most desirable where oratory held the highest place. Thus he chose his part with the "boni," whom he despised while he supported them, drifting on through vacillation into treachery, till "the ingredients of the poisoned chalice" were "commended to his own lips."

In Cicero Nature half-made a great man and left him uncompleted. Our characters are written in our forms, and the bust of Cicero is the key to his history. The brow is broad and strong, the nose large, the lips tightly compressed, the features lean and keen from restless intellectual energy. The loose bending figure, the neck, too weak for the weight of the head, explain the infirmity of will, the passion, the cunning, the vanity, the absence of manliness and veracity. He was born into an age of violence with which he was too feeble to contend. The gratitude of mankind for his literary excellence will forever preserve his memory from too harsh a judgment.

[1] Philippic ii. 35.

[2] Abridged from Dion Cassius, who probably gives no more than the traditionary version of Cicero's words.

[3] [Greek: emphutos chraestotaes] are Dion Cassius's words. Antony's language was differently reported, and perhaps there was no literal record of it. Dion Cassius, however, can hardly have himself composed the version which he gives in his history, for he calls the speech as ill-timed as it was brilliant.

[4] Abridged from Dion Cassius. xliv. 36.

[5] "In deorum numerum relatus est non ore modo decernentium sed et persuasione vulgi."--Suetonius.

[6] Near Gaeta.

CHAPTER XXVIII.

It remains to offer a few general remarks on the person whose life and actions I have endeavored to describe in the preceding pages.

In all conditions of human society distinguished men are the subjects of legend; but the character of the legend varies with the disposition of the time. In ages which we call heroic the saint works miracles, the warrior performs exploits beyond the strength of natural man. In ages less visionary which are given to ease and enjoyment the tendency is to bring a great man down to the common level, and to discover or invent faults which shall show that he is or was but a little man after all. Our vanity is soothed by evidence that those who have eclipsed us in the race of life are no better than ourselves, or in some respects are worse than ourselves; and if to these general impulses be added political or personal animosity, accusations of depravity are circulated as surely about such men, and are credited as readily, as under other influences are the marvellous achievements of a Cid or a St. Francis. In the present day we reject miracles and prodigies; we are on our guard against the mythology of hero worship, just as we disbelieve in the eminent superiority of any one of our contemporaries to another. We look less curiously into the mythology of scandal; we accept easily and willingly stories disparaging to illustrious persons in history, because similar stories are told and retold with so much confidence and fluency among the political adversaries of those who have the misfortune to be their successful rivals. The absurdity of a calumny may be as evident as the absurdity of a miracle; the ground for belief may be no more than a lightness of mind, and a less pardonable wish that it may be true. But the idle tale floats in society, and by and by is written down in books and passes into the region of established realities.

The tendency to idolize great men and the tendency to depreciate them arises alike in emotion; but the slanders of disparagement are as truly legends as the wonder-tales of saints and warriors; and anecdotes related of Caesar at patrician dinner-parties at Rome as little deserve attention as the information so freely given upon the habits of modern statesmen in the salons of London and Paris. They are read now by us in classic Latin, but they were recorded by men who hated Caesar and hated all that he had done; and that a poem has survived for two thousand years is no evidence that the author of it, even though he might be a Catullus, was uninfluenced by the common passions of humanity.

Caesar, it is allowed, had extraordinary talents, extraordinary energy, and some commendable qualities; but he was, as the elder Curio said, "omnium mulierum vir et omnium virorum mulier;" he had mistresses in every country which he visited, and he had liaisons with half the ladies in Rome. That Caesar's morality was altogether superior to that of the average of his contemporaries is in a high degree improbable. He was a man of the world, peculiarly attractive to women, and likely to have been attracted by them. On the other hand, the undiscriminating looseness attributed to him would have been peculiarly degrading in a man whose passions were so eminently under control, whose calmness was never known to be discomposed, and who, in everything which he did, acted always with deliberate will. Still worse would it be if, by his example, he made ridiculous his own laws against adultery and indulged himself in vices which he punished in others. What, then, is the evidence? The story of Nicomedes may be passed over. All that is required on that subject has been already said. It was never heard of before Caesar's consulship, and the proofs are no more than the libels of Bibulus, the satire of Catullus, and certain letters of Cicero's which were never published, but were circulated privately in Roman aristocratic society.[1] A story is suspicious which is first produced after twenty years in a moment of political excitement. Caesar spoke of it with stern disgust. He replied to Catullus with an invitation to dinner; otherwise he passed it over in silence--the only answer which an honorable man could give. Suetonius quotes a loose song sung by Caesar's soldiers at his triumph. We know in what terms British sailors often speak of their favorite commanders. Affection, when it expresses itself most emphatically, borrows the language of its opposites. Who would dream of introducing into a serious life of Nelson catches chanted in the forecastle of the "Victory"? But which of the soldiers sang these verses? Does Suetonius mean that the army sang them in chorus as they marched in procession? The very notion is preposterous. It is proved that during Caesar's lifetime scandal was busy with his name; and that it would be so busy, whether justified or not, is certain from the nature of things. Cicero says that no public man in Rome escaped from such imputations. He himself flung them broadcast, and they were equally returned upon himself. The surprise is rather that Caesar's name should have suffered so little, and that he should have been admitted on reflection by Suetonius to have been comparatively free from the abominable form of vice which was then so common.

As to his liaisons with women, the handsome, brilliant Caesar, surrounded by a halo of military glory, must have been a Paladin of romance to any woman who had a capacity of admiration in her. His own distaste for gluttony and hard drinking, and for the savage amusements in which the male Romans so much delighted, may have made the society of cultivated ladies more agreeable to him than that of men, and if he showed any such preference the coarsest interpretation would be inevitably placed upon it. These relations, perhaps, in so loose an age assumed occasionally a more intimate form; but it is to be observed that the first public act recorded of Caesar was his refusal to divorce his wife at Sylla's bidding; that he was passionately attached to his sister; that his mother, Aurelia, lived with him till she died, and that this mother was a Roman matron of the strictest and severest type. Many names were mentioned in connection with him, yet there is no record of any natural child save Brutus, and one other whose claims were denied and disproved.

Two intrigues, it may be said, are beyond dispute. His connection with the mother of Brutus was notorious. Cleopatra, in spite of Oppius, was living with him in his house at the time of his murder. That it was so believed a hundred years after his death is, of course, indisputable; but in both these cases the story is entangled with legends which show how busily imagination had been at work. Brutus was said to be Caesar's son, though Caesar was but fifteen when he was born; and Brutus, though he had the temper of an Orestes, was devotedly attached to his mother in spite of the supposed adultery, and professed to have loved Caesar when he offered him as a sacrifice to his country's liberty. Cleopatra is said to have joined Caesar at Rome after his return from Spain, and to have resided openly with him as his mistress. Supposing that she did come to Rome, it is still certain that Calpurnia was in Caesar's house when he was killed. Cleopatra must have been Calpurnia's guest as well as her husband's; and her presence, however commented upon in society, could not possibly have borne the avowed complexion which tradition assigned to it. On the other hand, it is quite intelligible that the young Queen of Egypt, who owed her position to Caesar, might have come, as other princes came, on a visit of courtesy, and that Caesar after their acquaintance at Alexandria should have invited her to stay with him. But was Cleopatra at Rome at all? The only real evidence for her presence there is to be found in a few words of Cicero: "Reginae fuga mihi non molesta."--"I am not sorry to hear of the flight of the queen." [2] There is nothing to show that the "queen" was the Egyptian queen. Granting that the word Egyptian is to be understood, Cicero may have referred to Arsino? who was called Queen as well as her sister, and had been sent to Rome to be shown at Caesar's triumph.

But enough and too much on this miserable subject. Men will continue to form their opinions about it, not upon the evidence, but according to their preconceived notions of what is probable or improbable. Ages of progress and equality are as credulous of evil as ages of faith are credulous of good, and reason will not modify convictions which do not originate in reason.

Let us pass on to surer ground.

In person Caesar was tall and slight. His features were more refined than was usual in Roman faces; the forehead was wide and high, the nose large and thin, the lips full, the eyes dark gray like an eagle's, the neck extremely thick and sinewy. His complexion was pale. His beard and mustache were kept carefully shaved. His hair was short and naturally scanty, falling off toward the end of his life and leaving him partially bald. His voice, especially when he spoke in public, was high and shrill. His health was uniformly strong until his last year, when he became subject to epileptic fits. He was a great bather, and scrupulously clean in all his habits, abstemious in his food, and careless in what it consisted, rarely or never touching wine, and noting sobriety as the highest of qualities when describing any new people. He was an athlete in early life, admirable in all manly exercises, and especially in riding. In Gaul, as has been said already, he rode a remarkable horse, which he had bred himself, and which would let no one but Caesar mount him. From his boyhood it was observed of him that he was the truest of friends, that he avoided quarrels, and was most easily appeased when offended. In manner he was quiet and gentlemanlike, with the natural courtesy of high-breeding. On an occasion when he was dining somewhere the other guests found the oil too rancid for them. Caesar took it without remark, to spare his entertainer's feelings. When on a journey through a forest with his friend Oppius, he came one night to a hut where there was a single bed. Oppius being unwell, Caesar gave it up to him, and slept on the ground.

In his public character he may be regarded under three aspects, as a politician, a soldier, and a man of letters.

Like Cicero, Caesar entered public life at the bar. He belonged by birth to the popular party, but he showed no disposition, like the Gracchi, to plunge into political agitation. His aims were practical. He made war only upon injustice and oppression; and when he commenced as a pleader he was noted for the energy with which he protected a client whom he believed to have been wronged. At a later period, before he was praetor, he was engaged in defending Masintha, a young Numidian prince, who had suffered some injury from Hiempsal, the father of Juba. Juba himself came to Rome on the occasion, bringing with him the means of influencing the judges which Jugurtha had found so effective. Caesar in his indignation seized Juba by the beard in the court; and when Masintha was sentenced to some unjust penalty Caesar carried him off, concealed him in his house, and took him to Spain in his carriage. When he rose into the Senate, his powers as a speaker became strikingly remarkable. Cicero, who often heard him, and was not a favorable judge, said that there was a pregnancy in his sentences and a dignity in his manner which no orator in Rome could approach. But he never spoke to court popularity; his aim from first to last was better government, the prevention of bribery and extortion, and the distribution among deserving citizens of some portion of the public land which the rich were stealing. The Julian laws, which excited the indignation of the aristocracy, had no other objects than these; and had they been observed they would have saved the Constitution. The obstinacy of faction and the civil war which grew out of it obliged him to extend his horizon, to contemplate more radical reforms--a large extension of the privileges of citizenship, with the introduction of the provincial nobility into the Senate, and the transfer of the administration from the Senate and annually elected magistrates to the permanent chief of the army. But his objects throughout were purely practical. The purpose of government he conceived to be the execution of justice; and a constitutional liberty under which justice was made impossible did not appear to him to be liberty at all.

The practicality which showed itself in his general aims appeared also in his mode of working. Caesar, it was observed, when anything was to be done, selected the man who was best able to do it, not caring particularly who or what he might be in other respects. To this faculty of discerning and choosing fit persons to execute his orders may be ascribed the extraordinary success of his own provincial administration, the enthusiasm which was felt for him in the North of Italy, and the perfect quiet of Gaul after the completion of the conquest. Caesar did not crush the Gauls under the weight of Italy. He took the best of them into the Roman service, promoted them, led them to associate the interests of the Empire with their personal advancement and the prosperity of their own people. No act of Caesar's showed more sagacity then the introduction of Gallic nobles into the Senate; none was more bitter to the Scipios and Metelli, who were compelled to share their august privileges with these despised barbarians.

It was by accident that Caesar took up the profession of a soldier; yet perhaps no commander who ever lived showed greater military genius. The conquest of Gaul was effected by a force numerically insignificant, which was worked with the precision of a machine. The variety of uses to which it was capable of being turned implied, in the first place, extraordinary forethought in the selection of materials. Men whose nominal duty was merely to fight were engineers, architects, mechanics of the highest order. In a few hours they could extemporize an impregnable fortress on an open hillside. They bridged the Rhine in a week. They built a fleet in a month. The legions at Alesia held twice their number pinned within their works, while they kept at bay the whole force of insurgent Gaul, entirely by scientific superiority. The machine, which was thus perfect, was composed of human beings who required supplies of tools, and arms, and clothes, and food, and shelter, and for all these it depended on the forethought of its commander. Maps there were none. Countries entirely unknown had to be surveyed; routes had to be laid out; the depths and courses of rivers, the character of mountain passes, had all to be ascertained. Allies had to be found among tribes as yet unheard of. Countless contingent difficulties had to be provided for, many of which must necessarily arise, though the exact nature of them could not be anticipated. When room for accidents is left open, accidents do not fail to be heard of. Yet Caesar was never defeated when personally present, save once at Gergovia, and once at Durazzo; and the failure at Gergovia was caused by the revolt of the Aedui; and the manner in which the failure at Durazzo was retrieved showed Caesar's greatness more than the most brilliant of his victories. He was rash, but with a calculated rashness, which the event never failed to justify. His greatest successes were due to the rapidity of his movements, which brought him on the enemy before they heard of his approach. He travelled sometimes a hundred miles a day, reading or writing in his carriage, though countries without roads, and crossing rivers without bridges. No obstacles stopped him when he had a definite end in view. In battle he sometimes rode; but he was more often on foot, bareheaded, and in a conspicuous dress, that he might be seen and recognized. Again and again by his own efforts he recovered a day that was half lost. He once seized a panic-stricken standard-bearer, turned him round, and told him that he had mistaken the direction of the enemy. He never misled his army as to an enemy's strength, or if he mis-stated their numbers it was only to exaggerate. In Africa, before Thapsus, when his officers were nervous at the reported approach of Juba, he called them together and said briefly, "You will understand that within a day King Juba will be here with the legions, thirty thousand horse, a hundred thousand skirmishers, and three hundred elephants. You are not to think or ask questions. I tell you the truth, and you must prepare for it. If any of you are alarmed, I shall send you home."

Yet he was singularly careful of his soldiers. He allowed his legions rest, though he allowed none to himself. He rarely fought a battle at a disadvantage. He never exposed his men to unnecessary danger, and the loss by wear and tear in the campaigns in Gaul was exceptionally and even astonishingly slight. When a gallant action was performed, he knew by whom it had been done, and every soldier, however humble, might feel assured that if he deserved praise he would have it. The army was Caesar's family. When Sabinus was cut off, he allowed his beard to grow, and he did not shave it till the disaster was avenged. If Quintus Cicero had been his own child, he could not have run greater personal risk to save him when shut up at Charleroy. In discipline he was lenient to ordinary faults, and not careful to make curious inquiries into such things. He liked his men to enjoy themselves. Military mistakes in his officers too he always endeavored to excuse, never blaming them for misfortunes, unless there had been a defect of courage as well as judgment. Mutiny and desertion only he never overlooked. And thus no general was ever more loved by, or had greater power over, the army which served under him. He brought the insurgent 10th legion into submission by a single word. When the civil war began and Labienus left him, he told all his officers who had served under Pompey that they were free to follow if they wished. Not another man forsook him.

Suetonius says that he was rapacious, that he plundered tribes in Spain who were allies of Rome, that he pillaged shrines and temples in Gaul, and destroyed cities merely for spoil. He adds a story which Cicero would not have left untold and uncommented on if he had been so fortunate as to hear of it: that Caesar when first consul took three thousand pounds weight of gold out of the Capitol and replaced it with gilded brass. A similar story is told of the Cid and of other heroes of fiction. How came Cicero to be ignorant of an act which, if done at all, was done under his own eyes? When praetor Caesar brought back money from Spain to the treasury; but he was never charged at the time with peculation or oppression there. In Gaul the war paid its own expenses; but what temples were there in Gaul which were worth spoiling? Of temples, he was, indeed, scrupulously careful. Varro had taken gold from the Temple of Hercules at Cadiz. Caesar replaced it. Metellus Scipio had threatened to plunder the Temple of Diana at Ephesus. Caesar protected it. In Gaul the Druids were his best friends; therefore he certainly had not outraged religion there; and the quiet of the province during the civil war is a sufficient answer to the accusation of gratuitous oppression.

The Gauls paid the expenses of their conquest in the prisoners taken in battle, who were sold to the slave merchants; and this is the real blot on Caesar's career. But the blot was not personally upon Caesar, but upon the age in which he lived. The great Pomponius Atticus himself was a dealer in human chattels. That prisoners of war should be sold as slaves was the law of the time, accepted alike by victors and vanquished; and the crowds of libertini who assisted at Caesar's funeral proved that he was not regarded as the enemy of these unfortunates, but as their special friend.

His leniency to the Pompeian faction has already been spoken of sufficiently.

It may have been politic, but it arose also from the disposition of the man. Cruelty originates in fear, and Caesar was too indifferent to death to fear anything. So far as his public action was concerned, he betrayed no passion save hatred of injustice; and he moved through life calm and irresistible, like a force of nature.

Cicero has said of Caesar's oratory that he surpassed those who had practised no other art. His praise of him as a man of letters is yet more delicately and gracefully emphatic. Most of his writings are lost; but there remain seven books of commentaries on the wars in Gaul (the eighth was added by another hand), and three books upon the civil war, containing an account of its causes and history. Of these it was that Cicero said, in an admirable image, that fools might think to improve on them, but that no wise man would try it; they were _nudi omni ornatu orationis, tanquam veste detracted--bare of ornament, the dress of style dispensed with, like an undraped human figure perfect in all its lines as nature made it. In his composition, as in his actions, Caesar is entirely simple. He indulges in no images, no labored descriptions, no conventional reflections. His art is unconscious, as the highest art always is. The actual fact of things stands out as it really was, not as mechanically photographed, but interpreted by the calmest intelligence, and described with unexaggerated feeling. No military narrative has approached the excellence of the history of the war in Gaul. Nothing is written down which could be dispensed with; nothing important is left untold; while the incidents themselves are set off by delicate and just observations on human character. The story is rendered attractive by complimentary anecdotes of persons; while details of the character and customs of an unknown and remarkable people show the attention which Caesar was always at leisure to bestow on anything which was worthy of interest, even when he was surrounded with danger and difficulty. The books on the civil war have the same simplicity and clearness, but a vein runs through them of strong if subdued emotion. They contain the history of a great revolution related by the principal actor in it; but no effort can be traced to set his own side in a favorable light, or to abuse or depreciate his adversaries. The coarse invectives which Cicero poured so freely upon those who differed from him are conspicuously absent. Caesar does not exult over his triumphs or parade the honesty of his motives. The facts are left to tell their own story; and the gallantry and endurance of his own troops are not related with more feeling than the contrast between the confident hopes of the patrician leaders at Pharsalia and the luxury of their camp with the overwhelming disaster which fell upon them. About himself and his own exploits there is not one word of self-complacency or self-admiration. In his writings, as in his life, Caesar is always the same--direct, straightforward, unmoved save by occasional tenderness, describing with unconscious simplicity how the work which had been forced upon him was accomplished. He wrote with extreme rapidity in the intervals of other labor; yet there is not a word misplaced, not a sign of haste anywhere, save that the conclusion of the Gallic war was left to be supplied by a weaker hand. The Commentaries, as an historical narrative, are as far superior to any other Latin composition of the kind as the person of Caesar himself stands out among the rest of his contemporaries.

His other compositions have perished, in consequence, perhaps, of the unforgiving republican sentiment which revived among men of letters after the death of Augustus--which rose to a height in the "Pharsalia" of Lucan--and which leaves so visible a mark in the writings of Tacitus and Suetonius. There was a book "De Analogi?" written by Caesar after the conference at Lucca, during the passage of the Alps. There was a book on the Auspices, which, coming from the head of the Roman religion, would have thrown a light much to be desired on this curious subject. In practice Caesar treated the auguries with contempt. He carried his laws in open disregard of them. He fought his battles careless whether the sacred chickens would eat or the calves' livers were of the proper color. His own account of such things in his capacity of Pontifex would have had a singular interest.

From the time of his boyhood he kept a common-place book, in which he entered down any valuable or witty sayings, inquiring carefully, as Cicero takes pains to tell us, after any smart observation of his own. Niebuhr remarks that no pointed sentences of Caesar's can have come down to us. Perhaps he had no gift that way, and admired in others what he did not possess.

He left in verse "an account of the stars"--some practical almanac, probably, in a shape to be easily remembered; and there was a journal in verse also, written on the return from Munda. Of all the lost writings, however, the most to be regretted is the "Anti-Cato." After Cato's death Cicero published a panegyric upon him. To praise Cato was to condemn Caesar; and Caesar replied with a sketch of the Martyr of Utica as he had himself known him. The pamphlet, had it survived, would have shown how far Caesar was able to extend the forbearance so conspicuous in his other writings to the most respectable and the most inveterate of his enemies. The verdict of fact and the verdict of literature on the great controversy between them have been summed up in the memorable line of Lucan--

Victrix causa Deis placuit, sed victa Catoni.

Was Cato right, or were the gods right? Perhaps both. There is a legend that at the death of Charles V. the accusing angel appeared in heaven with a catalogue of deeds which no advocate could palliate--countries laid desolate, cities sacked and burnt, lists of hundreds of thousands of widows and children brought to misery by the political ambition of a single man. The evil spirit demanded the offender's soul, and it seemed as if mercy itself could not refuse him the award. But at the last moment the Supreme Judge interfered. The Emperor, He said, had been sent into the world at a peculiar time, for a peculiar purpose, and was not to be tried by the ordinary rules. Titian has painted the scene: Charles kneeling before the Throne, with the consciousness, as became him, of human infirmities, written upon his countenance, yet neither afraid nor abject, relying in absolute faith that the Judge of all mankind would do right.

Of Caesar, too, it may be said that he came into the world at a special time and for a special object. The old religions were dead, from the Pillars of Hercules to the Euphrates and the Nile, and the principles on which human society had been constructed were dead also. There remained of spiritual conviction only the common and human sense of justice and morality; and out of this sense some ordered system of government had to be constructed, under which quiet men could live and labor and eat the fruit of their industry. Under a rule of this material kind there can be no enthusiasm, no chivalry, no saintly aspirations, no patriotism of the heroic type. It was not to last forever. A new life was about to dawn for mankind. Poetry, and faith, and devotion were to spring again out of the seeds which were sleeping in the heart of humanity. But the life which is to endure grows slowly; and as the soil must be prepared before the wheat can be sown, so before the Kingdom of Heaven could throw up its shoots there was needed a kingdom of this world where the nations were neither torn in pieces by violence nor were rushing after false ideals and spurious ambitions. Such a kingdom was the Empire of the Caesars--a kingdom where peaceful men could work, think, and speak as they pleased, and travel freely among provinces ruled for the most part by Gallios, who protected life and property, and forbade fanatics to tear each other in pieces for their religious opinions. "It is not lawful for us to put any man to death," was the complaint of the Jewish priests to the Roman governor. Had Europe and Asia been covered with independent nations, each with a local religion represented in its ruling powers, Christianity must have been stifled in its cradle. If St. Paul had escaped the Sanhedrim at Jerusalem, he would have been torn to pieces by the silver-smiths at Ephesus. The appeal to Caesar's judgment-seat was the shield of his mission, and alone made possible his success.

And this spirit, which confined government to its simplest duties, while it left opinion unfettered, was especially present in Julius Caesar himself. From cant of all kinds he was totally free. He was a friend of the people, but he indulged in no enthusiasm for liberty. He never dilated on the beauties of virtue, or complimented, as Cicero did, a Providence in which he did not believe. He was too sincere to stoop to unreality. He held to the facts of this life and to his own convictions; and as he found no reason for supposing that there was a life beyond the grave he did not pretend to expect it. He respected the religion of the Roman State as an institution established by the laws. He encouraged or left unmolested the creeds and practices of the uncounted sects or tribes who were gathered under the eagles. But his own writings contain nothing to indicate that he himself had any religious belief at all. He saw no evidence that the gods practically interfered in human affairs. He never pretended that Jupiter was on his side. He thanked his soldiers after a victory, but he did not order _Te Deums _to be sung for it; and in the absence of these conventionalisms he perhaps showed more real reverence than he could have displayed by the freest use of the formulas of pietism.

He fought his battles to establish some tolerable degree of justice in the government of this world; and he succeeded, though he was murdered for doing it.

Strange and startling resemblance between the fate of the founder of the kingdom of this world and of the Founder of the kingdom not of this world, for which the first was a preparation. Each was denounced for making himself a king. Each was maligned as the friend of publicans and sinners; each was betrayed by those whom he had loved and cared for; each was put to death; and Caesar also was believed to have risen again and ascended into heaven and become a divine being.

[1] Suetonius, Julius Caesar, 49.

[2] To Atticus, xiv. 8.

Made in the USA
Middletown, DE
14 September 2021

48257215R00205